BIBLE DRAMA

ONE HUNDRED AND THIRTY PLAYS, IN SIX PARTS

LAWRENCE WADDY

For the Hall family,
with best wishes
July 2005

Lawrence Waddy

Bible Drama

One hundred and thirty plays, in six parts

Lawrence Waddy

Published for Lawrence Waddy by Mountain N' Air Books
P.O. Box 12540, La Crescenta, CA 91224 U.S.A.

Bible Drama

Copyright © July 2004 by Lawrence Waddy

Lawrence Waddy , 1914–

1st edition, 2004

Published in the United States of America
for Lawrence Waddy by
Mountain N' Air Books – P.O. Box 12540 – La Crescenta, CA 91224 USA

Phone: (800) 446-9696, (818) 248-9345 and (800)303-5578 fax

E-mail Address: publishers@mountain-n-air.com

Cover and book layout/design   by Gilberto d' Urso

Cover photo from Mr. Lawrence Waddy personal archives

This book is an original paperback, published electronically, printed and on demand

Library of Congress Control Number: 2004110252

Bible Drama

ISBN 1-879415-41-0

1. Waddy, Lawrence, 2. Dramas—religious—Bible Studies—essay

ISBN: 1-879415-41-0

BIBLE DRAMA

ONE HUNDRED AND THIRTY PLAYS, IN SIX PARTS

LAWRENCE WADDY

FOREWORD

These scenes and plays are designed to supplement study of the Bible and make its stories easier to appreciate. Anyone who reads them through, compares them with the text, and discusses their meaning, will have a clearer picture of the main events of the Bible and of its teaching.

Here are some suggestions about the best use of the plays. The leader of the group which will be reading them must first study them carefully. They are not written for any one age group. Select the plays which will be best for your students to read and act.

Begin with READING. Assign roles, including someone who will read the stage directions where necessary. You will probably need a second reading, with some roles switched, to bring the scene to life.

A TAPE RECORDER, with a microphone able to pick up several voices, makes your reading far more valuable. Students love to hear how their voices sound, and they will quickly appreciate the need for audibility, pacing of lines, and vitality in portraying their characters. Encourage them to overact at first. If Jesus is angry, let him be really angry. If the Devil is mean, the meaner the better. You can always tone down excesses. Make several tape versions of each scene. It takes vey little time, and the rewards are great.

Let us suppose that after a few weeks you have read twenty or more scenes. You may at that point want to ACT some of them. I have indicated scenes which are most suitable for acting**. Scenes marked * are good for acting; those marked + are harder, but often well worth the effort. Others are marked for reading rather than acting. You can first present the acting scenes very simply, with part of your group performing in front of the others. Rehearsal is much easier if you make COPIES of a scene, paste them on stiff card, and highlight the actor's role. He or she can then hold the card during the rehearsal action, and discard it when the lines are known. The experience of standing in front of even a small group and playing a role is not only valuable but almost always exciting, even for a shy beginner.

Many of these scenes involve a crowd. Lines spoken by a crowd can make or ruin a scene. It is both challenging and enjoyable to make them work well. For example: Scene Seven in the JESUS series contains a crowd following Jesus on stage. The bigger the crowd the better. Divide them into three parts. At a signal from the director the first group says (or shouts) 'Let me get through, please!' The second group: 'Please, Jesus! Help me!' The third group: 'Out of my way! I must get near him!' They go on saying these words, perhaps three times, until Jesus shouts, very loud: 'Please be quiet!' Practice this until it is convincing. Later the same groups divide the crowd lines: 'It's true! He really healed the boy!' 'That's no trick. The boy never spoke before.' 'Jesus! Heal me next!' This will take careful direction, but if you make it successful the scenes involving crowds will be transformed.

In many scenes you will find lines which are not assigned to a character. These may be spoken by a Narrator. For example, lines introducing new scenes in RUTH and HOW MUCH LAND DOES A MAN REQUIRE?

Suppose now that after many sessions you have covered at least one part of the book: Old Testament, Jesus's Life and Parables, Acts of the Apostles, or Plays with Bible Themes. Your students would probably love to PRESENT some of these scenes to a bigger audience than their class. That is fine, as long as they are ready! Never ask an audience to watch a play unless it will be audible and well acted. Everyone will be depressed and discouraged if these standards are not met. Scenes may be very simple, but they must be efficient. Someone with a little acting experience will be able to teach the actors to keep their feet still unless they need to make a move, to face the audience when they speak, not to drop their voices at the end of a line, and to portray their characters with vigor and enthusiasm. Moses must defy Pharaoh with confidence and dignity; Ruth and Naomi must convince the audience of their affection and courage; Goliath must shout his scornful lines like a crude giant; and so on. The actors will feel tremendous satisfaction if they have made a scene come alive, however rough the quality of the acting.

From there you can go on to more ambitious presentations: school assembly, parish supper, an audience of parents and friends. Make quite sure that your TECHNICAL AIDS work well. I found out years ago that Satan is the patron saint of microphones: he will make them go wrong at the last moment if he possibly can—and the same is true of lighting. Make sure that these aids to a performance will not let the actors down.

For groups which reach the level of confident acting a MUSICAL may be the best possible form of presentation. An experienced, adaptable pianist is absolutely essential if you are to undertake this kind of production. The musicals can be fitted into worship services, and have proved to be powerful sermon material if they are acted with sincerity and enthusiasm, even if the cast's experience is small.

In short, there are endless ways to use everything in this book from the short-est scenes, intended only for reading, to longer plays like PILGRIM'S PROGRESS and THE GOOD SAMARITAN. No two group leaders will use the book in quite the same way, but my hope is that everyone who participates in reading and acting these scenes will find the Bible easier to understand and to love.

In both Old and New Testament plays, characters marked with a # are not named in the Bible story.

THE OLD TESTAMENT

INDEX OF SCENES

** SCENES: EXCELLENT TO ACT.

*SCENES: GOOD TO ACT.

+ SCENES, HARDER, BUT TRY IT!

Characters:

ABRAHAM:
    The call of Abraham*; Abraham and Lot*; Sacrifice of
    Isaac (Improvise)
MOSES:
    The Burning Bush**; Moses and Pharaoh (two scenes)**;
    The Golden Calf*; Moses and Joshua*.
RUTH*:
    Read it all, then act all or part of the story.
SAMUEL and DAVID:
    Praying for a son**; A coat for Samuel**; Call of Samuel**;
    A king is named+; Samuel anoints David+; David and
    Goliath+; The sin of David**
DAVID and ABSALOM:
    Read first, then choose scenes for acting.
SOLOMON:
    Solomon's prayer* ; Judgment of Solomon**; Queen of
    Sheba (improvise); Prosperity and moral decline+
THE PSALMS:
    Reading; perhaps act out Psalm 84.
ELIJAH** Read first, then try to act all scenes.
ELISHA and NAAMAN**:
    Read first, then try to act all scenes.
ISAIAH AND THE SIEGE OF JERUSALEM+
JEREMIAH:
    Read first, then act as appropriate.
THE EXILES IN BABYLON:
    Read first, then act as appropriate.
AFTER THE EXILE**:
    Attempt all Daniel scenes.

BEFORE ABRAHAM

The story of Abraham begins in the 11th chapter of Genesis. The chapters which precede this are not meant to be historical in a literal sense. They are vivid and true pictures of the stages of creation and human history up to Abraham's time. I say 'true pictures', for the stories of Adam and Eve, of Cain and Abel, of Noah and the Flood, are true in the same sense as Jesus' parables. They tell the truth through what are called myths: truth in the form of stories.

There was a real time when man and woman first lived, with a knowledge of good and evil, of beauty and truth. We do not know when or where this happened, but the myth or parable of the Garden of Eden told Jewish readers the truth about the significance of our creation. There was at least one catastrophic flood, remembered in the literature of Assyria and Greece as well as in the Hebrew scripture; but we cannot know that Noah was the name of a real survivor. (Among the verse plays you will find one about Noah, which you can read whenever it seems appropriate.) The stories are no less valuable because we recognize them as true rather than literal. We recognize the same value in great stories like the Iliad and Odyssey, which describe a true situation in the form of wonderfully crafted myths. The same is true of Shakespeare's Macbeth and Romeo and Juliet. When were murderers and lovers portrayed more truly?

Abraham is the first person who can be credibly placed in a historical context, though we cannot be sure when he lived. The story of a man being called by God to leave the comfort of his home (in what is now Iraq), with its many gods, and seek a promised land, is easy to believe. One day perhaps archeologists will find proof of Abraham's life. Until that happens we can place his story some time after 2000 BCE. With his journey to the land which God promised to him the history of the Jews begins.

ABRAHAM

Scene one:

THE CALL OF ABRAHAM*
BIBLE REFERENCE: GENESIS 12: 1-3

Characters: VOICE OF GOD
ABRAHAM
SARAH, his wife
LOT, his nephew

Almost two thousand years before the birth of Jesus, a prosperous man living in Haran, in Mesopotamia, found that he no longer believed in the gods of his people the Chaldees. His name was Abram, later changed to Abraham, and his wife was Sarai, later changed to Sarah. When God challenged Abraham to begin a new life he was ready to listen. Our scene shows him walking over his land.

VOICE OF GOD: Abraham!

ABRAHAM: Who is it? Where are you?

VOICE OF GOD: I am the Lord your God. I have work for you to do. Will you trust me, and do what I ask?

ABRAHAM:
(KNEELING)   If you think I am worthy—

VOICE OF GOD: I know that you are worthy. I have seen your yearning for the true God. You are to leave this place, Abraham, and take all of your kindred. Go towards the south. I will guide you, and make you the father of a great nation.

ABRAHAM: Yes, Lord, but—(SILENCE) Did I really hear God's voice?

SARAH:
(ENTERING)   I brought you—why, what is wrong, Abraham? Why are you down on your knees? You're not sick?

ABRAHAM:	(Laughing) No, Sarah, not sick. I have heard the voice of God. Lot! (HE CALLS LOUDLY) Lot! Come quickly!
LOT:	(Running In) What is it, uncle?
ABRAHAM:	I knew that God's call would come. Now he has told me my duty.
LOT:	You mean you had a vision?
ABRAHAM:	I heard his voice, as clearly as I hear yours now.
SARAH:	What did he say?
ABRAHAM:	We are to pack our possessions, and leave Haran.
LOT:	Leave? Which way?
ABRAHAM:	To the south. God has promised a new country, a nation under him.
SARAH:	But, Abraham—
ABRAHAM:	There are no 'buts', dear Sarah. We have been yearning for the true God, and he has spoken. Trust him, and trust me to do what is best for our family!

Scene two:
ABRAHAM AND LOT*
Bible Reference: Genesis 13: 5-12

Characters: ABRAHAM
                    SARAH
                    LOT

They came to Canaan, and camped in the hills. Trouble arose between servants of Abraham and Lot. One day, while Abraham and Sarah were sitting in their tent, Lot burst in.

LOT:	We've got to do something, uncle. I can't stand any more of this!
ABRAHAM:	Now, now, calm down. What is wrong?

LOT: You know as well as I do. Our herdsmen are quarreling. Mine say that your flocks have all the best pasture because—

ABRAHAM: Then they are wrong. I want no injustice, and if that is all that troubles you it can soon be cured. But it goes deeper than that.

LOT: What do you mean?

ABRAHAM: The time has come for us to separate, and build towns for our people.

LOT: But—I need you!

SARAH: Your uncle is right, Lot. You must learn to make your own decisions, and govern your own people.

ABRAHAM: God has brought us together to the land which he promised. Now we must spread out. You have seen the hills and the valleys towards Jordan. Where would you like to settle and build your home?

LOT: You are really giving me the choice?

ABRAHAM: Yes.

LOT: Then I must choose the valley. Why, uncle, the land is so rich, down towards Sodom and Gomorrah. Could we not both—

ABRAHAM: No. You go there. Sarah and I will stay in the hills. It is rough up here, but already I love these mountain tops. Perhaps I feel closer to God here. Collect your people, and go when you are ready.

SARAH: May God watch over us all, and give you a peaceful home and long life!

Scene three:

THE SACRIFICE OF ISAAC (improvise)
BIBLE REFERENCE: Genesis 22: 1-19

Now for a challenge! Read the story, and then improvise the scene. Abraham and Isaac are on the way to sacrifice on the mountain top. They walk with their servants. Isaac, a young boy, complains about the rough road. Abraham is quiet and grim. When they reach the top, Isaac asks where the animal is. The Bible does not say whether Isaac fought and protested when he found out that he was to be sacrificed. Ask the actor to react in his own way. After he has been tied, and laid ready for the sacrifice, the Voice of God intervenes dramatically.

In Biblical times the Jews did not practice human sacrifice, but their neighbors, for example the Moabites, often did. Look up the meaning of sacrifice in commentaries. It was basically a beautiful idea: that a people should give back to God the first and best of what he gave them, crops and herds. They also believed that an animal which was sacrificed carried away their sins with its death. It was a means of coming closer to God, not an act of cruelty.

The Jews believed that Abraham was enabled by God to lay the foundations of their new religion, breaking away from the polytheism which most ancient peoples practiced.

Among the VERSE PLAYS you will find: JOSEPH AND HIS BRETHREN

MOSES

Moses was born in Egypt, perhaps about 1250 years before the time of Jesus. Some of the Jews had lived in Egypt for many generations, since the time of Joseph. When Moses was born they were being treated as slave laborers, and male babies were being put to death.

The Book of Exodus describes how Moses' mother hid him in the rushes by the river Nile. He was discovered by the daughter of the Pharaoh who then ruled Egypt. She decided to adopt him as her child, and Moses' mother was assigned to nurse the baby. Moses was raised as a privileged Egyptian, but he never forgot the plight of his people.

When he became a man he saw the way in which his fellow Jews were being maltreated. One day he witnessed the beating of a Jew by an Egyptian overseer. Moses was so enraged that he killed the Egyptian. He then fled to the land of Midian. There he married Zipporah, the daughter of a priest of Midian. It was while Moses was in Midian that God called him back to become the leader of his people.

Scene one:

THE BURNING BUSH**
BIBLE REFERENCE: Exodus 3: 1-15

Characters: MOSES
ZIPPORAH, with her baby GERSHOM
VOICE OF GOD

SCENE:

Mount Horeb in Midian

(MOSES IS SEATED. ZIPPORAH ENTERS)

MOSES: Greetings, wife! What brings you so far from home?

ZIPPORAH: I came to bring you more food, and also news from Egypt.

MOSES: News? First sit down and rest. You must be tired, carrying our baby.

ZIPPORAH: My father came with me. Our mule is at the foot of the path. He went to see the other flock.

MOSES: Well, and how is my boy Gershom? How are you, stranger? (HE TAKES THE CHILD)

ZIPPORAH: He is a strong man, like his father.

(THEY LAUGH. MORE DIALOGUE ABOUT THE BABY MAY BE IMPROVISED)

MOSES: You said you had news from Egypt?

ZIPPORAH: Yes. A message from your brother Aaron. The boy who brought it arrived yesterday.

MOSES: What did he say?

ZIPPORAH: That things grow worse and worse since the old Pharaoh died. The work is always being increased, and the people are near to breaking point. And—

(PAUSE)

MOSES: Yes? What else?

ZIPPORAH:	Oh, Moses, I'm frightened! Are you going to leave me, and risk your life back in Egypt?
MOSES:	What was the rest of the message?
ZIPPORAH:	That every Jew with a strong right arm is needed to fight his people's battle. But we are so happy here, Moses! Must you go? What can one man do?
MOSES:	If we always asked that question, my dear, and shrank from risking our lives for what is right, nothing would ever be achieved. Go home now! Thank you for bringing the food, and for telling me news which you would rather have hidden. You are a good wife to me. Whatever happens, we will face it together, and Gershom will grow up to be our helper.
ZIPPORAH:	I will leave you then. My father will be wanting to visit the other shepherds. Come home as soon as you can!

(SHE GOES. MOSES SITS SILENT, THEN KNEELS AND PRAYS)

MOSES:	O God, when will you show mercy to our people? When shall we see any sign of relief? You are calling me to lead them, but what can I do to break their bondage? (AFTER ANOTHER PAUSE HE SUDDENLY TURNS TO ONE SIDE, AND SHADES HIS EYES WITH HIS HANDS) What is that light? O God! Is it a sign? The mountain is on fire, but the bush is not burned.
VOICE OF GOD:	Moses!
MOSES:	Yes, Lord?
VOICE OF GOD:	I am here, Moses. Take off your shoes, for you are standing on holy ground. I am the God of Abraham and Isaac and Jacob. I have seen my people's affliction, and I will deliver them from the Egyptians. They shall go to a good land, a land flowing with milk and honey, the land which I promised to Abraham.
MOSES:	(COVERING HIS FACE) Lord, why do you tell me this?
VOICE OF GOD:	Because you must lead them. Go to Pharaoh, and take my people out of Egypt!

MOSES:	Who am I to stand before Pharaoh? How will he or our people listen to me?
VOICE OF GOD:	Say that the God of their fathers, the only true God, the God I AM has sent you. That is my name. You shall serve me, and have no other god.
MOSES:	Yes, Lord. (PAUSE) The fire is quenched. May I have faith and strength to make his words come true!

Scene Two:

MOSES AND PHARAOH **
BIBLE REFERENCE: Exodus 5

Characters:	PHARAOH AN OFFICER MOSES AARON

Pharaoh is seated C. Bring out the anger in this scene.

PHARAOH:	Bring them here, and let us have done with this!
OFFICER:	(LEADING MOSES AND AARON IN) Kneel before the King, you dogs! (THEY BOW) Down on the floor! (HE PUSHES THEM DOWN ON THEIR KNEES) That's better! I don't know why you waste your time on these scum, Your Majesty.
PHARAOH:	I wish them to take a message to their people. Rise! (THEY RISE AND STAND TO ONE SIDE OF PHARAOH, HALF FACING THE AUDIENCE)
MOSES:	Your Majesty—
OFFICER:	Silence! How dare you interrupt the King?
MOSES:	I bring a message, to Pharaoh and to all Egypt.
PHARAOH:	Oh, really? A message from whom?
MOSES:	From the one true God.
PHARAOH:	The one true God? Is he an acquaintance of yours, Jew?

MOSES:	He sends this word through me, sir. Listen, if you value your life and the welfare of your people!
OFFICER:	Do you want me to throw them out, sir, and have them whipped?
PHARAOH:	No. Let us hear this socalled message.
MOSES:	Speak, Aaron! Tell the King the message of the Lord God!
AARON:	Thus says the Lord God of Israel: Let my people go, that they may hold a feast unto me in the wilderness! Let us go three days' journey into the desert, sir. That is the bidding of God.
PHARAOH:	The bidding of God? Thank you! He seems to be the God of scroungers and workshy idlers. I have heard about you two. That is why I called you here today. If you wish to be leaders of your people, you do as I say. Otherwise we will deal with you. Go and tell your Jews that I am not satisfied with their work. I expect longer hours and better results. My officers will see to it that idleness, waste, and disobedience are punished severely. Is that understood?
MOSES:	You refuse to listen?
PHARAOH:	Me? Pharaoh of Egypt listen to a common laborer? Go and tell your God that this is Egypt! The person who lays down laws here is the Pharaoh. If I hear one word more—
MOSES:	Then I warn you, Pharaoh of Egypt—
OFFICER:	Silence!
MOSES:	I warn you, that I will do the Lord's bidding.
AARON:	When Moses smites the river Nile with his rod the water will turn to blood—

PHARAOH: Stop! So, Jew, you will turn the Nile to blood? You do that! Meanwhile I will tell my taskmasters to double the work in your camps and cut the ration of food. Let us see who is God in Egypt! Let them go, Officer! I think they are madmen, not dangerous criminals.

Scene Three:

The same characters and setting.

MOSES: You would not listen, Pharaoh.

PHARAOH: No, Jew. I would not listen, and I will not listen! I demand an end to your magic and your threats, or I will have you flayed alive.

MOSES: No, Pharaoh. You dare not harm me. You are too much afraid.

PHARAOH: Look, Moses—and you, Aaron. I have tried to be reasonable. I wish you no harm.

AARON: We have heard that many times. Broken promises, soft words—you have seen what they have brought upon you and your people: plagues and suffering!

PHARAOH: Coincidences, you mean.

AARON: Do the Egyptian people think that they are coincidences?

PHARAOH: The Egyptian people are not there to think. They do as I tell them.

MOSES: Then there is no room for further discussion. We bid you goodbye.

PHARAOH: Wait! Can we not come to a compromise? I cannot let all of your people abandon their work.

MOSES: There can be no compromise. It is too late. Up to now the Lord has struck the land and the water, the crops and the animals. By this time tomorrow he will have struck you and your people. Your son will die, and so will the firstborn sons of every Egyptian family. Come, brother!

(THEY GO OUT, NOBODY PREVENTING THEM)

PHARAOH:	It cannot be true! Their God cannot have this power!
OFFICER:	But what if he does, Your Majesty? Must our sons die?
PHARAOH:	(SHOUTING HYSTERICALLY) I tell you I will not yield! Set extra guards over the Jews, so that they cannot plan any trick! I will not yield!

Scene four:

THE GOLDEN CALF+
BIBLE REFERENCE: Exodus 32

Characters:	AARON AHOLIAB MOSES JOSHUA JEWISH MEN and WOMEN

Moses led the Israelites out of Egypt, and turned towards the promised land of Canaan. It was a long, hard journey, which tested all his powers as a leader. He was called by God to climb Mount Sinai, so as to receive the commandments which would guide the people's lives. He was away a long time, and Aaron's faith wavered. The scene is a Jewish camp in the wilderness.

AARON:	Thank you. Thank you, my friends.

(STANDING BESIDE TWO LARGE BASKETS, WHILE MEN AND WOMEN FILE BY, DEPOSITING THEIR GIFTS OF GOLD)

WOMAN:	This is my wedding ring, sir.
AARON:	You are all generous. Tomorrow Aholiab will make the Golden Calf, and you will be able to worship it.
SECOND WOMAN:	My earrings. An Egyptian lady gave them to me.
AARON:	Thank you. Your gold is much better offered to God than worn as an ornament to your body.
AHOLIAB:	That is enough, Aaron. Let us take it to the furnace.
AARON:	Very well. My people, we have enough gifts. Keep what you stil have. We will assemble tomorrow for the evening sacrifice, and worship the Calf.

(THE PEOPLE DISPERSE)

AHOLIAB: Are you sure that Moses will understand why we are doing this?

AARON: I cannot be sure. But—he has been on the mountain so long, and the people need something to worship. They are afraid that Moses is dead, or has abandoned us.

AHOLIAB: Very well. I will make the Calf. It will be beautiful—I promise you that.

AARON: I know it. You are a fine craftsman. It will be so much easier for the people to pray to an image of gold—something they can see. Moses talks of God as a spirit, but do they understand? Still, I am afraid—

Next evening, the Calf is set up on an altar. Aaron stands by it, with the people kneeling.

AARON: O God, we have made our offerings to you, of all that was most precious among our possessions. We pray to you through this image of gold. We give you thanks for our deliverance from the land of Egypt. Now, in our sufferings and our need, we pray for strength and help. As we have offered our gold to fashion your image, so reward us with precious gifts, with food and drink and victory over our enemies, until we come to the promised land. O Calf of Gold, symbol of richness and fertility, give us your blessing, and lead us to a land of plenty and peace! (HE TURNS TO THE PEOPLE) Now, people of Israel, dance and sing before the image of our god! Strip off your robes, and dance!

(A WILD DANCE BEGINS, ACCOMPANIED BY MUSIC OF CYMBALS. MOSES RUNS IN, SHOUTING)

MOSES: In the name of God, stop! Stop! (SUDDEN SILENCE) What is this madness? My brother, what sacrilege have you committed?

AARON: You were away so long. We thought that perhaps you were dead.

MOSES: I would rather be dead than see my people wallowing in idol worship and betraying their God.

AARON:	We are not betraying God! We are trying to worship him through an image, like the Egyptians. It is so hard—
MOSES:	Silence! Some evil spirit has struck you with madness. I have come from the very presence of God on the mountain. I carried the tables of laws, the symbol of our covenant with the one true God. When I heard what was happening here, I broke the tables and ran to save you from this abomination.
AARON:	Were we so wrong?
MOSES:	You have denied the very heart of your faith. You have lowered our people to the level of barbarians, bowing before wood and stone, and mouthing spells. Where is Joshua?
JOSHUA:	I am here, Moses.
MOSES:	Take all the men you can trust, and kill the leaders of this madness! Not my brother, for I truly believe he was struck with a frenzy which he could not resist—but all those who have danced naked before this image. And you, Aaron, and Aholiab, take this evil thing to the furnace! Grind it to powder before my eyes, and we will mix it with the water which my people drink, They shall be made to taste and swallow their sin!
AARON:	They begged me to make them new Gods; they offered their gold freely—
MOSES:	Be silent! Pray that, if it be possible, God will forgive your crime! I will return to him in penitence, and bring back the Laws which he has written for us, if he will permit it. If not, may I be blotted out, and our people forgotten here in the wilderness! Do your work, Joshua!

This scene could be completed by having Moses read the Ten Commandments to the people. Then discuss them. Think especially about the meaning of a 'graven image'. We do not literally have images which we worship; but anything which stands between us and God and unbalances our lives is an idol. It may be money, or sport, or sex, or anything with which we become obsessed. You may wish to read now some of the four modern plays grouped under the title ANY GRAVEN IMAGE....

Scene five:

MOSES AND JOSHUA*
BIBLE REFERENCE: Numbers 13 and 27: 18-23:
Deuteronomy 30: 11-20, and 34

Characters: MOSES
JOSHUA

Scene:

Mount Pisgah, overlooking the Jordan Valley and the promised land. Moses is seated, gazing across the River Jordan.

JOSHUA:
(ENTERING)   Did you ask me to come, Moses?

MOSES: Yes, Joshua, I asked you to come. I must give you my last words of counsel and farewell.

JOSHUA: Farewell! Why—

MOSES: I know from the Lord that I can go no further. He has let me see the promised land, but I may not set foot on it. You must lead our people across Jordan.

JOSHUA: If it is God's will, but—

MOSES: We have come a long way together. We have seen victory and defeat, faith and betrayal. Now there lies our country, promised to Abraham and Isaac and Jacob. My part is done: yours is beginning. You fought by my side. You went to spy on the land of Canaan. You have been chosen to lead Israel. Keep his commandments faithfully!

JOSHUA: With all my heart.

MOSES: His commandment is not hidden, or far away. It is not in the sky or beyond the sea, but in your mouth and your heart. You must choose life and good, or death and evil. Walk in the ways of God, keep his word, and you will live and multiply. But if your heart turns away, and if you serve other gods, you will die, and with you all our people. There is life, and death: blessing, or a curse. Choose life! Now leave me to make my peace with God before I die. May he bless you and keep you always!

THE BOOK OF RUTH*

(read first, then select scenes for acting)

Characters: ELIMELECH of Bethlehem
NAOMI, his wife
MAHLON and CHILION, their sons
RUTH and ORPAH, sisters from Moab
BOAZ, kinsman of Elimelech
#HEZRON, kinsman of Elimelech, and other ELDERS

This beautiful story is set in the time of the Judges, which covered two centuries after the coming of the Jews from Egypt. The writer shows an unusual sympathy for foreigners. The refugee Jewish family is kindly treated in Moab; and Ruth the Moabitess, we learn at the end, was a greatgrandmother of King David himself. The book introduces us for the first time to Bethlehem.

BY THE RIVER JORDAN
(ELIMELECH AND HIS FAMILY DRAG THEMSELVES TO THE RIVER BANK)

NAOMI: Thank God! The river at last!

MAHLON: Water! (THEY ALL STOOP AND DRINK)

CHILION: Oh, wonderful! Better than any wine!

ELIMELECH: Yes. Jordan. Almost the end of our journey.

MAHLON: We have to rest, Father. We can't go on tonight.

ELIMELECH: No, Mahlon. We will rest tonight; but I'm afraid there is no food here, unless we can catch fish or trap a bird.

CHILION: We haven't the strength to try.

ELIMELECH: That is why we must cross into Moab tomorrow.

NAOMI: But—what if they drive us away, or worse than that?

ELIMELECH: We've been over that before, Naomi.

MAHLON: I'm scared. You know the stories they tell about Moabites and Edomites.

CHILION: And there may be famine in Moab too, Father.

ELIMELECH: You talk as if we had another choice. We don't. Now try to rest. We need all our strength for tomorrow.

MOAB

(THE FAMILY CRAWL UNDER A TREE, IN VERY BAD CONDITION)

NAOMI: It's no use. I can't go any further.

MAHLON: Nor I.

ELIMELECH: Don't give up! That smoke ahead has to mean a house, at least, probably a village. You three stay and rest. I will try to find somebody.

CHILION: It's our last chance.

NAOMI: God have mercy on us!

(ELIMELECH CRAWLS SOME DISTANCE. RUTH COMES FROM THE OPPOSITE DIRECTION, CARRYING A BASKET OR WATER POT)

RUTH: Oh, sir! Are you hurt?

ELIMELECH: My wife—and sons—dying!
(HE POINTS BACK AND COLLAPSES)

RUTH: Orpah! Quick! Come and help!

ORPAH: (RUNNING IN) What is it? Oh!

RUTH: He says his family are back there, dying. Are you from Israel, sir?

ELIMELECH: From Bethlehem-Judah.

RUTH: We will help you. Wait, and I will fetch my father.

ORPAH: And I will run to my uncle's house. Here, I will leave you water.

ELIMELECH: Thank God!

AGAIN BY JORDAN

The family of Ruth and Orpah took the Jewish refugees in, and they recovered. They made a new life for themselves in Moab. Mahlon and Chilion married Ruth and Orpah. Then disaster struck the family. All three husbands died, leaving Naomi and the two Moabite women widows. Naomi decided to go back to her native Bethlehem. Ruth and Orpah accompanied her to the border to say goodbye.

RUTH: Rest a little, Mother. We are nearly at the river.

NAOMI: There are the mountains of Judaea—my old country!

ORPAH: Oh, Mother dear, why don't you stay with us.

NAOMI: No, Orpah. I must go back to my own people. You two ought to rejoin your families. I am too old to find another husband, but you will marry again. Now, walk with me to the river and we will say goodbye.

RUTH: Mother, I have decided. I cannot go back.

ORPAH: Ruth! You can't leave Moab!

RUTH: Yes—I am going with my mother-in-law. Where she goes I will go; and where she dies I will die. Don't ask me to leave you, Mother! I have decided.

ORPAH: No, Ruth, no! Oh, I wish I had the courage!

NAOMI: You are sure, my child? Sure that you wish to go with me, alone, to a country far from your own home, where I may have been forgotten and you may find yourself among enemies?

RUTH: Yes, I am sure. Don't cry, my sister! We are different, you and I. Turn back now, and I will go with Naomi.

NAOMI: God will protect you, dear daughter. Perhaps one day we will all meet again.

(NAOMI AND RUTH WALK AWAY. ORPAH WATCHES THEM, AND WEEPS)

BETHLEHEM

Naomi and Ruth came to Bethlehem. Boaz watched them as they walked near his home.

BOAZ: Welcome, strangers!

NAOMI: Boaz!

BOAZ: You know my name? Who—why surely—-this cannot be Naomi?

NAOMI: I was called Naomi once. Now I need a name to match the bitterness of my life—Mara. I went away full, and come back empty—but not alone. This is Ruth of Moab, widow of my dead son. She chose to come with me.

BOAZ: (EMBRACES BOTH WOMEN) Welcome to Bethlehem, my child! I can hardly believe that it is really you, dear Naomi. Come in, and tell me all your news!

INSIDE BOAZ'S HOME NAOMI TOLD HER STORY.

BOAZ: (SEATED WITH THE TWO WOMEN) So they are all dead?

NAOMI: Yes. We three were left as widows. I thought it best to come back to my own kindred.

BOAZ: You were right. We will look after you.

NAOMI: You are a good man, Boaz. Care for Ruth also! She left everything for me.

BOAZ: This shall be her home. The love that she has shown for you needs to be repaid.

RUTH: I thank you, sir.

BOAZ: There has been too much enmity between Judah and Moab. Now I must see what can be done to find you somewhere to live; and of course you may follow the harvesters and glean corn from my fields.

Boaz found Naomi a home. He told his steward to see that the reapers would treat Ruth with kindness, and leave plenty of corn behind for her to glean. Soon everybody could see that Boaz was falling in love with Ruth. He called a meeting of the city elders by the gate.

(SEVERAL ELDERS ARE SEATED IN A HALF CIRCLE. NAOMI AND RUTH STAND TO ONE SIDE)

BOAZ:	I called this meeting because it is necessary to dispose of the property of Elimelech, now that we know him to be dead.
ELDER:	What do you propose, Boaz?
BOAZ:	You know our law. The closest kinsman of Elimelech should buy the land and property. That is you, Hezron.
HEZRON:	I am willing to do that, Boaz. What is the property?
BOAZ:	I have a list here. Of course you realize that in buying the property you will also purchase the wife of Elimelech's dead son, the Moabite girl Ruth. Will you make her your wife, and raise up the name of the dead?
HEZRON:	Oh, I think I understand. Well, Boaz— perhaps I should yield that right to you. You are the second closest kinsman, and—
BOAZ:	(EAGERLY) Are you sure, Hezron?
HEZRON:	Yes, certainly. You buy the property, and marry Ruth.
BOAZ:	Give me your shoe as a pledge of the agreement. (HEZRON TAKES OFF HIS SHOE, LAUGHING, AND GIVES IT TO BOAZ)
HEZRON:	There! Now it is yours to buy—and Ruth is yours to marry!
BOAZ:	You are a good friend. I call you all to witness that I accept Elimelech's inheritance, and that Ruth of Moab is my wife. (HE TAKES HER BY THE HAND)

Boaz and Ruth were married, and she bore a son named Obed. His son was Jesse, the father of David, the shepherdboy who became Israel's greatest king.

SAMUEL AND DAVID

With Samuel a new phase of Jewish history began. He was the first of the great prophets. Under God's guidance he chose and anointed the first two kings who united the tribes of Israel. The story began in the sacred precinct of Shiloh, where Eli was the priest.

Scene one:

PRAYING FOR A SON **
BIBLE REFERENCE: I Samuel 1: 1-18

Characters: ELKANAH
HANNAH and PENINNAH, his wives
TWO CHILDREN of Elkanah and Peninnah
ELI the priest

ELKANAH: Now that I have made my offering to God, let me give each of you your gifts.

PENINNAH: (IN A SHARP VOICE) Come here, children! Your father has gifts for you.

FIRST CHILD: Ooh! I wonder what I will get.

SECOND CHILD: Not as much as I will. I'm the eldest!

PENINNAH: Be quiet!

ELKANAH: Hannah, come and sit with us.

FIRST CHILD: Does she get a present too?

ELKANAH: My child, if you grow up to deserve a present as much as Hannah does, you will be a wonderful woman.

PENINNAH: Oh, yes! She never does anything wrong. It's a pity God doesn't—

ELKANAH: Be silent, Peninnah!

PENINNAH: Why? You always prefer her to me, and give her more. Why does she have no children? Tell me that! If she's so wonderful, why does God—

ELKANAH: I told you to be silent! Hannah, where are you going?

HANNAH: Leave me alone—please! I am going to pray. I cannot bear to be with you when she talks like that. (SHE RUNS TO THE OTHER SIDE OF THE STAGE)

ELKANAH: Peninnah, why can't you learn to control your tongue? I will double Hannah's portion, and set half of it aside for the child whom she may still bear. Your portion will be less, and your children's.

FIRST CHILD: That's not fair!

SECOND CHILD: No. Why—

ELKANAH: Be quiet! Go back to the carriage and wait for me! I will come soon.

PENINNAH: Come on, children! We're not wanted here. Leave her to her prayers! Much use they will be to her! (SHE GOES OUT WITH CHILDREN. ELKANAH WALKS ACROSS TO HANNAH, WHO KNEELS, PRAYING SILENTLY)

ELKANAH: Why are you crying, my dear?

HANNAH: How do you think I can bear any more of that? The insults of that woman and her greedy, vulgar children? I try to love them, but I am weak, I want my own child!

ELKANAH: I know, I know. Surely God will hear our prayers.

HANNAH: Leave me for a few minutes. I will come to the carriage.

(HE GOES OUT. AFTER A PAUSE ELI ENTERS)

ELI: What are you praying for, lady?

HANNAH: Oh, sir! I did not see you.

ELI: I saw your lips moving, and no words came. For a minute I thought you might be drunk; but I can see that you are deep in prayer, and weeping. Can I help?

HANNAH: I have lost hope that anyone can help me—even God.

ELI: What is it that you want so badly?

HANNAH: A son, sir! I love my husband so much, and he loves me, but we have no child. If I could only bear a son, I would bring him to you and let him serve the Lord.

ELI:	Go in peace! I will pray for you also. God will hear your prayers, and if it is his will you will bear a son.
HANNAH:	Thank you for your kindness, sir.

Scene Two:

A COAT FOR SAMUEL**
BIBLE REFERENCE: I Samuel 1: 19 to 2: 11

Characters: HANNAH
SAMUEL
ELI

Hannah bore a son named Samuel. As a boy he worked and studied at Shiloh under the guidance of Eli.
(SAMUEL, ABOUT TEN YEARS OLD, IS SWEEPING THE FLOOR)

HANNAH:	(Entering) Samuel!
SAMUEL:	Why, mother! I knew you would come. (THEY EMBRACE)
HANNAH:	My child! You've grown so tall! It was time I brought your new new coat. Look! (SHE HOLDS OUT A NEW COAT, WHICH HE PUTS ON)
SAMUEL:	Thank you! It's beautiful!
HANNAH:	I will pass the old one on to one of the village children.
ELI: (ENTERING)	Welcome, Hannah! What do you think of your son?
HANNAH:	Greetings, sir, from my husband! I have gifts for you. How he has grown!
ELI:	A new coat, I see. Samuel, go and ask your mother's servant to bring in the gifts. (SAMUEL GOES OUT) He is a fine boy, Hannah. God did more than answer your prayers.
HANNAH:	I know, sir. Each year I thank him more and more.

ELI:	Samuel has a special kind of faith, which brings him close to God. He will do great things one day. I will leave you to your prayers. (HE GOES OUT. HANNAH KNEELS)
HANNAH:	O Lord, my heart rejoices in you. You are the only God, the rock of our lives. You raise the poor out of the dust, and give children to the childless. Make us worthy of the happiness which you have given to us through our son Samuel!

Scene three:

THE CALL OF SAMUEL **
BIBLE REFERENCE: I Samuel 3.

Characters:	VOICE OF GOD
	SAMUEL
	ELI

One night Samuel lay asleep on the floor. Eli slept close by in a bed.

VOICE OF GOD:	Samuel!
SAMUEL (SITTING UP)	Yes? Here I am. (PAUSE. HE GOES AND STANDS BY ELI'S BED) Here I am, sir.
ELI: (HALF AWAKE)	What is it, my boy?
SAMUEL:	I heard you call, sir.
ELI:	No. I did not call. Go back to sleep. (A PAUSE. SAMUEL IS ASLEEP AGAIN)
VOICE OF GOD:	Samuel, wake up!
SAMUEL:	What? (HE GOES TO ELI) Yes, sir?
ELI:	What is it? Again, Samuel? You must be dreaming. Go back to bed!
SAMUEL:	I was sure—I am sorry, sir. (HE GOES BACK TO BED. A PAUSE)
VOICE OF GOD:	Samuel!

SAMUEL:	Yes? (HE GOES TO ELI) It happened again, sir. I could swear you called.
ELI:	No; but I believe there is a voice calling you. If it comes again, say, 'Speak, Lord, for thy servant heareth.' Can you remember that?
SAMUEL:	Yes, sir. I'm sorry I disturbed you. (HE GOES BACK TO BED. A PAUSE)
VOICE OF GOD:	Wake up, Samuel!
SAMUEL:	Speak, Lord, for thy servant heareth.
VOICE OF GOD:	Eli is right. It is I, the Lord, calling you. I want you to be my servant and messenger. Men's ears will tingle at the things which I will declare through you. There are hard days ahead for the people of Israel, but you must listen for my words, and follow my bidding. You shall be a prophet to my people, my own mouthpiece. Now sleep, Samuel, son of a noble father and of a blessed mother!

(SAMUEL LIES DOWN AGAIN AND GOES TO SLEEP)

Scene four:

A KING IS NAMED +
BIBLE REFERENCE: I SAMUEL 9 AND 10

Characters: SAUL, a young man of huge physique
His SERVANT
SAMUEL
CROWD of Jewish men and women

Samuel became the Lord's prophet. God told him that on a certain day a man named Saul, of the tribe of Benjamin, would come looking for his father's donkeys. This was the man whom Samuel was to anoint as the first king of Israel.
(SAUL AND HIS SERVANT ENTER, TIRED AND DISCOURAGED)

SAUL:	We're going to have to give up. It's no use.
SERVANT:	Yes, sir. I'm afraid the donkeys are lost. We can rest in this village.

(SEVERAL PEOPLE PASS BY. SAUL APPROACHES THEM)

SAUL:	Friends, have you by chance seen a herd of donkeys? My father is Kish, of the tribe of Benjamin. He sent me to look for them.
DIFFERENT PEOPLE REPLY:	I haven't seen them. How many? Have you tried down by the river? etc)
SAUL:	Isn't there a prophet who lives here?
MAN:	You mean Samuel. Yes, he is here.
SERVANT:	I will look for him, sir.
SAUL:	I have no gifts for him.
MAN:	He will not ask you for gifts.
WOMAN:	Here he comes! (SAMUEL ENTERS, AND LOOKS HARD AT SAUL)
SAUL:	Excuse me, sir. Are you Samuel the prophet?
SAMUEL:	Walk with me, Saul, son of Kish. I was expecting you. (THEY WALK ASIDE) Forget about the donkeys. They have been found.
SAUL:	How did you know—? Expecting me, did you say?
SAMUEL:	The Lord has spoken. Our people are divided, so that our enemies always defeat us piecemeal. What does Israel need most? A king, Saul! A strong man, to enforce unity. And the Lord has chosen you.
SAUL:	Me? A Benjamite, from an unknown family? You are mocking me.
SAMUEL:	This is no mockery, but the will of God. Come with me now! You must eat, and rest. Tomorrow I will anoint you king of all the tribes of Israel. Then we will go to Mizpeh, and proclaim God's will to the people.
SAUL:	But—how will they accept me, an unknown man?

SAMUEL: They will accept God's choice, at the bidding of God's prophet. I am chosen as his spokesman, you as his warrior chief. Do not be afraid! The spirit of the Lord will be within you, and you will fight with his strength as well as your own. Now call your servant, and we will go to my home!

Scene five:

SAMUEL ANOINTS THE BOY DAVID +
BIBLE REFERENCE: I SAMUEL 16: 1-13

CHARACTERS   SAMUEL
VOICE OF GOD
SEVEN SONS OF JESSE
DAVID

Saul fought hard to unite the tribes of Israel, but it was an uphill battle. They were not used to obeying one ruler, and their enemies were formidable, especially the Philistines. Saul was a brave man, but he had many failings. Samuel was told by God to go to Bethlehem and offer a sacrifice. There he found Jesse, grandson of Ruth the Moabitess, with his family.
(SAMUEL ENTERS JESSE'S HOUSE AND GREETS HIM)

SAMUEL: You are Jesse?

JESSE: Yes, sir. I am honored that the Lord's prophet has come to my home. What do you wish of me?

SAMUEL: Bring all your sons to me, beginning with the eldest.

JESSE: But— Have we done something wrong in the eyes of the Lord?

SAMUEL: No, Jesse. When I have seen your sons I will show you God's will.

JESSE: Very well. (HE CALLS LOUDLY) Eliab! Come here!
(SEVEN SONS COME ONE AFTER ANOTHER. THIS CAN EITHER BE ACTED OUT OR BRIEFLY EXPLAINRD BY THE NARRATOR. EACH ONE IS INTRODUCED BY JESSE, THEN DISMISSED BY SAMUEL)

SAMUEL: Have you no other son?

JESSE:	Only my youngest boy, David. I did not think you would wish—
SAMUEL:	Call him, please!
JESSE:	Very well. Eliab! Find David and send him. He is only a boy, and looks after our sheep. He's a good singer, too: makes up songs all the time and plays the guitar.
DAVID:	(RUNNING IN, BREATHLESS) You wanted me, Father?
JESSE:	David, this is the prophet Samuel—
SAMUEL:	(TO HIMSELF) God be praised! I have found him! (TO JESSE) Thank you, Jesse. Leave us alone, please.
JESSE:	(SHAKING HIS HEAD) If you say so. (HE GOES OUT)
SAMUEL:	David, I am the prophet of the Lord. I do not speak for myself, but for him. Kneel down! (DAVID KNEELS) David, neither you nor I can fully understand what God is asking us to do. It will be shown to us later. I anoint you in the name of God, as the chosen future king of Israel. Make yourself ready, by prayer, and by the training and dedication of your mind and body and soul! Do you understand and accept this responsibility?
DAVID:	If you say that it is God's will, I accept it. But Saul is our king. Surely it is my duty to serve him—
SAMUEL:	Yes. Your calling has not yet come. Go back to your sheep and sing your songs in God's praise! May his blessing be with you now and when you meet your greater challenges!

Scene six:

DAVID AND GOLIATH + (but try it)
BIBLE REFERENCE: I Samuel 17.

Characters:	ELIAB, ABINADAB, SHAMMAH , David's brothers DAVID KING SAUL GOLIATH the PHILISTINE SOLDIERS, Jewish and Philistine

Some time later King Saul and his army, including David's older brothers, were fighting the Philistines, who lived near the Mediterranean coast and aimed to conquer Israel. David's father and mother sent him with a donkey load of food for his brothers. He found them, and the rest of the army, in despair.

ELIAB: (SITTING WITH HIS BROTHERS ON THE GROUND) It's no use.

ABINADAB: No. Nobody can fight Goliath.

SHAMMAH: So we have to surrender?

ABINADAB: Yes, surrender and be humiliated.

ELIAB: Look, here comes David! (DAVID ENTERS)

ABINADAB: David! What in the world brings you here?

DAVID: My brothers! (THEY EMBRACE) Mother and Father send their greetings.

ELIAB: Are they well?

DAVID: Yes, everybody is well. They sent a load of food—some for you and some for King Saul.

SHAMMAH: Mother's bread, and parched corn! I can't wait! Not that it's much use—

DAVID: What is the matter? You all look worn out.

ELIAB: David, we are facing a crushing defeat. You see that man on the hill?

DAVID: God in heaven! A giant!

ELIAB: He has issued a challenge. Fight him singlehanded, or give up. The king doesn't know what to do.

SHAMMAH: Not even Saul dares to face that monster.

ABINADAB: He's a freak, and with that armor nobody can hope to touch him.

DAVID: (SPEAKING SOFTLY) Strong as an ox—but clumsy.

ELIAB: Not too clumsy to carve up anyone who comes within his reach.

DAVID: Within his reach, yes. Eliab, would they let me offer to fight him?

ELIAB: You? Don't be crazy!

DAVID: I'm not being crazy. You say nobody else will try?

SHAMMAH: It's impossible. We're not cowards, but—

DAVID: Not impossible. I can see a way—

ABINADAB: He's calling out the challenge again.

GOLIATH: (OFF STAGE OR AT A DISTANCE) This is your last chance, Jewish pigs! Will none of you be a man and face death? Fight before the sun passes its height, or surrender! My sword is thirsty for a Jewish cur's blood.

SHAMMAH: (AS THEY ALL STAND, AND SAUL APPROACHES) The king!

DAVID: (KNEELING) Your Majesty!

SAUL: Yes, boy. Who are you?

ELIAB: Our brother David, sir. He—

DAVID: I know a way to fight the Philistine, sir.

SHAMMAH: We've told him not to be foolish—

SAUL: My son, nobody can save us now.

DAVID: At least I could try. He's far too strong for anyone who fights at close quarters. If I come near him I will die—I know that. But I may be able to kill him before he can reach me.

SAUL: Kill him before—I don't know what you mean, boy.

DAVID: (SHOWS HIS SLING) With this. You see, sir, I'm in charge of our sheep at home. We have foxes and jackals, and sometimes a wolf, out to get at the flock. I've had to learn to hit them with a slingstone before—

ABINADAB: That's true, sir. He can hit anything.

SAUL: But a wolf has no armor, David.

DAVID: I know that. But even Goliath has to see. Look at his helmet! It leaves his eyes and nose and part of his forehead—

SAUL: You can aim for that? Impossible!

DAVID: No. I ought to hit a target that size, if I come as close as I dare. I may miss, and be killed, but that's better than not trying.

SAUL: (AFTER A PAUSE) David, do you think this is what God wants you to do?

DAVID: Truly I do, sir.

SAUL: Then at least wear my armor—

DAVID: No, no! . That would only hamper me. I have to have my arms free and use my sling.

SAUL: With no protection?

DAVID: My sling and pebbles are my protection. If I hit him, I need no armor. If I miss, no armor would save me. I have never worn any of these things.

SAUL: Then go, David! May your skill match your bravery!

GOLIATH: Time is nearly up, you dogs!

DAVID: (WALKING TOWARDS GOLIATH) I am coming, Philistine! I will fight you in the name of the Lord God of Israel!

GOLIATH: What? A boy? No sword or armor? What kind of joke is this? At least send me a man to kill.

DAVID: You will find out which of us is a man, Goliath.

GOLIATH: Very well, boy. Come over here, and I will give the dogs and vultures something to eat. You crazy little hero! (DAVID PUTS A PEBBLE IN HIS SLING) What's that you've got? Do Jews fight with pieces of string? (DAVID WALKS CLOSER, AND SLINGS A STONE. GOLIATH FALLS WITH A GROAN. THE ARMIES CRY OUT IN JOY AND AGONY)

Scene seven:

THE SIN OF DAVID **
BIBLE REFERENCE: 2 SAMUEL 11 AND 12: 1-25

Characters: KING DAVID
BATHSHEBA
NATHAN
SERVANT

David became King, and made Jerusalem the capital of Israel. He was the greatest leader of the Jews since Moses; but the Bible records his faults as well as his gifts and achievements. This scene takes place in his palace. David and Bathsheba the Queen are seated when a servant enters.

SERVANT: Your Majesty, the prophet Nathan is here.

DAVID: At this hour of the evening? Tell him to come tomorrow.

SERVANT: He is insistent on seeing you, sir.

DAVID: Very well, let him come. I have not seen Nathan since—since we were married.

BATHSHEBA: What is the matter, David? You look frightened.

DAVID: I? Frightened of Nathan? Why should I fear him?

SERVANT: The prophet Nathan, Your Majesty.

NATHAN: I am sorry to disturb you, Your Majesty, and your Queen. Is this the newborn prince?

DAVID: You have been away from our court, Nathan. What brings you back?

NATHAN: A case of injustice, sir. I would like you to hear it, and give your judgment.

DAVID: Surely it could have waited—

NATHAN: I come at the Lord's bidding, sir. When he gives me his word I do not wait.

DAVID: Very well. Will you take the child, Bathsheba, and go to your room.

BATHSHEBA: As you wish, my Lord.

NATHAN: No, sir. I would like Queen Bathsheba to hear what I say.

DAVID: You are taking a great deal on yourself, Nathan. Very well. Stay, Bathsheba, and listen!

NATHAN: This is the story of two men from your kingdom, sir. One is rich, and has everything he could wish for. The other is poor. He had only one ewe lamb, in comparison with all of the rich man's flocks. The lamb was like a child to him, they say, and ate and drank at his table. You understand, my lady?

BATHSHEBA: What is it to me?

NATHAN: Just a story. Now hear the end. A traveler came to visit the rich man. He was unwilling to kill one of his own sheep; so he took the poor man's lamb, killed it, and served it to his guest.

DAVID: But that is unforgivable! Tell me who he is, and I will see that justice is done. He must be forced to— Why do you look at me, Nathan?

NATHAN: Why do I look at you, David, King of Israel, conqueror of Jerusalem, rich and mighty ruler? I look at you because you are the man who did this thing. There beside you sits the wife of the faithful soldier whom you killed—oh, not with your own hands, but with cunning and cowardice. And there is the son born of your sinful marriage!

DAVID: Stop! If you must say these things to me, do not say them to her! She had no guilt. I have sinned, I know it—

NATHAN:	You have sinned, and you have brought shame and suffering on her. For the child will die, David. This son of yours will die, and there will be violence and discord among your other sons, because you despised the Lord's law. God is merciful, and will give you and the Queen other sons when this child is dead. But hear his word, and from now on do justice in his eyes!
BATHSHEBA:	David, stop him! I do not want my child to die!
DAVID:	I cannot silence the mouth of a prophet. I have sinned towards Uriah, whom I gave over to death, and towards you, whom I stole from him. May God forgive me!
NATHAN:	I will leave you now. When the child dies, mourn for him. Then turn to the work of God and pray that you may sin no more!

David and Absalom

BIBLE REFERENCE: 2 Samuel 14-18

David, like most rulers of his time, had several wives and a large number of children. This naturally led to jealousy and trouble. These scenes tell the dramatic story of the attempt by one of his sons, Absalom, to depose his father and become king.

Scene one:

ABSALOM WOOS THE PEOPLE (improvise)
BIBLE REFERENCE: 2 Samuel 15: 1-6

Absalom, young and handsome and vain, was determined to become king. He killed his eldest brother Amnon, and set out to ingratiate himself with the people. He is outside the gate of Jerusalem, stopping men and women as they walk past. Improvise his words and their replies. He says things such as:

'If I were king I could solve your problem.' 'My father is too old to be king. He ought to be allowed to retire in peace.'

Scene Two:

DAVID ON THE RUN (improvise)
BIBLE REFERENCE: 2 Samuel 15: 13-37

David is now old, and has lost his power of leadership. He has left Jerusalem. We find him 'weeping, barefoot, with his head covered.' Messengers bring bad news, which he receives with hopeless indifference. His loyal commander, Ittai the Gittite, refuses to abandon him. David asks Hushai to go and spy for him in Jerusalem. Improvise these conversations.

Scene three:

ABSALOM IS DECEIVED**
BIBLE REFERENCE: 2 SAMUEL 16: 15-23, AND 17

Characters: ABSALOM
AHITOPHEL
HUSHAI
ZADOK the priest
OFFICERS of Absalom

Absalom is seated with some of his officers, and Zadok the priest. He must decide on his strategy for defeating his father King David.

ABSALOM: So my father has run away, and left all his women behind. It's time for the old man to give up, isn't it? Tell the women not to be afraid. They belong to me now, like everything else in Jerusalem.

OFFICER: Yes, sir. (HE GOES OUT)

ABSALOM: Send for some food and wine. And bring Ahitophel here.

2nd OFFICER: Yes, sir. He is waiting outside. (HE GOES OUT. AHITOPHEL ENTERS)

ABSALOM: Well, my friend, we have him on the run. Jerusalem abandoned, and everyone flocking to join us. It's almost too good to be true!

AHITOPHEL: Yes, sir; and if we strike now we will finish the war in one day.

ABSALOM: Follow him at once?

AHITOPHEL: That's right. In war, initiative is everything. David has no heart to resist you. His people are in shock. Smash them now! Give me twelve thousand men, and I will have him back tomorrow, a prisoner.

OFFICER:	(ENTERNG)Excuse me, sir. Hushai the Archite is asking to see you.
ABSALOM:	Hushai? My father's oldest friend? What things war does to us! Bring him in.
AHITOPHEL:	Don't waste time on him, Absalom! Give me my answer!
HUSHAI:	(ENTERINGAND KNEELING) Your Majesty!
ABSALOM:	Is this your idea of loyalty? Sit over there! Why did you leave your king?
HUSHAI:	Long live Your Majesty! My friend and master must be the man chosen by the Lord and by the people. I will serve you as I have served your father.
ABSALOM:	Better, I hope. Well, since you are here, tell me your news.
HUSHAI:	You must not underestimate David, or his generals. They are like a bear robbed of her cubs. For a little while they are dangerous. The King—that is, the former King, has gone into hiding—I'm not sure where—and plans to ambush you—
AHITOPHEL:	He's lying! Our spies tell us that David is shattered, sitting with what is left of his army, weeping and wringing his hands. We have to strike now!
HUSHAI:	Your friend is wrong. Look, I have nothing to gain by joining you and watching you lose, have I? And you will lose, if you lead out an army that is unprepared, and fall into a trap.
ABSALOM:	What is your advice?
AHITOPHEL:	Don't listen! It's all lies!
HUSHAI:	Wait until you have all of your army, sir. People are flocking in from Dan to Beersheba to join you. In a few days you can wipe David out in the open, or pull apart with ropes any fortress he hides in. But don't attack now!
ABSALOM:	(AFTER A PAUSE) He's right, Ahitophel. If David is preparing an ambush...

AHITOPHEL:	If God wants to poison your mind there's nothing I can do. Accept a traitor's advice and reject mine! But I'm not going to wait and be tortured by David's soldiers. (HE RUNS OUT. OFFICER ENTERS)
OFFICER:	Your food and wine are ready in the hall, sir.
ABSALOM:	Good! Let us go. Hushai, join me, and you, Zadok.
ZADOK:	Yes, sir. (AS THEY LEAVE, HUSHAI PULLS ZADOK BACK)
HUSHAI:	May I speak to you for a moment?
ZADOK:	(NERVOUS) What is it?
HUSHAI:	We have to get a message to David. Can you do it?
ZADOK:	Yes. We have a girl here who can find Jonathan and Ahimaaz.
HUSHAI:	David must get across the river. He has a little breathing space. If he sits where he is it's all over.
ZADOK:	I understand. Quick! We must follow the others.

Scene four:

A MESSAGE TO DAVID (improvise)
BIBLE REFERENCE: 2 SAMUEL 17: 15-22

An exciting scene to improvise, but hard to act. The maid comes to a farm with Hushai's message. A boy hears her talking to the farmer's wife, and runs to tell Absalom's men. Jonathan and Ahimaaz listen to the maid's news, but soldiers are heard approaching. The farmer's wife hides them in her well, and the soldiers search unsuccessfully. Jonathan and Ahimaaz emerge, promise the women rewards for their courage, and hurry away to reach David.

(In the Bible story there are two farms.)

Scene five:

PREPARING FOR BATTLE *
BIBLE REFERENCE: 2 SAMUEL 18: 1-8

Characters:	DAVID
	JOAB, ABISHAI, and ITTAI, his Generals

David crossed the Jordan and reviewed his amy. Now it was time for them to join battle with Absalom's troops.

JOAB: (AS THE GENERALS ENTER WITH DAVID)
Sit down and rest, sir! You have done all that you can

DAVID: Thank you, Joab. You are right. I am tired.

ABISHAI: You have a fine army, sir, ready for victory.

DAVID: Victory? Over my own son, whom I love best of all ?

JOAB: Sir, Absalom has proved to be a traitor and a liar. He has put a price on your head. If you are halfhearted now, how do you expect us to fight?

ABISHAI: The sooner we can bring you proof of his death the better.

DAVID: No, no—not his death! Spare the boy, Joab!

JOAB: Sir, we are soldiers, loyal to our king. We fight to win at all costs.

DAVID: I will march with you.

ITTAI: No, sir. If we die, it does not matter. If you die, the traitors will have their reward. You are equal to ten thousand men on our side—too precious to be risked.

JOAB: Ittai is right.

DAVID: Very well. You three will command the three divisions. I will wait here.

ABISHAI: For God's sake, sir, pray for us! Don't go soft! We are ready to die for you.

DAVID: I know it, Abishai. Victory or defeat—either way is hard for me, but I will pray for my loyal friends.

Scene six:

THE DEATH OF ABSALOM*
BIBLE REFERENCE: 2 SAMUEL 18: 9-33

Characters: DAVID
OFFICERS
AHIMAAZ
MESSENGER (the Cushite or Ethiopian)

Absalom, defeated and riding away on a mule, was caught by his long hair in a tree. A soldier found him, and called Joab, who killed Absalom. Joab ordered a trumpeter to sound the 'Cease Fire!' Ahimaaz eagerly offered to tell David, but Joab knew that David might hate him for bringing bad news. He sent an Ethiopian messenger; but Ahimaaz persuaded him to let him go also, and he outran the Ethiopian.

DAVID: (SEATED, SURROUNDED BY OFFICERS) Still nothing!

OFFICER: No, sir. Wait! There's a man running across the plain.

DAVID: One man? A messenger from Joab! How near is he?

OFFICER: A long way. But look—

2nd OFFICER: There's another runner, overtaking him.

OFFICER: That's Ahimaaz. I can tell from the way he runs.

2nd OFFICER: You're right. (HE SHOUTS) Ahimaaz! What news?

AHIMAAZ: (FROM A LONG DISTANCE) Good news! Victory!

2nd OFFICER: Thank God, sir! Victory!

DAVID: Yes, but—Absalom!

AHIMAAZ: (RUNNING IN AND KNEELING, BREATHLESS) Victory, Your Majesty! We routed Absalom's men.

DAVID: Thank you, Ahimaaz. And my son—Absalom?

AHIMAAZ: I left at once, sir. There was a lot of confusion, I couldn't tell—

OFFICER:	Here comes the second messenger, sir.
DAVID:	Stand aside, Ahimaaz! (CUSHITE ENTERS AND KNEELS) Tell us your news!
MESSENGER:	Good tidings for my Lord the King! The Lord has delivered you from the enemies who rose against you.
DAVID:	And Absalom? What do you know of him?
MESSENGER:	May all your enemies end like him, sir!
DAVID:	(HEAD IN HANDS) O God! O Absalom, my son, my son! If it could only have been I who died! (HE WALKS OUT SLOWLY)
OFFICER:	Wait until Joab gets back. All the king cares about is that rat Absalom.
2nd OFFICER:	Poor old man! His sons have not given him much joy.
AHIMAAZ:	Well, he'd better pull himself together, and go to meet the men who fought for him.

Scene seven:
THE ANOINTING OF SOLOMON +
BIBLE REFERENCE: I Kings 1: 1-40

Characters: DAVID, an old man
ABISHAG, a young girl
BATHSHEBA
ZADOK the priest
BENAIAH
NATHAN

David grew old, and there were quarrels between his sons. This scene describes a crisis which arose just before he died. David is lying on a couch, with Abishag kneeling beside him, chafing his hands to keep them warm. Bathsheba is seated at the other side of the room when Nathan comes in and stands beside her.

NATHAN:	My lady, we know that the king no longer understands what is happening outside.
BATHSHEBA:	I know it, Nathan. His mind is wandering. Abishag is the only person he wants near him.

NATHAN:	Somehow you must make him understand. Adonijah has virtually proclaimed himself king. Solomon is in great danger of losing his throne and his life—which means your life too, and the lives of all who are faithful to Solomon.
BATHSHEBA:	I will do what I can. Wait here!
NATHAN:	I will, my lady.
BATHSHEBA:	(CROSSES TO STAND CLOSE TO DAVID) David, I must speak to you.
DAVID:	Who is it? I cannot see.
ABISHAG:	It is Queen Bathsheba, my Lord.
BATHSHEBA:	Let me come close to him, Abishag. All our lives are in danger. (ABISHAG RISES, AND BATHSHEBA KNEELS)
DAVID:	Don't leave me, girl! Where are you?
BATHSHEBA:	David, my Lord, it is I, Bathsheba. You must listen!
DAVID:	(SLOWLY) Bathsheba. Yes, yes. I—
BATHSHEBA:	You swore that our son Solomon would be king after you.
DAVID:	Solomon. Yes. But Absalom—
BATHSHEBA:	Absalom is dead, David.
DAVID:	Dead?
BATHSHEBA:	And Adonijah has proclaimed himself king. He has sacrificed at En-Rogel, and—
NATHAN:	(APPROACHING) May I speak to my Lord the king?
BATHSHEBA:	Nathan has come to tell you more: Nathan the prophet.
DAVID:	I am tired. Where is Abishag?

NATHAN: She is here. But first you must listen. You gave your oath to Queen Bathsheba, and to your loyal servants, that Solomon would be king. It is now or never!

BATHSHEBA: If Adonijah succeeds, you will be murdered. Only Solomon—

DAVID: (SUDDENLY ALERT, SITTING UP WITH AN EFFORT) You are right. My eyes and my mind are dim, but—what must I do?

NATHAN: Zadok is here, your Majesty, and Benaiah, your chief priest and faithful soldier. We have a paper proclaiming Solomon king. Seal it, and we will act.

DAVID: Call them in!

BATHSHEBA: God be praised! When Solomon is anointed you can rest in peace.

DAVID: Yes, yes—in my grave. I have tried to serve God—

BATHSHEBA: O, my Lord, you have served him, and your people love you.

(NATHAN BRINGS IN ZADOK AND BENAIAH)

ZADOK: (KNEELING WITH BENAIAH) Greetings, Your Majesty!

BENAIAH: Your Majesty!

DAVID: That is Zadok's voice, and—

BENAIAH: It is Benaiah, sir.

DAVID: Yes. You were with me in the old days—

NATHAN: Here is the decree, sir. Make your mark, and I will seal it with your seal. (HE HOLDS A PAPER WHILE DAVID MARKS IT WITH A PEN)

DAVID: Go to Solomon. Set him on my own mule, and bring him to Gihon. Zadok, and you, Nathan, anoint him king over Israel. Blow the trumpet, and cry, 'Long live King Solomon!' Then set him on my throne for all the people to see.

ZADOK: We will, sir. You have saved our people!

DAVID: (FALLING BACK) Now leave me. Abishag, I am cold!

SOLOMON

BIBLE REFERENCE: 1 KINGS, 1-11 AND 2 CHRONICLES1-9

Scene one:

SOLOMON'S PRAYER *
BIBLE REFERENCE: I KINGS 3: 3-15

Characters: Solomon
                     Voice of God

Solomon defeated Adonijah and his commander, Joab, and was made king. He longed for his people to enjoy peace and prosperity. Alone in the sanctuary at Gibeon he prayed for strength, and God answered his prayer.

SOLOMON: (KNEELING BESIDE A COUCH) Lord God, I thank you for the victory which you have granted to me and your people. Strengthen me now and always, that I may walk in the steps of my father, and lead Israel in the paths of justice and righteousness. (HE LIES ON THE COUCH AND SLEEPS)

VOICE OF GOD: I have heard your prayer, Solomon.

SOLOMON: (STILL LYING, AND SPEAKING AS IF IN A DREAM) Is it your voice, Lord?

VOICE OF GOD: Yes. You came to the shrine to ask for guidance, and I will give you whatever gift you ask for.

SOLOMON: (SITTING UP) Whatever I ask?

VOICE OF GOD: Yes. You are young, and the road ahead of you is hard. Ask what you think will help you most.

SOLOMON: You made my father king, Lord, and your love never left him. And now I am king over a people too great to number. Give me an understanding heart! Give me wisdom to govern your people, and help me to choose between good and evil!

VOICE OF GOD:	Your prayer will be answered. Because you did not ask for riches, or power, or victory in war, you shall indeed have the gift of wisdom; and you will be rich, and increase the greatness of your kingdom—so long as you remain humble and serve me faithfully. Now sleep in peace! Tomorrow your task begins!
	(SOLOMON LIES DOWN AGAIN)

Scene two:

THE JUDGMENT OF SOLOMON**
BIBLE REFERENCE: I Kings 3: 16-28

Characters: KING SOLOMON
#GEBER (his secretary),
#MIRIAM
#ESTHER

Solomon was a gifted leader. He became famous for his wisdom as a judge in his people's disputes.

SOLOMON:	(SEATED AT A TABLE) What is the next case?
GEBER:	(STANDING BESIDE HIM) Two women, Your Majesty. A dispute over a baby.
SOLOMON:	Very well. Bring them in.
GEBER:	Yes, sir. (WOMEN ENTER) Stand in front of the King That's right. Now kneel.
SOLOMON:	You may rise. Which is the petitioner.
MIRIAM:	I am, Your Majesty. You see—
SOLOMON:	Your name?
MIRIAM:	Miriam, Your Majesty
SOLOMON:	And yours?
ESTHER:	Esther, Your Majesty. This woman is lying—
SOLOMON:	Be quiet! Miriam, make your petition.

MIRIAM: We live in the same house, you see, Your Majesty—

GEBER: Call the King 'Sir'. You need not keep saying 'Your Majesty.'

MIRIAM: Yes, My Lord—sir. Well, each of us had a baby last week, sir. Hers was born three days after mine. It died, sir. She must have lain on it in the night. It was terrible.

ESTHER: It was her child that died.

MIRIAM: No, sir, she's lying. She got up in the night and took my son, while I was asleep, and put the dead baby in my bed. I woke up, sir, and got ready to feed my son, and—oh, sir, it was so awful! There was this baby, cold and dead. Then I saw it wasn't my baby at all, but hers.

ESTHER: Yes, that's what you said when you woke up, after crushing your child. She went half crazy, sir, and tried to tear my baby from me—

MIRIAM: I tell you it is my baby. You can't lie to the King.

SOLOMON: That's enough! I've heard all I need to know.

GEBER: I don't see how we can tell which of them is lying, sir. It's an impossible case.

SOLOMON: You think so? I think it's one of the simplest cases we have ever had to decide.

GEBER: Simple? I don't understand—

SOLOMON: Yes, simple. Where is the baby, by the way?

GEBER: Outside, sir, with one of the servants. I didn't want it squalling in here during the trial.

SOLOMON: Quite right, Geber. Well, fetch the baby in here.

GEBER: Yes, sir, but—

SOLOMON: And fetch my sword.

GEBER: Your—what, sir?

SOLOMON:	My sword. You're very slow this morning, Geber. Here is a case in which two women claim one baby. We can't give each of them a whole baby; so the only fair thing to do is to give them half a baby each.
GEBER:	Half a baby? Your Majesty, are you saying that you are going to cut this baby in half—kill it?
SOLOMON:	You can't cut it in half without killing it, Geber.
MIRIAM:	Oh no! Oh, God, you can't! My baby!
SOLOMON:	Fetch the baby, Geber, and fetch my sword.
GEBER:	Yes, sir. (WALKS TOWARDS DOOR)
MIRIAM:	Wait! I—oh, Your Majesty, don't kill the child!
SOLOMON:	It's the only way to give you both justice, isn't it, Esther?
ESTHER:	Yes, sir. It's better than letting her have my child.
MIRIAM:	Then give her the child, sir. If it has to be so, give her the baby!
SOLOMON:	Bring the baby and give him to his mother.
GEBER:	Yes, sir. But we don't know which the mother is.
SOLOMON:	Oh yes, we do, Geber. Miriam is his mother. She would not let her child die, even if it meant losing him.
ESTHER:	You tricked me—
SOLOMON:	It was you who tried to trick us, Esther. You have lied in this court, and you deserve to be punished. But God has already given you the heavy punishment of your baby's death. Go away, and from now on speak the truth! And Geber, see that Miriam is rewarded for her honesty.

Scene three:

THE QUEEN OF SHEBA (improvise)
BIBLE REFERENCE: I Kings 10

Read the chapter, and then choose actors to represent Solomon and the Queen. He shows her the marvels of his city, and describes the prosperity of the kingdom. She reacts with wonder.

Scene four:

PROSPERITY AND MORAL DECLINE +
BIBLE REFERENCE: I Kings 4-11

Characters: SOLOMON
SECRETARY
ADONIRAM, in charge of the labor force
ZADOK the priest
VOICE OF GOD

The Bible story of Solomon gives a vivid picture of a brilliant man whose judgment went wrong. He made the kingdom rich, but not the common people. He built a wonderful Temple, but in the eyes of ordinary Jews he spent too much on his own projects, at their expense. Eventually their discontent turned to active rebellion. Solomon did not train his son Rehoboam in leadership, with the result that when he was near to death one of his generals, Jeroboam, prepared to rebel. As soon as Solomon died the kingdom which David had extended and ruled with wisdom split into two parts, Judah in the south around Jerusalem, and Israel in the north, with its capital at Samaria. This scene shows Solomon's grip on his kingdom loosening. It is imaginary, but based on the Bible's description.

SOLOMON: (WALKING UP AND DOWN IMPATIENTLY) Make a note that I need a report from Ezion-Geber about the fleet.

SECRETARY: (SEATED AT A TABLE) Yes, sir.

SOLOMON: Are those returns in yet from the copper mines?

SECRETARY: Not yet, sir. The accountants—

SOLOMON: Tell the accountants from me that they are fired unless they produce the full figures tomorrow. And I need details of the stables at Megiddo, the new building in the Queens' quarters, and the repairs to the city wall. Is nobody able to finish a job unless I stand behind him?

SECRETARY: I will pass on your messages at once, sir.

SOLOMON: And now they tell me there is trouble with the labor force. Is Adoniram here?

SECRETARY: Yes, sir—ready to see you.

SOLOMON: Then go! Send him in!
(SECRETARY GOES OUT. ADONIRAM ENTERS)
You wanted to see me, Adoniram?

ADONIRAM: Not so much that, Your Majesty. I felt it was my duty to report to you.

SOLOMON: Really? You sound very stiff and formal today.

ADONIRAM: Look, sir, you have always told me to speak frankly.

SOLOMON: And I meant it. Come on, Adoniram. Sit down. There's something on your mind. let's have it!

ADONIRAM: (THEY SIT) Thank you, sir. Ever since you became king you've had one motto: Expand, expand, expand! You're a genius, and it has worked brilliantly—so far. We all recognize that. You have given us peace, and a standard of life beyond anything Israel has ever dreamed of; but—

SOLOMON: But it's hard to keep people grateful.

ADONIRAM: Grateful? The people you see are grateful, sir. They may complain of the taxes, but they know when they are well off. I'm talking about the people whose lives have been uprooted against their will—

SOLOMON: Your laborers? They get double the wages—

ADONIRAM: Sir, you must listen! I've done the job you told me to do. I've recruited labor for the mines and the building program and the fleet and the timber industry. But I'm warning you, some of the new projects are going to cause big trouble.

SOLOMON: Oh? Why should the new projects be any different from what has gone before?

ADONIRAM: Because, to be blunt, the people I have to shift from one job to another, the ordinary working folk, don't think you are building up the nation any more. They think your head has been turned, and that you want more and more for yourself, your wives, and—

SOLOMON: (SHOUTING) That's enough, Adoniram! Stick to your job! Don't tell me how to do mine!

ADONIRAM: Yes, sir. Well, at least I've said what I came to say. (HE GOES OUT. SOLOMON PACES UP AND DOWN. SECRETARY ENTERS, OBVIOUSLY NERVOUS)

SECRETARY: Excuse me, sir. The priest Zadok is here, asking to see you.

SOLOMON: (STILL ANGRY) Oh, he is, is he? I suppose he'd better come in. (SECRETARY GOES OUT. ZADOK ENTERS) Trouble as usual, Your Holiness?

ZADOK: Greetings, Your Majesty. There was a time when you would not have expected the Lord's priest to bring trouble.

SOLOMON: You're right. Those were good days, and you are a loyal servant of God. What do you want now?

ZADOK: I have just been shown the plans for the new shrines—that is what the architect calls them—which you have ordered to be built on the hill, behind the homes of your—ladies. A shrine to Milcom, a shrine to Chemosh, a shrine to Ashtoreth; and space left for others, no doubt. Is this true, Solomon?

SOLOMON: King Solomon, Zadok. Yes. It is no business of yours.

ZADOK: No business of the Lord's chosen priest? Are you mad? Is this the son of David, whom I anointed—

SOLOMON: (LOUD AND ANGRY) It is no business of yours because these shrines are not for our people. To strengthen our foreign ties I have been obliged to enter into political marriages. If my wives wish to remain faithful to their own gods, am I to—

ZADOK: Being faithful to Chemosh happens to involve the sacrifice of children, to be burned alive inside his brazen image.

SOLOMON: (HYSTERICAL) Get out of this room! I have made this kingdom great. Everything you eat, every offering in the Temple, is due to me. Do you think I will let a snivelling priest tell me what to do? Go! (ZADOK GOES. SECRETARY ENTERS)

SECRETARY: There are four more of your officers waiting—

SOLOMON: Tell them to go to hell! I don't want to see anybody.

SECRETARY: Excuse me, sir. I think you ought to know some bad news. Jeroboam—

SOLOMON: I gave orders that he was to be captured and put to death.

SECRETARY: He got away, sir, and headed for Egypt. They say he is in league with Hadad the Edomite. And you know that Rezon is in Damascus—

SOLOMON: Go away! Leave me in peace! (SECRETARY LEAVES) Nothing can touch me! God is on my side. (KNEELS) O God of my fathers, God of Abraham and Moses and David, what have I done? What have I done? Are you forsaking me now?

VOICE OF GOD: It is you who have forsaken me, Solomon.

SOLOMON: (HOARSE) Forsaken you, Lord?

VOICE OF GOD: Remember your dream at Gibeon. I warned you not to abandon your faith. I have tried to warn you often, but you were too busy to listen.

SOLOMON: Have I not made Israel great in the eyes of the world?

VOICE OF GOD: I called you be humble and faithful, not to be rich and powerful. Which do you think is more beautiful in my eyes, the flowers of the field, or you in all your glory?

SOLOMON: Give me one more chance!

VOICE OF GOD: It is too late. You must die, Solomon, and you cannot take with you any of your wives or your peacocks or your gold or copper. You have done great things for good, and for evil. Now your son must fight your battles.

SOLOMON: My son? Rehoboam? But—he isn't ready. He will lose everything.

VOICE OF GOD: If he does, whose fault is it? You were too busy making new fortunes to teach your son how to be king.

SOLOMON: Oh, God!
(HE FALLS TOHE GROUND, GROANING AND CHOKING)

SECRETARY: (RUNNING IN) Your Majesty! (SHOUTING) Send for a doctor! The King has fainted. A doctor! (HE KNEELS AND FEELS SOLOMON'S PULSE) He is dying!

THE PSALMS

In the psalms you willl find a great variety of sentiments, often expressed in words of surpassing beauty. The central theme is God, the almighty and ever-lasting, and his creation. He demands from his people righteousness and truth. Worship and sacrifice, and the Temple which was the center for worship, are constant themes. Some psalms are national, celebrating the king and his family, and the fortunes of the people, including their history as far back as Abraham, Jacob, Joseph, and Moses. Some are intensely personal, recording feelings of joy and anguish and penitence for sins.

Reading psalms together, and then discussing them, is a good exercise in Bible study. The leader of a group needs to prepare carefully by studying the context and meaning in a commentary.

Some of the psalms were originally used in processions. One, psalm 84, can be acted out to illustrate this.

Probably this psalm was sung during a procession from the Mount of Olives to the Temple. The view of Jerusalem from the mountain is spectacular. Here the worshippers stood, and said or sang: (I use the King James version)
How amiable are thy tabernacles, O Lord!
My soul longeth, yes, even fainteth for the courts of the Lord:
My heart and my flesh crieth out for the living God.

At this point they begin to process down into the valley. They sing about the birds which nest in the Temple, and the blessings which come to those who worship there and seek their strength from God.

In verse six, the 'valley of Baca' (or vale of misery) means the valley through which they are processing. The beautiful phrase, 'They will go from strength to strength' may have been a kind of stage direction:

'They cross from culvert to culvert.' Then they begin to climb the hill towards the Temple singing:

'Behold, O God our shield!'

As they enter the court, and pass the doorkeeper, they sing verse 10, celebrating their joy at being inside the Temple. The last verses of praise are sung there.

I have often led groups of young people from a distance to the door of our church, reciting this psalm. They can then sing or read other psalms, such as 24, 43, 65, 121, 122, 126, 127, and 150, with greater understanding.

KINGS AND PROPHETS

Now Israel was divided into two small kingdoms. This was the situation until an Assyrian army destroyed Samaria in 722 BCE. Jerusalem escaped destruction at that time, but in 597 the southern kingdom was defeated by the Babylonians. This, followed by a further defeat in 586, led to the exiling of a large number of Jews.

During these three and a half centuries there were many rulers in the two kingdoms. Their reigns are recorded in the Bible, sometimes in great detail, sometimes only in a single verse. They exercised little power, and were always dominated by one or another of the neighboring empires, Egypt, Assyria, or Babylon. The area of the middle east was like a sandwich, with thick slices of bread on either side, and a thin layer in the middle, the Jewish faith and culture, which gave the sandwich its taste. There are very few enduring achievements or ideas to remind us of the three empires which fought for dominance. But the weak, small people named Jews or Israelites left a spiritual legacy which has influenced the lives and thoughts of all subsequent generations. Both Christianity and Islam built much of their faith on the Hebrew scriptures,

The giants of that age were the prophets, not the kings. From the middle of the eighth century to the end of the fifth a series of prophets proclaimed God's message to the two kingdoms. Fortunately some of their words were recorded, and are part of the Bible. There were others, both men and women, whose work did not survive.

Some of these prophets lived courageous and dramatic lives, in addition to preaching God's word. Our next section records incidents from their lives in scenes which are based as closely as possible on the Bible text.

ELIJAH**

(Read first, then select scenes to act)

BIBLE REFERENCE: 1 KINGS 17-22

Characters: KING AHAB
QUEEN JEZEBEL
ELIJAH
WIDOW of Zarephath
NABOTH
an ANGEL

I am God's messenger—people often call us angels. This is the story of three people, a king, a queen, and a prophet. Let me take you to King Ahab's palace so that you may meet them.

ONE

ELIJAH: (STANDING BEFORE THE KING AND QUEEN, WHO ARE SEATED) So, Ahab, King of Israel, because you have given in to the wishes of your wife, and because you have proved too weak to lead your people, and because you have been unfaithful to Yahweh your God—

JEZEBEL: Stop him, Ahab! Kill him!

ELIJAH: —allowing the worship of Baal and the planting of groves where strange gods are venerated—for all these reasons you will be punished. In God's name I declare that no rain will fall in Israel for three years, unless he bids me give the word. Farewell, Ahab! (HE BOWS AND TURNS AWAY)

JEZEBEL: Are you going to allow this liar to cheat and insult you? Cut off his head and throw it to the dogs!

AHAB: My dear, we cannot do anthing hasty. The people respect Elijah, and—

JEZEBEL:	The people! Who cares what they think? Are you the King or not?
ELIJAH:	(AT THE DOOR) Think hard, Ahab! You can still save your people if you are true to the Lord God!

Elijah knew how powerful Jezebel was, and how bitterly she hated him. He fled into the countryside to avoid her revenge. As he had foretold, the land was parched with drought. God sent ravens to feed Elijah, until he came to the home of a poor widow in the village of Zarephath. She was gathering sticks outside her cottage when he approached.

TWO

ELIJAH:	Greetings, lady!
WIDOW:	Good day, sir.
ELIJAH:	I have come a long way. Will you let me have a drink of water?
WIDOW:	Yes, sir. We have little enough left, but I will fetch you a cup.
ELIJAH:	Can you spare a morsel of bread?
WIDOW:	Oh, sir, you don't know what you are asking. I and my son are close to starving. I was just going to light a fire and cook the last of our meal and oil.
ELIJAH:	I understand. But all will be well with you. I promise it in the name of the Lord. Your meal barrel and your oil vessel will never be empty until the rains return.

Elijah stayed at the widow's home, and his promise was fulfilled. There was always enough meal, and enough oil. But one day, while he was praying, she ran to him weeping.

THREE

WIDOW:	Oh, sir, come quickly! My son is dead!
ELIJAH:	Calm yourself, Sarah, and tell me what has happened. Where is he?

WIDOW:	In the loft above the barn. He was working there, when I heard him cry out. I ran to him, and there he lay on the floor, not breathing. God has forsaken us!
ELIJAH:	Never say that! Wait here while I go to him.

Elijah hurried to the boy. He prayed God to heal him, and three times he lay over him to give him the kiss of life. The boy began to breathe. Soon Elijah carried him back to his mother.

ELIJAH:	Here is your son.
WIDOW:	Is he—?
ELIJAH:	Alive and unharmed.
WOMAN:	My boy! Truly you are a man of God! May he bless you always!

The drought in Israel grew worse, and Jezebel's anger increased. Elijah returned to Ahab's palace.

FOUR

ELIJAH:	I have come back, Ahab.
AHAB:	So it is you, the enemy of Israel!
ELIJAH:	No. You are the cause of our people's suffering. Have I not proved to you that Yahweh is the true God, and that the gods of Jezebel are nothing but idols?
JEZEBEL:	Is there no limit to this man's insolence? Kill him!
ELIJAH:	The King does not dare kill me, Jezebel. Listen to my challenge! Collect all of your socalled prophets—the four hundred and fifty who serve Baal and the four hundred who minister in your groves and eat at your table. Let them set a bullock on an altar for sacrifice. I alone will do the same. We will put no fire beneath them, but we will pray, I to Yahweh and they to their spirits and idols. Let us see which god will answer the prayers!

FIVE

They did what Elijah said. The priests of Baal cried out all morning on Mount Carmel, and cut themselves with knives, but no fire came. Elijah taunted them.

VOICE OF ELIJAH:	Cry louder! He is a god. He may be talking, or out hunting, or on a journey, or perhaps asleep. Call him again! Louder!
	Evening came, and they had failed. Before night fell Elijah poured many barrels of water over his sacrifice. Then he prayed to Yahweh.
VOICE OF ELIJAH:	Lord God of Abraham, Isaac, and Jacob, let it be known this day that thou art God, and that I am thy servant.

The fire of the Lord descended, and consumed the sacrifice and the very stones of the altar, soaked in water. Then at Elijah's bidding the people slew all the priests of Baal; and at last it rained on the land. Jezebel's rage knew no bounds. She swore to kill Elijah. So he fled to the wilderness alone, and sank exhausted beneath a juniper tree. God sent me to him while he slept there.

SIX

ANGEL:	(BENDING OVER THE SLEEPING ELIJAH) Wake up, Elijah!
ELIJAH:	Who are you?
ANGEL:	A messenger sent by God to help you.
ELIJAH:	It's no use. I've done my best, but I can't go on. Let me die in peace!
ANGEL:	The Lord needs you alive, not dead. Drink this! (HE DRINKS FROM A CUP WHICH SHE GIVES TO HIM) That's good! Now you can sleep again.

I had given him honeyed wine, so that he clould sleep off his deep weariness. Then I woke him again.

ANGEL:	Elijah! It is time to wake up and eat.
ELIJAH:	(SITTING UP) O, God be praised for not abandoning me! I feel stronger already. What must I do now?
ANGEL:	First sleep again. One more rest, and you will be fit to face the Queen.

People think of God's angels as shining spirits with bright wings, far above mortals. But if you read the scriptures you will see how often he gives us practical tasks, such as I had that day. I fed Elijah once more. After sleep and refreshment he went away as strong as ever in body and spirit. Soon, on Mount Horeb, God spoke to him in the stillness of the mountain. Then he went to face Ahab and Jezebel. By now the Queen had added murder to her other sins.

SEVEN

JEZEBEL: My Lord Ahab, I have summoned Naboth, so that you may tell him your wishes.

NABOTH: (KNEELING) Your Majesty.

AHAB: O—yes, Naboth. You may rise. I–that is the Queen—well, it's about your vineyard, Naboth.

NABOTH: My vineyard, sir?

JEZEBEL: The vineyard which is by rights part of the palace gardens.

NABOTH: I beg your pardon, Your Majesty. That land has belonged to my family for more generations than I can count.

JEZEBEL: Don't be insolent! It belongs to the King.

AHAB: Now, my dear, leave this to me. Naboth, the fact is that we— the Queen, that is, and I—need that land for a herb garden.

NABOTH: A herb garden?

JEZEBEL: Yes, Naboth. My herb garden. You will be compensated for the exchange.

AHAB: The Queen means that another piece of land—excellent land, I believe—will be given to you in place of the vineyard..

NABOTH: I am sorry, sir, but that is out of the question.

AHAB: But, Naboth—

NABOTH: I cannot surrender the land which my fathers have owned and treasured.

JEZEBEL: If you refuse you are guilty of treason.

NABOTH: With all respect, Your Majesty, I do not think that you are familiar with the customs of Israel. We live by law, not by plunder. I am a loyal subject of King Ahab, and I think he understands—

AHAB: I know how you feel, but—

JEZEBEL: Let him go, my Lord. You have made him a generous offer, and he refused. Let him go.

NABOTH: Thank you. I am at your service, sir, to do anything which is consistent with the honor of my family.

By nightfall Naboth was dead, stoned by the servants of Jezebel. It was at this time that Elijah returned to Samaria.

EIGHT

(AHAB AND JEZEBEL ARE TOGETHER IN THE PALACE. ELIJAH ENTERS)

ELIJAH: So you are now a thief and a murderer, Ahab!

AHAB: Leave me alone! You have always been my enemy, and a troubler of Israel.

JEZEBEL: Send for the guards! Arrest him!

ELIJAH: Be silent, woman! You are the curse of the Lord's people. Soon the dogs will lick your blood in the place where you shed the blood of Naboth. You will be remembered as a failure, Ahab, a failure and a weakling. You have neither faith nor courage. You are not fit to be a king.

AHAB: (SHOUTING) No, Elijah, no! I didn't mean Naboth to be killed. It was Jezebel. Everything is her fault. Ask God to forgive me!

ELIJAH: It is too late. The Syrian army is marching against you. At least you can go out and fight like a man. And you, Jezebel, can wait here in your palace of ivory—but he will never return.

King Ahab went into battle, but he disguised himself to escape the notice of the enemy. A chance arrow struck him, and he died in his chariot. They cleaned the blood from the chariot in the herb garden of Jezebel, the place that had been Naboth's vineyard. In that same place Jezebel died, hurled from the palace tower by her servants. But Elijah the prophet was taken up to heaven in a chariot of fire, and is held in honor by all who read his story. Thanks be to God!

ELISHA AND NAAMAN THE SYRIAN**
BIBLE REFERENCE: 2 KINGS 5

Characters:

NAAMAN, Captain of the host of Syria
MIRIAM, his wife
TABITHA, a captive Jewish slave girl (the)
JORAM, friend of Naaman
GEHAZI, servant to Elisha
ELISHA

TABITHA: (STANDING AT ONE SIDE OF THE STAGE) Welcome, friends! My name is Tabitha. I was born of a Jewish family fourteen years ago. Last year the Syrian army attacked our country. The village where I lived was captured and burned. I try to forget that terrible day. I do not know what happened to my family. A few of us were brought here to Damascus as prisoners and given to Syrian masters. At least I was lucky to find myself the slave of the Captain of the army, General Naaman. He is a just man, and his wife is not cruel to me. They too have tragedy in their lives, for my master is a leper. He is held in high esteem by the king of Syria; but what is fame worth to a man who suffers so much? I have prayed that Yahweh may show pity to my master, though he is a worshiper of other gods. (A HAND BELL SOUNDS) My mistress is summoning me. Come with me and meet her and General Naaman!

ONE

(NAAMAN IS LYING ON A COUCH. MIRIAM ENTERS, LOOKS AT HIM, AND RINGS THE BELL)

MIRIAM: Are you asleep, my dear?

NAAMAN: No. I'm tired almost to death after that campaign, but I cannot sleep.

MIRIAM: The King has sent a message. He wants you to be at the palace at noon.

NAAMAN: To receive another medal, I suppose. I ought to be glad, but—

(TABITHA ENTERS WITH A TRAY)

MIRIAM:	Put the wine on the table, Tabitha.
TABITHA:	Yes, my lady.
NAAMAN:	So long as I carry this curse upon my skin how can I enjoy anything? I'd be better off as a slave like this kid than the way I am—the King's right hand man and a leper. O God! (HE BURIES HIS HEAD IN HIS HANDS)
TABITHA:	(SOFTLY) My lady.
MIRIAM:	Yes, Tabitha?
TABITHA:	I think I know how General Naaman can be cured.
MIRIAM:	Cured? Whatever do you mean, child? Some old wives' tale from Israel, I suppose.
TABITHA:	No, my lady. There is a prophet in my country who is famous both for his holiness and for curing many people. If General Naaman would go to him—
NAAMAN:	What is it, Miriam? What is the girl whispering?
MIRIAM:	Only some nonsense about a quack prophet. You may go, Tabitha!
NAAMAN:	Wait a minute! You, come here. What's your name?
TABITHA:	Tabitha, sir.
NAAMAN:	And who is this prophet, Tabitha?
TABITHA:	His name is Elisha. He is a man of God, and has healed many people.
NAAMAN:	Oh, he has? Well, I've tried everything, Miriam, and I'm no better off. Perhaps I should visit this prophet of Tabitha's. It will probably cost more than I made in booty from the war, but who cares?
MIRIAM:	You can't go begging to an Israelite—you, the head of the Syrian army!

NAAMAN: My dear, you don't have leprosy—not yet, anyway. This girl looks honest to me, and I'm desperate. Tell Joram that we will leave in the morning. We'll need the carriage, ten talents of silver and six of gold. Oh, and cloaks and robes—the best of what I brought back from the war. Will that be enough for your prophet, do you think, Tabitha?

TABITHA: I do not think that he will accept payment, sir.

NAAMAN: You don't? My child, you don't know much about the world. He will take all that he can squeeze out of me; but if he does me any good it will be worth every penny. Now leave me to rest! I must make an early start. My medal can wait.

TABITHA: (FROM ONE SIDE) So General Naaman started out in his carriage, with his companion, Captain Joram, and servants riding mules as his escort. I had given the General directions to the place where Elisha lived. They stopped the carriage outside the gate, and Naaman climbed down with difficulty to go towards the house door.

TWO

NAAMAN: Fetch out this man Elisha, Joram!

JORAM: Yes, sir. (HE KNOCKS. AFTER A PAUSE GEHAZI ENTERS)

GEHAZI: Good morning.

JORAM: Tell the prophet Elisha to come out.

GEHAZI: Who wants him, sir?

JORAM: My master, General Naaman. He wishes to consult him.

GEHAZI: (STAMMERING) General Naaman? Yes, my Lord, of course. I will tell him.

NAAMAN: You do that, Jew, and hurry! (GEHAZI GOES INSIDE) That's a fawning hypocrite if ever I saw one, Joram. I hope his master is not like him.

JORAM: So do I, sir. I didn't like his looks at all. (GEHAZI RETURNS) Well?

GEHAZI:	Excuse me, sir–my Lord. My master is at prayer, and does not wish to be disturbed—
NAAMAN:	At prayer? Of all the impudence! Did you tell him who I am?
GEHAZI:	Yes, my Lord. He sent you a message—
NAAMAN:	I didn't ask for a message from some crawling idiot like you. I told him to come out here.
GEHAZI:	I'm very sorry, my Lord. I—
NAAMAN:	Oh, stop whining and cringing, and tell me what this famous message is.
GEHAZI:	He said that your—your—
NAAMAN:	Come on, man! Out with it! My what?
GEHAZI:	Your—leprosy—will be cured if you bathe seven times in Jordan.
NAAMAN:	How in the name of Rimmon did he know about my leprosy? Did you tell him?
GEHAZI:	No, no, my Lord. I know nothing. He is a prophet. He knows—
NAAMAN:	I'm going home, Joram. My wife was quite right. The man is a quack. Tell your prophet I'll be back one day with the Syrian army to burn down his house, and I personally will hang him from the nearest tree.
JORAM:	My Lord, while we're here don't you think you ought to try—
NAAMAN:	What? Wade into some filthy Jewish river? Are you out of your mind? If I want a swim, we have Abana and Pharpar—real rivers. I came here for a cure, not for some witch doctor's mumbo-jumbo.
GEHAZI:	I beg you, my Lord, to do what the prophet said. The river is close by, at the foot of this hill.
JORAM:	He's right, sir. You've nothing to lose.

NAAMAN: Oh, very well. Drive to the river, and let's get it over.

TABITHA: They drove to the river bank. Naaman stripped off his cloak and his boots. As he stepped into the river he felt the power of God filling his body and uplifting his spirit. He began to tremble. Seven times he went in and out of the stream, letting the fresh water run over his skin. It was as the prophet had promised. He knelt on the river bank and wept for joy. Then he and Joram returned to the prophet's house. Inside, he talked with Elisha.

THREE

NAAMAN: (KNEELING. ELISHA IS SEATED) Elisha, I—

ELISHA: Don't kneel to me, Naaman! It is God whom you must thank.

NAAMAN: (SITTING) I will thank him every day for the rest of my life. There is no other God.

ELISHA: Then you will be his witness to your people.

NAAMAN: Elisha, you have saved my life. Now I have to ask you one thing more. You know who I am, and the position I hold in Syria. When I return, the whole of the Court will give thanks to Rimmon. If I say, Rimmon is no god—only Yahweh, I will lose my lob and probably my head.

ELISHA: Are you sure that is not what God is challenging you to do?

NAAMAN: I think he has restored my health so that I can use it, not throw it away. Let me load two of my mules with earth from your land. I will cover it with a shrine, and every day I will worship Yahweh. I have a slave girl, an Israelite, who told me to come to you. When I return I will set her free. If she will stay with us she can show me how to pray to your god. But I cannot forswear my belief in Rimmon. I will work to make our two countries be neighbors, at peace.

ELISHA: You have great faith, Naaman. Gehazi, see to the loading of the mules with earth.

GEHAZI: Yes, master.

NAAMAN:	Now let me give you the payment for what you have done. Nothing can match it, but you shall have gold and silver and—
ELISHA:	No gold or silver. Faith is not bought and sold.
NAAMAN:	I understand that you want nothing for yourself, but can I not pay for a temple—
ELISHA:	God's temple is his world, and the hearts of his faithful people. Give your money to the poor.
NAAMAN:	You really mean that you will accept nothing?
ELISHA:	Nothing except your thanks to God.
NAAMAN:	My slave girl was right. Will you give me your blessing?
ELISHA:	Yes, my friend. (NAAMAN KNEELS) The Lord bless you and keep you, the Lord make his face to shine upon you and give you peace, now and everrnore. (NAAMAN RISES) Goodbye, soldier of the true God!
NAAMAN:	Goodbye, faithful prophet .
GEHAZI:	(ENTERS AND WATCHES) The mules are ready, sir. What shall I do with the gifts from the General's wagon?
ELISHA:	Leave them where they are, in the wagon.
GEHAZI:	But, sir—
ELISHA:	You heard me, Gehazi. I have explained to General Naaman that we cannot accept his gifts.
GEHAZI:	As you wish, master.
TABITHA:	Naaman and Joram left in their carriage. Gehazi could not bear to see them go—all that silver and gold thrown away! He slipped out of the house, saddled a mule, and let himself out through a back gate. But Elisha knew in his heart what his servant was doing. Gehazi rode fast, and called out when he had almost overtaken them.

FOUR

GEHAZI:	(BREATHLESS) General Naaman!
NAAMAN:	Stop the carriage! What is it that you want?
GEHAZI:	A message from my master, sir.
NAAMAN:	Well?
GEHAZI:	After you left, he thought about the gifts you had offered, to the Lord, not to him. He felt he had been ungracious to refuse them.
NAAMAN:	So he has changed his mind.
GEHAZI:	He would like me to bring back just a portion of the gold and silver—
NAAMAN:	Do you believe this man, Joram?
JORAM:	He could be lying; but the simplest thing is to give him what he wants.
NAAMAN:	I agree. You, fellow, take what you can load on to your mule; but if you are lying may God strike you with the curse you deserve!
GEHAZI:	Lying, sir? How would I dare—
NAAMAN:	Help him, Joram! Don't break the mule's back, Jew!
GEHAZI:	Thank you, my Lord. May God bless you! (HE GOES OFF)
NAAMAN:	I have half a mind to go back and check his story.
JORAM:	Better not, sir. We need to hurry if we are to be home before nightfall.
NAAMAN:	You're right. Well, at least we met one man of God on our journey.

TABITHA:	My master returned home, cured of his leprosy. He and my lady Miriam set me free that very day. The General sent to Israel to try to find my parents, but no trace of them could be discovered. They asked me to stay in their home, and I serve them now as a free woman. I miss my home and my country, but I have their kindness to be thankful for. I have taught my master some of King David's psalms, and all of the laws of Moses which I can remember. We pray together standing on the soil of Israel—in secret. There is still enmity between Syria and Israel, but my master works to make peace. Oh—I forgot to tell you that my master sent Joram back later to give greetings to the prophet. There was a new servant at the gate. Elisha told Joram why.

FIVE

ELISHA:	(SEATED INSIDE HIS HOME) So you are back, Gehazi.
GEHAZI:	Back, master?
ELISHA:	That was what I said. You went out.
GEHAZI:	Just as far as the stable, sir.
ELISHA:	Do not lie to me! It was the gold, wasn't it?
GEHAZI:	I—I don't understand what you—
ELISHA:	Each lie makes it worse. You made your choice, and you shall have what you desired. The gold is yours.
GEHAZI:	I don't want all of it. I want to give part to God, and to you. I couldn't bear to see it wasted. Naaman wanted to give it to you. I only—
ELISHA:	You shall have it. Not God, not I. You.
GEHAZI:	You mean, keep all of it?
ELISHA:	All that he brought with him—including his leprosy.
GEHAZI:	(AFTER A PAUSE) No! No! You can't do that to me.

ELISHA: I have not done it. You made you own hell, paved with gold.

TABITHA: That ends my story. Captain Joram sometimes joins us when
                   we pray to Yahweh. I think he also comes because I am pleasing
                   to him. I pray that soon we will be man and wife. Truly the
                   ways of God are strange. Shalom, my friends!
THE LORD BE WITH YOU!

ISAIAH AND THE SIEGE OF JERUSALEM+
BIBLE REFERENCE: 2 KINGS 18:13 TO 19: 37

CHARACTERS   ISAIAH the prophet Inside Jerusalem
                   KING HEZEKIAH
                   ELIAKIM, Mayor of Jerusalem
                   SHEBNA the scribe

Outside the city   RABSHAKEH and RABSARIS, Assyrian Generals
                   JEWISH PRISONER

Isaiah, the author of most of the first 39 chapters of the book named for
him, was perhaps the greatest of the prophets whose books survive. Other
prophets were outstanding for particular sides of their message: among
them Amos in describing the righteousness of God, Hosea in describing his
tenderness, Ezekiel in the vividness of his spiritual visions. Isaiah seemed to
have every gift in rich measure: courage, vision, tenderness, and above all a
grasp of the majesty of God. His ministry covered the last forty years of the
8th century BCE.

The Assyrian army crushed the northern kingdom in 722. Archeology has
confirmed the terrible fate of Lachish in Judaea at that time. There was
every reason to believe that Jerusalem and the southern kingdsom of Judah
would be destroyed. Only the courage of Isaiah and a plague which struck
the Assyrians saved the city and the kingdom.

This scene is not easy to act, unless you have a hall with a gallery, but a
reading will give an idea of the thrilling events.

(KING HEZEKIAH IS SEATED LOOKING DOWN FROM THE CITY WALL. ISAIAH
AND OTHERS STAND BEHIND HIM, INCLUDING ELIAKIM AND SHEBNA)

ELIAKIM: The messenger has arrived, Your Majesty.

HEZEKIAH: Pray God that it is not more bad news!

MESSENGER: (RUNNING IN AND KNEELING) Your Majesty, the Assyrians are coming—the whole of Sennacherib's army. They have burned Lachish. I only just ecaped. It was horrible! (HE BREAKS DOWN IN TEARS)

HEZEKIAH: What are we to do? We have given him all that we have—even the gold from Solomon's Temple. Are we all to die or become slaves?

ISAIAH: No, Your Majesty! I know in my heart that God will save Jerusalem. You must stand firm. Bar the gates and trust in God!

SHOUTS FROM DIFFERENT VOICES OFF STAGE, SPEAKING TOGETHER:
'Look! They're coming!! 'You can see the dust rising.' 'And the flash of shields.' 'It's the Assyrians!'

HEZEKIAH: You know what happens to cities that resist them:
fire, and murder, and slavery—

ISAIAH: I know it, sir. I still say that God will save Jerusalem. He has sent me this message to proclaim to you.

HEZEKIAH: Shebna, and you, Eliakim, be ready to talk to them when they come close. See if we can make some kind if agreement.

SHEBNA: It won't work with Sennacherib's generals. They take everything or cut your throat.

ELIAKIM: Or both. We shall be lucky to be alive by nightfall.

(A LOUD VOICE HEARD FROM BELOW, WHERE RABSHAKEH AND RABSARIS ARE WITH A GROUP, INCLUDING A JEWISH PRISONER. SHEBNA AND ELIAKIM ADVANCE TOWARDS THE EDGE OF THE WALL)

RABSHAKEH: You up there! You Jews! Fetch your King to the wall!

RABSARIS: (AFTER A PAUSE) No answer. We'll have to burn the city.

RABSHAKEH: Oh, he'll come in a minute. These Jews are cowards.

RABSARIS: Try another summons.

RABSHAKEH:	Jews! For the last time. Bring out your King and open your gates!

(ELIAKIM AND SHEBNA APPEAR AT THE WALL)

SHEBNA:	King Hezekiah has sent us to answer you. What do you want with him?
RABSHAKEH:	I don't talk to underlings.
ELIAKIM:	I am Mayor of Jerusalem.
RABSHAKEH:	Not for long. If you interrupt me, I will have your tongue pulled out before I skewer you on a stake. You have five minutes to fetch your king.
SHEBNA:	What message shall we—
RABSHAKEH:	What message? Guess, Jewish rat! Or hear what your countryman has to say. (HE STRIKES THE PRISONER) Speak up, dog! Tell them what happens to the enemies of Assyria!
PRISONER:	Don't try to resist! Open the gates! They will spare your lives if you obey at once.
RABSHAKEH:	Now fetch your king!
SHEBNA:	Sir, may we confer with you in your language. We understand it—
RABSARIS:	So that your people won't know what you're saying? No, cur. Your five minutes are almost up. Jerusalem will make an excellent fire, and you will be roasted.

(ELIAKIM AND SHEBNA RETURN TO HEZEKIAH)

HEZEKIAH:	It's no use. Open the gates!
ISAIAH:	That is not the will of God. In my heart I know that he means us to have courage.
ELIAKIM:	It is now or never, sir.
HEZEKIAH:	(AFTER A PAUSE) I will trust in the Lord. Prepare to defend the city!

That night, while the Assyrians slept and the Jews waited in agony, Isaiah prayed alone. Towards dawn the King approached him close to the wall.

HEZEKIAH: It's quiet in their camp, but at dawn—

ISAIAH: (LOOKING DOWN) Not even sentries patrolling.

HEZEKIAH: That's strange.

ISAIAH: Almighty God! I think I understand. Don't you see? The angel of the Lord has struck them. They are not asleep—they are dead!

(BELOW, RABSARIS RUNS TO RABSHAKEH AND WAKES HIM)

RABSARIS: General Rabshakeh! For God's sake, sir, wake up!

RABSHAKEH: What is it? You're trembling like a leaf, man.

RABSARIS: They're stone dead, sir, thousands of them! Tongues blackened, eyes staring. It's the plague—or the god of the cursed Jews. You have no army left.

RABSHAKEH: Plague! (HE GOES FROM CORPSE TO CORPSE LYING ON THE GROUND)

RABSARIS: Don't touch them! You'll die yourself!

RABSHAKEH: (RECOVERING HIS MORALE) Muster all the men who can walk! Leave the sick behind! Put an arrow through any who try to follow us. We must get out of here before the plague destroys us all.

(ON THE WALL ABOVE THE KING STANDS WITH ISAIAH)

HEZEKIAH: O God of Abraham, Lord of our people, we have seen the deliverance which your hand has wrought. Make us worthy of your mercy! Speak to the people, Isaiah, faithful and true prophet! You have delivered us.

ISAIAH: Not I. I only speak what God puts in my mouth. Listen to me, all you citizens of Jerusalem!

Isaiah could now deliver a version of the parable of the vineyard, from chapter 5 of his book, verses 1-5. This time God has saved them, but they must heed his warning. They could all say or sing together Psalm 150, with as many instruments as possible.

JEREMIAH AND THE CAPTURE OF JERUSALEM
BIBLE REFERENCE: 2 KINGS 24: 1-17 AND THE BOOK OF JEREMIAH

Another great prophet, Jeremiah, lived through a forty year span of preaching and witness, from 626 BCE to at least 586. He endured even harder times than Isaiah. As always, Judah was sandwiched between Egypt to the south and a mighty neighbor to the north, now Babylon in place of Assyria. In the early years of his mInistry it seemed that a young King, Josiah, might reform and revitalize the faith of the Jews. But he was killed in battle with the Egyptians. Soon after that Judah became subject to Babylon. Jeremiah urged his people to remain loyal to Babylon, but in 597 a futile revolt took place against his advice. Worse still, the next King, Zedekiah, attempted another revolt in 586. Many of the ablebodied Jews were forced into exile in Babylon as a result of these two uprisings. Jeremiah still tried to deliver his message, urging the Jews to make a 'new covenant' with their God.

Scene one:

THE CAPTURE OF JERUSALEM +
BIBLE REFERENCE: 2 KINGS 24: 1-16

Characters: GRANDFATHER
GRANDMOTHER
MOTHER (MIRIAM)
SON, 18 (JACOB)
DAUGHTER, 17 (NAOMI)
SON, 6 (EZRA)
BABYLONIAN OFFICER and SOLDIERS

The city has fallen. It has been decreed that men and women between sixteen and forty will be marched to Babylon. Members of a typical family wait in their home. The names are all imaginary.

(THE FAMILY, EXCEPT FOR EZRA, ARE SITTING OR STANDING, NUMB WITH SHOCK AND MISERY)

GRANDFATHER: There, there, Miriam. Try not to lose heart.

MIRIAM:	Not lose heart, when my husband has been murdered by those animals from Babylon, and we are all to be slaves?
GRANDMOTHER:	(NERVOUS) Don't talk like that! It isn't safe.
EZRA:	(RUNNING IN) They're coming! An officer and four men just went into Ephraim's house.
MIRIAM:	Quick, Jacob! Under the floorboards!
JACOB:	It won't work, mother. They have all of our names.
MIRIAM:	It has to work! Somebody must live to take vengeance for your father.
JACOB:	All right; but if you're caught you know what they will do. (HE HIDES)
GRANDFATHER:	Pull the rug over the boards. Now sit, everyone.

(A LOUD KNOCK. OFFICER AND SOLDIERS ENTER)

OFFICER:	Stand up, all of you! (THEY OBEY) You won't be hurt if you do as you're told. Now, this is the house of Josiah-ben-Isaac. (HE CONSULTS A LIST) Killed in battle. Right?
MIRIAM:	Yes.
OFFICER:	Are you his wife? Well, that's war, lady. We don't want to harm you.
MIRIAM:	You cannot harm me. You have taken away my life already.
OFFICER:	Come, now! It's not that bad. These are your mother and father?
GRANDFATHER:	Yes.
OFFICER:	And you have sons, Jacob and Ezra, and a daughter, Naomi.
MIRIAM:	Jacob is dead.

OFFICER: Not according to your neighbor. Under persuasion he gave us a list of everyone on the street. You, girl—you're going to Babylon. Take her out!

NAOMI: No!

OFFICER: Come on! No trouble—take her out. (NAOMI IS REMOVED BY SOLDIERS. IMPROVISE FAMILY'S WORDS) Now, I want Jacob. I'll give you half a minute. Everyone his age goes to Babylon. If he isn't here we take this kid. Only he won't make it, and the ones who fall out are knocked on the head. It's your choice.

MIRIAM: O God, God! (WEEPING)

JACOB: (CLIMBING OUT OF HIS HIDING PLACE) I told you it was no use, Mother.

OFFICER: Good lad. Come with me! The rest of you stay in here until you have permission to move.

JACOB: (AS SOLDIERS HOLD HIM) Take your hands off me! I gave myself up.

OFFICER: Now then, calm down! Tie him up, just in case. We don't want any tricks.

(OFFICER, SOLDIERS, AND JACOB GO OUT)

GRANDFATHER: O God of Abraham, this is the hour of defeat and misery. If we are being punished for our sins, turn our hearts to repentance, and forgive us!

MIRIAM: What use is it to pray? God has deserted us. All I want is to die!

Scene two:

A PROPHET AND A KING *
BIBLE REFERENCE: Jeremiah 29 and 37-39. 2 Kings 25, 1-12

Characters: JEREMIAH
              BARUCH, his companion and scribe
              EBED-MELECH, his friend
              SHEPHATIAH, his enemy
              KING ZEDEKIAH

After the fall of Jerusalem in 597 the weak king Zedekiah did not know what to do—obey the Babylonians or try to revolt again. Jeremiah told him that resistance was hopeless, and would only cause further ruin; but his enemies, led by Shephatiah, labelled Jeremiah a coward and urged the king to fight. Jeremiah was thrown down a cistern and kept a prisoner, but two of his friends pulled him out. One of these was Baruch, his faithful companion and the recorder of his prophecies. They carry Jeremiah and lay him on a rug. He is emaciated and covered with mud.

EBED-MELECH: Gently! In the shade.

BARUCH: Watch over him! I will fetch some wine

JEREMIAH: (FAINTLY) Water, please!

EBED-MELECH: Yes. I don't suppose he could swallow wine or food yet. (HE GOES OUT)

BARUCH: He looks terrible. Master! Can you hear me?

JEREMIAH: My eyes ache. The light—it hurts. Where am I?

BARUCH: Safe! We'll wash away this slime, and you'll feel better. Ebed-Melech saved your life, and persuaded the King to see you.

JEREMIAH: (HIS VOICE STRONGER) Poor Zedekiah! He can't make up his mind. First he gives me special rations, then he has me buried in a cistern.

EBED-MELECH: (RETURNING WITH WATER)
                 Here, drink this! (GIVES HIM WATER)

JEREMIAH: Thank you! (DRINKS) Wonderful! You're a brave man.

EBED-MELECH: Did the ropes hurt your arms? When we pulled you up I was afraid—

JEREMIAH: I'm sore all over, and I stink to high heaven, but I will recover.

SHEPHATIAH: (HURRYING IN) What is this? Who gave orders for the removal of ths man—

EBED-MELECH: King Zedekiah gave the orders, Shephatiah—just in time to save you from a charge of murder.

SHEPHATIAH: This is your doing! We'll see that you pay for it. Shielding a traitor!

JEREMIAH: What is the charge against me? There has been no trial—

SHEPHATIAH: With a Babylonian army outside the walls we don't have time for trials—or need them. You are charged with deserting to the enemy.

JEREMIAH: Which you know to be a lie.

SHEPHATIAH: Worse than that, you have encouraged other people to become traitors, telling them that only those who defect to the enemy will live—

JEREMIAH: That is a lie also.

SHEPHATIAH: —and that the city is bound to fall soon, so get out while you can.

JEREMIAH: Yes, I said that. If facing reality is treachery then I am a traitor.

ZEDEKIAH: (HURRYING IN) Are you safe, Jeremiah?

JEREMIAH: I will live, sir. It takes more than the efforts of Shephatiah and his friends to silence me.

SHEPHATIAH: Let me remind you, sir, that you gave orders—

ZEDEKIAH: You forced me to do it—and you behaved like savages.

SHEPHATIAH: Nothing is too bad for this traitor.

ZEDEKIAH: Go, go! All of you! If anyone asks, you have not seen me here. This meeting is to be secret. Is that understood?

SHEPHATIAH: If you say so.

EBED-MELECH: We understand, Your Majesty.

ZEDEKIAH: Who is this man?

EBED-MELECH: Baruch, the prophet's friend. You can trust him.

ZEDEKIAH: Thank you for saving Jeremiah's life. I will remember. Now leave us!

(ALL GO OUT EXCEPT ZEDEKIAH AND JEREMIAH)

JEREMIAH: You want my advice?

ZEDEKIAH: I need you. I'm sorry—

JEREMIAH: Sorry that I was almost murdered? Thank you. Do I have your assurance that I will not be handed back to them?

ZEDEKIAH: Stay here, for your own safety. Ebed-Melech will protect you. Now tell me what to do. I am going mad with fear and uncertainty.

JEREMIAH: I have told you. God's word does not change. Surrender yourself and the city to the Babylonians. Then you and all of us will be saved. Resist, and what is left of Jerusalem will be destroyed and our people wiped out.

ZEDEKIAH: God, God, God! I can't do it! You are right, I can see that, but what would happen to me? They wll hand me over to the Jews who have already defected to Babylon—

JEREMIAH: Don't think about the danger! Choose what is right, and act like a king! Those Jewish puppets won't hurt you. Babylon despises them. Surrender, and live, or resist, and hear your own wives curse you as they are dragged away to Babylon!

ZEDEKIAH: Is there no hope that Egypt—

JEREMIAH: I have told you, Pharaoh and his army are doomed. They will be bitten to death like a heifer, when the gadflies from the north attack them.

ZEDEKIAH: You have no comfort for me?

JEREMIAH: Yes. The comfort of the truth. One word: surrender!

ZEDEKIAH: (PACING UP AND DOWN) Don't tell anyone what we have said. Say that I came to make sure you were free—

JEREMIAH:	And you will do nothing. We will all pay the price.
ZEDEKIAH:	I—O God, I must think! Whichever way I turn—
JEREMIAH:	I have said all I can, and I am tired. Please fetch my friends.
ZEDEKIAH:	Yes. I will try to protect you—
JEREMIAH:	Think about your duty, not about me! May you find the strength to do what is right!

Zedekiah did not surrender. He was blinded, and taken to Babylon. The tribulations of Jerusalem grew worse, and Jeremiah ended his life as an exile in Egypt.

THE EXILES IN BABYLON

Scene one:

JEREMIAH'S LETTER
BIBLE REFERENCE: JEREMIAH 29: 1-14

Characters: OBADIAH, a Jewish exile
ELASAH and GEMARIAH, messengers from Jerusalem
JEWISH MEN AND WOMEN

The exiled Jews waited anxiously for news from Jerusalem. Messengers came from time to time, telling of the hardships of those who had been left behind. In the home of an exiled Jew, Obadiah, a group gathered because of the news that two men had arrived from Jerusalem. They sat crowded together on rugs, while Obadiah stood with the new arrivals.

OBADIAH:	My friends, I gathered you together to hear the news which these two messengers have brought. They have letters for many of you from your families, and a letter to all of us from our prophet Jeremiah. I will ask Elasah to read you that letter.

ELASAH: Thank you, Obadiah. Greetings to all of from the remnant of our people! I will give you your letters after I have read what Jeremiah wrote, and Gemariah and I will answer your questions to the best of our ability. Here is the prophet's letter: Fellow Israelites, amid the sufferings of our people I send you greetings, and bid you never lose your faith in God. He has caused you to be led away into captivity.

Now he says this to you: Build houses, and live in them! Plant gardens, and eat the fruit that grows in them! Marry, and raise your families in Babylon, so that your numbers may grow in the time of your exile, instead of dwindling away! Work for the peace and prosperity of Babylon! Yes, pray for your masters! In their peace you will enjoy peace.

Take no notice of false prophets, who talk of doom or resistance! Your exile must last a man's lifetime; but then, says the Lord, I will come to you and lead you back to the land of your fathers. I have thoughts of peace towards you, not of evil. I will hear your prayers. If you seek for me with your whole heart you will find me. I will gather you back from exile and restore you to Israel when the time is ripe.

That is the prophet's message, my fellow Israelites. He says the same to those who are left in Jerusalem and in the countryside. Life is hard, but if we have courage nothing can defeat our faith.

(LOOK UP JEREMIAH 40-42 AND LAMENTATIONS 5 FOR A PICTURE OF THE SUFFERINGS OF THE PEOPLE LEFT IN JERUSALEM)

Scene three:

THE VISION OF EZEKIEL
BIBLE REFERENCE: Ezekiel 37: 1-14

Characters: EZEKIEL
VOICE OF GOD

Things were at their worst for the Jews. Defeat and exile would have broken the spirit of most nations; but the exiles in Babylon enjoyed the leadership of their prophets. Ezekiel was a young priest who was taken to Babylon. His courage and vision gave inspiration to his fellow exiles. The most famous of his spiritual experiences resulted in the parable of the Valley of Dry Bones.

(EZEKIEL IS ALONE, STANDING IN SILENCE. AFTER A PAUSE, HE SPEAKS)

EZEKIEL:	I am here, Lord.
VOICE OF GOD:	Yes, Ezekiel. You heard my call.
EZEKIEL:	Why here, Lord, where all the garbage from the city is thrown out into the valley?
VOICE OF GOD:	Look over there, where all those bones are scattered.
EZEKIEL:	I see them, Lord.
VOICE OF GOD:	They are human bones, the bones of the dead. Do you think that they could become the bodies of living men and women?
EZEKIEL:	After being broken and scattered? Only you know how that could be.
VOICE OF GOD:	Pray, Ezekiel! Pray over these bones. First, that they may come together, bone to his bone.
EZEKIEL:	In your name I pray that these bones may be joined as they once were.
VOICE OF GOD:	You see? Your prayer is being answered. These are the skeletons of the dead. Now pray that they have flesh and sinews, and be covered with skin!
EZEKIEL:	In your name I make that prayer, Lord.
VOICE OF GOD:	Now you see the bodies of the dead, but they have no breath within them. Cry to the wind, and say: 'Come from the north and south and east and west! Put breath into these dead, that they may live!'
EZEKIEL:	My Lord and my God! I understand what you are telling me. These are the bones of your people, broken and scattered. In God's name, live! Live and breathe!
VOICE OF GOD:	When you awake, tell the people what you saw. You are called to give them hope, and when the time is due the broken will be mended and the scattered brought together. Tell them never to despair!

Scene three:
THE LATER YEARS OF EXILE
BIBLE REFERENCE: Isaiah 40, 42, 44, 53

Characters: A TEACHER
(the writer of the second part of the book of Isaiah)
STUDENTS. The lines can be divided betweenseveral.

Inside a small house a teacher stands in front of his class. Boys and girls seated on the floor.

TEACHER: That ends today's lesson from the scriptures. Do you have questions?

BOY: Do you remember Jerusalem, sir?

TEACHER: No, Ezra. I was born soon after my mother and father came here.

GIRL: Do you think we will ever see Jerusalem?

TEACHER: I think so, Sarah. I know that our people will return there one day. I truly believe that the trials of Jerusalem are nearly over. God has promised forgiveness after our sins have been punished. When that forgiveness comes, the glory of the Lord will be revealed to all the world.

BOY: But we can't fight the Babylonians, sir, can we? Do you think they will change, and allow us to go back?

TEACHER: Nobody can tell how it will happen. I don't think God chose our people to be victors in war or rulers of an empire. He can measure the ocean in the hollow of his hand, and weigh the mountains on scales. Human boasting and worldly success mean nothing in his eyes, only righteousness and mercy. I know that he watches over us with tenderness, like a shepherd guarding his sheep. One day he will send a Messiah to save us—

BOY: Then we will win battles, surely.

TEACHER:	Perhaps. But I think God's Messiah will come as a servant, not a tyrant. I think he will open the eyes of the blind and free the prisoners. Love will be his weapon, and the victories of love far outweigh those of war. If we are to follow him it is that kind of victory that we must seek.
GIRL:	Will people follow a leader like that? Won't they think him weak?
TEACHER:	I don't know. He may be despised and rejected by some, but others will understand that it is for us that he will face wounds and punishment and humiliation. We have to hope that when he comes some at least will understand what true leadership means.
GIRL:	Some people say that God has ceased to care for us. My aunt Miriam—
TEACHER:	That is foolish. Does your aunt think that the everlasting God grows faint and tired? I think it is the faint and tired whom he tries to help. When things are bad, we must look ahead and trust in his love. One day we will soar back like eagles.
BOY:	One day! How can we ever beat the Babylonian army? And look at their temples! Is our god stronger than theirs?
TEACHER:	Numbers mean nothing to God—nothing! Nations are like a drop in a bucket to him. He is so great that it's as though the sky is only the size of a tent . As for humans, in his eyes we are no bigger than grasshoppers. And what are temples, Ezra, and the idols inside them? Wood and stone! They take half a tree and make it into the image of a god, and burn the other half! Those things don't last, any more than grass or flowers. But God's glory never withers or fades.
BOY:	Grasshoppers? Are we that small?
TEACHER:	How about fleas—the smallest thing you can think of? That's what we are—and that includes the King of Babylon! It's our hearts that matter, not muscles or bulk. Even if we are like fleas in comparison with the sun and the stars, God cares about us. He never, never forgets! (A BELL SOUNDS) There goes the bell. Learn your lesson well, and we will talk more about it tomorrow.

The exile lasted about sixty years. The Babylonians were not senselessly cruel, like the Assyrians. The Jews prospered in exile, and prophets like Ezekiel and the Second Isaiah kept them from forgetting their heritage. How often Jews who were enduring unspeakable sufferings during World War 11 must have read the words of these prophets!

Read Psalm 137, and think about what it was like for families to be broken up and homes destroyed. A boy and girl could improvise a scene in which Jacob and Naomi, the brother and sister of scene one, are unexpectedly reunited during the exile.

Scene four:

THE END OF THE EXILE
BIBLE REFERENCE: Ezra 1 and Psalm 126

Characters: CYRUS, King of Persia
SECRETARY
JEWISH LEADERS, an old man and a younger priest

In the year 539 Babylon fell to the Persians, and the Jews received a new master. What would happen to the exiles? The answer was given quickly. Soon after the fall of the city Cyrus was in Babylon making decisions about his new subjects. The scene is imaginary.

(CYRUS SITS AT A TABLE, WRITING. HIS SECRETARY STANDS AT HIS SIDE)

CYRUS: Well, who comes next?

SECRETARY: Representatives of the Jews, sir, or Israelites, they are sometimes called.

CYRUS: Oh, yes, I've heard of them. Forced to come here when Nebuchadnezzar overran their country. Is that right?

SECRETARY: Yes, sir. According to the records, some have been here for two generations. There are several thousands of them. They keep to themselves, and work hard. Lawabiding people, I'm told—religious.

CYRUS: Let me see what they say.

(SECRETARY GOES OUT, AND USHERS IN THE TWO JEWS. THEY BOW)

CYRUS: You are representatives of the Jewish people?

OLD MAN: Of the exiled Jews in Babylon, Your Majesty. Our people still live in their own land, but they are poor.

CYRUS: Because the Babylonians carried off everything, including your sons and daughters? It's a familiar story. I have heard good reports of your people here. What is it you wish to ask me?

PRIEST: My Lord, most of our people have never seen our Holy City, Jerusalem. Except for a very few, like my friend here, we have been born in exile. We ask your permission for those who wish it to return to their country.

CYRUS: To a poor country? I understand that many of you are rich men here in Babylon.

PRIEST: That is true, sir; but what are riches without God's love? We will not all go; but we beg to be free to choose. We can help our fellow Jews by sending strong men and women to Jerusalem. Perhaps with your blessing they can rebuild our city.

CYRUS: We have no quarrel with your people. Go, or stay! Only be loyal to Persia and to me.

OLD MAN: God be praised! You are as they say, sir, a just man.

PRIEST: We will repay you, sir. We will be loyal, and work for peace and prosperity. Now let us go and tell our people this great news.

CYRUS: You may do so. I will sign and seal a decree. As for the treasures which the Babylonians stole from your city, some reparation will be made. We want our subjects to live good lives, not to cherish hatred.

OLD MAN: May God bless you for ever, Your Majesty!

(THE TWO JEWS GO OUT. A CROWD IS WAITING FOR THEM OUTSIDE. THEY ASK FOR SILENCE, AND GIVE THE NEWS, AMID SHOUTING AND CHEERING. THE PRIEST CAN LEAD THEM IN SAYING OR SINGING PSALM 126)

After the Exile

Most of the Old Testament was written and edited before the return of the Jews from Babylon. Slowly the nation recovered, but it remained small and weak under a series of different masters. For two centuries Persia was the power to the north, and Egypt, now usually less powerful than in earlier times, was always there in the south.

In 333 Alexander the Great of Macedon achieved an amazing series of conquests, which destroyed the rule of Persia. He died at an early age, leaving his vast empire divided between his generals. The Greek kingdom based on Syria absorbed the Jews, and they experienced periods of tight control alternating with times of greater independence. Eventually Pompey, a conqueror as great as Alexander, brought Roman rule to Egypt and Syria. Judaea became part of the Roman province of Syria from 63 BCE.

The last of the prophets lived during the century after the return from Babylon. After that three great books were added, different from anything which had gone before. The book of Jonah is included among the minor prophets, but it is a parable rather than a prophecy, a wonderful story of a prophet who tried to run away from God, and found himself preaching unwillingly to the Ninevites. The book of Job is another parable, built up from a short story into a long, beautifully written book. It is a deep, poetic study of the meaning of suffering. (You will find JOB among "The VERSE PLAYS.")

The book of Daniel was probably written at the time when a Jewish revolt against one of the Hellenistic kings of Syria was taking place. It is made up of two parts: a narrative about young Jews during the exile four hundred years earlier, and the visions of one of them, Daniel. The writer is not trying to give an accurate historical picture. His book describes the courage and moral victories of Daniel and his friends. It is similar in spirit to the book of Esther and the Apocryphal book of Judith.

DANIEL**

(Attempt all Daniel scenes)

BIBLE REFERENCE: The book of Daniel

This is the story of Daniel the prophet, whose faith and courage are described in the book named after him. The writer imagines a group of young Jews living in exile in Babylon. King Nebuchadnezzar ordered his minister Ashpenaz to find some clever, handsome Jewish boys and teach them the language and learning of the Chaldeans. They were well treated, and given food and drink from the King's table. However, Daniel refused to eat food which as a Jew he believed to be unclean. Ashpenaz tried to persuade him and his friends to change their minds.

Scene one:

WHAT KIND OF FOOD? *

Characters: ASHPENAZ
DANIEL
SHADRACH, MESHECH, ABEDNEGO, his friends

(ASHPENAZ IS SEATED. THE BOYS STAND IN FRONT OF HIM)

ASHPENAZ: Why not be reasonable, Daniel?

DANIEL: I cannot be what you call reasonable, sir. I was raised a Jew. I must be faithful to my religion.

ASHPENAZ: Look, boys, you know that I have gone out of my way to help you—

ABEDNEGO: Yes, sir.

SHADRACH: We know that, sir.

MESHECH: And we are grateful.

ASHPENAZ: But not grateful enough to do what I ask.

DANIEL: Sir, is it a big thing that we are asking?

ABEDNEGO: All we need is simple, plain food.

ASHPENAZ: Yes, but—

SHADRACH: Rich dishes are fine for the king, but—

ASHPENAZ: You need rich food at your age.

MESHECH: But, sir—

ASHPENAZ: You're putting me in a very hard position. If the King sees you looking like sick skeletons he will blame me. You know what that means.

DANIEL:	Look, sir, give us a chance! Please let us eat plain Jewish food for ten days. After that, see how we look, and weigh us on the scales.
SHADRACH:	If you tell us we look bad, or find we are not doing our work, we will eat the king's food.
ASHPENAZ:	Is that a promise?
ALL:	Yes, we promise.
ASHPENAZ:	Then I suppose I must try it.

Scene two:

THE KING AND THE MAGICIANS*

Characters: KING NEBUCHADNEZZAR
ASHPENAZ
ARIOCH, Captain of the Guard
MELZAR, a magician
MAGICIANS and ASTROLOGERS (Optional)

The Jewish boys won their argument, and flourished on their simple diet. After ten days they were brought before the king, who said that he had never seen their equals in looks and physical strength. As for their learning and wisdom, they outstripped the sages of the Chaldeans. Daniel especially was expert in interpreting dreams and visions. This proved fortunate, because King Nebuchdnezzar began to be troubled by bad dreams. He could not remember what he had dreamed, but he demanded help from his magicians and astrologers.

(NEBUCHADNEZZAR IS SEATED ON HIS THRONE. ASHPENAZ AND ARIOCH STAND BY HIS SIDE. THE MAGICIANS ARE KNEELING IN FRONT OF HIM)

KING:	Another nightmare last night! Explain it to me!
ASHPENAZ:	O King, live for ever! Tell your servants the dream! They will interpret it.
KING:	How can I tell it when I have forgotten it? It is for you to tell me. That is what I pay you to do—so get on with it!
MELZAR:	But, sir, that is not possible.

KING:	Not possible? That will be too bad for you, Melzar. Either you tell me what I dreamed, in which case you will get a rich reward; or you turn out to be a fake and a failure—and in that case all of you will be hacked to pieces, and your houses made into a dunghill.
ASHPENAZ:	Your Majesty, if you could only remember something—
KING:	I thought I made it plain, you dog, that I remember nothing. You claim to be magicians. I want results—now!
MELZAR:	Only the gods could tell you what you are asking—
KING:	So you are liars and hypocrites! I thought so. Arioch!
ARIOCH:	Sir!
KING:	Take these men and execute them, and the whole pack of socalled wise men.
MELZAR:	Your Majesty, have mercy!
WISE MEN:	Mercy! Mercy!
KING:	Now, Arioch!
ARIOCH:	Yes, sir.

(ASHPENAZ, MELCAR, AND MAGICIANS CRY FOR MERCY AS THEY ARE REMOVED)

Scene three:

DANIEL TELLS THE KING HIS DREAM**

Characters: KING NEBUCHADNEZZAR
ARIOCH
DANIEL

Arioch told Daniel and his friends that they must die along with the other wise men. Daniel begged for one night, in which he might pray God to show him the King's dream. His wish was granted, and during the night God revealed the dream and its meaning. In the morning Daniel pleaded to Arioch to postpone the execution of the other wise men until he had been granted an interview with the King. When Daniel was brought in, the King was on his throne, surrounded by his courtiers.

ARIOCH:	O king, live for ever! I have found one of the captives from Judah, who will make known to the King his dream and its meaning.
KING:	Is this true? Who is this man?
ARIOCH:	His name is Daniel, sir.
KING:	Daniel? Yes, I remember him. Fetch him at once!
ARIOCH:	Yes, sir. (SHOUTS) Bring in the Jew, Daniel! (GUARDS LEAD DANIEL IN)
KING:	Well, Daniel, is it true? You know what I dreamed?
DANIEL:	Not I, sir, but the God to whom I pray. No astrologer can find the truth without his help and guidance.
KING:	So you claim he has helped and guided you? Prove it!
DANIEL:	Your dream foretold things which are to happen in days to come.
KING:	(SHOUTING) Tell me what I dreamed!
DANIEL:	You saw a great image—a statue. There was bright light around it—
KING:	Yes! The image—the light blinded me. It was terrible!
DANIEL:	Its head was of gold, its breast and arms of silver and its thighs of brass—
KING:	Go on!
DANIEL:	Its legs were of iron, but it had feet of clay. You saw a stone come crashing against the feet of the image. It fell, and was shattered.
KING:	It is true—everything you say! The fragments were no bigger than chaff.
DANIEL:	The stone which had broken the image grew, as large as a mountain.

KING: Yes! But what does it mean, Daniel? I must know!

DANIEL: The head of gold can be none other than yourself, for you are a king of kings, and your glory shines like gold. After you will come other kingdoms, of silver and of brass, whose glory will be far less than yours. Then shall come a kingdom as strong as iron. It will bruise and break the other kingdoms. Where you saw the iron turn into feet of clay, God showed you the kingdom growing weak, so that the stone could overthrow it, bringing the kingdom crashing down to earth. That stone is another kingdom which God will raise up. It will never be destroyed.

KING: Daniel, no man is equal to you. Let Daniel have anything he asks for! Burn incense in his honor!

DANIEL: No, sir. Honor the one true God, whose servant I am.

KING: If he is your god, then he is the true god. From today you are Governor of Babylon. See that this is proclaimed to all the people, Arioch!

ARIOCH: Yes, sir.

DANIEL: I will serve you faithfully, sir. I ask that three of my friends may work with me.

KING: Anything you say. After what you have done for me you only have to give an order, and it will be carried out.

Scene four:

THE FIERY FURNACE**

Characters: KING NEBUCHADNEZZAR
ARIOCH
SHADRACH, MESHECH, and ABEDNEGO
GUARDS

But trouble soon fell upon Daniel and his friends. King Nebuchadnezzar built a huge image of gold, and it was decreed that when trumpets and harps and flutes sounded everyone must fall down and worship that image. The enemies of Daniel were glad, because they knew that the Jews would refuse to bow down before an idol. Arioch seized Shadrach, Meshech, and Abednego and dragged then before the King.

KING: (SEATED) What is the trouble, Arioch?

ARIOCH: May the king live for ever! Treason, Your Majesty! These Jews, who have wormed their way into your favor, refuse to obey your express commands. They will not fall down before your holy image.

KING: Is ths true, Jew?

SHADRACH: Your Majesty, we are your faithful servants—

KING: (SHOUTING) Answer me, dog! Did you refuse to fall down before the image?

SHADRACH: Yes.

KING: And you, Jewish swine? Did you refuse?

MESHECH: Our faith prevents us—

ABEDNEGO: We cannot do what God forbids.

KING: You dare to disobey me? Is the furnace hot, Arioch?

ARIOCH: It is, sir; hotter than ever before. I thought that you would want these men done away with at once.

KING: Throw them in, now! Burn them!

ARIOCH: With pleasure, sir. Guards! Open the doors and throw them in!

(GUARDS DRAG THE JEWS OFF STAGE. ARIOCH FOLLOWS. SOON THE GUARDS ARE HEARD YELLING: "A-a-h! I'm on fire! Help! The fire!"

VOICES OF THE JEWS:(OFF STAGE) The Lord is my shepherd. Though I walk through the valley of the shadow of death I will fear no evil.

KING: Well, are they dead?

ARIOCH: (ENTERING) God in heaven! I–I don't believe it!

KING: What is it, man? Stop staring at me like an idiot!

ARIOCH: Sir, come here! Please! (KING GOES TO THE SIDE OF THE STAGE) I'm going mad. The guards who opened the doors are dead, but—

KING: Arioch, there are four! We threw three men into the furnace, and there are four. And the fourth is like the Son of God! (HE FALLS TO HIS KNEES) Forgive me! Be merciful, and forgive me! (THE THREE JEWS REENTER) Are you truly alive, untouched by the fire?

SHADRACH: By God's grace we are.

ABEDNEGO: Touch our clothes.

KING: Truly you have humbled me. You were ready to die for your faith, and your God saved you by a miracle. Blessed be the God of Shadrach, Meshech, and Abednego, who sent his angel to deliver his servants! Let no man speak against their God, on pain of death! Let them be raised to high office in our kingdom!

Scene five:

THE LIONS' DEN**

Characters: KING DARIUS
TWO COUNSELLORS
DANIEL

Daniel continued to interpret the dreams of the king and of his son Belshazzar, who succeeded him. Belshazzar worshipped idols. One night, at a drunken feast, he and his courtiers used the holy vessels taken from King Solomon's Temple in Jerusalem as cups. While they were doing this a finger wrote on the wall a message which noone could understand. The Queen remembered Daniel's wisdom, and he was summoned. He read the writing on the wall, and told the King that it prophesied his death and the end of his kingdom. That very night Belshazzar was killed, and the Persian King Darius took possession of Babylon. Darius kept Daniel as Governor of Babylon, and because of his wisdom it appeared that he would be set over the whole of the King's realm. Then all of the King's courtiers grew jealous of Daniel, and set a trap for him.

SEVERAL RAPID VOICES OFF STAGE:	The only way to harm him is through his faith.
	I have an idea—
	What is it?
	Suggest to the King that nobody may make a prayer or petition for thirty days, except to the King himself—
	How will that help?
	Don't you see? Daniel prays to his God all the time—
	Yes, of course!
	Thrown to the lions! Just what he deserves!

They succeeded in their plan. They caught Daniel praying to the God of the Jews, and dragged him before the King, seated on his throne.

1st COUNSELLOR:	Here is Daniel the Jew, Your Majesty
2nd COUNSELLOR:	He broke the law.
FIRST:	We found him praying to his god.
DARIUS:	That is not a crime. He is my faithful servant and friend.
SECOND:	Not a crime, Your Majesty? Your decree was absolutely clear.
FIRST:	No petitions except to you. Throw him to the lions!
DANIEL:	These men have set a trap for both of us, Your Majesty. Put me in the lions' den, and I will pray God to deliver me.
DARIUS:	O, Daniel! I have no choice. May your God protect you!
FIRST:	Bind him, and throw him in!
SECOND:	Into the den with the Jew!
DANIEL:	You have no need to bind me. Open the door, if you have the courage. I will go in.
SECOND:	I will fetch one of the guards—
FIRST:	We don't want any tricks—

DANIEL: Your Majesty, since these brave men will not open the door, I will. May the King live for ever! (HE OPENS THE DOOR OFF STAGE. THE LIONS ROAR ONCE, THEN ARE QUIET)

FIRST: Put the bar across quickly!

SECOND: Now, sir, set your seal on the outside, so that we know he cannot slip away.

DARIUS: Yes, I will seal it. Here, take my ring and make the seal! But woe to you if Daniel's prayers are heard! You have tried to slay my friend, and your trick succeeded; but if Daniel lives until dawn be very sure that you will take his place in the lions' den.

That night Darius fasted, and prayed for Daniel. Very early next morning he arose, and came to the door of the lions' den.

DARIUS: Daniel, O Daniel, servant of the living God, is your God able to save you from the lions?

DANIEL: (OFF STAGE) O King, live for ever! My God sent his angel and shut the lions' mouths. They have not hurt me.

DARIUS: God be praised! Guards! Open the door! (THEY DO SO. DANIEL WALKS ON STAGE. THE LIONS ROAR AGAIN)

DANIEL: (KNEELING) Your Majesty!

DARIUS: I cannot believe it. Now I know that you worship the one true God. Guards, seize the men who accused Daniel, with their families, and throw them to the lions! Let it be decreed in my kingdom that all men tremble before the God of Daniel, who has shown such mighty signs and works!

Daniel was restored to power, and lived in peace. His visions are recorded in the book of the Bible named for him.

JESUS!
His Life and Parables
SCENES FROM THE LIFE OF JESUS

**scenes, excellent to act. *scenes, good to act.
+scenes, hard to act, but try them.

1. Joseph and Mary**
2. The Innkeeper**
3. The animal who did not speak**
4. Rabbis in Jerusalem*
5. Temptation**
6. John the Baptist*
7. Cana of Galilee*
8. The call of four fishermen**
9. Healing the sick**
10. Women who came to Jesus**
11. Lepers**
12. Five loaves and two fish**
13. What is righteousness?*
14. Critics**
15. Who are you, Lord?**
16. The road to Jerusalem**
17. Fish for breakfast**

Before starting to act a scene, read the FOREWORD TO ALL SECTIONS carefully. In many of these scenes the crowd represents the biggest acting challenge. Characters marked with # are not named in the Bible.

Scene One:

JOSEPH AND MARY**
BIBLE REFERENCE: Matthew 1:18-24; Luke 1:26-38

CHARACTERS: MARY
                    JOSEPH

The story of the Annunciation is very familiar: the angel Gabriel comes to tell Mary about the coming birth of Jesus. That scene has been the subject of many great paintings. Matthew's account of Joseph's dream is less familiar; but it was this dream which convinced him that he should take Mary as his wife. The scene takes place at Mary's home in Nazareth. She is seated, sewing, when Joseph knocks at the door. She lets him in.

MARY: Joseph !

JOSEPH: Mary, my dearest. Oh, it's so good to see you! (HE EMBRACES HER)

MARY: And you, Joseph. I have been so bewildered and troubled.

JOSEPH: I want you to stop worrying. You're coming home with me.

MARY: You mean you're going through with the marriage?

JOSEPH: Yes, dear. You know how deeply I care for you; and now God has sent me a clear command.

MARY: You also?

JOSEPH: Yes, a dream. I know that you had a vision of the angel Gabriel. I have always believed in you, Mary—you know that. But until last night I didn't know what to do.

MARY: Tell me what happened. It makes me so happy to hear it.

JOSEPH: I went to sleep worrying about us, and what people would say when they found out about the baby. While I was asleep I heard a voice, which seemed to come out of a bright light. I knew that it was the angel of the Lord.

MARY: He came to you too? Oh, thank God!

JOSEPH: The voice said, 'Joseph, son of David, do not be afraid to take Mary into your home She has conceived her baby through the power of the Holy Spirit. She will bear a son, whose name will be Jesus, the Savior.'

MARY: It was the same vision. God has spoken to both of us.

JOSEPH: He reminded me of the prophet Isaiah's words: that a maiden will conceive and bear a son, called Emmanuel, 'God with us.' Then I woke up, and hurried over here to tell you.

MARY: Oh, Joseph I cannot tell why this has happened to us. I only know that I must do my best to serve him. I could not do it alone, but with your help I can.

JOSEPH: You shall not be alone, Mary. I am proud that God has chosen me to give you and your son a home. Now, get ready. I want to carry out his command without delay.

Scene Two:

THE INNKEEPER **
BIBLE REFERENCE: Luke 2: 1-7

CHARACTERS: INNKEEPER
A MAN and a WOMAN, guests
MAID
JOSEPH
MARY

SCENE:

The Inn at Bethlehem: A table and two chairs. A chair by the fireplace. The scene is imaginary. Guests would not have had 'rooms' in the modern sense, and we do not know what kind of man the Innkeeper was; but the spirit of the scene is faithful to the gospel story. It may help to make the situation of Joseph and Mary clearer.

The story of Jesus begins in Bethlehem. Joseph and Mary came there from Galilee to be 'taxed' or 'registered'. Herod, the local ruler who governed Judaea under the Roman rule, kept his people under strict control. A few hours before Jesus was born the travelers arrived in Bethlehem, and could find nowhere to stay.

INNKEEPER:	(TO THE GUESTS SEATED AT THE TABLE) I hope you're enjoying your meal.
MAN:	It tastes great after that tough journey.
INNKEEPER:	You came from Jerusalem?
MAN:	That's right. We ran into snow.
INNKEEPER:	That's quite rare for this time of year.
WOMAN:	We feel so lucky to have got the last room.
INNKEEPER:	Yes. We've had a dozen people ask for a room since you arrived. (BELL) There's another. Susannah!
MAID:	(COMING IN WITH A DISH) Yes, sir?
INNKEEPER:	Answer the door. Remember, we're full—no room.
MAID:	Yes, sir. (SHE OPENS THE DOOR)
JOSEPH:	(FROM OUTSIDE) Good evening. May I speak to the innkeeper?
MAID:	I'm sorry, sir. He's busy; and we don't have any room.
JOSEPH:	I understand that. We've tried several places. But may I just have a word—
INNKEEPER:	What's the trouble, Susannah? There's a draught coming through that door. I'm sorry, sir. We don't have an inch of room left.
JOSEPH:	May I come in for a minute? We have an emergency.
INNKEEPER:	An emergency? All right, then Come in (JOSEPH AND MARY ENTER)
JOSEPH:	Come inside, Mary dear. It will be warmer in here.
MAID:	Come and sit by the fire. (SHE LEADS MARY TO A CHAIR)

JOSEPH:	She's very near her time. The rough journey has been too much for her.
INNKEEPER:	She's going to have a baby? Where have you come from?
JOSEPH:	Nazareth.
INNKEEPER:	Nazareth? In Galilee? You must be mad!
JOSEPH:	When the Romans give an order you obey it, pregnant or not.
INNKEEPER:	I don't know what to do. We've already doubled up in most rooms.
WOMAN:	We'd like to help, but I don't see how—
MAN:	Keep out of this! Anna It's not our business.
WOMAN:	It has to be somebody's business.
JOSEPH:	I know you have no rooms; but what we really need is any kind of shelter. She'll die out there in the cold.
INNKEEPER:	This is what happens in our trade. Feast or famine. A month ago every room was empty.
MAID:	They could go in the stables, sir.
INNKEEPER:	Let a baby be born in the stables?
MAID:	That's where the animals keep their young ones warm. (TO MARY) I'll help you if my Master will let me.
JOSEPH:	We'll accept that gladly, and pay you.
MARY:	Please, sir!
INNKEEPER:	I don't know what to say.
JOSEPH:	Then say yes!
MARY:	God will bless you if you let us stay. (PAUSE WHILE HE CONSIDERS)

INNKEEPER:	All right. Susannah, show them where to go, and send some food from the kitchen. But don't linger out there! We have too much to do as it is.
MARY:	We will never forget your kindness.
INNKEEPER:	Kindness? I don't know. We'll do what we can for you, but—a manger in a stable? What a way to be born.

Scene Three:

THE ANIMAL WHO DID NOT SPEAK**

CHARACTERS: THE HORSE
THE OX
THE CAMEL
THE DONKEY

This scene is taken from a legend: that as Christmas morning begins at midnight animals are able to speak for just one minute. On the first Christmas morning four of them were watching what was happening at one manger in their stable. A baby was coming to life, and there were strange rumors that the child would become some kind of king—although it seemed most unlikely.

HORSE:	You heard what they were saying? A king
OX:	That kid? It's a little hard to believe.
CAMEL:	You never know. Stranger things have happened.
HORSE:	One thing I do know. If he grows up to be a king, he will need a fine horse; a stallion like me, for instance, so that he can ride in processions and be seen by his subjects.
CAMEL:	Processions? That won't do him much good. He will need to make long journeys to faroff lands. That is where I can help him. Communications are the key to a king's strength.
OX:	I am sure you can each be useful—in a minor degree. But a king's power depends on the lands which he rules, and it is my strength which pulls the plow. If this baby is really a king he will need me most.
DONKEY:	Excuse me—

HORSE: Probably the rumors are groundless.

CAMEL: His father and mother look like very common people.

OX: Provincials, I'd say from their accent: Galileans.

The minute was up. The poor donkey never got in a word, and the other animals took no notice of him. In spite of that it was the donkey who carried the baby to safety in Egypt, and the donkey who bore the Son of God into Jerusalem.

(The could read G.K.Chesterton's poem, THE DONKEY, at the end of the scene. It can be found in the Oxford Book of English Verse, number 931.)

Scene Four:

RABBIS AT JERUSALEM*
BIBLE REFERENCE: LUKE 2: 41-51

CHARACTERS: TWO RABBIS
                   JESUS
                   JOSEPH
                   MARY

Luke tells us that when Jesus was twelve years old his parents took him with them on their annual visit to Jerusalem, at the Feast of the Passover. A large company went from Galilee. After the Feast they started on their way home. Mary and Joseph thought that Jesus was somewhere among the group, but after a day's journey they could not find him. They turned back towards the city, anxious and puzzled. It was only on the third day that they found him in the Temple.

JESUS: (SEATED ON A MAT ON THE FLOOR) But, Rabbi, what is the true meaning of sacrifice?

RABBI 1:   Read the scriptures, my son. Listen to what your teachers say. You are too young to be questioning such things.

JESUS: I know the scriptures, sir. Burnt offerings. Peace offerings. Sin offerings. Clean and unclean animals. I have studied all this.

RABBI 2:   Then you have learned all that a boy should know, Why—

JESUS:	Yes, sir. But in our class at school I asked our teacher to explain why Micah the Prophet wrote: 'I desire mercy, and not sacrifice,' and King David said in his psalm, 'Sacrifice and meat-offerings thou wouldest not—'
RABBI 1:	This is indeed a boy who searches the scriptures. But be careful, child! Remember the proverb: 'Make your ear attentive to wisdom, and incline your heart to understanding—'
JESUS:	That's just the point, sir It goes on—don't you remember? 'If you cry out for insight and raise your voice for understanding.' Surely we are meant to think for ourselves, and to try to find out God's will?
RABBI 2:	To think for yourself? No, no, my son! Learn from your masters, and from those who have gone before you. It is dangerous to put yourself forward—
JOSEPH:	(ENTERING WITH MARY) Jesus. What are you doing here?
MARY:	Oh, my boy. You gave us such a fright.
RABBI 1:	Is this your son?
JOSEPH:	Yes, sir. We have looked for him everywhere, and—
JESUS:	Oh, Mother, Father. I'm sorry! I was so excited, coming to Jerusalem. You mean you left without me?
MARY:	We thought you were with all the other children in the caravan.
JESUS:	I didn't mean to cause you trouble.
JOSEPH:	I hope he hasn't been making a nuisance of himself, sir.
RABBI 2:	Far from it. This is a remarkable boy.
RABBI 1:	He has great potential, for good or for harm. Watch over him carefully!
RABBI 2:	He has amazed us—the things he has said—
RABBI 1:	—and his knowledge is Incredible.

JESUS: I had to do my Father's work. I could think of nothing else.

MARY: Your father's work? You can't work for him here. He needs you in the carpenter's shop at home.

JESUS: Oh, Mother, you don't understand. I have to do the work to which my Father in Heaven calls me.

Scene Five:

TEMPTATION **
BIBLE REFERENCE: MATTHEW 4: 1-11; LUKE 4: 1-13

CHARACTERS: JESUS
SATAN

SCENE:

A MOUNTAIN TOP IN THE WILDERNESS.

That is all we know about the youth of Jesus. In the gospels he enters his ministry as a mature man, strong in body and mind and spirit. He is ready for the work to which he is called. Now he goes to the wilderness to prepare for the change in his life. There, as he thinks how to use the great gifts of power and love which he has brought to the world, Satan vainly tries to tempt him to cheapen and misuse them.

JESUS: (KNEELING) Father, I am ready. Show me your will, and I will go and find laborers for your vineyard.

SATAN: (ENTERING) You have fasted enough, Jesus. Now it is time for you to eat.

JESUS: Is that your voice, Satan? Can you never stop trying to tear down and spoil the love of God?

SATAN: Whatever I do is always misinterpreted. I am not trying to tear down, but to build up. First, you must build your strength. You can do no work for your father while you are fainting with hunger. Pray that these stones may be turned into bread, and eat !

JESUS: Man does not live by bread alone, Satan. I will eat when it is time to eat.

SATAN:	Very well. You know best about that. But now you are ready to show God's people your power. They are waiting for you, Jesus! They are longing to know that the Messiah has come. Climb with me to the Temple roof! Descend among the crowd, and reveal your power! He has said himself, 'He will give his angels charge over you. They will bear you in their arms, lest you strike your foot against a stone.'
JESUS:	Yes, he said that. It is also written in his book: 'You shall not tempt the Lord your God.'
SATAN:	Tempt? I am not tempting you, Jesus, I am offering to help you. You are so hesitant, so weak! Together we could rule the world. Look! Don't you see? All the kingdoms of the world, waiting for you! Work for me, work with me, and nothing can resist us.
JESUS:	Oh, Satan, go! You have no power over me. You have forgotten the only truth that matters: 'Worship the Lord your God, and serve him and him alone.' Go, and leave me to my prayers!
SATAN:	You weak, goody-goody fool! Milksop! Do you really think mankind is worth what you are doing? Love Service! They will mock you first, then beat you, then murder you. God has gone mad, sending you here in rags—mad, mad!

Scene six:

JOHN THE BAPTIST*

BIBLE REFERENCE: MATTHEW 3: 1-12

John, son of the priest Zacharias and Elizabeth, was a cousin of Jesus. He was surely one of the most unselfish great figures in history. His whole message was that he was preparing the way for another far greater than himself, the coming Messiah. His call to baptism and repentance met with a ready response; but he was watched by the Jewish authorities, in case he might prove to be dangerous. Some of Jesus' disciples had been followers of John, as we learn in John 1:40.

CHARACTERS:	A Pharisee
	A Sadducee
	A Priest
	A Levite
	John the Baptist
	A Soldier

A Tax Collector
Andrew
Crowd

The Scene is a desert place near Bethabara, east of the Jordan River. The Pharisee and Sadducee approach each other across the stage.

PHARISEE: Greetings, Ezra! What brings you to this wild place?

SADDUCEE: Nicodemus! I might ask you the same thing; but I can guess the answer.

PHARISEE: The socalled Baptist, John?

SADDUCEE: Exactly. I have come to find out what is really happening.

PHARISEE: I too. They say he is coming this way soon, with a crowd at his heels.

SADDUCEE: A fine man, I hear. Austere—they say he eats simple desert food, wild honey and locusts—disciplined, knows the Law well.

PHARISEE: And a magnetic speaker. Oh, yes. The question is, are his views orthodox?

SADDUCEE: You and I might diagree about what that means. (NOISE OF CROWD OFF STAGE) Well, here they come We shall soon know.

(JOHN ENTERS, FOLLOWED BY A CROWD)

SOLDIER: Stop and talk to us, Master!

LEVITE: Sir, I want to ask you a question.

ANDREW: Please, Master, give me an answer !

JOHN: Very well, my friends! Stop here, and ask your questions. I see we have distinguished visitors from the City. Good evening, gentlemen.

SADDUCEE: You are John-ben-Zacharias? I am Ezra, a Sadducee, from Jerusalem.

PHARISEE: And I am Nicodemus, a Pharisee from that city.

JOHN:	I have no soft, smooth words to say to you. Go back and tell the leaders in Jerusalem that I see in them a generation of vipers, bloodsuckers, and traitors to God's word! Repent, and be washed clean by baptism, if you truly wish to humble yourselves before God!
PHARISEE:	You dare to say that to us, the children of Abraham?
JOHN:	Oh, Abraham! If God wanted to do so, he could take these stones and turn them into children of Abraham.
PRIEST:	That is blasphemy.
JOHN:	I say to you what the prophet Isaiah proclaimed: 'Prepare the way of the Lord, the coming Messiah. '
SOLDIER:	But if I seek baptism what will it mean? I'm a soldier. How can I follow you, and do my job?
JOHN:	A soldier? Then you are trained to observe discipline and preserve peace. Don't use your power to oppress the people you are sworn to protect. Do your job without cruelty and favoritism.
TAX COLLECTOR:	And I, master? I'm a tax collector.
JOHN:	It's the same with you, friend. Be fair and honest, avoid extortion, and follow God's law. Listen, all of you! This is a call to simple justice and love. If you have spare clothes, and plenty to eat, share what you have with the poor and hungry.
LEVITE:	May I ask what your authority is for saying these things?
JOHN:	Indeed you may. I have no authority, except that God has sent me to make the way clear and straight for the Savior who is coming.
PRIEST:	The Messiah? You really believe that?
JOHN:	If you have read the scriptures how can you not believe it? What I say or do is not important. I am only here to point the way for him who is to come soon—a leader so great that I am not good enough to kneel and untie his shoelaces.

ANDREW: And what does it mean, being baptized?

JOHN: Washing away your sins, after true repentance. I can see you are a man of faith, my friend. I only baptize with water, but he who is coming after me will baptize you with God's holy spirit. It will be like fire, filling your life.

ANDREW: This leader—how shall we know him when he comes?

JOHN: Oh, you will know him, if you look for him with pure eyes. But first a lot of dead wood has to be cleared away from among our people. I tell you, the axe is ready to strike, and to cut down those who refuse to recognize the Messiah.

PHARISEE: Why do you preach out here in the wilderness?

SADDUCEE: And wear that camel's hair shirt?

JOHN: Out here nobody can accuse me of hypocrisy. I am no popular preacher, seeking gold, and eating fine food. I stand for simple, stark repentance, to make men and women ready for the coming of the Christ.

PRIEST: And if he does not come?

JOHN: God forgive you for your unbelief, sir! He will come, I promise you, and soon!

Scene seven:

CANA OF GALILEE *
BIBLE REFERENCE: John 2: 1-12

CHARACTERS: #JACOB and MIRIAM, father and mother of the bride
#MATTHEW and BARTHOLOMEW, servants
MARY
JESUS
#EZRA, Master of Ceremonies

SCENE:

A HOME IN CANA. A TABLE AND DISHES.

John tells us that at the beginning of his ministry Jesus was invited with his mother to a wedding. He accepted, and when he joined the party afterwards he found himself challenged to help people with an urgent need. It was his first miracle. It tells us three things. First, that God never refuses an invitation to come into our lives. He is not too busy, and he does not make excuses. Second, that if you ask him to help you in a crisis he will do so without fail, but not necessarily in the way you expect. Third, that the longer you maintain a close relationship with God the richer it becomes. The 'good wine' is kept to the last.

(THE SERVANTS ARE WORKING AT THE TABLE. MIRIAM ENTERS IN A HURRY)

MIRIAM: We need more cakes and fruit, Matthew.

MATTHEW: As quick as we can, Ma'am. We don't seem to be able to keep up.

BARTHOLOMEW: What a mob! And eat! I never saw such appetites.

MIRIAM: I suppose I ought to be thankful that everyone came, but—

JACOB: (BURSTING IN) Miriam! In heaven's name hurry up and bring in more wine!

MIRIAM: More wine? I don't believe it. They can't have drunk it all.

JACOB: They have. We have to get hold of some more.

MIRIAM: That's your job, Jacob. I'm having enough trouble keeping them fed. Whoever would have thought that Jonas would come, and Joanna with all her children, and that flock of cousins from Magdala?

JACOB: Well, they came, and they have to eat and drink.

MARY: (ENTERING) Is there anything I can do to help you, Miriam?

MIRIAM: Oh, Mary! We're at our wits' end. We're running out of wine.

MARY: Don't worry! It's one of the most beautiful weddings I have ever seen.

JACOB: But we've got to do something. I'll go back and see that whatever we have left is served. Then—I don't know. (HE GOES OUT)

MIRIAM: There's a small amount left in the storeroom. I'll fetch that.

MATTHEW: One flagon? That won't be much help, not with this lot. (SHE GOES OUT)

MARY: Wait, both of you! I have an idea. (SHE GOES OUT)

BARTHOLOMEW: Come on, Matt! Let's load up this stuff. At least they can eat.

MARY: (RETURNING WITH JESUS) Can you help them, Jesus? Miriam and Jacob have been so hospitable.

MATTHEW: Let's go, Bart.

BARTHOLOMEW: All set. (THEY HURRY OUT)

JESUS: You really believe in me, don't you, Mother? You think I am ready to show signs in God's name.

MARY: I think your gift of love is strong enough to meet the needs of people who turn to you.

JESUS: Thank you, Mother dear. You understand a great deal. (SERVANTS RETURN) Will you please fill those pitchers in the yard with water?

BARTHOLOMEW: Look, sir, if you'll excuse us. We're rushed off our feet.

JESUS: Please do what I ask. I want to help your mistress.

MATTHEW: O.K. If you say so. Come on, Bart

JESUS: I will come with you. (THEY GO OUT. MIRIAM RETURNS)

MIRIAM: If only there were a store open, or the vineyard were closer. There's no way—

MARY: Wait just a moment. I think everything will be all right.

MIRIAM: I don't see how—(JESUS AND SERVANTS RETURN, CARRYING SMALL PITCHERS) Whatever is that?

MATTHEW: The young gentleman told us to bring it in, Ma'am. To serve to the guests, he said. Water from the pitchers.

JACOB: That's it! We're out of wine!

MIRIAM: Wait! I want to taste this. It's—why, it's not like anything I ever tasted.

JACOB: (TASTING) It's wine, all right—good wine. Get it in there quick, Matt! How did you find it?

MIRIAM: I don't know. You'll have to ask Mary that—or Jesus. Hurry, Matthew, and carry it in! (SERVANTS GO OUT)

JACOB: What has Jesus to do with it? You're a carpenter, aren't you?

EZRA: (HURRYING IN) Jacob! Miriam! What are you doing in the kitchen? Come back to the guests—and you, Mary and Jesus!

JACOB: We're coming, Ezra.

EZRA: I thought the party was breaking up, but your servants gave us a surprise, and we're ready for a new round of toasts. Where did you get that new vintage?

JACOB: You mean, the wine that came from those pitchers?

EZRA: Whatever it is I can't place it. Very unusual—and great wine!

JACOB: There's something unusual about this whole thing. Never mind! We'll figure it out later.

EZRA: The funny thing is, most people serve their best wine first, and make do with something cheaper later in the day. Why did you and Miriam hold back this great stuff to the last?

JACOB: Why did we, Miriam?

MIRIAM: We'll find out later. This is Rebekah's wedding. I'm so thankful we found what we need. You know that, Jesus, don't you? And Mary?

MARY: Yes, Miriam, we know.

MIRIAM: Let's go back to our guests.

Scene eight:

THE CALL OF FOUR FISHERMEN **
BIBLE REFERENCE: LUKE 5: 1-11

CHARACTERS: PETER and ANDREW. brothers
JAMES and JOHN, sons of Zebedee
JESUS

SCENE:

BY THE SEA OF GALILEE. A TABLE FOR A BOAT, AND NETS.

Jesus needed trustworthy friends, who were ready to make a big sacrifice in order to follow him. He found four of them by the lake of Galilee. These were not poor laborers, but fishermen who were partners in a business, Zebedee and Sons. We know that fish from Galilee was pickled and put in barrels for export at Magdala (its other name was Tarichaea, 'Pickletown').

ANDREW: (WASHING HIS NETS WITH PETER) Another blank night!

PETER: That's right. Not a fish to be seen.

ANDREW: Well, that's Galilee for you: shoals of fish, or none.

PETER: Hey, James, John Catch anything?

JAMES: (FROM OFF STAGE) A few miserable little fish. We threw them back.

PETER: Too bad! Well, let's get these nets done, and go home to bed.

CROWD: (DIFFERENT VOICES HEARD FROM OFF STAGE) Jesus! Jesus of Nazareth! Heal my son! Help us, Master Don't leave us!

JESUS: (ENTERING. THE CROWD MAY BE ON STAGE OR INVISIBLE) Be quiet, my friends! Please be quiet!

ANDREW: Good morning, Jesus.

PETER: Do you need help? That crowd sounded ready to get out of hand.

JESUS: Thank you both. If I could step into your boat —

PETER:	Of course.
JESUS:	It means putting off that sleep for a few minutes, Peter.
PETER:	How did you know I was thinking about that?
JESUS:	By looking at the rims around your eyes.
ANDREW:	Climb in (JESUS DOES SO. CROWD SURGES FORWARD ON STAGE, CALLING OUT: Don't go, Jesus! Don't leave us! Heal my son! We need you etc.)
JESUS:	(SHOUTING) Friends! Please! Please! (THEY FALL SILENT) I am not leaving you. I will pray with everyone who seeks healing. But you mustn't press forward, or more people will be hurt, not healed. That is why I asked these fishermen to lend me their boat. You see them mending their nets? The Kingdom of Heaven is like a net. The fisherman draws it into his boat and sorts out the fish—the good ones, and those that are tasteless and rotten. He throws those back into the water. So God has sent me to gather into his kingdom all who are clean and who seek to be near him; but those who reject him it is hard for him not to reject. Now please walk back quietly to the town square, and lay your sick down there. I will follow you, and pray for them to be healed, if it is God's will.

(CROWD GOES OFF, DIFFERENT MEMBERS SAYING: Let's go! It's all right, Jonathan. Don't Cry! Come along! He promised. Jesus is coming)

PETER:	Let me give you a hand. (JESUS STEPS DOWN) There!
JESUS:	Thank you, Peter.
PETER:	That's all right, Master. Any time.
ANDREW:	We'll do anything to help you, Jesus.
JESUS:	Is that true? Let me put you to the test. How about postponing that sleep a little longer, and catching some fish?
PETER:	Catching some—Look, Jesus, I meant we'd do anything which makes sense. There aren't any fish out there. We tried all night. You're a carpenter, not a fisherman.

ANDREW: He means it, Simon.

JESUS: Andrew is right. I promise that, if you launch out into the deep water you will catch fish without number. Your lives will never be the same again, but you will catch fish.

PETER: All right. It's crazy, but let's get it over. Hey, James, John! We're going out .

JOHN: (OFF STAGE) You must be kidding!

JAMES: You said yourself—

PETER: All right, we're kidding. Come on, get ready

Simon Peter and Andrew launched their boat, followed by James and John. They were not prepared for what happened next.

ANDREW: (OFF STAGE) Here, what's going on?

PETER: Heavens above! It's a shoal! James! John! Quick!

JOHN: What is it?

JAMES: They're sinking. Get your oar! Hold on, Simon! (SOUNDS OF A STRUGGLE. THE FOUR COME BACK. PETER KNEELS)

PETER: Master, Leave me alone! I'm a sinner. You've shown me that.

JESUS: Don't be afraid! I wanted to prove to you that I need you.

PETER: Need me?

JESUS: Yes. You and Andrew, and the sons of Zebedee. I need all of you.

ANDREW: We're just four ordinary fishermen, Jesus.

JESUS: That is what I need: ordinary men and women with faith and courage. Fishers of men.

PETER: If you say so, Master, it must be true. What do you want us to do?

JESUS:	First let us go the town. The people are waiting for me. Perhaps after that we can meet at your home, Peter. I would like to know your family.

Scene nine:

HEALING THE SICK **

BIBLE REFERENCE: MANY STORIES OF HEALING. THIS SCENE IS A COMPOSITE.

CHARACTERS:	JESUS MOTHER TWO MEN, BYSTANDERS WOMAN BYSTANDER #LEBBAEUS TWO RABBIS CROWD

SCENE:

A STREET

CROWD VOICES:	Let me get through, please! Please, Jesus Help me! Out of my way! I must get near him!
JESUS:	(SHOUTING) Please be quiet (SILENCE AFTER A FEW SECONDS) That's better (SMILING) You make me sound like a Roman Centurion. Be patient, and I will come and pray with each of you. And you must all pray for each other. Lady, you have waited a long time. Is this your son?
MOTHER:	Yes, Master. He's deaf and dumb. Please, in God's name—
JESUS:	You have had faith, to bring him to me. What is his name?
MOTHER:	Lebbaeus, sir.
JESUS:	Come, Lebbaeus! Let me touch your ears and your lips. (HE PICKS UP EARTH AND MOISTENS IT WITH HIS TONGUE) Pray, all of you! Let the ears and mouth of Lebbaeus be opened, and his spirit be filled with peace and joy!
MAN 1:	The old mud and spit cure.
MAN 2:	Much good that will do him!

JESUS:	Please be quiet! Nothing can be done for this boy unless he is surrounded and supported by prayer. Now, Lebbaeus, open your ears (LOUDER) Open your ears! And loose your tongue! Do you hear me, Lebbaeus? You—can—hear.
WOMAN:	God! He nodded his head.
MAN 1:	It's a trick.
JESUS:	Lebbaeus, you hear me? Good Now say, 'I hear you, Master.' Speak! (LOUD) Speak!
LEBBAEUS:	I—hear—you.
MOTHER:	(HYSTERICALLY) Oh, no It can't be true. My boy! My boy!
LEBBAEUS:	It is true, Mother. I can hear, and speak. Don't cry, Mother!
CROWD VOICES:	It's true! He really healed the boy. That's no trick. The boy never spoke before. Jesus, Heal me next!
RABBI 1:	(ON ONE SIDE) Well, Rabbi, what did you think of that?
RABBI 2:	I don't know what to think. Where did he get this power over men and spirits?
RABBI 1:	What power? Don't ask me to believe that the son of Joseph the carpenter has power to heal sickness and forgive sins. He casts out devils through Beelzebub, the chief of the devils.
RABBI 2:	But you saw—the boy—
RABBI 1:	Very convincing. We'll see what the High Priest has to say when he hears about it. Come along, Rabbi! We must go and make our report.

Scene ten:

WOMEN WHO CAME TO JESUS **
BIBLE REFERENCES:
SCENES 1 AND 2: MARK 5: 22-49;
SCENE 3: JOHN 8: 1-11;
SCENE 4: MARK 7: 24-30;
SCENE 5: LUKE 7: 36-50.

This was only one of many healings which Jesus performed. 'As many as touched him were made whole,' Matthew (14:36) and Mark (6:56) wrote. We hear more of the men who left their work to follow him, the twelve whom he called Apostles. But there were also many women who turned to him.

CROWD VOICES: Make way! There's a girl dying! Let Jesus through! Come on, where's he going? To Jairus' house, the Synagogue leader. His daughter's dying. Make way, please!

JESUS: Stop!

PETER: What is it, Jesus?

JESUS: Who touched me?

PETER: Who TOUCHED you? Are you—

JESUS: Am I losing my mind? No, Peter. I know people are jostling us all the time, but this was different. Was it you, lady?

WOMAN: (KNEELING) Oh, sir, I'm sorry I didn't mean—

JESUS: You didn't mean me to know? You touched the hem of my robe. Did your wonderful faith bring you healing?

WOMAN: (SOBBING) I feel—I don't know—the flow of blood has stopped, after all these years.

JESUS: I knew, as soon as you touched me, that strength had gone from me to heal you. How wonderful that you believed in God's power to heal!

JAIRUS: Please, Jesus, hurry! My little girl—

JESUS: I'm coming, Jairus. God bless you, my daughter! May you be whole in body and spirit!

At Jairus' home Jesus fought for the girl's life. They had run out to tell him that the girl was dead; but he came and stood at her bedside,

JESUS: She is not dead. She is asleep.

MOTHER: Asleep! Don't mock me! She's dead—dead!

DOCTOR: You are talking nonsense, sir. I happen to be a doctor, and—

JESUS: Please be quiet! I must wake her. Sarah! Sarah! Wake up!

MOTHER: Leave her alone! Can't she even die in peace?

JAIRUS: Be quiet, my dear! Jesus is a great healer.

JESUS: I understand how you feel; but you can help me by praying for her. Sarah, sit up! You're a big girl, Sarah. I can't lift you if you won't help. Now, sit up! (LOUD) Up That's right—good girl—up!

DOCTOR: God almighty! It's incredible!

JESUS: Look after the doctor, Jairus. I think he's going to faint.

MOTHER: Oh, Sarah, my darling I—I'm sorry—

JESUS: She'll be all right now. Don't make a fuss over her. Give her something to eat.

John tells of a woman caught in adultery.

MAN 1: There she is, Jesus of Nazareth! Caught in the act!

MAN 2: We found her in bed, and now she is going to die.

JESUS: Of course. That is what she deserves, isn't it?

MAN: Let's get on with it!

JESUS: May I make a suggestion? You are going to stone this woman. Let the man who is without sin among you come forward and cast the first stone. (SILENCE) Well? (ONE MAN TURNS AND LEAVES, FOLLOWED BY THE REST) What is your name?

WOMAN: Susanna, sir.

JESUS: Susanna, the men who were going to stone you have gone away.

WOMAN: You saved my life

JESUS: Yes. Go, and sin no more! Make your life an act of thanksgiving to God.

Once a Phoenician woman pleaded for her child's life.

WOMAN: Sir, please heal my little girl!

JESUS: Woman, I am a Jew, sent to minister to my own people.

WOMAN: Sir, I need you. My daughter is dying. Please, please help!

JESUS: (SMILING) Do you think I can take the children's food and throw it to the dogs?

WOMAN: People give the dogs scraps, sir. Surely you can spare a little from the table.

JESUS: I cannot refuse faith like yours. Go home! You will find your little girl cured, not by me, but by your own shining faith.

In the home of a Pharisee a woman knelt at Jesus' feet.

SIMON: Sit down, Jesus. Supper will be ready soon.

JESUS: Thank you, Simon.

SIMON: There are some important questions which I need to ask you.

SERVANT: (ENTERING) Excuse me, sir—

SIMON: Yes? What is it? I asked you not to disturb me.

SERVANT: This woman, sir. I tried to keep her out, but—

WOMAN: (ENTERING AND KNEELING BY JESUS) Let me wash your feet, Master! I will not disturb you.

SIMON: Get the woman out of here! She's nothing but a common prostitute. This is a respectable household.

JESUS: Leave her alone, Simon! You wanted to question me?

SIMON:	How can we talk with that woman here? Don't you know what she is? I thought you were meant to be a prophet.
JESUS:	I know what she is. A sinner, who hates her sin, and is seeking God's love. You gave me no water to wash my feet. She is washing them with her tears, and drying them with her hair. You offered me no oil. She is anointing my feet with perfume. You were cold and correct. She is warm and full of love. God protect me from the chill of righteousness!
SIMON:	I'm only trying to tell you what this woman is—
JESUS:	And I tell you I know what she is. Have you finished, Mary?
WOMAN:	Yes, sir.
JESUS:	Thank you. You are asking for forgiveness and a fresh start?
WOMAN:	Oh yes, sir If I could only—
JESUS:	Your faith has earned you a new life. Go away now, and be strong! Now, Simon, your questions?

Scene eleven:

LEPERS**
BIBLE REFERENCE: LUKE 17: 12-19

CHARACTERS:	JESUS PETER JAMES JOHN #PHINEHAS #BENJAMIN and other lepers
PETER:	There's the city gate.
JAMES:	At last! Will I be glad to get to Mark's house and take the weight off my feet !
JOHN:	Aren't you tired, Jesus?
JESUS:	A little. It was a full day.

JAMES: Hello! Who are these?

PETER: Whoever they are, they've seen us.

JOHN: And they're coming on fast.

JESUS: They are lepers.

JOHN: Of course! There's a colony of them living in the hills.

JESUS: Stand behind me.

PETER: Yes, Lord. (LEPERS ENTER RUNNING)

PHINEHAS: Is one of you Jesus?

JESUS: I am Jesus.

PHINEHAS: We heard you were on your way to Jerusalem.

LEPERS: (DIVIDE THE WORDS AMONG THE GROUP)
Is it true? Can you heal us? Don't run away, Jesus! Help us, Master!

JESUS: (INTERRUPTING) Listen, please! I heard your questions. No, I will not run away. Yes, you deserve God's mercy. Can I heal you? Yes, if you do as I ask. You, friend, speak for the rest. What is your name?

PHINEHAS: Phinehas, sir.

JESUS: Well then, Phinehas, I ask you, in the name of all these lepers, do you have faith in God's power to make you whole?

PHINEHAS: I—Can it be true?

JESUS: If you believe in his mercy and love, it is true. Even Moses had his hand struck with leprosy, and then healed, to show God's power.

PHINEHAS: Yes, yes. I believe you have come from God to heal us!

JESUS: You all agree?

LEPERS:	(SHOUTING DIFFERENT PHRASES) O God, yes! It's a miracle! He says he can heal us! Jesus, Jesus, have mercy!
JESUS:	Then this is what you must all do. To be declared free from leprosy you must go to a priest and prove it, mustn't you?
PHINEHAS:	That's right.
JESUS:	And is there a priest close by?
PHINEHAS:	A mile away, in the village.
JESUS:	Then what are you waiting for?
PHINEHAS:	But—
JESUS:	No, Phinehas. No delays. Go! (LEPERS RUN OFF, SHOUTING)
PETER:	Is it true? Can you heal them all, just like that?
JESUS:	Peter, I have told you over and over. I do not heal the sick. I give them the faith which heals them.
JAMES:	Look! One of them has turned back.
JOHN:	Lost his nerve, do you think?
JAMES:	Or couldn't keep up with the rest?
JESUS:	No, I don't think that is the reason. (BENJAMIN RUNS IN AND KNEELS) What is it, my friend?
BENJAMIN:	(BREATHLESS) I suddenly thought—we didn't even say thank you.
JESUS:	That was easy to forgive; but I'm glad you came back. Look at your arms.
BENJAMIN:	O, great God It's true! (HE WEEPS)
JESUS:	Tears are good. Let your joy out. Who are you, and where is your home?
BENJAMIN:	Back home, in Samaria, they called me Benjamin.

JESUS:	Samaria. I thought so from your voice. So it was a foreigner who came to thank a Jew. You have a long journey back to your family. Come with us first to the city, and eat. I will take you to a priest to confirm that you are cured.

Scene twelve:

FIVE LOAVES AND TWO FISH**
BIBLE REFERENCE; JOHN 6: 1-14

CHARACTERS:	PETER JESUS ANDREW JAMES PHILIP BOY

Scene:

The countryside outside Capernaum

PETER:	Master, don't you think we should turn back?
JESUS:	Perhaps we should, Peter.
ANDREW:	There must be five thousand people out there.
JAMES:	I'm afraid they're going to get restless. It's been a long morning, and everyone's hungry.
JESUS:	I agree, James. they need to rest and eat.
PETER:	That's the point, Master. We're five miles from the nearest village. No stores, no food.
JESUS:	How about it, Philip? How do you think we can give these people bread?
PHILIP:	You know the answer to that, Jesus. We'd need hundreds of dollars to buy them a meal, even if it was possible.
JESUS:	Well, first let us ask them to rest. There's plenty of grass. Get everyone to sit down. Don't bunch them together too close; seat them by companies.

PETER: That's all very well, but—

JESUS: Would you do as I say, Peter? Please remember a morning when you didn't want to go fishing.

PETER: Oh, all right, Lord. I'll do it if you say so. Come on! Let's get them seated.

VOICES: Would you all sit down? Some of you over here. What's the idea? I'm hungry. I have to get home. Please sit down! The Master will tell you what to do. Where's the food? I don't know. I only know he wants you all to sit down)

BOY: Sir.

ANDREW: Yes? What is it, boy?

BOY: Can I speak to you?

ANDREW: That's what you're doing now.

BOY: No, I mean over here, where it's quiet. (HE DRAWS HIM ASIDE)

ANDREW: Now, what's your name, and what can I do for you?

BOY: I'm Levi, sir, from Bethsaida.

ANDREW: That's my home town too, Levi.

BOY: Yes, sir, I know. I've seen your boat by the lake.

ANDREW: Well, Levi?

BOY: I've got this, sir.

ANDREW: Your lunch? Good! You're luckier than most of us. Oh, I see. You want to share it?

BOY: Well, sir, I wondered. I mean—if it's any use to the Master—to Jesus. I thought—

ANDREW: Thank you, Levi. That's wonderful! Why don't we ask him?

BOY:	Oh no, sir! I couldn't do that. I thought you might take it to him. I mean, I didn't think you'd tell me it was a dumb thing to do, bringing it—
ANDREW:	It's not a dumb thing to do, Levi. I want you to come and meet Jesus. (THEY WALK TO HIM)
JESUS:	Who is this, Andrew?
ANDREW:	This is Levi, Master, from Bethsaida. He wants to give you something.
JESUS:	How do you do, Levi? Is this what your mother gave you?
BOY:	Yes, sir. She made me wait while she got it ready. Can you—I mean, is it any use, sir?
JESUS:	Five bread rolls and two lake fish, beautifully grilled? Yes, Levi. Sit down over there, and we will ask God how we can use your gift. Later I'd like to walk with you on the way home.
BOY:	Yes, sir. Thank you very much, sir. (HE WALKS AWAY AND SITS)
JESUS:	Out of the mouths of babes and sucklings! Oh, Andrew, it isn't the rich who give of their riches, but the simplehearted who give all that they have. Bless you, Andrew, for the love which showed in your face and brought that boy to me! And now, Father, consecrate this precious gift to your glory, and feed the hungry!

NOTE: To me this story goes side by side with the story of David and Goliath. Each is about a boy, who had something which he was ready to share. David had a sling and pebbles, this boy had his lunch. With those small things one killed a giant and the other fed five thousand people. Each of us has the equivalent of the sling or the bread and fish. How can we offer what we have? Perhaps it will help to kill the giants who threaten our communities: drugs, greed, violence, and many more.

Scene thirteen:

WHAT IS RIGHTEOUSNESS?**
BIBLE REFERENCE: SERMON ON THE MOUNT; LUKE 18: 9-14.

Characters: JESUS
ANDREW
JAMES
JOHN
VOICE OF PHARISEE
VOICE OF TAX COLLECTOR

ANDREW: How would you define righteousness, Master? How can we be truly righteous in God's eyes?

JESUS: I'm not sure I know the answer, Andrew. I didn't come to look for righteous people. If I had, I'm afraid it would have been a disappointing search.

JAMES: Is nobody righteous then?

JESUS: Put it like this, James. Happy are they who hunger and thirst after righteousness! Those are the people I came to find. They will never rest content, or think themselves good enough.

JOHN: But the Law gives so many rules, Jesus. If you try to keep them all—

JESUS: I don't want to destroy the Law. I want to fulfill it; but in the spirit, not merely the letter. The Law is dead without love. Let me tell you a story. Two men went up into the Temple to pray. One, who sat down in the front row, was a Pharisee—a good man. You can imagine his prayer.

VOICE OF PHARISEE: (HEARD FROM OFF STAGE, OR ACTED ON ONE SIDE) Lord God, I give thanks that I am not as other men are—not like those tax collectors sitting near the door! Why people like that bother to come and pray, I can't understand: adulterers, criminals, extortioners. Thank God I am not like them I keep the Law, Lord, to the letter. I pay all my dues, observe all the fasts—

JESUS: So you see? Here was a righteous man, but so far from God, if he only knew it! Listen to the prayer of the tax collector back by the door.

TAX COLLECTOR: Oh God, God, have mercy on me! I know that I have sinned. I have done evil, and left so much good undone. Be merciful to me, Lord!

JESUS:	I tell you, my friends, he went home closer to God than the Pharisee. God loves the humble. The proud and the virtuous so often shut him out.

Scene fourteen:

CRITICS**

BIBLE REFERENCE: MANY PASSAGES IN THE GOSPELS.

CHARACTERS:	JESUS and four VOICES (ON OR OFF STAGE)
VOICE 1:	Is it lawful to pay tribute to Caesar, Jesus? (HOSTILE AND AGGRESSIVE)
VOICE 2:	Why do your disciples not keep the fasts, Jesus?
VOICE 3:	Why do you eat with tax collectors and sinners, Jesus?
VOICE 4:	How can you heal on the Sabbath, Jesus? Why do you break the Law?
JESUS:	Please, gentlemen! One question at a time! I love to observe the Sabbath as much as you do; but the Sabbath was made for men and women, not they for the Sabbath. You asked me that question, sir?
VOICE 4:	Yes, I did. I want to know why you healed a man on the Sabbath.
JESUS:	Surely the important thing is that he was healed.
VOICE 4:	That's not the point—
JESUS:	Oh, yes, it is the point. If you are honest, you will admit that you would lift one of your sheep out of a ditch on the Sabbath, not wait and let it die.
VOICE 4:	This man would not have died if you had waited—
JESUS:	Oh, my dear sir! Aren't you making rules stand above the love of God? It seems to me God is much more like a shepherd than a Rabbi. God does not love by rule. He will search for one of his lost sheep at any time, day or night, Sabbath or not.

VOICE 1:	So you are our interpreter of God's will: you, a Galilean workman.
JESUS:	God is your shepherd, and I am the door of the sheep. That is the task he has laid upon me.
VOICE 2:	Blasphemy!
VOICE 3:	I have heard enough. Let's go!

Scene fifteen:

WHO ARE YOU, LORD? **
BIBLE REFERENCE: MANY PASSAGES, INCLUDING JOHN 14: 1-6

CHARACTERS: PETER
JESUS
ANDREW
JAMES
JOHN
THOMAS
PHILIP
JUDAS, and five others who do not speak

SCENE:

A HILLSIDE. SOME CAN SIT ON 'ROCKS', SOME STAND.

As they grew closer to Jesus, the Apostles knew that he was not simply another teacher and healer. God was calling them to follow the Way, the Truth, and the Life. But who was Jesus, and what was his relationship with Almighty God?

PETER:	Master, we have left our homes and our jobs to follow you. We don't regret it. But isn't it time you told us who and what you are, and what you want us to do?
JESUS:	Yes, Peter, it is time.
ANDREW:	Who are you, Lord? (EAGER, INSISTENT)
JESUS:	Whom do men say that I am?
JAMES:	Some people say that you are Elijah come back again.

JOHN:	Yes, I've heard that. Some say Jeremiah, or one of the prophets.
JESUS:	So that is what they say. What do you think yourselves?
PETER:	We think there is only one answer, Master. You are the long awaited Messiah—and you are the Son of God.
JESUS:	Oh, Peter! Blessings be on you! God the Father has shown you the truth. You are indeed like rock—the kind of rock my church will need for its foundation.
JOHN:	So it is true God has come down among us
JESUS:	Yes, John. God has loved his world so much that he has given his Son. Those who follow him faithfully will inherit eternal life in his presence.
THOMAS:	I don't understand. I'll follow you anywhere, Lord, but this talk puzzles me.
JESUS:	I'm sorry, Thomas. I don't mean to bewilder you. You have learned the way to follow, and I want you all to know where that way is leading me.
THOMAS:	But that's just it, Lord! We don't know where you are going, so how can we find our way?
JESUS:	I am the way, Thomas. You have to come to the Father through me. You have been loyal to me, so now you are close to the Father.
PHILIP:	Can't you show us the Father, Jesus? Show him to us, and we will be satisfied.
JESUS:	Don't you know me yet, Philip? After all this time we have been together? I am one with the Father. If you have seen me, you have seen him.
JUDAS:	That means you can show your power, Lord, and establish your kingdom. That is what we are waiting for. (JUDAS IS CALCULATING AND EAGER FOR POWER)

JESUS:	I can show power, Judas. I can plant the seed of my kingdom; but it is not the kind of kingdom you expect. My kingdom is not of this world.

Scene sixteen:

THE ROAD TO JERUSALEM**
BIBLE REFERENCE: LUKE 19: 1-10

CHARACTERS:	JESUS
	TWO MEN
	WOMAN
	ZACCHAEUS
	#MIRIAM

When he knew that the time was right, Jesus made his way to Jerusalem. He passed through Jericho, where a crowd greeted his arrival.

VOICES:	Here he comes! Look, on the donkey! It's Jesus! Make way there! Don't push! Jesus! Let me get close!
JESUS:	(LOUD) Thank you for your greeting, friends. Please stand back!
MAN 1:	Do you need a lodging for the night, Master?
WOMAN:	You can stay at our home.
MAN 2:	All the sick will be brought to the marketplace an hour before sunset.
WOMAN:	Please come with us, sir
JESUS:	Thank you. Thank you all. I see one of you even thought it worth while to climb a tree to greet me.
MAN 1:	Don't talk to him! That's Zacchaeus—the swine!
ZACCHAEUS:	Take no notice of me, Master. I just wanted to see you—and you can see I am too short.
JESUS:	Thank you for the trouble you took, Zacchaeus. May I invite myself to stay at your home, if it isn't too much trouble?
MAN 2:	Not with him, Jesus! He's a tax collector—a swindler!

JESUS:	Sometimes I find the swindlers need me more that those whom they swindle. May I come, Zacchaeus?
ZACCHAEUS:	Of course, Master, if you wish. But—
JESUS:	Don't worry about being unworthy. You climbed a tree. That was an act of faith. Shall we go?
WOMAN:	Doesn't the great Jesus know a crook when he sees one?
MAN 1:	A shame I call it!
MAN 2:	Turning down respectable people! (JESUS, ZACCHAEUS GO OFF TOGETHER. CHANGE SCENE TO ZACCHAEUS' HOME: TABLE, 3 CHAIRS)
	Later, at the home of Zacchaeus and Miriam, Jesus talked again of his journey to Jerusalem.
ZACCHAEUS:	Can't I come with you, Lord? I'd give up everything to follow you.
JESUS:	No, Zacchaeus. Your witness must be here in Jericho. You have promised to pay back all that you owe, and to do your work with honesty and compassion. Think what a testimony to God's love that will be!
ZACCHAEUS:	I swear I will, Lord. Life can never be the same again—not since you called me down from that tree.
JESUS:	And you, Miriam? Will you help your husband to keep his promise?
MIRIAM:	Yes, sir. I'm so happy! I never wanted all this money. It only made everyone hate us.
JESUS:	You see, Zacchaeus? If you stay here you will be serving me best. God's righteousness at the tax collector's table!
ZACCHAEUS:	At first noone will believe it.
MIRIAM:	My husband an honest man! That will be the biggest story ever in Jericho! (ALL LAUGHING)

ZACCHAEUS: The truth is, Lord. this is the happiest day of my life. I wish you could put off your journey and stay with us a little while.

JESUS: I wish I could do that. Your hospitality and your newfound joy warm my heart. But the passover is near, and I must do my Father's bidding. Now let us go to the marketplace. The sick will be waiting for me.

From Jericho Jesus and his friends started out on the steep, dusty road which led to Jerusalem.

These scenes do not cover the final days of Jesus' life, the Crucifixion, and the Resurrection. GOOD FRIDAY, one of the 'Verse Plays,' may be read to fill this gap.

Scene seventeen:

FISH FOR BREAKFAST **
BIBLE REFERENCE: John 21 and Acts 1: 1-4

CHARACTERS: JESUS
PETER
JAMES
JOHN

'Wait !' What a difficult piece of advice this can be, especially for people as impatient as Peter and the Sons of Thunder, James and John. John describes one of the times when Jesus came to his friends after his Resurrection. Here that scene is linked to Jesus' final words spoken before his Ascension. The scene is the shore of the Sea of Galilee, early one morning. Jesus has built a fire near the water's edge. John says that seven of the Apostles were together in the boats. For simplification the lines are here assigned to only three.

JESUS: (CALLING TO THE FISHERMEN IN THE DISTANCE) Have you caught anything?

JAMES: (FROM OFF STAGE) Nothing.

JOHN: We're giving up.

PETER: Who is that?

JAMES: I can't see. Whoever it is, he's lit a fire.

JESUS: Cast your net on the right side of the boat!

JOHN: No use. There are no fish. Wait! Is it you, Lord?

PETER: It is! (SHOUTING) I'm coming.

JAMES: Quick! Make a cast!

PETER: (RUNS IN TOWARDS JESUS, AND KNEELS) Oh, Lord and Master!

JESUS: You left your friends to catch our breakfast, Peter.

PETER: I couldn't wait. I had to come to you.

JESUS: Here have I been trying over and over again to teach you that waiting is important Never mind. I love you for your impetuosity. Put some more sticks on the fire.

PETER: Yes, Lord. (HE ATTENDS TO THE FIRE)

JESUS: (CALLING) Was I right?

JOHN: Of course you were, Master. A whole shoal. We'll be with you in a minute.

PETER: You told us to come back to Galilee, Master. We didn't know what to do while we were waiting for you, so we went fishing.

JESUS: That was wise of you. Waiting isn't easy, is it? It helps if you get on with the work that is familiar to you. (JAMES AND JOHN ENTER, CARRYING FISH) Well done, friends! Now we can cook our breakfast. I brought bread with me, and a pan.

JOHN: You promised to come, but—

JAMES: We were afraid it was all a dream—you being with us in Jerusalem.

JESUS:	It wasn't a dream. You be the cook, John, and I will explain to you why I have come back among you. This time together was very much needed. You all went through so much shock in those days after we left Jericho and went to Jerusalem. You went from anxiety and fear to despair, and then back to hope. I have tried to build your faith again by joining you in simple ways. Poor Judas would have wanted me to swoop down from the Temple roof and dazzle everyone into believing that I was alive. He never could believe that love doesn't work in those ways.
PETER:	I think I see what you mean. You met Nathanael and Thaddeus at Emmaus, just walking with them and eating. You came and sat with us in the Upper Room.
JAMES:	And now here we are eating breakfast back where you first called us to follow you.
JESUS:	Yes. You are starting to understand. Your new life is just beginning, and it will be hard, as well as full of joy. You need to be patient, and let your call come in my Father's good time. You needed these forty days to grow accustomed to my presence. Forty days! How well I remember that I too needed that time to make myself ready to do his work. Satan tried to hustle me then, and to tempt me. Don't let him do the same to you. Wait for the promise of the Spirit.
JOHN:	Are you leaving us now, Master?
JESUS:	Soon. All of you who are committed to carry on my work must gather together three days from now at Bethany. I want the women there with you. We will say goodbye, and after that I want you to wait in Jerusalem until your clear call comes. Wait in the room where we had supper that night, and pray.
PETER:	Life will seem empty, Lord.
JESUS:	It will if you look backwards, Peter, and think that you have lost me. If you look ahead, knowing how much I need you, there will be no time for regrets.
JAMES:	How will we know when that call comes?

JESUS: (LAUGHING) When the Spirit desends on you you will know, James. You will feel as though you are on fire, and blown away by the wind, all at the same time. By yourselves you would just be a small company of ordinary men and women. With the memories that we share, and the power which the Father will give you, you will win over the world. That fish smells just right, John. I will break the loaf, and we can eat.

PARABLES OF JESUS

ALL OF THESE ARE ** SCENES, EXCELLENT FOR ACTING

THE LOST COIN
THE RICH FARMER
THE TALENTS
TWO CARS ON A HILL
THE WIDOW AND THE JUDGE
GUESTS FROM OUT OF TOWN
THE LOST SHEEP
THE GOOD SAMARITAN

One:

THE LOST COIN
BIBLE REFERENCE: LUKE 15: 8-10.

CHARACTERS: #MARIA
#PABLO, her husband
#Mrs. JACKSON and #Mrs. BARTON, neighbors

SCENE:

Mrs. Maria Martinez' tiny house. Table,
three chairs, rug, broom, coins in bag.

MARIA: (SEATED AT TABLE. A LIGHTED CANDLE WOULD SHOW THAT IT IS STILL DARK) There! Soon we will be able to buy our new home, and there won't be all these dirty corners, and this leaky roof. Let me count them again! (POURS MONEY. SOME COINS FALL) Not so fast Careful! You don't want to run away from me, do you? Now: 1,2,3,4,5,6,7,8,9—oh, no It can't be— where is it? Oh God! Where's the tenth coin? (SHOUTING) Pablo! Quick, quick! I've lost a coin. Hurry !

PABLO: (ENTERING, SLEEPY) What is it, Maria? What are you doing up at this hour? It isn't even light yet.

MARIA: I've lost one of our coins. We have to find it! We have to!

PABLO: How could you be so careless?

MARIA:	Stop blaming me and look for it!
PABLO:	I never should have let you keep the coins—
MARIA:	You are too lazy to do anything.
PABLO:	(SHOUTS) Lazy? At least I don't throw away our money.

(ENTER JACKSON AND BARTON)

JACKSON:	Whatever is the matter with you people?
BARTON:	You're waking up the whole street. What is it?
MARIA:	It's nothing. Please go away and leave us alone.
PABLO:	Nothing! You lose a tenth of our savings and call it nothing?
JACKSON:	Savings? You mean you've lost some money?
MARIA:	Yes, but I'll find it. Pablo, hand me that broom. (ALL BUMP INTO EACH OTHER SEARCHING)
BARTON:	Try under the rug.
MARIA:	I've looked there. Oh, I wish you'd leave me alone.
JACKSON:	We're only trying to help you, Maria.
MARIA:	There! Thank God I've found it.
PABLO:	That's a blessing! In future, don't be so—
MARIA:	Stop scolding me, Pablo, and put the coffee on. We're all going to celebrate.
PABLO:	Celebrate what? I don't see—
MARIA:	You wouldn't. You're only a man. Sit down, neighbors.
BARTON:	Thank you, Maria.
JACKSON:	Isn't that wonderful for you?

MARIA:	Oh, yes, it's wonderful. To think of it—I thought my coin was lost, and now I've found it.

Our society is full of 'lost coins': people who are lonely or shunned or too shy to fit in with a group. What we need is more brooms: people sensitive enough to understand when someone is lost, and to look for them. It takes so little effort—a smile and a few words, perhaps—to make a big difference. Compare with this parable the plays CAMELS FOR THE ARK and GLAD TO SEE YOU BACK, in 'Modern Scenes."

Two:

THE RICH FARMER
BIBLE REFERENCE: Luke 12: 15-21

CHARACTERS:	#TOM (the farmer) #LEN (the architect) #NORA (Tom's wife); DOCTOR

SCENE:

Tom's living room.
A couch center; a table; two chairs; cell phone for LEN.

LEN:	You're sure you want a silo that big, Tom?
TOM::	What do you mean? You're a builder, aren't you? Get on and build what I ask for!
LEN:	Oh, sure. I'll build it. I just don't want you to change your mind when it's half done.
TOM::	Look, Len, I've worked my heart out on this land, and now I've got my reward. Since I bought out Stevens, and added the land beyond the highway, I've trebled my crop. And it's going on up and up. I need that silo, quick
(NORA ENTERS)	
LEN:	O.K. I'll have it up for you in three months.
TOM::	Make it two, Len.
LEN:	What's the mad rush?

TOM::	(SHOUTING) To store my crop, man! I can't let good grain rot. We've got to expand.
NORA:	Here's your coffee. Don't get excited, Tom. You know what Doctor Bennett said.
LEN:	That's right, Tom. Take it easy. What's the sense in trying to be twice as rich as you are already?
TOM::	Stop bugging me, both of you! (SHOUTING) Do I own this place or do I not? I want that barn pulled down, and the new silo built by— (HE COLLAPSES)
LEN:	Put a pillow under his head. I'll loosen his collar.
NORA:	Oh, God Tom, Tom! (LEN USES PHONE)
LEN:	Doc Bennett? Len Davis. I'm at Tom's. He's had a heart attack, I think. Yeah. At once. (TO NORA) He'll be here as soon as he can.
TOM::	What happened? I—
LEN:	Now, Tom, don't try to talk.
TOM::	Build—the silo!
LEN:	Yes, yes, Tom. Don't worry.
NORA:	Oh, Tom We don't need more money. I only want you well. I wish I knew what to give him.
LEN:	He's unconscious.
NORA:	I'll fetch some water.
LEN:	I think I hear Doc Bennett's car.

(DOCTOR HURRIES IN)

NORA:	Oh, doctor, thanks for coming so quickly.
DOCTOR:	All right, let's have a look at him. (EXAMINES TOM) Hm.

NORA:	Well, doctor. How is he?
DOCTOR:	Nora, you're a brave woman, and I've known you a long time. It's no use telling you lies. Tom is dying. It's his heart.
NORA:	Oh, no! Why couldn't he slow down? Why did he have to drive himself to death?
DOCTOR:	That's the way he is, Nora. Tom had to have things bigger and bigger.
LEN:	The last thing he said to me was: 'Build the silo!'
DOCTOR:	Poor old Tom I'm afraid that silo was one excitement too many. I'll do what I can, Nora; but I don't want you to have any false hopes. Would Tom like to see the pastor, do you think? He may regain consciousness.
NORA:	Yes, please call him, and ask him to come. Tom is a good man. If only—
LEN:	If he'd only given himself time to live.
NORA:	We were going on a trip. He talked about retiring, after the silo was finished.
DOCTOR:	With people like Tom there's always one more thing, Nora. Now how about you drinking a cup of that coffee? And I'll call Pastor Bowman.

Three:

THE TALENTS
BIBLE REFERENCE: MATTHEW 25: 14-30

Characters: The CEO of Talents.com
#Mr. or Mrs GOLDMAN
#Tom or Tammy Brown
#Stan or Susan Parsons
#John Turner

Scene:

The CEO's office.

A table with four chairs. Desk telephone. Papers.

PRESIDENT: (SEATED, USING DESK PHONE)
Celia? Ask Tom Brown to come in, will you?

BROWN: (ENTERING AFTER A PAUSE)
You wanted me?

PRESIDENT: Yes, Tom. Sit down, will you?

BROWN: Thanks.

PRESIDENT: As you know, Tom, I will be traveling for almost six months. We have to expand our foreign markets, and I think I can open up something big. But it will put a lot of responsibility on you.

BROWN: I think I can take it.

PRESIDENT: So do I. Now here's my idea. You will be in charge of production while I am gone. You'll be spending millions each month— big money, Tom. But you know the opportunities we have, if we're ready to use them.

BROWN: Yes, sir. Don't you worry. I can't wait to get my teeth into it.

PRESIDENT: Great! One more thing. I'm going to leave sales in the hands of Stan Parsons. That's another big job. Do you think you two can work together?

BROWN: He's the right man. He'll do a fine job, and I'm sure we can work smoothly.

PRESIDENT: As you know, that will leave John Turner. He might have been in line for either job, but—well—

BROWN: I think I know what you mean. John's O.K. while he works under your eye, but— Could he look after our downtown store, sir?

PRESIDENT: Just what I had in mind. I'm glad you agree. It gives him a job, but outside our main operation. Well, thanks, Tom. You've been a great help. I'll talk to the other two, and get back to you. Good luck!

BROWN: And to you, Mr. Goldman. Have a good trip, and bust the market open!

(AFTER A PAUSE THE PRESIDENT ASKS CELIA TO SEND IN PARSONS)

PARSONS: You wanted to see me, Mr. Goldman?

PRESIDENT: Yes, Stan. It won't take long, and I hope it's good news. Sit down.

PARSONS: Thank you, sir.

PRESIDENT: Here it is in a nutshell. While I'm away, I want you to take over our sales organization. That means supervising our eighteen sales representatives, keeping an eye on pricing, advertising, and a hundred other things. A big job. Will you do it?

PARSONS: Will I do it? Wow! That's the best tonic I ever had, sir. Yes!

PRESIDENT: Good, Stan. I like your spirit. We'll meet with Tom Brown tomorrow. He's taking over production. I wanted to get the main decisions made today.

PARSONS: Thanks, Mr. Goldman. I promise you won't regret it.
(HE GOES OUT. PAUSE. PRESIDENT PICKS UP PHONE)

PRESIDENT: Celia, if John Turner is in his office ask him to come in. (KNOCK AFTER A PAUSE) Come in John, take a seat.

TURNER: (SLOUCHING IN, SHABBILY DRESSED)
Thank you, Mr. Goldman.

PRESIDENT: I've been talking to Tom Brown about our operations during the time when I'll be away.

TURNER: Oh, yes, sir. We're certainly going to miss you. Things depend on you so much.

PRESIDENT:	Nobody's indispensable, John. You'll all have some extra responsibilty.
TURNER:	Yes, of course.
PRESIDENT:	What I'd like you to do is take charge of our downtown store. Can I count on you to do that?
TURNER:	The downtown store? Yes, sir, if that's what you'd like me to do. Things have been a bit slow down there lately, haven't they?
PRESIDENT:	All the more challenge to turn it around. See what you can do.
TURNER:	Yes, sir. I'll try to keep things from slipping any further.
PRESIDENT:	Look over this report, and come and see me later in the week.
TURNER:	Yes, sir. I expect I'll have a lot of questions.

(SIX MONTHS LATER ALL FOUR ARE IN THE OFFICE)

PRESIDENT:	Well, that's the picture from my end. Now let me hear from you. Tom?
BROWN:	Here are the figures, sir. We've had a great year. As you can see, production rose by 30%. We were able to—
PRESIDENT:	O.K., Tom. You've said enough. I'll study the details later. Thirty percent! Fantastic! I sure chose the right man for the job.
BROWN:	Wait till you hear what Stan has to say. He gave me first class support.
PRESIDENT:	Well, Stan?
PARSONS:	The full effect of Tom's production increase won't be felt till next year; but sales have already risen by 20 %. Here's a summary of the sales reps' reports, and—

PRESIDENT:	The best thing for me to do is to go away again You two have worked miracles. I know it meant long hours and real loyalty to the company. Now, John, how did things work out downtown?
TURNER:	So-so, Mr. Goldman. There were a lot of problems to contend with, you know, and—
PRESIDENT:	I don't want to hear about the problems. What were the results?
TURNER:	Well, my report isn't quite ready yet, but I think we should just about break even for the time you were away.
PRESIDENT:	With production up 30% and sales 20%? That isn't good enough, John, is it?
TURNER:	But, sir, you have to make allowances—
PRESIDENT:	That's where you're wrong, John. I'm tired of making allowances for you. You're capable, but you just don't have what it takes. You're fired, John. Look for something easier to do somewhere else. Tom, make arrangements to take over John's work, will you?
TURNER:	But sir—

Four:

TWO CARS ON A HILL
BIBLE REFERENCE: LUKE 18: 9-15

Characters:	#HENRY and HELEN, in the Cadillac #JOHN and FLORA, in the old car

SCENE:

A highway with a steep climb.
(You will need ingenuity to portray the 'cars' and the progress up the hill.)

FLORA:	Oh, John, are we ever going to get to the top of this hill?
JOHN:	Don't worry! We will some time.

FLORA:	Here comes a Cadillac. Maybe they'll help. (SHE WAVES) No use. What do they care about people like us?
HENRY:	(AS HE DRIVES PAST) Cars like that ought not to be allowed on the road.
JOHN:	If we can just change that wheel and get her to start we'll make it.
FLORA:	Oh, John! All that?
HENRY:	(AT TOP OF HILL, STALLED) What's wrong with this car?
HELEN:	Try starting it again, dear.
HENRY:	What do you think I'm doing? These modern engines are worthless.
HELEN:	I hardly like to mention it, but do you think we might be out of gas?
HENRY:	Out of gas? You know I never run out of gas.
HELEN:	The gauge does say empty.
HENRY:	Then it must be out of order. I KNOW I had plenty of gas.
HELEN:	Yes, dear. Only—
HENRY:	Look, Helen, if you don't have anything more helpful to say please keep quiet. I tell you, I never ran out of gas in my life.
HELEN:	No, dear. Then we'll wait for someone to come by.
FLORA:	(AT BOTTOM OF HILL) That sounds more hopeful.
JOHN:	I believe she's going to start.
FLORA:	Poor John! You do look a sight.
JOHN:	Who cares? let's go (THEY CLIMB THE HILL)
HELEN:	Here comes someone. Oh, it's that old car that was stuck at the bottom of the hill.

JOHN: (GETTING OUT OF CAR) Can we help you, sir?

HENRY: Thank you. If you would be so good as to call the Auto Club and ask them to come and tow us in—

JOHN: What's the trouble?

HENRY: Just the usual bad workmanship. None of the cars are properly built today.

JOHN: Mind if I have a look? I just fixed this old bus up.

HENRY: If you like. (HE GETS OUT. BOY CLIMBS IN)

JOHN: Sir, I think I know what's wrong.

HENRY: Oh, really? What is it?

JOHN: You're out of gas.

HENRY: Don't be ridiculous! Do you think I don't know how much gas I have? Please call the Auto Club.

JOHN: But all you need is a little gas. As it happens I have a spare can.

HENRY: Look, boy, I asked you a simple question. Will you, or will you not, go and call the Auto Club? I am not out of gas.

HELEN: Henry, please.

HENRY: Be quiet, Helen. You know nothing about the car.

FLORA: Come on, John Let's go.

JOHN: O.K. If that's the way he wants it. But even a Cadillac won't run without gas.

NOTE: This may seem like an unfair way to portray the Pharisee of Jesus' parable, for the Pharisees were, as Jesus knew, good men; but the parable brings out the fact that this Pharisee was spiritually 'out of gas.' He did not realize how badly he needed to ask for forgiveness for his pride and insensitivity. Jesus was able to help sinners and sick people because they knew that they needed him. He found it much harder to talk to those who believed that they were righteous.

Five:

THE WIDOW AND THE JUDGE
Bible reference: Luke 18: 1-5

CHARACTERS: #Judge Walters
                     His golfing partner
                     The Widow

SCENE:

A golf course. A golf bag. A seat to one side.

JUDGE: Wonderful morning for a round, Tom!

PARTNER: It sure beats sitting in the office.

JUDGE: Or in Court. Monday is usually a heavy day for me, but I manage to dodge it whenever I can.

PARTNER: Your drive, Jim.

JUDGE: O.K. (HE MIMES PUTTING DOWN HIS BALL AND PREPARING TO DRIVE)

WIDOW: (RUNNING IN) Judge Walters

JUDGE: Who are you? What are you doing here?

WIDOW: I have to talk to you.

JUDGE: Out here? This is my day off. Call my secretary for an appointment.

WOMAN: I have called, many times. You're always too busy to see a woman with no money.

PARTNER: Now look here, lady, you're being a nuisance. Go away!

WIDOW: A nuisance! You big, fat slob! If you'd suffered as I have, you'd be a nuisance. I'm going to make the Judge listen, if I have to follow you all around the course.

JUDGE: For the last time, will you leave me alone?

WIDOW: For the last time, no! I want justice. You may be the laziest man in the city, but you are the judge. Now will you listen or will you not?

JUDGE: I will not. In a minute I'll call the Club Secretary and have you removed.

WIDOW: All right. You asked for it. (SHE PICKS UP HIS GOLF BAG AND RUNS)

JUDGE: Stop! What do you think you're doing? Stop her, somebody! Look—come back here, and tell me what you want.

WIDOW: You mean that?

JUDGE: Yes, yes. Anything to get rid of you.

WIDOW: (RETURNING) Very well. You've made a promise. If you'll just listen it won't take five minutes.

JUDGE: Sorry, Tom. It's the only thing to do. Now sit down, and tell me what's on your mind. (THEY SIT)

WIDOW: It's my landlord—

Note: This is really a very funny short story. Jesus is saying: Do you think that God is asleep or unwilling to listen when you pray? Isn't it in fact just the opposite? He is always listening for your prayers and ready with his love. You don't need to chase after him to get his attention.

Six:

GUESTS FROM OUT OF TOWN
BIBLE REFERENCE: LUKE 11: 5-10

Characters: HUSBAND
       WIFE
       NEIGHBOR (unseen)

SCENE:

A home, at midnight. Husband and wife asleep on mattresses. Children may be asleep also. A clock strikes midnight, and there is a loud knock.

HUSBAND: What in the world was that?

WIFE: Mm?

HUSBAND: I thought I heard something.

WIFE: Mm?

HUSBAND: I suppose it was a dream. (PAUSE, FOLLOWED BY ANOTHER LOUD KNOCK) Who can that be?

NEIGHBOR: (FROM OFF STAGE) Jim! Sally! Are you there?

HUSBAND: Who is that? What do you want?

NEIGHBOR: Jim, we've just had guests arrive from out of town. Could I borrow some bread?

HUSBAND: At this time of night? Go away, for heaven's sake!

NEIGHBOR: Oh, come along, Jim! I really need it. These people—

HUSBAND: Look, we're all in bed. Can't you leave us alone?

NEIGHBOR: What kind of neighbor are you? Can't you see this is a crisis?

HUSBAND: Sally! Sally! Can't you get rid of the man? Give him his bread, and maybe he'll go away!

WIFE: Mm?

HUSBAND: Oh, Sally, you're hopeless!

NEIGHBOR: I wouldn't bother you if there were any stores open, but—

HUSBAND: A-a-a-a-gh! (HE JUMPS OUT OF BED AND FETCHES BREAD FROM THE KITCHEN, THEN GOES TO THE DOOR AND OPENS IT) Take your bread and get out of here! I hope it's stale.

NEIGHBOR: Well, don't make such a song and dance out of it. I only asked for a little bread. Some people just can't—

HUSBAND: (SLAMMING THE DOOR AND GETTING BACK INTO BED) A-a-a-agh! Guests from out of town Now! I'll never get back to sleep.

WIFE: Mm?

REPEAT THE PLAY, WITH THE HUSBAND SLEEPING AND THE WIFE AWAKE.

Seven:

THE LOST SHEEP
Bible reference: Luke 15: 3-7

CHARACTERS: The Shepherd
A flock of sheep
The lost sheep

SCENE:

In the countryside. Improvise an enclosure with an opening.
This scene is suitable for small children, with the teacher or an older student as shepherd.

(AS THE SHEEP CRAWL INTO THE FOLD, THE SHEPHERD TOUCHES EACH ONE GENTLY WITH HIS CROOK.)

SHEPHERD: Come on, now! Don't push! Plenty of time. 24, 25— Easy, there, Dusty! You'll get in much quicker if you don't knock each other over. (THE SHEEP BAA AND JOSTLE EACH OTHER) 86, 87. Nearly home now! Time for a rest. 98, 99—Oh, no! One missing? In you go! (HE SHUTS THE GATE) Now you keep quiet and look after yourselves while I find number 100. Don't worry! No wolf can jump that wall.

(HE WALKS AROUND THE STAGE, CALLING. AFTER A NUMBER OF CALLS OF "Where are you?' A FEEBLE BAA IS HEARD)

SHEPHERD: O.K. I heard you. Call again!

SHEEP: (A LITTLE LOUDER) Baa! Baa!

SHEPHERD: Over there, are you? You silly animal. I still can't find you.

(THE SEARCH MAY CONTINUE FOR SOME TIME. AT LENGTH A LOUD 'BAA' ENABLES THE SHEPHERD TO FIND THE SHEEP)

SHEPHERD: There! Trust you to fall into the first ditch you came across! (HE LIFTS THE SHEEP AND WALKS BACK TO THE FOLD) Hurt? No, I don't believe you are. Just lost and frightened; and that isn't so good, is it, funny face? Never mind! We'll soon have you back where you belong. (LOUD BAA'S FROM THE FOLD AS THEY APPROACH, ANSWERED BY THE LOST SHEEP) See? Your friends hear us coming. Welcome home! That's what they're saying. (HE DROPS THE SHEEP INTO THE FOLD) There you go! Just try to keep out of trouble in the future, will you? To oblige me? I have enough walking to do without going back to look for stragglers. All right, now. Settle down, all of you, I'll sing you David's song.

(HE SINGS THE 23rd PSALM IN SOME FORM: FOR EXAMPLE, BROTHER JAMES' AIR OR THE HYMN, 'THE KING OF LOVE MY SHEPHERD IS')

Eight:

THE GOOD SAMARITAN
Bible reference: Luke 10: 25-37

CHARACTERS: A MERCHANT (with two SERVANTS)
TWO BANDITS
A PRIEST and A LEVITE
THE GOOD SAMARITAN (with two SERVANTS)
THE INNKEEPER

The first scene is a roadside. A sign reads: Jerusalem 15: Jericho 15. The Merchant and his servants walk on.

FIRST SERVANT: The inn is just around that corner.

SECOND SERVANT: Great! I'm worn out.

MERCHANT: I'll buy you a bottle of wine when we get there—

(BANDITS RUN ON, SHOUTING, AND MUG THE MERCHANT. HE FALLS, CRYING OUT. THE SERVANTS DROP THE BAGS AND RUN)

MERCHANT: Don't run away! Help! Aagh!

FIRST BANDIT: Get his wallet.

SECOND BANDIT:	(ROLLING THE MERCHANT OVER) Here it is .
FIRST BANDIT:	Is he dead?
SECOND BANDIT:	Not yet. He won't last long out here. You take that bag.
FIRST BANDIT:	Right. Let's go! (THEY RUN OFF. A PAUSE. MERCHANT GROANS. THE PRIEST ENTERS)
MERCHANT:	Help! I've been mugged!
PRIEST:	Mugged? (HE HESITATES, THEN RUNS OFF) I—I'll find help.
MERCHANT:	O God, I'm going to die. (PAUSE. THE LEVITE ENTERS) Sir, for God's sake help me! I'm bleeding to death.
LEVITE:	Who—what happened?
MERCHANT:	Bandits. They—
LEVITE:	Bandits! i can't stop. It would be suicide.
MERCHANT:	Don't leave me to die!
LEVITE:	(RUNNING OFF) I'm sorry. I'll see what I can do to help. (MERCHANT WEEPS AND GROANS, THEN LIES STILL. THE SAMARITAN COMES ON WITH HIS SERVANTS.)
SAMARITAN:	Almost there. Hello! What's this? (HE KNEELS)
FIRST SERVANT:	He's been mugged.
SECOND SERVANT:	Watch out, sir! This could be dangerous.
FIRST SERVANT:	Hadn't we better go to the inn?
SAMARITAN:	And leave him here? Certainly not! Here, drink this. (HE GIVES THE MERCHANT WATER) Now help me lift him. It's all right, sir. We'll look after you. (THEY CARRY THE MERCHANT OFF. THE SIGN IS MOVED, AND REPLACED BY ANOTHER: 'THE HALFWAY INN'. THE SAMARITAN REENTERS AND KNOCKS AT THE DOOR)
SAMARITAN:	Open up, please! We have an injured man.

INNKEEPER: (APPEARING AT THE DOOR) What's this? Trouble?

SAMARITAN: He's been attacked by bandits. Can we have a room for him, and send for a doctor?

INNKEEPER: Of course. (SHOUTING) Sarah! Number 17. Get ready for a guest! Bring him in. (THE SERVANTS CARRY THE MERCHANT OFF STAGE. THE PRIEST AND LEVITE COME OUT AT ONE SIDE, LISTENING)

INNKEEPER: He's certainly lucky to have a friend like you, sir.

SAMARITAN: He's a stranger to me. I never saw him before.

INNKEEPER: A stranger?

SAMARITAN: Yes. But travellers have to stick together, don't they? We're all neighbors on the road. I would hope somebody would do the same for me.

INNKEEPER: Do you mind if I ask about the gentleman's check, sir?

SAMARITAN: Oh, yes. (HE GIVES THE INNKEEPER COINS) I expect he has money at home, but of course they stripped him clean. Take this. I will be coming back this way after my business in Jericho is completed. We can settle up then.

PRIEST: Perhaps I and my friend could help.

LEVITE: I have a little money with me.

INNKEEPER: Come inside. We can work it out together over supper. May I ask where you are from, sir?

SAMARITAN: I am a Samaritan.

PRIEST AND LEVITE: A Samaritan!

INNKEEPER: Well, you're a brave man, and unselfish too. Come to think of it, you two just came down that road. Funny you didn't see anything—or did you?

(THEY FREEZE IN PLACE. YOU COULD THEN ASK THE PRIEST AND LEVITE TO ANSWER THE QUESTION)

Other parables will be found among the VERSE PLAYS. These are also musicals. The scores are available if you wish to order them; but the text alone is suitable for reading and discussion.

> THE PRODIGAL SON
> THE GOOD SAMARITAN (a longer version)
> THE WEDDING FEAST
> A PENNY A DAY (The Laborers in the Vineyard)
> THE UNJUST STEWARD

ACTS OF THE APOSTLES

A DRAMA PRESENTATION

Luke was the only one of the gospel compilers who wrote a second book. In it he described the work of the first missionaries, who extended the church throughout the eastern half of the Roman empire, and as far as Rome itself. Paul's letters complement Luke's narrative. Between them they tell a thrilling story, with many heroes and heroines taking part in the trials and adventures of the young church.

In these scenes I have concentrated on the story of Paul. He was a giant among the early Christians, but we must remember that there were undoubtedly many other men and women whose courage and leadership are not recorded.

In the New Testament non-Christians are described from a Christian viewpoint. Luke is on the whole very fair. We see the Roman authorities standing for justice and efficiency, though they punish severely any breach of the peace. The Jews are the adversaries, especially in the early chapters. If we could ask Caiaphas whether he is fairly portrayed in the Bible, he would probably protest that his position as High Priest was almost impossible. He had to keep the peace, in order to prevent the Romans from intervening. To him, the Christians were troublemakers who rocked the boat. His office involved compromise and often injustice, but it would not have been easy for a High Priest to act with courage and high principles side by side with a governor like Pilate. Unlike Gallio of Achaea, Sergius Paulus of Cyprus, and other Romans mentioned in Acts, Pilate was a weak and indecisive official.

To an extraordinary degree Paul was a representative of the three main linguistic groups in this story: Jews, Greeks, Romans. He was a Greekspeaking Jew and a Roman citizen. Peter was unmistakably a Jew, just as Gallio was unmistakably a Roman. Many others in these scenes crossed the lines of culture and language. Stephen was a 'Hellenistic' Jew, with a Greek speaking background. Barnabas was from Cyprus and Luke from the province of Asia. The list of Christians in the church at Rome (Romans 16) contains a variety of Roman, Greek, and Jewish names, some of them probably the names of slaves. The transformation of the Church from a handful of Jesus' Jewish friends to an inclusive body from every class and background is amazing. Some of the original apostles found it hard to accept, but Peter, to his great credit, and Paul, more easily, led the way.

It is essential that you have an atlas of the Roman Empire when you read these scenes. You will see that only a few scenes are marked as excellent for acting. I suggest that you read through the scenes and discuss them. After that choose which scenes are appropriate for your group to act.

1. Pentecost (Improvise)
2. A miracle at the Temple*
3. Peter and John before the Council+
4. Repression and growth+
5. Stephen (Imp)
6. The Baptism of Paul**
7. Peter and the baptism of Cornelius (read)
8. Barnabas and Paul*
9. 'Go ye out into all the world' (Imp)
10. Confrontation in Cyprus*
11. Jews and gentiles at Lystra*
12. The Council at Jerusalem (Imp)
13. The guidance of the Spirit (read)
14. The prison at Philippi+
15. Turning the world upside down+
16. Paul at Athens**
17. Corinth: Roman justice+
18. Problems and opportunities in a young church*
19. The riot at Ephesus+
20. Farewell at Miletus (Imp)
21. The warning of Agabus+
22. Danger at Jerusalem (read)
23. Paul before a king and a governor+
24. Shipwreck+
25. A prisoner at Rome**

Scene one:

PENTECOST (improvise)

Before we embark on the story of Paul it is important to look at the very first days of the church. On the day of Jesus' Ascension his followers were told by an angel to 'wait for the promise of the Father' (Acts 1:4). How hard it must have been to wait! Peter was not a patient man. Simon 'the Zealot' (perhaps a nickname for his impetuosity), and James and John, whom Jesus once called 'the sons of thunder', do not sound like men who enjoyed waiting.

Acts 1:12-14 describes how a large group of Jesus' closest friends gathered in an upper room and prayed and waited. There were the apostles, the mother and brothers of Jesus, and 'the women', perhaps including Mary Magdalene, Mary the wife of Cleopas, Joanna, and Susanna. It is important to remember that when so many people were in one room they were very close together. We live in much larger rooms than an average Jerusalem family of that time. Imagine the growing excitement and impatience as they prayed together, elbow to elbow, sitting on chairs or rugs. They may have been in the same upper room in which the Last Supper took place.

You could at this point sit very close together, and improvise a dialogue: prayers from different people; discussion of the Resurrection experiences; speculation about the High Priest's reactions; anticipation of what the angel meant by 'the promise of the Father'. One thing which they did at this time was to pray over the replacement for Judas Iscariot. Two candidates were named, and Matthias was then chosen by lot.

Now imagine the moment when they are filled with the Holy Spirit. Different voices offer up prayers together, as the excitement mounts. Then the time comes when they 'catch fire'. They feel driven, as if by a strong wind, to run out into the streets and proclaim their faith.

Here is how you might act it out. Divide these lines between you, to be spoken and repeated, until Peter leads you out.

Come, Lord Jesus...The Spirit of the Lord is upon us...Show us your power, Lord...
He has come down...The Spirit of the Lord...Fill my heart, Lord...
My heart is on fire...Use me, Lord...

PETER: (LOUD) Yes! It is the spirit of the Lord, the wind of God. His fire, his power! Come with me!

They all follow hlm, crying:

Into the streets...to the Temple...Domine Christe...Spiritus Sanctus... Eloi! Eloi!...Kyrie Christe! (These cries in Latin, Greek, and Aramaic illustrate Luke's statement that they spoke in other languages)

Now have some of your group act as people on the street, amazed at what is going on. Comments like:

Who are they?... Here, watch where you're going!
That man looks like a Galilean...sounds like one, too...
Like that Jesus, the one who was crucified...He's talking Greek, I think...
I believe they're drunk...Disgraceful! At this hour of the morning...

ANDREW: No, no, you don't understand. Peter, they think we're drunk.

PEER: Drunk? No, my friends. (RAISING HIS VOICE) That is not what fills us with power and joy.

CROWD MEMBERS: What is going on, then?...Pushing everyone around...talking a lot of foreign gabble.

PETER:	Let me try to explain. (SHOUTING) Listen, friends, please! All of you, please listen! (CROWD GROWS QUIET) I can understand why you are puzzled. But have you never read the prophet Joel? 'I will pour forth my spirit upon all flesh'—you remember? 'Your sons and your daughters will prophesy, and your young men will see visions.' I tell you, that is what has happened to us. This is the day of the coming of God's spirit! You know about Jesus, who was crucified. He is risen from the dead! We know—we have seen him, talked with him. Turn to him, men of Israel! His works of power and love proved that he came from God—and he is risen!
CROWD VOICES:	What must we do?...Tell us what to do!...Don't listen to him! Blasphemy—that's what it is!...They're mad...drunk
PETER:	Change your hearts! Repent, and have faith in him! You can be baptized with water and the Spirit, now! You will be rich with the gifts which we have.
VOICES:	Praise God!... I repent!... I believe in him. ..Save me, Jesus!
PETER:	God be thanked for this day! His promise has been fulfilled. Come with us, friends! Baptize our new brothers and sisters whom Jesus has called!

Scene two:

A MIRACLE AT THE TEMPLE +
BIBLE REFERENCE: Acts 3:1 to 4:4

CHARACTERS:	#ELIAS, a cripple TWO MEN who carry him in PETER JOHN TWO JEWISH POLICEMEN, One a Captain. CROWD

The Apostles believed that the power of the Spirit enabled them to help anyone who came to them in need. Peter and John soon found a challenge. They had seen Jesus heal the sick. Could they do the same in his name? Sick men and women were often laid near to the Temple gate. This is where our next scene takes place. Two men are carrying a friend.

FIRST MAN:	There you are, Elias.

SECOND MAN: Comfortable? Here, let me shift this pillow.

ELIAS: Thank you, friends.

FIRST: Got all you need? We'll be back for you before sunset.

SECOND MAN: Send a message if you need anything.

ELIAS: Blessings on both of you! Goodbye. (THEY GO OUT. SEVERAL PEOPLE WALK PAST ELIAS. TO EACH HE SAYS, 'Can you help a cripple, sir, (or lady?) SOME GIVE HIM A COIN, SOME TAKE NO NOTICE. THEN PETER AND JOHN ENTER)

ELIAS: Can you help a cripple, sir?

PETER: Help a cripple?

ELIAS: Just something small, if you can spare it.

JOHN: No, friend. We cannot give you something small.

PETER: We have no silver or gold.

ELIAS: All right. No offense, I'm sure. Why are you looking at me like that?

PETER: If you have faith we will make you whole in the name of Jesus.

ELIAS: Jesus? The one who healed a blind man? The one they—

JOHN: Yes, the one they crucified. But he is not dead, and he still makes people whole in mind and body.

PETER: He sent us here today.

ELIAS: It isn't any use. I've tried everything.

PETER: You have not tried putting your faith in Jesus. Many who were dumb and blind—or paralyzed like you—came to him when they had tried everything. People with sick hearts also.

JOHN: Can you put your trust in him, and rise and walk?

ELIAS: You mean it, don't you? You're not lying to me.

PETER:	I swear by God Almighty that we are speaking the truth. What is your name, and what injury keeps you from walking?
ELIAS:	Elias Ben-Joseph. It's my ankles and my feet. I haven't walked in fifteen years.
PETER:	Hold my hands, Elias. No, tightly! Now, trust in the power of Jesus! (LOUDER) Get up! Up! (WITH GREAT EFFORT, PETER PULLS ELIAS TO HIS FEET) That's right. Stand! You can do it. Now take a step towards me! (PETER'S LOUD VOICE CAUSES A CROWD TO GATHER.)
VOICES:	'What's happening?' 'What's going on?' 'That's Elias!' 'Who are these men?'
PETER:	You've done it! You can walk! Stand and walk! Believe it, and you can do it!
ELIAS:	It's true! God, I can walk! I can walk! God Almighty, I'm healed!
VOICES:	'It's a trick!' 'That's Elias, for sure.' 'No, it can't be.' 'Who are you?' Let's get out of here!' 'If its Elias, it's a miracle.'
PETER:	Why stare at us, friends? Is this so astonishing? We have done nothing. It is God's power, his love, working in our world through Jesus.
MAN IN CROWD :	Jesus? Jesus of Nazareth? He's dead.
JOHN:	No! He rose from the dead, and—
WOMAN IN CROWD:	Don't give me that! I saw him crucified.
MAN:	You don't rise from the dead when the Romans are finished with you.
JOHN:	I tell you, the tomb could not hold him.
ELIAS:	I'm walking. Can't you see? If Jesus did that he isn't dead.
PETER:	It is true. Jesus has healed this man through faith. Jesus gave his life for us, but he has been raised in glory. He will bring healing and—
MAN:	Look out! Police! (CROWD DISPERSES HURRIEDLY)

POLICE CAPTAIN:	What's this disturbance?
PETER:	No disturbance, Officer.
ELIAS:	They healed me! You know me, Elias. I'm here every day.
POLICEMAN:	You aren't Elias. He's a cripple.
CAPTAIN:	Just a minute. There's something funny here. This IS Elias.
ELIAS:	They healed me—in Jesus' name, they said.
POLICEMAN:	Oh, they did, did they? We'll see what the High Priest has to say about that.
OFFICER:	Elias, you'd better go home, and keep quiet about this. As for you two—
POLICEMAN:	Do you think we'd better arrest them, sir?
ELIAS:	What? For healing me? That's crazy!
CAPTAIN:	Watch what you say, Elias! You two, come with us!
PETER:	We will come. Elias, give thanks to God, and bear witness to Jesus' power—
POLICEMAN:	That's enough from you. Make way, there! (THEY ARE LED AWAY)

Scene three:

PETER AND JOHN BEFORE THE COUNCIL+
BIBLE REFERENCE: ACTS 4: 5-22.
FOR ANNAS AND CAIAPHAS SEE MATTHEW 26: 3-5; MARK 14: 53-65,
JOHN 11, 47-53, AND ACTS 4 THROUGH 9.

CHARACTERS: CAIAPHAS, the High Priest
ANNAS, his father-in-law
ALEXANDER, and other members of his family
POLICE CAPTAIN
PETER and JOHN
#ELIAS the cripple
Members of the COUNCIL

The High Priestly caste represented the Jews under Roman rule. One rich family, of which Annas was the most powerful representative, provided eight High Priests in the first century CE. They steered a difficult course as religious and political leaders. Their money came largely from Temple sacrifices. The 'tables of the moneychangers' which Jesus overthrew were known as Booths of Annas.

Any new religious movement was a threat to them. They could exert strong pressure on a Roman official like Pilate, if they kept the Jewish people at peace. Jesus' popularity was dangerous. Hence their determination to get rid of him, and to suppress his followers. In their own eyes they were doing what was best for their people—and of course for their own survival. Our sources depict Caiaphas as a crafty, unattractive character. Annas wielded the real power. Alexander appears here as a violent, unthinking enemy of the Jesus movement, but this is imaginary.

(COUNCIL MEMBERS SEATED IN A HALF CIRCLE)

CAIAPHAS: Call the prisoners in, and the socalled cripple. Ask Captain Nathanael to come in also.

ATTENDANT: Yes, sir. (HE GOES OUT)

CAIAPHAS: This is a delicate matter. I ask you all to listen carefully, and to avoid making hasty judgments.

ALEXANDER: It's obvious that the whole thing is a fraud—

ANNAS: Here they come. We will be able to judge for ourselves.

(PETER AND JOHN ARE LED IN, AND STAND ON ONE SIDE. CAPTAIN ENTERS)

CAIAPHAS: Captain Nathanael, step forward, please.

ANNAS: I understand, Captain, that you arrested these two men after a disturbance near the Temple yesterday.

CAPTAIN: Yes, sir.

ANNAS: What are your names, and where do you come from?

PETER: I am Simon-bar-Jonah, of Bethsaida in Galilee. This is my friend, John-bar-Zebedee.

CAIAPHAS: Galileans! I suspected as much.

ANNAS: You are accused of having caused a public disturbance and claiming to work a miraculous cure in order to attract notoriety.

JOHN: It is a fact, sir, not a claim. Our friend stands here healed.

ANNAS: Your friend stands here, and you and he claim that he is healed. There is not a jot of proof that you are speaking the truth. You admit that you are responsible for what happened?

PETER: We healed him. If that caused a disturbance, as you call it, of course we are responsible.

ALEXANDER: And how did you perform this remarkable cure, Galilean?

PETER: Councillors, I find it strange that we are here, accused of healing a man. But since you ask by what power we healed him I can asnwer simply: we did it through Jesus of Nazareth. (REACTIONS OF SURPRISE AND ANGER. CAIAPHAS NODS. HE HAD EXPECTED THIS ANSWER) He was crucified, but he rose again, and told us to preach and heal in his name, by which alone men can be brought to salvation.

ANNAS: These men are peasants. What right have they to talk such nonsense?

JOHN: Sir, the man stands here healed.

ALEXANDER: Be silent, prisoner! How dare you answer back?

CAIAPHAS: It would be wise, I think, to send these men out while we reach a decision.

ANNAS: I should like to hear what Captain Nathanael has to say.

CAIAPHAS: Take them outside! (THEY ARE LED OUT) Well, Captain? How do you view the situation in the streets?

CAPTAIN: To be frank, sir, it is not good. Since this cripple Elias was headed—

ANNAS: Come now, Captain! Surely you have not fallen for that story.

CAPTAIN: Well, sir, you asked me to speak. I've known Elias for years. He begs every day by the Beautiful Gate: never any trouble before. He's over forty. In my opinion—

CAIAPHAS: We can do without your opinion, Captain. Tell us what other people believe about this healing.

CAPTAIN: The majority are skeptical, but they weren't there when it happened. Plenty of witnesses can swear to the change in Elias. It has certainly stirred up interest in this Jesus they talk about.

ANNAS: All right, Captain. You may go. (HE GOES OUT)

CAIAPHAS: As I said, a delicate matter.

ALEXANDER: Why not make an example of this Elias? Give him a beating which will cripple him for good?

ANNAS: That would be most unwise. We want to avoid publicity. Besides—

CAIAPHAS: The healing may be genuine. Was that what you were going to say?

ANNAS: God may have healed him. We cannot be sure. The point is that to deny it outright might be unadvisable.

ALEXANDER: Then punish these Galileans!

CAIAPHAS: Alexander, punishment is an excellent thing if it is effective. Punishment for its own sake has no value. This excitement over Jesus will die down. It would be folly to fan it by open persecution.

ANNAS: Then what do you suggest?

CAIAPHAS: A stiff warning. If that does not work, harsher measures.

ANNAS: Is that agreed?

ALL: Yes. Agreed.

CAIAPHAS: Call the prisoners back. (THEY ARE LED IN) Simon and John, your case has been considered. We have decided to be lenient. You will not on this occasion be punished; but it is our duty to warn you bluntly that any further claims made in the name of Jesus wil lead you into serious trouble.

PETER: Sir, we have no wish to speak with disrespect before this Council. We are Jews who love our faith. But you are asking us to put your commands above those of God.

ALEXANDER: How do ignorant men like you think that you know what he commands?

PETER: We know what we see and hear, sir.

ALEXANDER: Stupid, obstinate fools!

CAIAPHAS: Think it over. You have been warned what will happen to you if you oppose the authority of this Council. It is for us to interpret the will of God, not for individuals with no training in the Law. You may go now.

ANNAS: I trust that we will have no further trouble from you.

Scene four:

REPRESSION AND GROWTH +
BIBLE REFERENCE: Acts 5:27 to 6:6

CHARACTERS: A group of the Christians who were gathered at Pentecost. The scene is imaginary, but based closely on the text. Peter and John return to their friends after the beating described 1n 5:40. The home of Mark and his mother Mary may have been a regular meeting place, since Peter returned there after his imprisonment (Acts 12). Rhoda is there named as their servant.
Names can be confusing in the New Testament.

MARY. There are five or six: Jesus' mother; Mary Magdalene; Mary, wife of Cleopas (John), perhaps the same as Mary, mother of James and Joses (Matthew); Mary, sister of Martha and Lazarus; Mary, mother of John Mark.

JAMES and JOHN and SIMON and PHILIP and JUDAS (Jude) can also cause confusion. When these names occur, look them up in a concordance or commentary.

Mary, mother of Mark, is in her home with Rhoda and several of the apostles. Mark and Andrew hurry in.

MARK: Mother! Peter and John are coming. They are both hurt.

MARY:	I know, my son. Thaddeus saw you coming along the street.
RHODA:	We have beds ready for them.
MARY:	How badly are they injured?
ANDREW:	Not seriously, we hope. Beaten, as they expected. (PETER AND JOHN ARE HELPED IN BY MATTHEW, JAMES, AND THOMAS)
MARY:	Over here, Thomas.
THOMAS:	Good! You're ready for us. Easy, Peter!
JOHN:	I'm all right. Don't—
MATTHEW:	Sit down, John. Take it easy. I'll get you some water.
PETER:	Ah! That's better. All I need is a little rest.
RHODA:	Turn around, so that I can bathe your back.
PETER:	Ouch! That Police Captain had a strong arm.
JOHN:	They treated you far worse than me, Peter.
PETER:	(TRYING TO LAUGH) Perhaps because I did more talking.
ANDREW:	Can you tell us about it? Don't, if you're not up to it.
JOHN:	You rest, Peter. I'll tell them. (PETER LIES DOWN. JOHN RESTS AGAINST THE WALL. THE OTHERS GATHER AROUND THEM. RHODA GOES OUT)
MARY:	Drink this first, John.
JOHN:	Thank you, Mary. Where would we be without your home and all you do for us? Oh, that tastes good!
MARY:	Mark, go and fill the pitcher, please.
MARK:	Yes, Mother. (HE GOES OUT)

JOHN: There's really not much to tell. We were arrested near the Temple Gate just like last time. After two hours of waiting we were taken to the Council Room. All the same people were there, but this time Gamaliel the Pharisee was with them, luckily for us.

PHILIP: I've heard of him. The greatest teacher in Jerusalem, they call him.

JOHN: They repeated what they said last time. Why did you go on teaching about Jesus? Of course Peter said, 'We can't obey you rather than God.' I tell you, at that moment I thought it might be the end. That brute Alexander was howling for us to be lynched, and Caiaphas seemed to be on his side—

ANDREW: Surely they couldn't do that. The Romans–

PETER: I wouldn't be too sure. The way they looked—

JOHN: Rest, Peter! I'll do the talking. Anyway, this Gamaliel really saved us. He asked permission to speak, and he has a way with him that makes everyone listen. He told them to take a hard look at what they were doing. If God wanted us to fail we would fail, but if we were speaking God's word nothing could stop us. I tell you, they didn't like it; but I think Caiaphas, the old fox, was swung over by Gamaliel. He was glad to have Alexander and some of the others calmed down.

THOMAS: So what happened then?

JOHN: They chose the obvious way out: beat us, and avoid friction with Pilate. I kept quiet, and got off lightly; but when the captain was ready to beat Peter Alexander said to him, 'This will muzzle you, Mister Fisherman,' and Peter said—

PETER: It was waste of breath. I should have held my tongue.

ANDREW: What did you say?

JOHN: He said, 'You can't muzzle the word of God'—and of course the Captain laid into him all the harder.

PETER (SITTING UP): I feel better. What happened at your meeting today?

ANDREW: Later, brother. There's no hurry.

PETER:	No, no. Jesus' business cannot be held up by a few bruises. What decisions did you make?
MATTHEW:	None. We heard the representatives of the Greek speaking brothers.
PETER:	What was their complaint?
THOMAS:	That some of their widows are not being fairly treated in the food distributions.
ANDREW:	We told them a decision must wait for a full meeting of the Twelve.
PETER:	The Twelve! We are too few to know all their needs. With thousands joining us and turning to the Lord, how can we preach the good news and distribute bread and watch the money? It isn't like the old days in Galilee.
JAMES:	I have a plan. Peter. Rather than try to do all these things ourselves, let us appoint some helpers to do those jobs—look after the money, I mean, and the food?
JOHN:	That's right. It was the word that Jesus entrusted to us—the good news. I agree with James. If we are to be free for witness and healing, we must choose others for other tasks.
PETER:	Yes, that is what we must do. We ought to be thankful that the growth of the Church makes it necessary. Andrew and Philip, you know best about the Greeks among our number. Choose with prayer those whom you think to be best suited for that kind of work.
MARY:	Now, no more business for today. Rhoda has supper ready. You two need rest.

Scene five:

STEPHEN (improvise)
BIBLE REFERENCE: Acts 6-7

In these chapters the story of Stephen is told. He was one of seven deacons, or ministers, chosen for practical work; but Stephen proved also to be a brilliant speaker. He made such an impression that the High Priest's circle were determined to stop him. They called him before the Council, and his answer to their warnings was so eloquent and provocative that they were in a frenzy. To kill a man without the permission of the Romans was rash, and it only seems to have happened on this one occasion.

Saul (Paul) enters the story at this point. He was a young Jewish scholar with a great reputation. The Council asked him to look into the beliefs and organization of the Jesus movement, and if necessary to arrest its leaders. When they suddenly ordered the execution of Stephen Saul was designated to see that it was carried out.

It seems likely that Saul would have met with some of the Christians, to find out what they believed and to warn them not to preach heresy. You could improvise a meeting between Saul and Stephen. Saul goes to a Christian meeting, and afterwards asks Stephen to talk with him. What would each of them have said? Saul would surely have been disturbed and fascinated by Stephen's eloquence, and by all that he said about Jesus' message.

For Saul, watching the horror of a stoning must have been almost unbearable. You could improvise the scene, with a battered and dying Stephen saying his words of forgiveness as he looks at Saul. I picture Saul as never really getting over it. When he was ordered to go to Damascus and suppress the Christians there, he knew that he might have to repeat that awful process of murder. And had he been wrong about the Christians? Was Stephen's witness true? On the long ride from Jerusalem Saul had many hours in which to think about this. At the end of the journey his vision occurred.

This can be another improvisation. Saul's companions point to Damascus, now in sight from the road. Suddenly he cries out, covers his eyes, and falls. The dialogue in Acts 9 :4-6 follows. His astonished companions lift him up, while a crowd gathers. Everyone asks what is happening, and different people say: 'Did you hear that voice?' 'I heard something, but—' 'I was too confused to listen' 'There was a bright light'. 'Let's take him into the city.'

Scene six:

THE BAPTISM OF PAUL **
BIBLE REFERENCE:
Acts 9:9-22. Galatians 1:13-17. 2 Corinthians 11:32-33

CHARACTERS: SAUL (PAUL)
JUDAS
#SUSANNA
ANANIAS

It appears that Saul's companions left him when he went blind after his vision. He was taken in by a Christian family. This scene takes place in the house of Judas and his wife Susanna (she is not mentioned in Luke's account). They are watching him as he lies on a bed, restless and groaning.

SAUL: (LOUD) Who are you, Lord? Ananias, help me!

SUSANNA:	It's all right, Saul. It's all right. We are your friends. Three whole days unconscious! He must be so weak.
JUDAS:	Saul, can you hear me? Saul! Rest! You'll be all right.
SAUL:	(LOUDER) Ananias, help me!
JUDAS:	Who can this Ananias be? It's such a common name.
SUSANNA:	He doesn't know what he is saying.
JUDAS:	Wait a minute! I think he's opening his eyes.
SAUL:	Where am I? Who—
SUSANNA:	He's conscious!
SAUL:	(SLOW) Please tell me! How did I come here?
JUDAS:	We don't really know, Saul. You are Saul of Tarsus, aren't you?
SAUL:	Yes. Yes, I am Saul.
JUDAS:	That's what they said when I found you. It was near the South Gate. You were stumbling along by the wall, with a lot of frightened people watching. Nobody seemed to want to do anything.
SAUL:	I remember. Someone spoke to me. Was it you?
JUDAS:	Yes. I don't mind telling you, I was frightened too. I mean, what we had heard—
SAUL:	Why were you frightened? (PAUSE) You don't mean that you—
SUSANNA:	Yes, Saul. We're Christians.
SAUL:	And you still helped me?
JUDAS:	We had to. I'm no hero, but the spirit of Jesus seemed to push me forward. So I brought you here. My name is Judas, and this is Susanna, my wife.
SUSANNA:	How do you feel?

SAUL:	I can see nothing. My right arm is numb. But I feel my strength coming back.
SUSANNA:	You're shivering. I will fetch another blanket. (KNOCK) O God! Who can that be? Not the police!
JUDAS:	I will see. Don't worry! (OPENS DOOR) Ananias!
ANANIAS:	Greetings, Judas, and Susanna. I—O, it's true!
JUDAS:	This is Saul of Tarsus.
ANANIAS:	I know.
SAUL:	Ananias! I was sure that you would come!
JUDAS:	I don't understand
ANANIAS:	The Lord told me in a vision that I must come here and find you, Saul. I had just got back from work, and I don't know whether I was awake or had nodded off. All of a sudden there was this voice. I could hardly believe it—
JUDAS:	So that was why you kept talking about Ananias, Saul.
SAUL:	Did I? My mind is still confused. I know that the voice which spoke to me on the road has kept telling me that a man would come to heal my sight—Ananias.
ANANIAS:	That's it! The Lord sent the vision to each of us.
SAUL:	How could you believe it? You knew who I was, and why—
ANANIAS:	I didn't want to believe it, I can tell you. I can remember arguing. That's good, isn't it? Me arguing with the Lord! But I had to come.
SAUL:	So it is true that Jesus is Messiah! I should have known! I saw Stephen die, heard him— O God, God, God!
SUSANNA:	Rest now, Saul! Don't think about that !
JUDAS:	If it is God's will that you are to be one of us, look forward! Think of what lies ahead!

SAUL:	Yes. (PAUSE) Though I don't know what else can lie ahead for me but death, when they know at Jerusalem—
ANANIAS:	Saul, the Lord has told us one thing clearly. I am to pray with you that your sight may return. Lie back now. I want you to surrender yourself to faith in Jesus. He will make you whole.
JUDAS:	We will all pray. (ANANIAS LAYS HIS HANDS OVER SAUL'S EYES)
ANANIAS:	Lord Jesus, you have sent me here to our brother Saul, to give him back his sight, and to pray for him to be filled with your Holy Spirit. Let my hands be your hands, Lord! Come with healing power! Come! Heal! (A LONG SILENCE)
SAUL:	(SITS UP SLOWLY) I can see. My head feels strange, but I can see.
SUSANNA:	(AS SAUL TRIES TO STAND) No! Lie down! Before you do anything else you must eat. You have had nothing but water for three days.
SAUL:	Before everything else, my beloved friends, my brave, wonderful new friends, I must witness to you that I give my life to my savior.
ANANIAS:	Let us baptize him at once! Please, Susanna, fetch water. (SHE GOES OUT) Judas, you are the head of the household. Give our brother baptism!
SAUL:	Wait! Am I worthy to receive baptism, after what I have done?
JUDAS:	We all came to him as sinners. If you repent, and believe in your heart that Jesus is Lord, you should be baptized.
SAUL:	I do believe. He came to me in my need. Jesus is Lord!
JUDAS:	Saul—
SAUL:	No! That name is dead—stained with all my sins. Call me Paul, my name among the Romans. (SUSANNA HAS BROUGHT WATER)
JUDAS:	Paul, I baptize you in the name of the Father, and of the Son, and of the Holy Spirit. You are sealed as his servant for ever. Now say with us the prayer which he taught us! (THEY ALL SAY THE LORD'S PRAYER)

SUSANNA:	Wrap this around you. I will fetch your food. (GIVES HIM A SECOND BLANKET, AND GOES OUT)
SAUL:	Tell me what I can do to serve you.
ANANIAS:	Get back your strength first.
SAUL:	But if I stay here you will be in danger.
ANANIAS:	Danger is part of following the Lord. 'Take up the Cross, and follow me!' His words. So far we have not been interfered with here in Damascus. We always knew it would happen one day. After what happened to you I suppose it will be worse.
JUDAS:	What matters is that we all share it. Danger is lighter that way.
SAUL:	I only ask one thing. As I have stood in public places and denounced Jesus, let me soon go out into the streets and witness to him. After that I will wait for his guidance and for your advice.
SUSANNA:	(RETURNING) Here is food, Paul.

Scene seven:

PETER AND THE BAPTISM OF CORNELIUS (for reading)
BIBLE REFERENCE: ACTS 11: 1-18

CHARACTERS: PETER
JAMES, brother of Jesus
BARTHOLOMEW
THADDEUS

The scene is imaginary, but based on the text. The influence of the 'circumcision party' (verse 2) often appears in Acts and in Paul's letters. They were afraid of the growing influence of Gentiles. I have chosen Bartholomew and Thaddeus as their representatives because of their Jewish names (unlike the Greek names of Andrew and Philip). By using them we avoid introducing another Judas or Simon.

James, brother of the Lord, is now in charge of the Church in Jerusalem. He and two of the more conservative apostles are with Peter, seated in a home in Jerusalem. It is about fifteen years after the crucifixion and resurrection of Jesus.

JAMES:	We want to talk to you, Peter, before this evening's meeting.
BARTHOLOMEW:	I'm sure you realize that the rumors about what happened at Caesarea have made some people uneasy.

PETER: I certainly do. I agree that you should know all the facts, before it becomes a matter of general discussion. I keep telling myself that for all of you here in Jerusalem it must be impossible to understand news like this learned at second hand.

JAMES: Tell us exactly what happened.

PETER: I was staying at Joppa, with a wonderful Jewish family, Simon the tanner, his wife and children. They have all accepted Jesus and been baptized. Up there, and in Caesarea, there are many more Gentiles studying our faith than here in Jerusalem. Quite a few Romans in the army read the Law and the Prophets, and nobody can help admiring their enthusiasm. I met several of them, and I was puzzled.

THADDEUS: I can understand that. It's a new situation. We met so few Gentiles when we were with Jesus.

BARTHOLOMEW: But he always listened to them, and treated them with love and respect. However, that's a very different thing from—

PETER: Wait, please! Don't make up your minds until you hear my story.

JAMES: Go on, Peter.

PETER: I was puzzled, as I say, because with Jesus we were a band of Jews, united in worship and sacrifice and the Law—and here were these people, trained to read the scriptures, but not circumcised.

THADDEUS: Surely that is the point. Jesus never said—

PETER: Wait, Thaddeus, wait! One day I came in tired to Simon's place, and sat down to rest before supper. I suppose I was thinking about food, and my mind was confused about these Gentile families. Anyway I must have fallen asleep, because suddenly there in front of me was the most vivid sign from the Lord that I have seen since the Mount of Transfiguration. There was a kind of tablecloth, lowered from above me. On it there were all the kinds of flesh which you and I are forbidden to eat, every unclean animal you can think of, all piled on dishes in front of me. I felt myself recoil. Then Jesus' voice came—you won't believe this at first, but it's true. He spoke in that same half-humorous voice that he would use when he was trying to make us understand something, and we were being obstinate. Remember?

BARTHOLOMEW: (LAUGHING) Yes—like when he called James and John 'Sons of Thunder', and none of us could stop laughing—they were so embarrassed!

JAMES: What did he say, Peter?

PETER: 'Get up, Peter! Kill and eat!'

THADDEUS: WHAT?

PETER: It was just as clear as when you speak to me now. 'Kill and eat!' Of course I said, 'You can't mean that, Lord—not the pork and all those unclean things.' But all he kept saying was, 'Kill and eat!' It happened three separate times. When I kept protesting, he would say, 'You must not call what God has cleansed unclean.' Well, imagine what happened then! I felt my host shaking me, and saying, 'Wake up, Peter! Someone wants you.' So I got up, still dazed and confused, and went to the door. That was when I knew that Jesus meant me to baptize my first Gentile converts.

JAMES: Why?

PETER: Because at the door were two Jews, men I knew slightly, from Caesarea. They had been sent by a Roman Centurion stationed there, Cornelius. He had seen a vision, just like me, they said. The Lord had told him to ask me to come to him. Would you have refused to go, in face of that?

BARTHOLOMEW: No, you could not refuse.

PETER: That was the turningpoint. I found Cornelius to be a fine man, well known for his generosity, and a student of the scriptures. He was as sure as I was that the Lord's messenger had stood beside him and told him to send for me. So I said to him, in front of a whole company of our Jewish friends, 'Cornelius, this goes against all that I was brought up to believe, but I can see that Jesus is driving us forward to a new understanding. I have heard his voice in a vision also. He has shown me that the old rules about "clean" and "unclean" are not binding any more. Do you believe that Jesus is Lord?' He said, 'Yes, I believe.' That was it! I baptized him, and his dear wife, and their two children, and a God-fearing slave.

JAMES: (AFTER A PAUSE) When you tell that story to the meeting, Peter, I don't see how anyone can deny that you did God's will.

THADDEUS: I hope you are right. It will still be hard for some of the company to accept this. They are so afraid that we are moving too far and too fast, and losing the basis of our belief. But I know that my doubts have vanished.

BARTHOLOMEW: Mine also. Thank God the sign was so clear!

JAMES: Now we will be able to back you up. Thank you. Peter. It's time to be on our way.

Scene eight:

BARNABAS AND PAUL *
BIBLE REFERENCE: Acts 11: 19-24

CHARACTERS: PAUL
                 His FATHER
                 His MOTHER
                 BARNABAS

Fourteen years had passed since Paul's conversion. He lived quietly, probably at his home in Tarsus most of the time. It seems that Peter and the other apostles forgave his earlier conduct and never forgot him. We know from Galatians 1: 18 that Paul and Peter met for fifteen days in Jerusalem not long after Paul's conversion. During that time they surely shared everything between them. Now Paul's gifts were badly needed. Barnabas, who was always a bridgebuilder and peacemaker, was sent to ask Paul for his help. It was time for the church to send missionaries to other parts of the Roman empire. Paul was a Roman citizen, far better educated than any of the apostles. Would Barnabas be able to persuade him to begin a new life? All we know of Paul's father is that he earned citizenship. He must have been a prominent leader in Tarsus, a magistrate and probably a merchant in the canvas trade, as Paul sometimes worked in this trade during his missionary journeys. Canvas for sails and tents was in great demand. We can picture Paul's family as prosperous. We know from Acts 23: 16 that Paul had one sister.

This scene takes place in Paul's home. His parents are seated when Paul comes in.

PAUL: Here I am!

FATHER: You're later than usual. Busy day?

PAUL: We had a long meeting with an army contractor. A big order for tents. With that, and the sails for Calpurnius, things are going to be humming.

MOTHER: You'll be wanting your supper.

PAUL: I'm ready. (KNOCK. PAUL OPENS THE DOOR) Barnabas! It can't be!

BARNABAS: Greetings, Paul!

PAUL: Come in! Mother, Father, this is my old friend Barnabas, who was so wonderful to me in Jerusalem. Why, it's been ten years!

MOTHER: I was about to prepare supper. You must stay and join us.

FATHER: It's a pleasure to welcome you here.

BARNABAS: And for me to be here, sir. I have often tried to picture Paul's home.

FATHER: I'll leave you two to yourselves before supper. You must have a lot to talk about. (HE LEAVES)

PAUL: Sit down, and tell me why you are here, and about the church at Antioch, and Jerusalem, and how Peter is, and—

BARNABAS: Hold on, Paul! All in good time! Be patient, and don't shout ten questions at me all at once. Tell me first, are you well?

PAUL: Strong as a horse! My eyes are not very good, and I still have trouble with this hand; but I work a ten hour day—and then there's my ministry to the sick—you know, for the church.

BARNABAS: We hear reports. It gives us joy to know that the word is being preached here. Now let me tell you why I have come. I have a message for you.

PAUL: For me?

BARNABAS: From Simon Niger and the others at Antioch. You can read it later, but I can tell you what it says. We need you, Paul.

PAUL: Me? I don't see how—

BARNABAS:	The whole range of the gospel is changing. Nobody sees it more clearly than Peter. When I last saw him we talked about you.
PAUL:	I still find it hard to believe that I am trusted.
BARNABAS:	Of course you are! The persecution is in the past—buried. Nobody has been more faithful than you. Now we need your experience and knowledge.
PAUL:	I want to help, but I still feel ashamed to put myself forward.
BARNABAS:	But you have proved yourself, and the bigger our work grows the more we need your gifts.
PAUL:	It seems to me I can give so little.
BARNABAS:	Nonsense! Except for Silas you are the only Roman citizen in our number. You have the prestige of your father's position, and you have far greater learning than any of us.
PAUL:	Jesus didn't choose people for their learning.
BARNABAS:	He chose them so that they could give whatever they had to offer— the widow's two farthings or your wisdom. He fed a crowd with a boy's lunch, Paul. What do you think he can do with your brains and your courage?
PAUL:	Let me think and pray! And stay and talk to my parents. They are sensible, dedicated people, and they love the Lord.
BARNABAS:	Of course I will do that.
PAUL:	Because you are the one whom they sent it is an easier decision to make. Without your understanding I don't think Peter and the rest could have accepted me. To say no to you won't be easy, but I must search my heart first. (BELL RINGS) Come and join us for supper!

Scene nine :

'GO YE OUT INTO ALL THE WORLD' (improvise)
BIBLE REFERENCE: Acts 13: 1-4

CHARACTERS:	SIMEON NIGER MANAEN LUCIUS of CYRENE

PAUL
BARNABAS

This short passage marks the beginning of the 'Missionary Journeys', a new and momentous chapter in the Church's advance. The scene may be improvised. The five men are in a room together. They begin with silent prayer. Simeon then asks them to share their thoughts. Barnabas, who came from Cyprus, says that he knows there is a need for churches to be founded there. Why only there, others ask? The time is ripe for a wider mission. Paul keeps quiet, unwilling to put himself forward. Simeon says that the Spirit has kept on showing him Barnabas and Paul in a ship. Manaen says he too is sure that the Lord wants Paul to go on a journey. Lucius talks about his native Cyrene, and dreams of a mission there. Let him talk about it, and recollect that Simon of Cyrene carried Jesus' cross.

Simeon sums up their thoughts. The Spirit is guiding them to send Barnabas and Paul, with Cyprus as their first objective. Paul, hesitant at first, agrees to go if Barnabas will be the leader. They agree with this plan, and talk about Cyprus and the neighboring provinces of Cilicia and Asia, in modern Turkey. They discuss the opposition which they will meet: Roman officials may be friendly or hostile, Jews will be sharply split over Jesus' message, pagan priests will be bitterly opposed. Finally the other three lay their hands on Barnabas and Paul, and pray for the power of the Spirit to be with them on their journey.

Scene ten:

CONFRONTATION IN CYPRUS*
BIBLE REFERENCE: ACTS 13: 4-12

CHARACTERS: SERGIUS PAULUS, Governor of Cyprus
ELYMAS BAR-JESUS, a Jewish 'sorcerer'
PAUL, BARNABAS, and JOHN MARK

The characters of Sergius Paulus and Elymas are guesswork; but it it is not unlikely that an intelligent Roman Governor would take a keen interest in Judaism, and have at his headquarters a 'wise man' or sorcerer. Elymas' blindness may have been temporary, like Paul's at Damascus. Nothing is known of the life of Sergius after this incident.

Barnabas and Paul went first to Cyprus, which Barnabas knew well. At Salamis, as also at later places of call, they went first to the synagogues—there must have been a large Jewish population—without any special incident or confrontation. On the far side of the island, at Paphos, the Governor called them in to explain their message. There they sat and engaged in a heated dispute with the Jewish wise man Elymas. This scene breaks into the middle of the argument.

ELYMAS:	Your Excellency, I don't know what more I can say. This man is telling you a string of fairy tales: miracle healings, rising from the dead, and a garbled mixture of Jewish teachings dressed up as some new religious fad.
PAUL:	I warn you, Elymas, not to fight against the truth. Your spells and cheap magic tricks can never stand up against the love of Jesus. But when we try to reason with you all we hear is screaming and venomous accusations.
SERGIUS:	Gentlemen, you are not here to bicker, but to explain your views to me in a civilized way. Paul is right, Elymas: you do refuse to listen. Your only answer to him is abuse.
ELYMAS:	(SHOUTING) These men are liars! Their cheap carpenter Messiah is a fake! Why should I even try to answer them?
PAUL:	Elymas, beware! The power of Jesus is the power of love, but you cannot curse him and escape the wrath of God.
ELYMAS:	Who are you to tell me what I can or cannot do?
SERGIUS:	Stop! Paul, I am deeply impressed by what you have said. I would like to speak to you privately. Elymas—
ELYMAS:	Don't do it, sir! They will cast their spells and cheat you—
PAUL:	You swindler! You rascal! Now you have gone too far. You are trying to distort the straight ways of the Lord, you son of the Devil and enemy of all that is good! May the hand of God strike you, as he struck me when I fought against the light! You shall be blind, Elymas—blind!
ELYMAS:	(CRYING OUT AND FALLING) O God! Mercy, mercy! My eyes!
SERGIUS:	God in heaven! Is this true?
BARNABAS:	We will care for him, Your Excellency. (HE KNEELS BY ELYMAS, WHO IS MOANING) Be at peace, Elymas! Jesus can make you whole again if you trust in him. Mark, help me!

SERGIUS: Carry him to his room! Slaves, help them and show them the way! (MARK AND BARNABAS WITH SLAVES CARRY ELYMAS OUT) Paul, I believe in Jesus as Lord, not because of what happened to this poor man, but because of your witness, and what I see in the eyes of you and your friends.

PAUL: May this day be forever blessed! Tonight, sir, if you wish, you shall be baptized, and share in the Lord's supper. But remember! Ours is not an easy road. It led Jesus to the cross. Are you sure that you can follow him without shrinking, even if your rulers and your friends shun you?

SERGIUS: Which of us is sure of his courage? I know that you have shown me the way and the truth and the life. Go now and help poor Elymas! I will be with you this evening.

Scene eleven :

JEWS AND GENTILES AT LYSTRA +
BIBLE REFERENCE: Acts 14:8-23

CHARACTERS: PAUL
BARNABAS
*PHRIXUS, a cripple
*HIERON, a Jew of Pisidian Antioch
*FUSCUS, a Jew of Iconium
*JULIUS, a man in the crowd
LOIS, EUNICE, TIMOTHY, Christians of Antioch
CROWD of Gentiles
JEWS, companions of Hieron and Fuscus

From Cyprus Barnabas and Paul made the short crossing—to what is now Turkey. Their journey had already been fruitful and adventurous when they came to Lystra. Now they faced a crowd which was partly hostile and partly eager to listen. Paul stood on some steps and preached to them.

PAUL: And so, my friends, though Jesus was a Jew, as I am, and lived among Jews, he is the Savior of all people. We have Greeks in our number. We have a Roman Centurion and his family. We have people of every race. God sent his Son to us to heal the sick and the lame and to open every heart. Now we come to you in Lystra—

JULIUS: (AMONG THE CROWD, NEXT TO PHRIXUS) Here, look! This sick man is trying to come to you.

BARNABAS:	Bring him forward!
JULIUS:	Come on, Phrixus. I'll help you.
PHRIXUS:	Sir, is it true—that Jesus can heal a lame man?
BARNABAS:	Set him down here.
JULIUS:	No use trying it on him. He has never walked.
PHRIXUS:	You said you could heal me.
PAUL:	Yes, my friend. What is your name?
PHRIXUS:	Phrixus, sir.
PAUL:	Phrixus, God gave you life. Now I pray to him to heal you if it is his will, and if you have faith.
CROWD COMMENTS:	What's happening... Isn't that Phrixus?...What are they trying to do?...They won't heal him. He's a hopeless case.
BARNABAS:	Please keep back! Keep away from the steps, or someone will get hurt! Be quiet, and we will pray for our brother to be healed.
PAUL:	People of Lystra, God can heal our brother Phrixus. But you must pray, pray to Jesus! And you must believe. Phrixus, give me your hands. Now look at me, and say after me: Lord Jesus, (PHRIXUS REPEATS EACH PHRASE) I know that you can heal me, if it is your will. I am going to stand and walk. Now, stand up! Up on your feet! Come on, Phrixus! Stand! (WITH BARNABAS HELPING, PAUL LIFTS PHRIXUS UP) Throw away those crutches! Burn them! (THEY SUPPORT PHRIXUS)
CROWD COMMENTS:	Great Jupiter! He's standing up. That's Phrixus—he's on his feet!
PHRIXUS:	I can stand! Hold me—let me try to walk!
PAUL:	Friends, do not be amazed at what God has done. Help Phrixus to his home. Is it far, Phrixus?
PHRIXUS:	Around that corner. They never carry me far. What am I saying? I won't need to be carried!

PAUL: Will you two help him? And someone run ahead and warn his family.

BARNABAS: Have something to eat and drink, Phrixus. We will come and visit you later. (PHRIXUS IS LED OFF, WALKING SLOWLY)

JULIUS: People of Lystra, the gods have come to us! Can you doubt it? (YELLS FROM THE CROWD) I know nothing about Jesus; but this man must surely be Mercury, the way he speaks; and here is mighty Jupiter himself! (HE POINTS AT BARNABAS)

PAUL: Don't say that! It's blasphemy!

JULIUS: (WITH SHOUTS OF APPROVAL FROM THE CROWD) I say we should make a sacrifice to them. Take them to the Temple and sacrifice oxen! (VOICES: Yes, yes! They are gods! etc.)

PAUL: Stop! Stop! (SILENCE) Oh, my friends, don't speak like that! We are ordinary men like you. It is God who has done this, through Jesus. We have come to turn you away from superstitions—

LOUD VOICES: To the Temple! Fetch the priests! (FUSCUS, HIERON, AND OTHER JEWS ENTER)

PAUL: For the last time, listen! We are men, like you. It is Jesus—

HIERON: (SHOUTING) They are liars, troublemakers.

FUSCUS: Devils, not gods! (CROWD VOICES: Who are you? What do you mean? Who are these men?)

PAUL: Hieron, may God forgive you for this!

HIERON: Traitor! Listen, everyone! I am Hieron, from Antioch.

FUSCUS: And I am Fuscus of Iconium. We came to warn you about these moneygrubbing, cheating hypocrites.

PAUL: Don't listen! They are enemies of the true God!

HIERON: Wherever these men go, trouble follows. They pervert our Jewish faith—

FUSCUS:	They tried this trick in Iconium. There was a riot, and we chased them out—
PAUL:	Wherever we go, the powers of darkness turn against us.
HIERON:	Now they are pretending to be gods—
BARNABAS:	That is a lie. We—
FUSCUS:	Drive them out of your city!
JULIUS:	He's right! They cheated us! (VOICES: Wait a minute! Yes! It was a fake! Chase them away! Stone them!) (PAUL AND BARNABAS ARE SURROUNDED. STONES ARE THROWN, PAUL FALLS, WHILE BARNABAS RUNS OUT. THE CROWD DISPERSES, AND AFTER A PAUSE PAUL SITS UP. BARNABAS ENTERS WITH TIMOTHY, LOIS, AND EUNICE)
BARNABAS:	Paul! Paul! Thank God you're alive!
PAUL:	(SLOWLY) I will be all right.
LOIS:	We must get your head washed and bandaged.
TIMOTHY:	Hurry! We must get both of them out of the city.
PAUL:	Not so fast! I don't intend to be driven away by men like Hieron and Fuscus. I'm grateful to you. It's courageous of you—Lois, Eunice, Timothy—to offer to help. Barnabas, go and see that Phrixus is all right. If you will help me, Timothy, I can walk to your home. Later we will join in the Lord's supper.
EUNICE:	I will go ahead and prepare for you.
PAUL:	That crowd will cool off. Then those whom the Lord calls will join us.

NOTE: We do not know that Lois, Eunice, and Timothy (mentioned in 2 Timothy 1:5) were already Christians; but as Timothy later joined Paul (Acts 16:4) it seems likely.

Scene twelve:

THE COUNCIL AT JERUSALEM (improvise)
BIBLE REFERENCE: Acts 15
CHARACTERS:

The APOSTLES, except for James, son of Zebedee, who had been killed by Herod (Acts 12).
JAMES, brother of Jesus, who presided (Acts 15:13)
JUDAS BARSABBAS and SILAS, chosen as envoys (verse 22)
ELDERS and THE PHARISAIC PARTY (verse 4)

This meeting marked a turningpoint in the Church. The Apostles, who had worked with Jesus in a Jewish context within Judaea, now faced honest disagreements within the expanding community. Could it be true that membership in the Christian body was open to Gentiles who did not first accept Jewish traditions? Did Jesus' parables of seed and growth mean that his message was to be shared by everyone in the world?

You could improvise this scene, reading Romans 14, I Corinthians 10, and Galatians 1-2 to complete the picture of what was discussed. Choose actors to represent James, the chairman, a moderate conservative, Paul and Barnabas, fresh from their experiences in Cyprus and Asia, , and on the conservative side (against the admission of Gentiles) other Apostles. After vigorous discussion, James reads verses 13-21. Then they all pray for unity. Judas Barsabbas and Silas are appointed to carry the decision to Antioch.

The Council did not end the disagreements over admission to the church, but it marked the beginning of widespread missionary enterprises. We only know about Paul and his companions; but Peter also went as far as Rome, and probably to other parts of the Empire, and others, certainly including Barnabas and Mark, must also have made journeys of which we have no record.

Scene thirteen:

THE GUIDANCE OF THE SPIRIT (for reading)
BIBLE REFERENCE: Acts 16: 6-10

This short passage is very important. We have shown how the Holy Spirit came to a group at Pentecost, and to the assembled leaders in Jerusalem. Now we read about individuals asking for that guidance on their journeys, and receiving it in different ways. In the first episode we see Paul, Silas, and Timothy in a house somewhere in the southwestern part of the province of Asia (Turkey). They have been praying for guidance about their journey. After a time of silent prayer they speak.

FIRST EPISODE

CHARACTERS: PAUL
SILAS
TIMOTHY

SILAS:	I saw a straight road leading to the north. There were other roads to the left and right, but I knew that we ought not to take them.
PAUL:	It's strange that you should say that. I was thinking of Ephesus, and how I long to go and preach there, in front of Diana's temple. But I felt the Lord saying, 'Not yet, Paul!' Timothy?
TIMOTHY:	I am still confused. I thank God for counting me worthy to be with you, but I must do as you say.
PAUL:	It is clear to me that the Lord is directing us towards the north, through Mysia. That is what we must do next, and then seek more guidance.

SECOND EPISODE

This may be improvised. In Mysia the three are staying with a family. Assign roles to family members. Their host tells them about the big cities in Bithynia, on the north coast of Turkey. That would be a fruitful mission field. Then a letter is brought by a Christian from Troas. It is from Carpus (see 2 Timothy 4). Paul reads the letter aloud. Carpus has heard about Paul's journey, and begs him to come to Troas, using his home as a base for preaching. He mentions that a physician named Luke is staying with him. They agree that this is the guidance of the Spirit. Bithynia, like Ephesus, must wait.

THIRD EPISODE

CHARACTERS: CARPUS
LUKE
SILAS
TIMOTHY
PAUL

Improvise this scene, in the home of Carpus. Paul is still sleeping, but the other four are eating breakfast. Since Paul later left some parchments at Carpus' home (2 Timothy 4:13) they could be discussing the need to write down the story of Jesus. Luke, they say, should keep written notes of all that he hears or sees. Paul bursts in and says that he has had a dream, described in verse 5. They discuss Macedonia: the cities, Philippi, Neapolis, Thessalonica, Berea; the types of people they may meet there; and the chances of finding a ship leaving for a Macedonian port. Luke will go with Paul and Silas.

Scene fourteen:

THE PRISON AT PHILIPPI**
(hard, but very much worth while)
BIBLE REFERENCE: Acts 16: 19-40

CHARACTERS: PAUL
SILAS
*PHLEGON, the jailer
*LUCIA, his wife
Their two CHILDREN
Voices of PRISONERS

In Macedonia Paul and Silas went from the port of Neapolis to Philippi, a Roman colony, or center for veteran soldiers. Apparently there was no synagogue. Paul went to the open air place of prayer by the river. There he met Lydia, a 'seller of purple', one of the many women who helped Paul in the foundation of house churches. He antagonized some of the local merchants by healing a girl who had 'brought her masters much gain by soothsaying.' The merchants had Paul and Silas thrown into jail. There they sat, their feet chained. They sang this or another hymn, which could be heard by the other prisoners in a room close by.

PAUL and SILAS: (SINGING) In the cross of Christ I glory,
Towering o'er the wrecks of time.
All the light of sacred story
Gathers round its head sublime.

PRISONERS' VOICES: Go on! Sing some more! Don't stop!

PHLEGON: (ENTERING) What is this cross you were singing about?

SILAS: The Son of God was nailed to a cross in Judaea, jailer, to save the world.

PHLEGON: Son of God?

PAUL: Yes: Jesus of Nazareth, your friend and savior. What is your name?

PHLEGON: Phlegon, sir. Here, what am I doing calling a prisoner 'sir'?

VOICES: Here, you! Sing!

SILAS: They want us to tell the story of Jesus, Phlegon.

PAUL and SILAS:	(SINGING) When the woes of life o'ertake me, Hopes deceive, and fears annoy, Never shall the cross forsake me. Lo, it glows with peace and joy.
PHLEGON:	I like that song. Tell me—

(AN EARTHQUAKE SHAKES THE PRISON. LIGHTS GO OUT, SHOUTING)

PAUL:	Don't panic! You won't be hurt!
PHLEGON!	O God! The doors are open! I shall be beheaded for this. (HE DRAWS HIS SWORD)
PAUL:	Don't harm yourself, Phlegon! We won't run away.
SILAS:	Are you all right, Paul?
PAUL:	Just shaken. It did me no harm. And you?
SILAS:	The same. We seem to be free of our chains.
PHLEGON:	Lights! Lights! Lucia! (LUCIA ENTERS WITH A LAMP, HER CHILDREN WITH HER) O, thank God! Are you safe? And the children?
GIRL:	We weren't hurt, Daddy.
BOY:	Wow! Didn't it make a terrible noise!
LUCIA:	The quake seemed to shake the prison without harming our house.
PAUL:	Thank you for bringing the light. Everyone keep calm! You'd better count the prisoners. I don't think you'll find any missing. (PHLEGON GOES NEXT DOOR)
SILAS:	They're too scared to run far.
LUCIA:	Who are you, sir? You're not like any other prisoners.
PAUL:	I am Paul of Tarsus, and this is my friend Silas. We were brought here because we are followers of Jesus, Son of God.
LUCIA:	You were beaten and put in jail for that?

PAUL: Partly for that. Some of your merchants thought we were harming their pockets.

SILAS: So naturally they wanted us out of the way.

PHLEGON: (returning) I can't believe it ! Everyone is here, and noone hurt. There's more going on tonight than I can understand.

SILAS: The hand of God is upon us. He wants to show you his power, and lead you to salvation.

PHLEGON: What must I do to have salvation?

LUCIA: Before you worry about that, let me bathe their bruises. Fancy putting gentlemen like this in prison!

PAUL: Our bruises can wait. The important thing is our souls. Phlegon, this Jesus whom we worship is God himself, but for the love of us he humbled himself, and came to live among us in the form of a man—not a king or a general, but an ordinary carpenter in Judaea. He sent us here tonight to give you the good news. This earthquake is a sign, but his real power lies in acts of love and service. Do you understand this and believe it?

PHLEGON: I don't know, sir. I trust you to speak the truth: that I know.

LUCIA: Please, sir, come to our home and drink some wine. I'll get some breakfast ready. Come and help me, children!

PAUL: Thank you, Lucia. We will come, and tell you more about Jesus. Then you can all be baptized. (LUCIA AND CHILDREN GO OUT)

SILAS: Give us some food to take to the other prisoners. We want to speak to them also.

PHLEGON: That's very irregular, but—oh, it's too much for me! I'll do what you say. I expect the magistrates will send someone to free you in the morning.

PAUL: Oh no, Phlegon! I've decided to give our friends at City Hall a lesson. They have beaten and imprisoned two Romans without trial, and—

PHLEGON: Romans! You mean you let them beat you, and never said—

PAUL:	We had good reasons. Jesus allowed himself to be scourged and crucified. We will tell you about his death later, and how he rose from the dead to assure us of everlasting life.
SILAS:	There was another reason. If the magistrates are uneasy about having broken the law by imprisoning us, they will be less likely to make trouble for Jesus' followers here after we have gone.
PAUL:	If you are to be one of us, Phlegon, you must meet those wonderful people: Lydia, the dye merchant, and Epaphras, and Euodias and Syntyche, and the rest.
LUCIA:	(CALLING) Aren't you coming?
PAUL:	Yes, Lucia. My back does feel sore. Food and a bath will be very welcome. (CALLING TO THE PRISONERS) We will be in to see you soon, friends. Food is on the way.

SILAS:	Let's sing them another verse, Paul
	    When the sun of bliss is beaming
	    Light and love upon my way,
	    From the cross the radiance streaming
	    Adds new luster to the day.

Scene fifteen:

TURNING THE WORLD UPSIDE DOWN + BIBLE REFERENCE: Acts 17: 1-10

CHARACTERS: JASON
#ARETE, his wife
#PHORMIO, their son
PAUL and SILAS
#SOSIPATER, #XANTHE, #LYSIPPUS, Jewish Christians
#JULIA and #ANTIPHON, Gentile Christians
#PAMPHILUS, leader of the Synagogue
#TITIUS, a Roman official

At Philippi it was merchants who alerted the Romans to Paul's actions. At Thessalonica it was angry Jews, who accused him and his converts of 'turning the world upside down'. Things came to a head while Paul was at an evening meeting in the home of Jason, a Jew converted to Christianity.

(ALL OF THE CHARACTERS EXCEPT SOSIPATER, PAMPHILUS AND TITIUS ARE SEATED IN JASON'S HOME. THEY ARE SINGING A HYMN SUCH AS THIS, OR PSALM 67)

ALL SINGING: Jesus, my Lord, my God, my all,
 Hear me, blest Savior, when I call!
 Hear me, and from thy dwelling place
 Pour down the riches of thy grace!
 Jesus, my Lord, I thee adore.
 O make me love thee more and more!

(AS THEY END, SOSIPATER ENTERS)

JASON: Welcome, Sosipater! Come and join us!

SOSIPATER: First I think you ought to know that there is something going on in your street.

ARETE: Outside our house?

SOSIPATER: Yes, or at least that is what it looks like. Some young men are standing out there—a rough-looking bunch—on the far side of the road. They jeered at me as I approached your door.

LYSIPPUS: Did you recognize any of them?

SOSIPATER: No. I got the impression that they are waiting for someone.

JASON: Phormio, take a look. Try the back first. Then stay at the window of the store. Let us know at once if anyone comes near our door.

PHORMIO: I will Father. (HE GOES OUT)

JASON: If he gives us a warning, Paul, you and Silas leave at once by the back door, as we agreed.

PAUL: We will. Now let us quickly finish our business. Silas, you have a report?

SILAS: I have worked with Lysippus and Sosipater to make a list of all who have made their commitment to the Lord. Sosipater, you can speak for the Jewish community.

SOSIPATER: Yes. Nine families have joined us, God be praised! It has caused bitter feelings in the Synagogue, as you know, especially since we began to meet with our gentile brothers and sisters.

SILAS: It happens everywhere we go.

JASON:	Still, we believe we have a core strong enough to make our church secure.
PAUL:	I believe that also. Three Sabbaths in the Synagogue! So much has happened in this short time.
XANTHE:	May we speak?
SILAS:	Of course, Xanthe. I was going to ask Lysippus to speak next for the gentiles.
LYSIPPUS:	(LAUGHING) I think Xanthe and I were growing uncomfortable at all of you talking about 'our church' and its 'strong core'.
XANTHE:	It sounded as if we had no part to play, except to make up the numbers.
SILAS:	You know that we do not feel that! Paul and I have always gone to the Synagogue first, because—
PAUL:	We take the Messiah to those who should welcome him; but in God's eyes all are equally precious.
SOSIPATER:	Don't think that when Paul has left us our Jewish families will look down on you! We all desperately need each other to survive.
PAUL:	You could put it like this. Jews have special responsibilities in our churches. They need to interpret the Eucharist, the Law, and the Scriptures, which you would find hard to understand without their guidance. They are the cement of the Church, but they have no special privileges.
XANTHE:	We understand that. Jesus means too much to us for party strife or jealousy to be possible.
PAUL:	I never cease to be amazed at the courage and leadership which women are providing wherever I go. Here it is you and Julia and many more, firm as a rock, Jews and gentiles. I see a great future—
PHORMIO:	(ENTERING HURRIEDLY) It looks bad, Father. The crowd has grown. There's a group with torches walking down the street. I heard them shouting 'Paul', 'Jason.' (HE GOES OUT AGAIN)
JULIA:	The Lord protect us!

ARETE: This way, Paul, quickly!

JASON: Send us news. We will get a message to you in Berea.

PAUL: God bless you all!

SILAS: Goodbye, friends! (PAUL, SILAS, ARETE GO OUT)

JASON: Everyone sit down again.

JULIA: We aren't breaking any laws. Surely they can't—

PHORMIO: (RETURNING) Antiphon and Pamphilus are coming to the door.

JASON: So it is the Synagogue leaders.

PHORMIO: There's another man with them, and a crowd of thirty or forty—
(LOUD KNOCK. JASON OPENS THE DOOR. ARETE RETURNS FROM THE BACK)

ANTIPHON: This is the house, Officer.

PAMPHILUS: And this man is Jason. He is one of them.

JASON: May I ask why you have come here?

TITIUS: You are Jason?

JASON: Yes.

TITIUS: Which of these men is Paul?

LYSIPPUS: Paul is not here. He was with us earlier, but he left.

ANTIPHON: Where did he go?

JASON: Just a minute! Antiphon, I know that you and Pamphilus bear us
                ill will. I am very sorry for that. But this is a Roman city. We are not
                breaking any laws—

ANTIPHON: Wherever Paul goes, he turns the world upside down. We are going
                to see that here at least decent people are protected from you
                Christians.

LYSIPPUS: Officer, what do you want with us?

ANTIPHON: This man is a gentile! Is that what you have come to, Jason—eating and drinking with unclean scum?

TITIUS: That's enough! I want to know what is going on here. We've had complaints about you, Jason—

JASON: Of course, from these men. The fact that they hate us does not mean that we are disloyal. Have you a warrant to arrest us?

TITIUS: Nobody is talking about arrests. I have to ask you all to come to headquarters for questioning.

JASON: And leave the mob outside to ransack our home?

TITIUS: No. Before we go, Antiphon, you're to see to it that all those people are dispersed. We don't tolerate mob violence in this city.

PAMPHILUS: Just you wait, Jason! This is only the beginning.

TITIUS: Go out there, both of you, and get rid of them! As for you, Jason, since Paul is not here you will be held responsible for any charges brought against Christians. You will have every chance to answer for yourselves. Now let us go.

ARETE: You don't want our son.

TITIUS: No. He can stay and watch rhe house,

JASON: Don't worry, Phormio! We'll be back soon.

PHORMIO: I'll be all right. Take care of Mother!

TITIUS: The rest of you follow me!

Scene sixteen:

PAUL AT ATHENS **
BIBLE REFERENCE: Acts 17: 16-34

CHARACTERS: #CHRYSIPPUS, a Stoic philosopher
#ATHENAGORAS, an Epicurean philosopher
DIONYSIUS, a member of the Areopagus Council

DAMARIS, a Christian convert PAUL

Paul and Silas travelled from Thessalonica to Berea. But Paul was anxious to go to Athens, the intellectual center of the Greco-Roman world. His stay there proved to be as frustrating as any experience in his life. To be patronized was almost worse for Paul than to be beaten and imprisoned. Chrysippus and Athenagoras are imaginary characters, but their types are implied in Luke's text. The Areopagus was an old religious and cultural body. After having become almost obsolete it had recovered Its prestige under Roman rule.

(CHRYSIPPUS, ATHENAGORAS AND DIONYSIUS ARE WALKING ACROSS THE AGORA, THE MAIN BUSINESS CENTER OF ATHENS)

CHRYSIPPUS: Well, what did you think of our Jewish friend?

ATHENAGORAS: Paul? Impressive, I thought. A forceful speech, but with a lot of eastern absurdity mixed up in it.

CHRYSIPPUS: You didn't swallow the resurrection of this Jesus, I suppose. You Epicureans don't give an inch on immortality, do you?

ATHENAGORAS: We prefer our myths in books of fiction, not dressed up as history. For an educated man with a good mind, Paul believes some remarkable things.

CHRYSIPPUS: You're very quiet, Dionysius. What did you think?

DIONYSIUS: You really want to know? What I heard today was the first true message of hope that ever got through to me. I don't know what to believe about Paul yet, or about Jesus. I only know I have to find out more. If it is even half true, it's the most important thing that ever happened in the history of mankind.

CHRYSIPPUS: Come now! Don't get carried away?

DIONYSIUS: Why not? In God's name, Chrysippus, you and I have hung around Athens, discussing every dead philosophical idea, for so many years that it sickens me. Here comes a man who is real, and tells us from his own experience that God cares—God is love—

ATHENAGORAS: But is the experience real? I'm sure Paul believes it, but you know what these easterners are like.

CHRYSIPPUS: There he is, talking to that woman. Who is she?

DIONYSIUS: That's Damaris. She has a flax import business. Paul is in the canvas trade. He has been lodging at her home.

CHRYSIPPUS: A tradesman philosopher! That's something new.

ATHENAGORAS: (AS PAUL AND DAMARIS ENTER) Paul—excuse me for interrupting, madam, but we were just talking about your friend. My name is Athenagoras, and this is Chrysippus. I think you know Dionysius. That was a very able talk you gave, Paul.

PAUL: Thank you. Talk is like seed. The important thing is where it falls, and what fruit it bears.

ATHENAGORAS: You certainly scattered some unusual seed today. Your argument flew around like a sparrow, scavenging a little from every religion.

PAUL: Then it should be suitable for an Athenian audience, sir. There are more dead religions here than in the rest of the Empire, I would say.

CHRYSIPPUS: That is offensive, Jew! Don't forget that you are enjoying our city's hospitality. What right have you—

PAUL: I mean no offence. I say what God commands me, in Jesus' name and through the power of the Spirit. I bear you no ill will, but today I have spoken to men who seem to be all intellect and no heart, no lifeblood. If you patronize my Lord and Savior, it is a waste of time to talk to you.

DIONYSIUS: Paul, may I—

PAUL: Come with me, Dionysius! I watched you at the Council. I know that you are seeking for Jesus, and are called to follow him.

DAMARIS: Come with us to my home. Several others are gathering there to hear more from Paul.

CHRYSIPPUS: Well! Another new sect! I didn't know you went in for eastern fads.

PAUL: Chrysippus, I pray from the bottom of my heart that you will one day find out how blind you are. May Jesus come to you both in his love, and enter your hearts.

CHRYSIPPUS: Goodbye, Dionysius. Be careful what lies you swallow. This man would outtalk Socrates. (PAUL, DAMARIS, AND DIONYSIUS GO OUT) Remarkable! I'm all in favor of new approaches, but—

ATHENAGORAS: I can see what Dionysius means. The man is sincere. If it were not for the fairy tales, Jesus' teaching would be an original contribution to religious thought.

CHRYSIPPUS: Let us walk down to the gymnasium. It will be interesting to see how it struck some of the others.

Scene seventeen:

CORINTH: ROMAN JUSTICE +
BIBLE REFERENCE: Acts 18: 1-20. I Corinthians 8 , 11:17-24, and 13

Corinth was a big, cosmopolitan port. The church contained a mixture of converts from many religious backgrounds. Paul's letters to this church refer to many problems, but he obviously cared for the people deeply. Gallio came from a famous family, which included the philosopher Seneca and the poet Lucan. Like most Roman aristocrats, he was just and intelligent. His aim was to preserve peace in a turbulent community, without involving himself unnecessarily. Today the court room is packed with excitable Jews and Christians.

CHARACTERS: GALLIO, Governor of Achaea (Greece)
A ROMAN COURT OFFICIAL
SOSTHENES, Leader of the Synagogue
PAUL

OFFICIAL: Silence in the Court! All rise! (GALLIO ENTERS AND SITS)

GALLIO: You may be seated. (HE CONSULTS A DOCUMENT) This is an informal hearing of a complaint by the Jewish community against Saul, also called Paul, and his associates, of the sect known as Christians. I wish to establish whether there is a case which should be tried under Roman law. Who represents the Jews?

SOSTHENES: (RISING) I do, Your excellency. My name is Sosthenes, leader of the Synagogue.

GALLIO: Which of you is Paul?

PAUL: (STANDING) I am, Your Excellency.

GALLIO:	Sosthenes, state your case. Please be brief.
SOSTHENES:	It is very simple. For a long time we Jews have been loyal and lawabiding citizens of Corinth. Roman law offers us protection, and recognizes our rights. But for more than a year our community has been torn by disloyalty and dissension—ever since this Paul arrived.
GALLIO:	One moment. Paul, I understand that you are a Roman citizren.
PAUL:	I am, sir.
GALLIO:	But you are a Jew?
PAUL:	Yes, sir, by birth and upbringing—
SOSTHENES:	But a traitor and a renegade—
GALLIO:	Be silent! This Court will be conducted in an orderly manner. Answer only when I direct a question to you. Is that understood?
SOSTHENES:	I apologize, Your Excellency.
PAUL:	I am a Jew, sir, but I am a follower of Jesus, the Christ, the Son of God. He too lived as a Jew, but he taught us that love and faith have no limits of race.
GALLIO:	That hardly seems like a dangerous belief. What is your objection to Paul's teaching, Sosthenes?
SOSTHENES:	It is his behavior that has broken up our community. We keep to ourselves, and observe our own Law, which is precious in our eyes. This man ingratiated himself with some of our members and recruited them to his sect. We regard this Jesus as an impostor. Paul puts out a debased, cheap corruption of our belief. We demand that you—
GALLIO:	Stop! You do not demand anything, and I am not interested in your beliefs. What results of his actions do you object to?
SOSTHENES:	First he persuaded our leader to turn Christian. Then he hauled in half the riffraff of Corinth—dock slaves, loose women, criminals, to be a part of his wonderful church!

GALLIO: That is no concern of mine.

SOSTHENES: With respect, sir, if it imperils the peace of the city and our rights as Jews. Ask him whether his Christians—

PAUL: May I speak, sir?

GALLIO: Yes, Paul. In a few words, what is your reply to these charges?

PAUL: We are not disloyal. We have caused no upheaval. To us a Phrygian dockworker is equal to a Jewish rabbi or a Roman General. We preach love, joy, and peace to all. God does not look at us as Roman or Jew, rich or poor.

GALLIO: Thank you. There is no case here to be tried in a Roman court. Religious disagreement is as old as the human race. I am inclined to believe, Sosthenes, that the upheaval of which you speak has come from your party, not Paul's. But I offer no judgment, because it does not concern me as Governor. I urge you to solve your differences in a civilized manner. I warn you to avoid violence. That is all.

SOSTHENES: Your Excellency, I protest—

GALLIO: I did not invite you to speak again.

SOSTHENES: No, sir, but—

GALLIO: You are all dismissed.

OFFICIAL: Court dismissed! (A BUZZ OF COMMENT AS THEY ALL LEAVE)

GALLIO: Paul, I would like a word with you.

PAUL: Certainly, sir.

GALLIO: Sit down. I confess I am puzzled to find a man of your background mixed up in a revivalist movement. I would have placed you as a professor of some kind.

PAUL: You would have been right—if my life had not been changed by Jesus.

GALLIO: You knew this man?

PAUL:	Not in his lifetime. He appeared to me—
OFFICIAL:	(RUNNING IN) Excuse me, sir. There's trouble outside.
GALLIO:	What kind of trouble?
OFFICIAL:	That Sosthenes. There's a mixed crowd, and he isn't popular with some of them. He got into a fight—
GALLIO:	Is it out of hand? Are our men involved?
OFFICIAL:	No, sir. Just a brawl so far, but I thought you ought to know.
GALLIO:	Quite right, Metellus. Keep an eye on the situation, but don't interfere unless you have to. It's no concern of ours.
OFFICIAL:	Yes, sir. (HE GOES OUT)
GALLIO:	Part of your love and peace, Paul?
PAUL:	My friends are sworn to avoid violence. Jesus taught us to love our enemies.
GALLIO:	Then it's a good thing you have the Roman army to keep the peace.
OFFICIAL:	(ENTERING) The crowd has broken up, sir, but I think Sosthenes is hurt. He's lying in the street.
PAUL:	May I go and help him?
OFFICIAL:	I think some of your people are doing that—the ones who were in court.
GALLIO:	Loving the enemy? All right, go and help. I hope we will have another chance to talk. But keep your people out of trouble. I understand that your Jesus finished up on a cross.
PAUL:	He didn't finish. His work has just begun. We face trouble if it comes, but we don't cause it. Thank you for impartiality, sir. I would like to talk with you again.

Scene eighteen:

PROBLEMS AND OPPORTUNITIES IN A YOUNG CHURCH *

BIBLE REFERENCE: Acts 18: 1-22 and Paul's letters

CHARACTERS:
PAUL
CRISPUS, formerly leader of the Synagogue
GAIUS ((I Corinthians 1: 14)
STEPHANAS and his family (I Corinthians 1: 16)
SILAS
TIMOTHY
PHOEBE (Romans 16: 1)
EPAINETUS (Romans 16: 5)

The scene is imaginary, but it pulls together different parts of the Bible text. it follows closely on the last scene. Paul baptized the household of Stephanas (I Corinthians 1: 16). His home could well have been the church's meetingplace. Or It could have been the home of Justus (Acts 18: 7).Here in a Christian home a group of members discuss the problems which they had to deal with in a cosmopolitan church. 'Our colleague Sosthenes' (I Corinthians 1: 14) may be the same as Sosthenes of the last scene, but we cannot be sure.

In the living room of a home in Corinth Paul is sitting with a group of his new friends. Phoebe enters from another room.

PAUL: How is Sosthenes, Phoebe?

PHOEBE: Much better. He seems to have relaxed since Silas prayed with him. We made him drink some milk. I think he will sleep soon.

STEPHANAS: Come and join us, unless you are needed in there.

PHOEBE: Your wife and daughter will look after him, Stephanas.

PAUL: We need to think hard about what happened today, and how it will affect our work. Now that we have shared in the Eucharist, does any of you have a comment?

EPAINETUS: May I speak? You know I was the first to be baptized here in Corinth, five years ago. I've seen this trouble coming ever since. I don't think we can run away from it. Jesus told us to baptize all nations, and in Corinth that means just about every people you can think of. So, let us face it, we clash with orthodox Jews.

STEPHANAS: And we have to stand up for the truth.

TIMOTHY: Truth tempered with love. When Phoebe and Priscilla bandaged Sosthenes' head today they achieved more than a month of sermons.

AQUILA: What worries me is the Jewish tactics, getting us in trouble with the Romans. Priscilla and I have already had to leave Rome. We don't want to be hounded from city to city.

SILAS: Most Roman officials have a lot of common sense. They can be rough in their methods—Paul and I know that; but I must say I was encouraged by Gallio today.

PHOEBE: We have had no trouble with the authorities in Cenchreae. I suppose we are better off than you in Corinth, because we have very few Jews living there.

STEPHANAS: You're very quiet, Paul.

PAUL: I wanted to listen before telling you what I think. I feel deeply thankful for what the Lord did today. Not for the shedding of blood, but for the chance to witness, even a little, before a man like Gallio, and for the fact that Sosthenes is here in Stephanas' home. Corinth seems made for trouble, but it is also full of opportunities. Where there is vitality you will find hatred, not a dead wall of polite cynicism such as I met with in Athens. I agree with Timothy that tying up Sosthenes' head was a wonderful piece of witness. Faith may bring us to Jesus, but the witness of love is beyond price. Eloquence, prophecy, almsgiving, even martyrdom—only if love shines through them will they win souls. Here in Corinth, with Venus' temple breeding vice on one side, and the dock slums on the other, we need to show a patient, selfeffacing love. Let us treat Sosthenes with courtesy and trust. We won't take advantage of him, far less gloat over what happened today. Avoid quarrels, and concentrate on what we share with our Jewish brothers and sisters. Forgive them for bringing us to court. Perhaps that will win them over, so that we can seek for truth together. I worry sometimes about our emphasis on prophecy and on speaking with tongues. All our knowledge is incomplete—waiting to grow up, as it were. We can only see a blurred reflection in a mirror, but if we hold fast to the gospel we will one day see reality, whole and clear, and through our faith others will be led to see it. We need faith—plenty of it. We need hope, because the road is hard. Most of all we need love. That was so clear today in the case of Sosthenes.

STEPHANAS' WIFE: (ENTERING) Paul, Sosthenes would like to speak to you.

PAUL: I will come at once. (THEY GO OUT)

AQUILA: That man is a giant.

EPAINETUS: Just when things seem too bad to be true he cuts through to the essentials, and you see it all differently. (A KNOCK)

PRISCILLA: I expect that is Crispus. (SHE LETS HIM IN)

SILAS: What news?

CRISPUS: Everything is quiet. I called on Nathanael. He told me the synagogue people are upset about what happened to Sosthenes.

TIMOTHY: Do they know where he is?

CRISPUS: Yes. Several of them saw us carry him away. They know we are trying to help, and they are grateful.

PRISCILLA: What is the next step, Crispus?

SOSTHENES: Some friends of Sosthenes will be here soon, to take him home if he can be moved.

PHOEBE: He should be ready, unless he falls asleep. Who started the riot?

CRISPUS: Nobody seems to know. Sosthenes has a lot of enemies. Perhaps it just happened, with noone really planning it.

PHOEBE: When trouble arises everyone turns on a Jew. Have you eaten, Crispus?

CRISPUS: No, I'm famished.

STEPAHANAS' WIFE: We kept some supper for you. Here! (SHE BRINGS IT TO HIM)

CRISPUS: Thank you. (HE SEES MEAT ON THE PLATE) Oh, I—

AQUILA: Worried about the meat?

CRISPUS: It's no use. Every time I eat in a Gentile home the Law comes back and hits me.

TIMOTHY:	That's only natural. I wish you could have heard Paul just now. He was telling us—here he is! (PAUL ENTERS)
CRISPUS:	Paul, I need a lesson in charity. I almost refused to eat meat, without even asking where it was bought.
PAUL:	(LAUGHING) From head of the synagogue to membership in our hotchpotch of a church is a big step; but the only rules which matter are those that your heart and conscience tell you to keep. It took me time to learn that. We need to reverence the bread and wine of his supper more and more, and not to care about what else we eat.
CRISPUS:	It tastes good, Stephanas!
STEPHANAS:	And you needn't worry. My wife doesn't buy from pagan temple shops.
AQUILA:	Crispus tells us that Sosthenes' friends are coming to fetch him.
PAUL:	Good! He began the day hating us bitterly. I have found out that he believed some strange lies about our church. It's terrifying how two sets of people, each believing in God, can live in the same town and work up a storm of hatred and prejudice. At least we have broken down part of that. There won't be such a wall between us any more. Sosthenes is a good man, a very loyal Jew. Perhaps one day he will understand, and come to Jesus. I will go and tell him that his friends are on the way.

Scene nineteen:

THE RIOT AT EPHESUS +
BIBLE REFERENCE: Acts 19: 8-41

CHARACTERS: PAUL
AQUILA
PRISCILLA, his wife
GAIUS
ARISTARCHUS

Paul went back to Jerusalem, but soon set out again for Asia. In Ephesus he met the same kind of opposition which had led to his imprisonment at Philippi, but this time on a larger scale. Just as Stratford-on-Avon thrives on its Shakespeare

trade, so Ephesus grew rich partly through the cult of the goddess Diana.
You would not be popular in Stratford if you proved that Shakespeare did not
write the plays attributed to him; and Paul infuriated the silversmiths of Ephesus
by denouncing Diana worship. Jesus had done something similar at the Temple in
Jerusalem, denouncing the profits made by those who sold animals for sacrifice.
The scene is imaginary, but it enables us to act out an important, vivid event. Paul
might well stay at the home of Aquila and Priscilla if they were at Ephesus during
his visit. They were his hosts in Corinth (I Corinthians 16: 18). Alexander may be
the same man as 'the coppersmith' of 2 Timothy 4: 14.

(AQUILA, PRISCILLA, AND PAUL ARE IN AQUILA'S HOME. THE THEATRE IS CLOSE BY,
AND WE HEAR CONTINUOUS SHOUTS: 'Great is Diana of the Ephesians!' 'Bring Paul
here!' etc.)

PAUL: Let me go! I—

AQUILA: No, Paul. You know we all agreed—

PAUL: To protect me, and allow Gaius and Aristarchus to be lynched?

AQUILA: To do what is best for the church, not for any one of us.

PAUL: I watched Stephen die, stoned by a mob. Do you think I can let it
               happen again?

PRISCILLA: They make a lot of noise, but this is a Roman city. Things will calm
               down—

PAUL: Jerusalem was a Roman city. Let me go, Aquila! I want to be Jesus'
               wiiness.

PRISCILLA: You cannot go back on what we all decided
(LOUD SHOUTS OF 'Silence!' IN THE THEATRE. 'In the name of the Emperor, silence!'
AT LENGTH THE MOB STOPS SHOUTING)

AQUILA: What's happening? They have stopped—

PAUL: Some Roman has arrived. Whoever told that crowd to be quiet is a
               brave man.
(KNOCK. GAIUS AND ARISTARCHUS ENTER)

AQUILA: Thank God you're both safe! Come in!

PAUL: Are you hurt?

ARISTARCHUS: Nobody was hurt. I think the worst is over.

GAIUS: We were hurried off the stage by Roman police.

PAUL: Go back to the beginning.

GAIUS: Well, you probably know that the riot began with the silversmiths. Several of them came to my house, led by a man named Demetrius. They expected to find Paul.

ARISTARCHUS: You had left less than an hour earlier.

GAIUS: They were out for blood, and they forced us to go to the theatre. We weren't hurt—just hustled along. But it was terrifying going into that place. I thought of what you have said about the armor of God. Talk about needing the shield of faith!

ARISTARCHUS: We had managed to tell Tychicus to follow you here, and warn Aquila to keep you out of the way.

PAUL: That was generous, but it was wrong.

GAIUS: No, Paul. It was plain common sense. If you had been there, none of us would have got out alive.

ARISTARCHUS: When we arrived, the theatre was amost full. More people were pressing in. They were working themselves into a frenzy. Then that man Alexander got on the stage—

PAUL: The coppersmith?

GAIUS: Yes. Nobody would listen to him. I think he was saying that the Jews had nothing to do with your attack on the Diana cult, but he may have trying to help us. Anyway, what the crowd wanted was you. Demetrius got up and harangued them about you being the enemy of Ephesus. He pointed at us, and shouted that if they couldn't find Paul they could teach his friends a lesson.

ARISTARCHUS: Just then the police arrived, and behind them some troops. Was I glad to see a Roman soldier! They got between us and Demetrius, then edged us back and out behind the stage. I found myself on Harbor Street. They told me to get lost.

GAIUS: I was behind Aristarchus. As I left I heard a Roman with a voice like Mithras' bull, shouting: 'Silence for His Excellency the Town Clerk!'

PAUL: So you were saved by the Romans! They crucified Jesus, and now they rescue us.

AQUILA: You knew this might happen. You can't hurt the merchants' profits and not cause trouble.

PAUL: But it was not I who faced the mob.

AQUILA: Do you think anyone is going to call you a coward? You have risked death over and over, and it was our decision to keep you here. The question is what next?

ARISTARCHUS: We should call a church meeting, tonight if possible. But where?

PRISCILLA: Here. We are used to risks.

PAUL: O, my friends! I seem to bring trouble wherever I go.

GAIUS: You preach the cross. That means trouble, as well as joy and salvation.

PAUL: Very well. Let us meet tonight. I must go and pray. Perhaps I ought to leave Ephesus and let things die down. I have promised to go back to Macedonia.

ARISTARCHUS: Remember that you can stay with my parents in Thessalonica any time you wish.

PAUL: I know. I have dedicated friends in city after city. But I must be clear in my mind what is right. I hate to run away from here because of danger.

AQUILA: Leave the decision to the church. We will call the meeting for an hour after sunset.

Scene Twenty:

FAREWELL AT MILETUS (improvise)
BIBLE REFERENCE: ACTS 20: 15-38

CHARACTERS: PAUL and all of the friends listed in 20: 4

This is an improvised scene. Paul explains his eagerness to visit Jerusalem (v.16). He asks for reports from the cities represented by the people who are present. Look up Revelation, chapters 2 and 3. Assign different cities to your actors, and ask each to give a short report from his or her church. Then Paul and his companions describe the situation in Macedonia, and the plot attempted against him in Greece (v. 3). Preparing these reports will call for careful reading and imagination.

Paul says goodbye, using the material given in verses 15-38. He blesses all of his friends, and they embrace and exchange good wishes

Scene twenty one:

THE WARNING OF AGABUS +
BIBLE REFERENCE: ACTS 21: 8-14

CHARACTERS: PAUL
                     LUKE
                     PHILIP
                     HIS WIFE (and four daughters if you wish to include them)
                     AGABUS

Paul has reached the port of Caesarea, on his way to Jerusalem. He is staying at the home of Philip, who like Stephen was one of the seven deacons. Agabus acts like some of the Old Testament prophets (Isaiah 20: 2, Jeremiah 13: 1, Ezekiel 4: 1) He performs a sign which is a symbol of God's will for the future.

(ALL THE CHARACTERS EXCEPT AGABUS ARE SEATED IN PHILIP'S HOME)

PAUL: My friends, it is wonderful to be here with you, This is a very happy day for me, whatever the future holds.

PHILIP' WIFE: And for us, Paul. We have longed to meet you, ever since we heard of your baptism at Damascus.

PAUL: But before that I was your bitter enemy. Oh, Philip! I can't forget that Stephen and you were close friends.

PHILIP: I don't forget it either; but Jesus used Stephen's martyrdom to bring you to us. None of us bears you any ill will.

PAUL: Let us share our memories. I will tell you what happened on the road to Damascus. Luke can testify to what made him one of us, and what adventures he has seen. Then let all of you tell us about your lives. You begin, Philip!

(PHILIP DESCRIBES THE EVENTS OF ACTS 8: 4-40. YOU COULD IMPROVISE STORIES TOLD BY HIS WIFE AND DAUGHTERS, OR HAVE AGABUS KNOCK AS PHILIP FINISHES. ONE OF THE GIRLS OPENS THE DOOR)

PHILIP:	Come in, Agabus!
PAUL:	Agabus! It must be seven years. (THEY EMBRACE)
AGABUS:	Yes, at Antioch.
PAUL:	How are you?
AGABUS:	Well, thank God. I have heard so much about your adventures. You have been through hard times.
PAUL:	The joys have far outweighed the sufferings. This is Luke, my friend and companion. Luke, Agabus is revered for his gifts as a prophet.
LUKE:	I know. You predicted the famine, Agabus, didn't you?
AGABUS:	And you and Barnabas took our gifts to Jerusalem. It seems so long ago—and so much has happened.
PHILIP:	Great things! Now Paul is on his way to Jerusalem.
AGABUS:	I heard that. In fact, it is the reason for my coming here.
PAUL:	To go with me?
AGABUS:	No, Paul, though I would gladly do that. I am here to warn you that it will be dangerous.
PAUL:	What we do is always dangerous.
AGABUS:	Yes, but this is different. Give me your belt!
PAUL:	My belt? Why—
AGABUS:	Give it to me! (HE TAKES THE BELT, AND BEGINS TO TIE HIS HANDS AND FEET) I had a vision two nights ago. The Spirit told me clearly: 'The man to whom this girdle belongs will be bound like this by the Jews in Jerusalem, and handed over to the Gentiles.'
PHILIP'S WIFE:	Paul, if this is true—
LUKE:	It's a warning. Ought you not to take notice of it?
PAUL:	Thank you, Agabus. You were right to come here.

PHILIP:	Will you leave Judaea?
PAUL:	Oh, no. I will go to Jerusalem, as I planned.
PHILIP:	But Paul—
PAUL:	Of course we must all pray tonight, and be sure that it is God's will. But in my heart I am sure. Don't cry, Melanippe! You all know that Jesus turned his face towards Jerusalem, understanding what faced him there. None of you would hesitate if you were in my shoes. Nor do I think that God means me to die there. I think he wants me to go to Rome—which I have never yet seen.
PHILIP'S WIFE:	Now that Agabus is here you can all eat supper. But don't stop talking! There is so much more that we all want to hear. Come on, girls!

Scene twenty-two:

DANGER AT JERUSALEM
(read first, then choose scenes to act)
BIBLE REFERENCE: Acts 21-23

This series of incidents illustrates three important elements in the story of the young Church. (1) The violent hatred which some Jews felt towards Paul. They thought that he was a traitor to his faith, because he had become a leader in a heretical sect in which gentiles were mixed with Jews. (2) Paul's courage, and his witness to the gospel under the threat of danger. (3) The determination of the Romans to see justice done. The book of Acts contains many examples of these things. Here they are brought together in an exciting story.

FIRST EPISODE

CHARACTERS: PAUL
FOUR JEWISH CHRISTIANS (verse 24)
A CROWD OF JEWS
CLAUDIUS LYSIAS, Roman Commander
ROMAN SOLDIERS
CENTURION

Improvise this episode. The Praetorium, headquarters of the Roman garrison, was next to the Temple courtyard. Paul is walking across the yard with four Jewish Christians. They are talking about finding the official who can confirm that they have taken their vows and been purified, so that they can enter the Temple. Paul did all he could to conciliate hostile Jewish opinion in Jerusalem, where he was suspected of showing too little respect for the Law.

Several Jews see him. They were 'Jews of Asia', who perhaps recognized Paul from some previous encounter. They cry out:

Look! There's Paul—Traitor!—Are you sure?— I'm certain.— Who are those men with him?—Gentiles!—Paul is bringing gentiles into the Temple!— Get the traitor!—Drag them all outside!—Lynch Paul!

There is a rush towards Paul, and a scuffle. One of Paul's companions runs to the steps of the praetorium, shouting for help. The Commander, with a Centurion and some soldiers, runs down the steps. Paul is tied up and lifted through the angry, protesting crowd.

SECOND EPISODE

CHARACTERS: The same as in the first episode.

  With the crowd still shouting, 'Kill him!' Paul is set down at the top of the steps.

PAUL: Colonel, may I have a chance to—

CLAUDIUS: You speak Greek, do you? I thought you were Egyptian.

PAUL: Egyptian? Why did you think that?

CLAUDIUS: We were told to keep an eye out for an Egyptian terrorist.

PAUL: (LAUGHING) I've been called many things in my lifetime, but never that. I am a Jew, sir, from Tarsus in Cilicia, a citizen of a great city.

CLAUDIUS: Well, what do you want?

PAUL: These people also made a mistake. They thought I was breaking the Law by taking gentiles into the Temple. If you let me speak to them, I think they will quiet down.

CLAUDIUS: All right, go ahead! At least it will show me what this is all about. (HE YELLS TO THE CROWD FOR SILENCE) That's better! Now listen to what this man has to say.

(PAUL DELIVERS A SPEECH BASED ON Acts 22: 1-21. READ IT, OR IMPROVISE A SCENE BUILT AROUND IT, WITH INTERRUPTIONS)

THIRD EPISODE

CHARACTERS: PAUL
                    CLAUDIUS LYSIAS
                    #REGULUS, a Centurion
                    SOLDIERS

Soldiers pushed Paul into a room at the top of the stairs. The Commander and Centurion entered with him.

CLAUDIUS: That's right. In here. Centurion, keep a section of your men on the steps. Nobody is to come up.

REGULUS: Yes, sir. Calvus, form Number Two Section halfway down the steps. Report to me here if you have any trouble. (SOME SOLDIERS GO OUT) What about this prisoner, sir?

CLAUDIUS: Yes, we have to deal with him. You seem to be the cause of a lot of trouble, Jew. I'm not convinced that we've got to the bottom of it. Centurion, tie him up and lash him! Then he'll be more in the mood to give us some straight answers. I'm going back outside,

REGULUS: Yes, sir. Tie him to that table! (SOLDIERS BEGIN TO DO SO)

PAUL: Centurion, do you intend to flog a Roman citizen without trial?

REGULUS: Don't give me that! Are you crazy, pretending to be a Roman? You could be flogged to death for that.

PAUL: You and your Commander could be in bad trouble if you hurt me. I want to avoid that if I can.

REGULUS: Are you serious? Here, Metellus, tell the Commander he's needed. At the double! (A SOLDIER RUNS OUT) You'd better be speaking the truth, sir, or I wouldn't like to be in your shoes.

CLAUDIUS: (ENTERING) What is it, Centurion?

REGULUS: I think you should talk to this man, sir, before we lash him.

PAUL: I have been telling the centurion that since I am a Roman citizen it would cause you both—

CLAUDIUS: You a Roman?

PAUL: Naturally you will want to verify that. I have my diploma at my lodging. I am registered at Tarsus in Cilicia.

CLAUDIUS: How could someone like you afford to buy citizenship?

PAUL: I was born a citzen, Colonel. My father was one of the Duumviri in our city before my birth.

CLAUDIUS: And it cost me three years' pay! I have to believe you, I suppose. I'm sorry we handled you roughly—

PAUL: You saved my life, and I'm grateful. Now I am saving you from flogging a Roman without a court order.

CLAUDIUS: Look, sir, if you had to keep order in a place like this you'd soon find that legal forms don't mean much. It's a nightmare—all the fanatics in Jerusalem! I'm sorry, I know you're a Jew, but if you'd seen what happens here—

PAUL: (REMEMBERING HIS OWN PART IN THE DEATH OF STEPHEN) Yes, I know what you mean. What do you want to do with me now?

CLAUDIUS: These cases involving religion are impossible. We'll have to hold you for your own safety. Tomorrow i'll know whether a charge is being brought against you. Probably it will blow over,

PAUL: It may, but I doubt it.

CLAUDIUS: Meanwhile I'll have a room prepared for you, and check on your story.

PAUL: Thank you both. It's not the first time I have owed my life to Rome. If Pontius Pilate had been a man like you—

CLAUDIUS: Pilate? Wasn't he Prefect here in Tiberius' time?

PAUL: Yes. Perhaps I can tell you about him one day. But you probably want to get me out of here.

CLAUDIUS: Yes. Please come this way. We'll put you on the side of the building away from the Temple. Regulus, watch the situation here until I come back!

FOURTH EPISODE

CHARACTERS: PAUL
#JONATHAN, his nephew
CLAUDIUS LYSIAS
SOLDIER

Soon after the last episode Paul is in a small room, writing at a table. A SOLDIER opens the door and brings in JONATHAN, a boy about sixteen.

SOLDIER: Visitor for you, sir. He says it's urgent.

PAUL: Thank you, Metellus. Jonathan! (THEY EMBRACE)

JONATHAN: Uncle Paul, I had to come. I never thought they'd let me in.

PAUL: Get your breath back, and tell me what has happened.

SOLDIER: The Commander is on his way up, sir. He gave us orders to take the boy to you. I'll be outside the door if you need me.

PAUL: Thank you. (SOLDIER GOES OUT) Now, Jonathan.

JONATHAN: There's a plot to kill you, Uncle. I heard about it from Phinehas Bar-Tolmai, whose father is one of the Sanhedrin.

PAUL: What kind of plot? I know that there are many people who hate what I have done—or what they think I have done.

JONATHAN: This is serious. I told James and some of the elders. They agreed that I had the best chance to get to you.

(SOLDIER OPENS THE DOOR, STANDS AT ATTENTION, AND LETS CLAUDIUS PASS)

CLAUDIUS: Wait outside. (SOLDIER GOES OUT) What's the trouble?

PAUL: This is my sister's son, Jonathan, a student here in Jerusalem. He says there is a plot to kill me. I think you can rely on him. He was sent here by our Church's leaders.

CLAUDIUS: You were quite right to come, Jonathan. Try to give us the facts simply and briefly.

JONATHAN: What I heard was this, sir. Forty Jews have taken an oath to kill my uncle. They say they won't eat or drink until he is dead.

CLAUDIUS: They may be very hungry before they're through. How do they mean to reach him?

JONATHAN: They went to the High Priest this morning. The plan was to ask for Uncle Paul to be brought in for questioning tomorrow. On the way they will kill him in the street.

CLAUDIUS: The part about the Council is true. The request from the High Priest came an hour ago. Thank you, Jonathan. Don't tell anyone you came here. We'll let you out at the back. I promise you no Jewish gang is going to catch my troops unawares. Now run along! Get in touch with me here if you have to, but keep out of the way—mouth shut!

PAUL: The Lord bless you, Jonathan! I will send you a message when I can. Tell your mother I pray for her every day. (JONATHAN GOES OUT)

CLAUDIUS: A good lad.

PAUL: Yes, he is. What will you do now?

CLAUDIUS: I didn't want to tell you in front of the boy. It's better he shouldn't know, in case they catch him. You're leaving Jerusalem, Paul.

PAUL: Alone?

CLAUDIUS: Not on your life! If there's one thing I can't stand it's a lynching mob. You're going to the Governor at Caesarea, and you will arrive with a whole skin, if it takes half my troops to get you there.

PAUL: Thank you, Colonel. I am at your disposal any time. I would like to say how much I appreciate your concern and your professionalism.

CLAUDIUS: It's my job. Apart from that I am intrigued by you. By the way, I checked; you are a citizen!

PAUL: There's only one thing I regret.

CLAUDIUS: What's that?

PAUL: That I won't have time to tell you about Pontius Pilate.

Scene twenty-three:

PAUL BEFORE A KING AND A GOVERNOR +
BIBLE REFERENCE: ACTS 25 AND 26.

CHARACTERS: FESTUS, Governor of Judaea
KING HEROD AGRIPPA
BERNICE, his sister
ROMAN OFFICERS

JEWISH LEADERS

At Caesarea Paul was brought before the Prefect Felix. For two years he was held there, living comfortably and able to see his friends. Luke's guess is that Felx hoped for a bribe to set him free. Then a new Prefect arrived, Festus. Paul's accusers had followed him from Jerusalem and demanded that he be brought to trial. Festus consulted King Herod Agrippa II, the puppet king who under Rome's supervision governed parts of Judaea. Agrippa was Jewish, and Festus hoped that he would shed light on this perplexing case which was causing so many passions in Jerusalem. We are in an audience chamber. Paul stands on one side, guarded by soldiers. Festus escorts Agrippa and Bernice to chairs in the center.

FESTUS: Your Majesty, will you sit here? And you, Princess, on this side? (THEY SIT. PAUL AND HIS GUARDS REMAIN STANDING)

AGRIPPA: Is this the prisoner Paul?

FESTUS: Yes, sir. I will go over the facts of the case briefly. As I told you, the Jewish authorities approached me as soon as I arrived here, demanding that I put this man on trial. They wanted a death sentence. In fact they had plotted to assassinate him illegally. That shows how strongly they feel. But Paul, quite within his rights, has refused to be tried in Jerusalem. He has appealed to Caesar. That puts me in an awkward position, and I hope you can help me. I have no clear charges to send to Rome. So I thought that a preliminary hearing today might help to clear my mind.

AGRIPPA: I and my sister wish to hear him explain this faith of his which has made such an impact.

FESTUS: Paul, you have our permission to speak.

(PAUL DELIVERS THE SPEECH FROM ACTS 26: 2-23. EITHER READ IT, OR MAKE UP YOUR OWN VERSION)

FESTUS:	A great deal of that is crazy talk, Paul. Too much booklearning must have driven you mad.
PAUL:	Ask King Agrippa whether he thinks me mad, sir. He knows the background of my story. I can speak freely in front of him.
AGRIPPA:	He's right, Festus. I can see how this Jesus movement arose out of Jewish beliefs, but I'm not surprised that the High Priest is upset over it.
PAUL:	You see, Your Excellency? I am very far from mad. I am speaking the truth, plain and simple.
BERNICE:	We have heard accounts of this Jesus. I had no idea how far the movement has spread.
FESTUS:	If these Jewish representatives have their way it won't spread any further.
PAUL:	Nothing can stop the spreading of the good news! You can silence me, but you cannot muzzle our Church.
AGRIPPA:	It's a fascinating story, Paul.
PAUL:	Fascinating? Yes, I suppose you can call it that. The vital thing is that it is true. You know our Scriptures and the message of the prophets. If you accept what they say, surely you can—
AGRIPPA:	Wait a minute! Festus, I think you had better take us away from this man. He's dangerous!
BERNICE:	No, Agrippa! I want to hear more.
AGRIPPA:	It's not safe, my dear. With his eloquence he'll be turning us into Christians, if we stay any longer.
PAUL:	I wish to God I could turn you to Jesus. I wish that both of you, and you also, Festus, could share all that Jesus has given to me, and stand where I stand—except for these chains!
BERNICE:	Why is he kept a prisoner, Festus?
AGRIPPA:	Yes, Governor. I'd like an answer to that. You surely don't consider his preaching a criminal offence.

FESTUS:	No, sir. As far as I can see, no formal charge against him would stick for a moment, though of course I felt bound to take seriously the strong pressure brought to bear by his influential accusers. Paul would have been discharged if he had not appealed to Caesar. Once that appeal has been made by a citizen, it is irreversible.
AGRIPPA:	A pity.
PAUL:	No, sir, it is not a pity. It will enable me to preach the good news in Rome.
BERNICE:	You really believe in this Jesus, don't you?
PAUL:	It is the only reality in my life. Jesus is my Savior, and yours. I pray fervently that you will understand that one day, and give yourself to him.
BERNICE:	Are you sure that we must go, brother?
AGRIPPA:	Yes, my dear. We can't afford to get involved in a hornet's nest like this.
FESTUS:	Will you come this way, Your Majesty?

Scene twenty-four:

SHIPWRECK + (but try it)
BIBLE REFERENCE: Acts 27

CHARACTERS: PAUL
#TROPHIMUS, Captain of the ship
JULIUS, in charge of the prisoners
#BALBUS, owner of the ship
BOATSWAIN
SAILORS and PRISONERS

Read the chapter first to familiarize yourself with the story. The corn ships plying from the eastern Mediterranean to Rome were the largest vessels of that time. Ship's Captains tried to avoid taking them to sea after mid-September, since the weather then became treacherous. I have given names to the Captain and owner. Before you begin, imagine the tension and panic, especially among the helpless prisoners, who know that the crew will save themselves first.

It is nighttime on board a large sailing ship. Everyone, from the Captain and the

— 228 —

owner to the prisoners shackled below deck, is terrified and exhausted. For two weeks rough seas and high winds have left the ship helpless, since she left the southern coast of Crete. Now she is close to land, which presents a new and terrible danger. Paul is on deck, with the owner, the Captain, and the Roman Centurion in charge of the prisoners. A sailor is taking a sounding at one side.

TROPHIMUS: What is the sounding?

SAILOR: Twenty fathoms, sir.

BALBUS: Twenty! That means land not far off. We'll lose the ship.

JULIUS: More important than the ship are my two hundred and fifty prisoners.

TROPHIMUS: For God's sake stop arguing! What's the sounding now?

SAILOR: Fifteen, sir.

TROPHIMUS: (SHOUTING) Drop the four stern anchors! Boatswain, can you hear me?

BOATSWAIN: (OFF STAGE) Ay, ay, sir. Stern party, drop your four anchors!

JULIUS: Will they hold us?

TROPHIMUS: They may and they may not. Just leave me alone! I am Captain of this ship, and I am trying to get you ashore alive.

PAUL: (TO ONE SIDE OF THE GROUP) We will all get to shore alive.

BALBUS: What do you mean?

PAUL: I know it. God has assured me.

BALBUS: What's going on there in the bows?

TROPHIMUS: I can't see a thing.

BOATSWAIN: (RUNNING IN) Sir, some of the crew are lowering the boat. They pretended to drop the forward anchors, but—

JULIUS: Lowering the boat? You mean they're trying to sneak away?

PAUL: Stop them! Unless they stay in the ship everyone may die.

TROPHIMUS: Boatswain, cut the boat loose!

BOATSWAIN: Ay, ay, sir. (HE RUNS OFF)

BALBUS: That's our only boat, Captain. Why do you listen to this man?

TROPHIMUS: Because he has more guts and common sense than the rest of you put together. Thanks, Paul! I think we saved a mutiny. (BOATSWAIN RETURNS) Did you manage it?

BOATSWAIN: Yes, sir. Just in time. I put two men under arrest.

JULIUS: (LAUGHING) Two more prisoners! What worries me is that some of these brutes down below may make a break for it. I'll have to be ready to kill them if there's danger of that.

PAUL: Don't touch them! We will all reach the shore alive, and none of them can get away.

BALBUS: I suppose God told you that.

PAUL: Yes. He has told me what we should do, and what will happen.

JULIUS: The storm seems a little less fierce. You have no idea where we are, Captain?

TROPHIMUS: After drifting for fourteen days? I've told you, we can be anywhere south of Crete—Carthage, Cyrene, the Syrtes—

BALBUS: So what is the great Paul's plan?

TROPHIMUS: Yes, Paul. What do you want me to do?

PAUL: First, distribute as much food as the men can eat. We're all weak from hunger, and this is a chance to eat before morning. If we need to swim ashore we will need all of our strength.

TROPHIMUS: You're right again. I'll see to it. Boatswain! (HE GOES OUT)

BALBUS: Of all the crazy situations I ever saw this is the strangest! A prisoner gives orders to the three of us.

PAUL: They are not my orders. Jesus sent me here to save your lives.

BALBUS: Jesus? That's a new one. Who's he?

JULIUS: Paul has been telling me about Jesus ever since he was handed over to me at Caesarea. I've never had a prisoner like this. I'd give a year of my pension to see him set free.

PAUL: And I would give my life to see you accept Jesus in your heart, Julius. As for me, he means me to go to Rome and witness for him. What happens after that is in his hands.

BALBUS: It's beginning to get light. (TROPHIMUS RETURNS WITH A TRAY OF FOOD AND CUPS) Any clues to where we are, Captain?

TROPHIMUS: No, but the lookout thinks there's a sandy bay southwest of us. Here, eat some of this.

PAUL: Have the prisoners had food?

TROPHIMUS: Don't worry! Everyone has some. Your friend Luke is helping down below. We'll dump everything overboard, and drop an anchor an hour after dawn.

BALBUS: Can you save the ship?

TROPHIMUS: Not a hope. If we stay out here another day the anchors will drag. We'll end up on those rocks. The way the wind is now we might make it through the currents to that cove. You can see it now. If we don't, we all drown. If we do, we beach the ship and jump.

PAUL: We shall all be safe. Don't worry about the prisoners, Julius! I will go and break bread with them. I will tell them how you thought you might have to kill them, but that you changed your mind. I promise you that they will not try to escape. When we come close to the shore, Luke and I will help those who are sick. Now eat and drink with thankful hearts, my friends! If we show no fear, the crew and prisoners will follow us. (PAUL GOES OUT)

BALBUS: I can't believe it! I hope I never have another voyage like this.

TROPHIMUS: Without that man we'd all be dead. Who this Jesus is I have no idea, but Paul—you can't help respecting a man like that.

JULIUS:	He told me he has been close to death many times because of preaching this new religion. If I get to Rome alive I am going to find out about it.
BALBUS:	You'll forget the whole thing in a week. Religion is fine in a storm at sea, but if I get to Rome all I will be interested in is my insurance money for the ship.
TROPHIMUS:	You're a hard man, Balbus! Well, you'll soon know whether it is to be insurance or a tombstone. Boatswain! (SHOUTING) Assemble both watches, and raise the anchors! Hoist the foresail, and unlash the steering paddles!
BOATSWAIN:	(FROM OFF STAGE) Ay, ay, Captain!
BALBUS:	May the gods protect us!
JULIUS:	Time for a prayer, Balbus? I know I trust more in Paul and his prayers than in what little faith I ever had in our gods.
BOATSWAIN:	(OFF STAGE) Both watches fall in on the after deck!
JULIUS:	Now, Jesus, if you are really God's son, watch over us!

Scene twenty-five:

A PRISONER AT ROME **
BIBLE REFERENCE: ACTS 28: 16-31 AND PAUL'S LETTER TO PHILEMON.

CHARACTERS: PAUL
MARK
ONESIMUS
#MARIUS, a Roman soldier

Everyone in the ship reached land safely in Malta. From there Paul and the other prisoners were taken to Rome. It is uncertain what happened to Paul after his imprisonment in Rome. He may have remained a prisoner there until his death, or he may have been released and made some further journeys, before a second imprisonment. Luke ends his two volume story with the picture of Paul living at Rome, a prisoner, but able to preach and write.

Onesimus was a slave who ran away from his master Philemon. Paul sent him back, with the short letter (Philemon) included in the New Testament. Onesimus means 'profitable' (compare Onassis, from the same root). Paul makes more than one pun on the name in his letter. You could adapt it by calling him Nicholas and making a pun on nickels. Marius is an imaginary name for Paul's guard.

In his prison room at Rome Paul sits at a table with Mark. Marius stands near the door. Onesimus is preparing a meal. The room is plainly furnished.

PAUL: Is breakfast almost ready, Onesimus?

ONESIMUS: Coming up in a minute.

MARK: Do you need help?

ONESIMUS: No, Mark. I can manage. It was much harder work at Philemon's.

PAUL: Marius, you must join us. It's our custom here for the guard to eat with us.

MARIUS: That's what they told me. It's not your everyday prison assignment, they said. They're certainly right!

PAUL: (LAUGHING) I'm glad. I am a prisoner, and I don't intend to run away. We don't have to shed tears over it. We can be friends.

MARIUS: When will the Emperor's court hear your case?

MARK: If we knew that we'd be wiser than the Emperor.

PAUL: We don't know, so we have to be patient. Now, Mark, what is happening today?

MARK: A group of Greek freedmen are coming soon. Rufus and Amplias later this afternoon. We hope that Tychicus will be here by evening. He got into Puteoli two days ago.

PAUL: Good! That will mean news from Ephesus. Meanwhile we can try to finish the letters to Laodicea and Colosse; and I have to write to Philemon about our runaway friend here.

ONESIMUS: Breakfast!

MARK: I'll clear these things off the table.

PAUL: Marius, you haven't met our cook. This is Onesimus, a slave of Philemon, from Colosse.

MARIUS:	Colosse in Asia? You're a long way from your master.
PAUL:	Let's be honest with Marius. He ran away.
MARIUS:	Ran away! (HE WHISTLES IN ASTONISHMENT) That wasn't very smart.
PAUL:	Not what you'd expect from an 'Onesimus'? We're keeping him useful. One day he'll go back to his master and live up to his name.
MARIUS:	If he goes back he'll be lucky to live at all.
ONESIMUS:	That's what you would expect, but I believe I can go and tell Philemon that I am sorry. I think he will accept me back.
MARIUS:	You mean he'll believe you?
PAUL:	Philemon is a kind of son to me. I brought him to Jesus six years ago, with his wife Apphia and their son Archippus.
MARIUS:	You keep talking about this Jesus. I know he has something to do with you being a prisoner.
PAUL:	That's true. I'm his prisoner, not the Emperor's. Later we'll tell you about it. But now it's time for my letters. Clear the dishes, Onesimus! Then you can tell Marius how you found joy in the Lord, while Mark and I get to work.

Here the Acts of the Apostles ends. The final word in greek, AKOLUTOS, means that Paul wrote and preached 'without restrictions.' The gospel had come a very long way since the meeting in the upper room at Pentecost.

Modern Plays with a Bible Theme

In planning Drama Schools I have learned to mix Bible scenes with others which have a contemporary theme. Each one of these plays can easily be linked to the Bible. They are designed, like the Bible plays, for reading, acting, and discussion. Some are hard to act, others easily adaptable to any kind of stage. If you plan a course of play reading, mix some of these plays in with the Bible scenes, and you will find that they go well together, dealing with the same questions.

1. GRANNY IS COMING FOR CHRISTMAS**
2. FINDING THE DENTIST**
3. GLAD TO SEE YOU BACK**
4. HONOR YOUR FATHER*
5. GODPARENTS**
6. MARTIN THE COBBLER+
7. HOW MUCH LAND DOES A MAN REQUIRE?+
8. WHO IS MY NEIGHBOR? (read)
9. THE PERFECT HOUSE(read)
10. THE CHAMPION (read)
11. THE EMPIRE (read)
12. CAMELS FOR THE ARK (read)
13. PILGRIM'S PROGRESS (read)
14. GOD'S TUMBLER(read)
15. SATAN'S GUIDE TO THE TEN COMMANDMENTS (read)
16. A VIETNAM PARABLE (read)

ONE:

GRANNY IS COMING FOR CHRISTMAS **

CHARACTERS: MOTHER
                FATHER
                KATHY, 17
                JERRY, 10

This play, which may be acted by people of any age, is especially suitable for Advent. It is a parable in which Granny stands for Jesus. The setting is a home at breakfast time on a school day. Scene one might be called: WHO'D WANT TO BE GRANNY?

KATHY: (ENTERING) Mom! Isn't breakfast ready yet? I have to leave.

MOTHER: Why can't you get your own breakfast for a change? is Jerry up yet?

KATHY: How would I know? (SHE SITS)

FATHER: (ENTERING) Don't talk to your mother like that, Kathy. Where's the paper?

MOTHER: I don't suppose anyone brought it in yet. It's Jerry's job.

JERRY: (ENTERING) Hurry up, Mom! I need my breakfast.

MOTHER: You need— You have a nerve, coming in late, looking as though you haven't even washed your face.

FATHER: Go fetch the newspaper—fast!

JERRY: Don't bug me! (HE SITS)

MOTHER: Look, all of you. Granny's arriving at 3.30 to day. Jerry, I told you to have your things out of your room, so that I can get it ready. And Kathy, don't forget you're to pick her up at the airport.

KATHY: Today? Oh, Mom, I forgot all about it. Dan wants me to—

FATHER: Oh, for crying out loud! You forgot—that's all you kids ever do—forget. Here's Granny coming for Christmas, your mother needs help, and all I hear is 'I forgot, I can't, I don't want to.'

JERRY: Why do I have to move out of my room? It's such a drag. Why doesn't Kathy move out?

MOTHER: (SITS DOWN, WEEPING) I can't stand it! You all shout at each other and complain. I wish Granny weren't coming at all. I wish there was no such thing as Christmas. What a curse you make of Christmas with your bickering!

Part Two:

Same scene
I CAN'T WAIT TO SEE GRANNY!

KATHY: (ENTERING) Need any help, Mom?

MOTHER: No, dear, it's all ready. Give Jerry a hand with his things, will you? I need to get his room ready for Granny.

KATHY: He already did most of it. 3.30 at the airport. I can't wait to see Granny!

FATHER: (ENTERING) Time you sat down and had your own breakfast, honey. Morning, Kathy! (HE KISSES HER)

MOTHER: It's all on the table. Start in, Jerry!

JERRY: Coming, Mom! (ENTERS) Here's the paper, Dad. The Rovers won in overtime.

FATHER: They did? That's good. Thanks, Jerry.

MOTHER: Is your room ready?

JERRY: Almost. Will Granny be here when I get back from school?

FATHER: If the flight's on time, yes. I'll be home early today.

MOTHER: Maybe we can all walk down to the beach before dark, if she's not too tired.

KATHY: It really feels like Christmas when Granny comes. We must get the decorations up.

FATHER: Don't forget you're coming with me to fetch the tree tomorrow, Jerry.

JERRY: Can we take Granny with us?

FATHER: Certainly, if she wants to come.

MOTHER:	Time for you two to leave. I'll finish your room, Jerry. Have a good day! And Kathy, drive carefully this afternoon. Christmas traffic at the airport is bad.
KATHY:	I will, Mom. 'Bye, Dad!
JERRY:	'Bye, Mom, Dad! See you! (THEY GO OUT)
FATHER:	It's time for me to leave too. You know something? I'm proud to have Granny come to our home.

Two:

FINDING THE DENTIST **

CHARACTERS:	SCHOOL PRINCIPAL
	Her SECRETARY
	TOMMY ROWE (10)
	GAS STATION ATTENDANT
	STEVE COOK
	SMALL GIRL
	DOCTOR BAKER
	NARRATOR

SEEK, AND YE SHALL FIND. This is a play for children, or for children and adults.

It is not always easy to find God. This play is a parable about the need to keep on trying and looking. The play opens in the Principal's office at an elementary school. The Principal is at her desk. A knock at the door.

PRINCIPAL:	Come in!
SECRETARY:	Excuse me, Mrs. Jameson. There's a boy here with a toothache.
PRINCIPAL:	You'd better bring him in, Carol. (SHE DOES SO)
SECRETARY:	It's Tommy Rowe.
PRINCIPAL:	Hi, Tommy! Tooth hurting, is it?
TOMMY:	Yes, Ma'am. A filling came out, and it started to ache.
PRINCIPAL:	You don't look too good. We must get you to a dentist. Shall I call your mother?

TOMMY: That's the trouble. My Mom's gone to visit my Auntie at Marston, and my Dad's out of town.

PRINCIPAL: I see. There's nobody else who can take you? How did you get to school?

TOMMY: I rode my bike. I could get to Doctor Baker's, I think.

PRINCIPAL: Where's his office?

TOMMY: I know it's Diamond Street. I'm not sure of the number. It's only about ten blocks.

PRINCIPAL: I'd take you myself, but I have a meeting coming up. (SHE LOOKS IN A DIRECTORY) Here we are: 4827 Diamond. Listen, Tommy, you ask Mrs. Butler in the office to draw you a map, and I'll call Doctor Baker to say that you are coming. We'll say it's an emergency.

TOMMY: Yes, Ma'am.

PRINCIPAL: Sure you'll be O.K?

TOMMY: I'll manage. (HE GOES OUT)

So Tommy started out on his bike. There was a cold wind, and his tooth was aching. Perhaps that was why he missed a turning, and found himself on an unfamiliar street. He decided to ask his way at a gas station. He wheeled his bike to where the attendant was standing.

ATTENDANT: Hi, there! What can I do for you?

TOMMY: Which way is Diamond Street?

ATTENDANT: Diamond? What number are you looking for?

TOMMY: 4827. Doctor Baker's.

ATTENDANT: I know Doc Baker well. He's often in for gas. Drives a cream Chevy. Nice fellow. Take the next right, by the church there, then the second left—that's Merton. Two blocks, and make a right to Diamond. Doc's house is on the left. Tooth bad?

TOMMY: Pretty bad. Thanks a lot.

ATTENDANT: Doc Baker will fix you up in no time. (TOMMY RIDES OFF)

Tommy rode away. He was still a little confused, so on Warburton he decided to ask a pleasant-looking man who was getting out of his car. (AGAIN TOMMY WHEELS HIS BIKE ON STAGE)

TOMMY: Excuse me, sir.

STEVE: Yes?

TOMMY: Could you tell me where 4827 Diamond is? Doctor Baker's office?

STEVE: I sure can. I know Doc Baker well. See him every week at Rotary, and on the golf course. Straight on that way, and first right. Tell Doc that Steve Cook put you on your way. What's your name?

TOMMY: Tommy Rowe.

STEVE: Well, good luck,Tommy! Doc wil make it all right.

Tommy reached the 4800 block on Diamond. He still wasn't quite sure which was the right house. A small girl was playing with a jump rope in her front yard.

TOMMY: Hi!

GIRL: Hi!

TOM:MY: Do you know which house is Doctor Baker's?

GIRL: He's my daddy. He lives here.

TOMMY: Thanks. Can I leave my bike?

GIRL: Put it against the wall. I'll call my Daddy.
             (SHE RUNS OFF. SOON DOCTOR BAKER APPEARS)

BAKER: Hello there, Tommy!

TOMMY: Hello, sir.

BAKER: Come on in, and I'll see what I can do for you.

So Tommy found the dentist. On his short journey Tommy learned quite a lot about Doctor Baker. He knew his address. He knew that he was a nice fellow, who drove a cream Chevy, played golf, and went to Ro— something. Tommy did not quite understand this. He knew that he had a daughter with a jump rope. There was much more that he did not know, but this was enough. It is the same kind of journey which we undertake when we look for God.

Three:

GLAD TO SEE YOU BACK**

CHARACTERS: Mrs. MARIE EDWARDS , a teacher
DELIA, 15, a student
HENRY, a teacher, and STUDENTS (optional)

This is a play for a student and an adult, or for two students. In a crowded corridor at a High School, Henry and Marie are making their way towards Marie's classroom. The opening lines may be described or acted. It is difficult to act out the sounds and movements of a group, but it is valuable to try.

HENRY: (IN AMONG THE CROWD) Try to make it by 4.30, Marie.

MARIE: I'll try. Oh! How are we ever going to get through?

HENRY: Follow me. You guys, let us through, will you? (STUDENT VOICES)

MARIE: Hi, Donna! Thanks. Hi, Vince! Delia, glad to see you back.

DELIA: Thanks, Mrs. Edwards. (DOOR OPENS. MARIE AND HENRY GO INTO HER ROOM)

HENRY: That's better. Who was that girl you spoke to?

MARIE: Delia? I can't remember her last name.

HENRY: She looked kind of lost.

MARIE: She was in my class last year. Very quiet, but a good kid. See you later.

Next morning Marie Edwards was in her room, marking her class's notebooks, when there was a knock on the door.

MARIE: Come in! (DELIA ENTERS) Oh, hi, Delia! Do you want to see me?

DELIA: If you have a minute, Mrs. Edwards.

MARIE:	Of course. Sit down, won't you?
DELIA:	Thank you. (SHE SITS. A PAUSE)
MARIE:	What can I do for you?
DELIA:	It's—well, I came to thank you for what you did yesterday.
MARIE:	What I did? There must be some mistake. I didn't do anything for you.
DELIA:	Oh, yes, you did. In the corridor, when you passed me.
MARIE:	I—oh, yes, I remember, but—
DELIA:	You know what you said?
MARIE:	I'm not sure. Something silly or trivial. Was it 'Hi!'?
DELIA:	No. You said you were glad to see me back.
MARIE:	(SHAKEN, AFTER A PAUSE) Yes, I suppose I did say that.
DELIA:	Did you—do you know why I was out of school?
MARIE:	No. It was pure chance I remembered you were out at all. What happened?
DELIA:	It was my sister. Do you mind if I tell you?
MARIE:	Of course not, if it helps.
DELIA:	I mean, I'm not in your class, or anything. I don't want to waste your time.
MARIE:	I don't think talking like this is ever a waste of time. Tell me!
DELIA:	My sister and I are twins--were. She was always the leader, and—it's hard to explain if you haven't been a twin. She was—well, most of my life. It was almost as if we were inside each other. We fought sometimes, but that didn't matter.
MARIE:	I understand. But she didn't come to this school, did she?

DELIA: No. You see she got sick when we were in 8th grade. At first they didn't know what it was. Then they found out. Bone cancer. She was just fifteen, Mrs. Edwards.

MARIE: Oh, Delia! I'm so sorry.

DELIA: I used to go home and tell her about everything. I still depended on her a lot. She was—special. (SHE IS CRYING) I'm sorry.

MARIE: You don't have to be sorry. You stayed home because she was dying?

DELIA: Yes. She died four days ago. The funeral was yesterday.

MARIE: What can I say, Delia dear? I don't think death is any kind of disaster to fear, for a person like her; but it's very hard for you and your family—you especially.

DELIA: I'm not sorry about her dying. It was going to happen anyway, and I don't think at the end it hurt too badly. But it's myself I keep thinking about—and then I feel so mean. I ought to be caring about her, not about how I can get along without her.

MARIE: It's only human to think about that. She is in good hands. You are the one with a tough battle to fight.

DELIA: Coming back yesterday I was scared. I wasn't even sure I wanted to go on living. A few of the kids knew about it, but most of them didn't. I felt so lost, Mrs. Edwards. (CRYING)

MARIE: (KNEELING BY HER) There's plenty of kleenex. Let some of the hurt out, dear girl. It helps to cry sometimes. Do you believe in God?

DELIA: Yes—yes, I do. We don't go to church much. I'm not sure what Mom and Dad believe. But I do, especially now—only—

MARIE: Let me tell you something. I may be very simple, but I think God meant you to come and talk to me. You see, dear, what I said to you yesterday was sheer chance. Don't be offended if I say this, will you? I wasn't really glad to see you back. I was saying it, the way we all say polite, meaningless things. Only he didn't want it to be meaningless. Do you understand?

DELIA:	Yes, I can understand that. It was what I needed so much, but you didn't know.
MARIE:	Anyway, let's be thankful it happened. You see now I really am glad to see you; and if I can help you any way, any time, you'll know that I am here.
DELIA:	Yes, Mrs. Edwards.
MARIE:	We're both due back in class, aren't we? Can you make it, do you think? Or would you rather stay in here for a while? I can tell Mr. Ross.
DELIA:	No, it's O.K. I'd rather go. I enjoyed your class last year. You probably didn't realize that. I know I didn't say much, but it was a good class.
MARIE:	I'm glad. (THEY BOTH LAUGH) There's that word again! This time I really mean it. I didn't know you then. but from now on let's have no barriers. It was a privilege to talk to you, Delia. Now we must go; but come back soon!

Four:

HONOR YOUR FATHER *

(harder, but excellent for an adult group)

CHARACTERS:	STAN FORSBERG and his wife ETHEL (50's) GLORIA FORSBERG HOLT and her husband DESMOND (50's) PETER FORSBERG and his wife HARRIET (late 40's) MARGE FORSBERG (mid-40's) AUNT DORA

SCENE:

The simple home of Jacob Forsberg in a remote country area. He is in his 80's. It is the day of his wife's funeral. Four of his five children are returning from it. His sister Dora has looked after him while they were away. The characters in this play are adults, but students may also read or act it.

MARGE:	(AS THE SEVEN ENTER BY THE FRONT DOOR) Quietly! He may be asleep. (SHE CROSSES TO THE BEDROOM DOOR)
GLORIA:	I have to sit down. I'm exhausted.
DESMOND:	Over here, dear. (HE STEERS HER TO THE ONLY COUCH)

PETER: Leave room for Harriet, Gloria.

GLORIA: What do you mean leave room? I'm not that large, Peter.

HARRIET: I'll be all right here. (SHE SITS ON A CHAIR)

PETER: We don't have enough chairs for everyone.

STAN: I'll fetch two more.

ETHEL: No, Stan. I'll get them. (SHE GOES OUT OF ONE DOOR, AS MARGE COMES WITH DORA FROM THE BEDROOM)

MARGE: Father's fast asleep.

GLORIA: Good! That gives us a chance to talk.

MARGE: Aunt Dora, I don't think you've met Harriet, Peter's wife.

DORA: Pleased to meet you, Harriet. I'm Mr. Forsberg's sister.

ETHEL: (RETURNING WITH TWO CHAIRS) Sit here, Aunt Dora.

DORA: Thank you, Ethel dear.

GLORIA: Is there a drink in the house?

STAN: You know Father never kept liquor in our home, Gloria

PETER: Well, let's get our discussion over, and we can go back to the motel.

GLORIA: Who's going to begin?

PETER: First there's the will. Did Mother leave one?

STAN: She made a will last year, when she knew she was sick. Just five lines. She left everything to Father.

MARGE: Mr. Jensen, the attorney in White Falls, said it was a good idea—not that she had much to leave.

GLORIA: There's her wedding china. She always said I should have that.

PETER:	Always? That can hardly include the last thirty years. You've hardly seen her.
GLORIA:	You know what I mean. When we were all at home.
MARGE:	A lot of things were different when we were all at home, Gloria.
STAN:	It makes no difference. It all belongs to father.
GLORIA:	What use is it to him? I mean, he can't—
PETER:	Can't what? Why don't you come out and say it?
DORA:	You two still quarreling, like when you were kids? You should be ashamed! Nobody's going to move that china while I have anything to do with looking after your father. Memories are all he has now— memories, and Marge's care—with Stan and Ethel to help.
HARRIET:	But—how much does he understand? I mean, isn't he—
MARGE:	Feeble-minded? You're a doctor, Desmond. What would you say?
DESMOND:	Oh, it's not my line at all. You'd need an expert opinion. Of course no doctor would ever use that term.
STAN:	It doesn't take a doctor to see that Father forgets things, and needs help with his food, and a lot more. But what difference does it make?
PETER:	Well, Stan, none, I suppose—unless—
GLORIA:	Peter's worried Father may need to go into a home of some kind, and then he'd have to help pay for it.
HARRIET:	Gloria, you've no right—
GLORIA:	Oh, come off it, Harriet! It's true, and you know it.
PETER:	I haven't noticed the noble Doctor Holt and his wife offering to lift a finger to help.
DESMOND:	You watch what you're saying, Peter! Of course Gloria and I will do anything we can.

MARGE: You mean that, Desmond?

DESMOND: (ALARMED) Certainly! I--don't think I quite understand you.

MARGE: I think it's time we got right down to what we are going to do. A home is no place for Father. He'd give up, and die. And don't try to tell me that would be merciful, Gloria!

GLORIA: I never—

MARGE: You hinted at it in your last letter.

STAN: Well, he's not going to a home. so we can forget it.

PETER: Then that clears the air.

ETHEL: Does it, Peter?

PETER: Yes. I mean, you've agreed that what he really needs is Marge, and—

ETHEL: What he needs is for his children to care for him, and repay some of what he and Mother did for them.

DORA: 'Honor your father and your mother, that your days may be long in the land which the Lord God gave to you.'

GLORIA: That's fine for you to say, Aunt Dora; but Desmond and I aren't in any position to help.

ETHEL: And Marge is—

GLORIA: Of course she is! She's always lived at home, and has no ties—

STAN: Why don't you tell them, sis?

PETER: Tell us what, for God's sake?

MARGE: I'm thinking of getting married. (A HORRIFIED PAUSE)

GLORIA: Married? You?

MARGE: Yes, Gloria. It's not impossible, you know. You've managed it twice.

PETER: But—what would happen to—

DORA: To your father? That's the point, Peter. It's for the four of you to work out together, isn't it? At least you came for the funeral. I hear Norman didn't even answer Stan's telegram. So you can write him off.

GLORIA: It isn't for the four of us. It's nothing to do with me! I got myself out of this place thirty years ago—

STAN: So, if Marge gets married, you'll do nothing? It's not what Desmond said a moment ago.

DESMOND: Naturally we would do what we can. I could put you in touch with the right doctors, and help to make any arrangements. But, as Gloria says, our commitments—

STAN: It's not doctors we need. We're agreed Father is not going to be shunted off into a home.

PETER: I'm still staggered. I can't believe it. Marge, are you sure—

MARGE: No, I'm not sure. A decent man, a widower, has asked me to marry him. While Mother was alive I never gave it much thought. Now I think it's up to you to help me make up my mind.

PETER: Tell her about some of the pitfalls of matrimony, Gloria!

ETHEL: It's not a joke, Peter.

PETER: No, it's not. I apologize. My nerves are on edge. If we could only help—

STAN: There's no 'if', Peter. Between the four of us we have a solemn duty to care for the father who worked himself to the bone to give us all we have. Aunt Dora said it in Bible terms. I'm saying to you, you're not going to run away from your responsibilities.

GLORIA: I need that drink. Isn't there anything?

DORA: Brandy, but you're not sick enough for that.

DESMOND: Are you suggesting that your father might live—stay—with each of us in turn?

STAN: I'm not ruling anything out. The only place where there has been too little room is here—right here, where Marge has put up with it for twenty years. You have plenty of room. So does Peter. We can fit Father in, by shifting the kids to the living room.

GLORIA: (AFTER A LONG SILENCE) If nobody else will say it, I will. This is one world—yours. Where we live is another world. You can't mix them. Isn't that right, Peter?

PETER: I never even thought of it. I mean, we knew Mother couldn't travel, so we never suggested—

DORA: But your father could travel, Peter, if he had to.

MARGE: Be honest, you two! You've let Stan and me do everything all your lives, and now you can't believe we won't stand between you and any kind of burden. Not that it is a burden. 'Honor your father and your mother.' Well, it comes back to you, like in the parable, a hundredfold. I've seen you every few years, Gloria, and I wouldn't have changed places with you. Oh, I've envied you and Peter sometimes. I'm no saint. But in the end I'd take the life I've lived over all of your money, and your moves, and your marriages. I love Father—yes, and honor him. I'm happy and proud to have held Mother's hand as she died, and seen her eyes open wide to let in the light of heaven. And I'll tell you something else. I wouldn't let Father go and visit either of you, and feel your discomfort and your shame, and hear you try to get out of explaining to your flashy friends who it is tucked away in a back room. He's not so feebleminded that he can't tell the difference between love and its opposite. If I get married—and I think I will—I will go on caring for Father. It will be possible, because of Stan and Ethel, who are worth a dozen of you two, and because of Aunt Dora, and because my Steve is a decent, generous fellow. But this house needs a lot of changes: an extra room, a toilet and a bath, a new heating system. I'll send you the bills, divided in half. That's the least you can do. It's also all you can do. I'm not a fool, Gloria. You did cut yourself off when you went away. It's not really your fault. And if we've said some hard things today perhaps that's good. From now on we can be more honest. (PAUSE) That's the longest speech i ever remember making.

GLORIA: (AFTER A PAUSE, GOES AND EMBRACES MARGE) I wish I could—

MARGE: That's all right, Gloria. There's plenty you can do, if we work together.

ETHEL:	Why don't you all go out and have dinner? You too, Aunt Dora. Stan and I will stay with Father.
PETER:	No. I'd like to stay, if you don't mind. Father didn't know me earlier. If I sit with him a while, and talk about the old days—
DORA:	That's good, Peter. It's decided. You stay. I stay. I don't like hotel food. Off you go, all of you!

Five:

GODPARENTS **
(for older students or adults)

CHARACTERS:	LORNA, a single mother in her thirties PHIL and EVIE, her friends

Godparents often take their duties lightly, but when a family faces a crisis strong and loyal godparents may be lifesavers. Lorna's husband has left her. She and her son Tim live alone. She is fighting a drinking problem. Tonight she sits in her living room, which shows signs of neglect. She is listening to music, a glass in her hand, when the bell rings. She disregards it, but it rings again.

LORNA:	Oh, shoot! Who'd be visiting me this late? (SHE SHUFFLES TO THE DOOR) Who is it?
PHIL:	(FROM OUTSIDE) It's Evie and Phil, Lorna.
LORNA:	Oh, God! (OPENS DOOR) You'd better come in, I suppose.
EVIE:	(EMBRACING HER) Hi, Lorna!

(LORNA STANDS NEAR THE DOOR, NOT MAKING ROOM FOR THEM TO COME IN)

PHIL:	We heard things are not so good, so we wanted to—
EVIE:	Is there anything we can do?
LORNA:	That's big of you. Suppose I tell you it's none of your damned business.
PHIL:	We'll try to convince you that you're wrong. A friend's troubles are a friend's business.

EVIE: Can we sit down?

LORNA: (MOVING BACK) Oh, sure! Sit down! Make yourselves at home, and take no notice of me. I've had a couple of drinks. Want a drink?

EVIE: No, Lorna. Not now.

PHIL: We heard from your mother that Jeff had left you, and money is pretty tight. Is that right?

EVIE: We're not trying to be nosey. You'd do the same for me.

LORNA: Good old dependable Evie! Damn you, you shouldn't have come here.

EVIE: But Lorna—

LORNA: (RAISING HER VOICE) Damn you! Do you think I want my friends to see me like this?

PHIL: No, I understand that; but not to come would be worse, wouldn't it?

LORNA: Could anything be worse?

PHIL: And besides that there's Tim.

LORNA: (IN TEARS) Why can't you leave me alone?

EVIE: Is he asleep, Lorna?

LORNA: (AFTER A LONG PAUSE, PULLING HERSELF TOGETHER) Yes, thank God! I don't—do this until he's in bed.

EVIE: You're a wonderful mother to him.

LORNA: Wonderful mother! Don't try to kid me! I'm a mess. I worried so much about Jeff—all his lies, and his women, and the money—I don't know what to do.

PHIL: For a start, don't be too proud to ask for help. We are Tim's godparents, you know.

LORNA: Godparents? What does that have to do with it?

PHIL:	A great deal. Do you know what we promised at his baptism?
LORNA:	That was six years ago. You always remember his birthday, but—
EVIE:	We promised to see that he grew up to know God, and—
LORNA:	So you've come to spy on me, to see if I take him to church every Sunday—
EVIE:	You know us better than that. We're not sure how best to help, but you've been my friend since grade school, and both of us feel a big responsibility as Tim's godparents.
LORNA:	(AFTER A LONG PAUSE) You know, you're really something, you two. You mean it, don't you? (SHE BURSTS INTO TEARS) Perhaps it isn't such a lousy world after all.
EVIE:	We feel so badly. We've got everything. We love each other. Phil has a good job. We have our children, our home, our church—
PHIL:	Don't refuse some common sense help. It isn't charity.
EVIE:	For a start I'm going to make some coffee. Then we'll work out a plan. O.K?
LORNA:	You win. (PAUSE) Godparents! I can't believe it!

Six:

MARTIN THE COBBLER
(more challenging)+

This play and the next have been adapted from stories by Leo Tolstoy, the great Russian writer. He was the author of classic novels, WAR AND PEACE, ANNA KARENINA, and others. Late in his life he turned to short stories, in which he tried to put his belief in a simple context. The story of Martin is one of the first which my parents read to me.

Music for the simple songs is available, but the play can be presented without music.

It can also be presented by a single actor representing Martin and the Narrator. With small adaptations in the text, Martin can describe the visits of Stepanitch and the others. For example he will say: 'Martin poured Stepanitch a cup of tea, and another for himself….' 'Martin took the baby and sat down at his bench…' 'Martin hurried out into the street,' etc.

CHARACTERS: MARTIN THE COBBLER
A PILGRIM
STEPANITCH, an old soldier
A YOUNG WOMAN with a baby
AN OLD WOMAN
A BOY
VOICE OF JESUS
NARRATOR
CHORUS (if desired)

The scene is simple. A table and chair center, with a candlestick. Martin's work bench right center need only be a chair with a stool or table in front of it. Everything else can be imagined, unless you wish to include a 'stove' and samovar and cups on the left side of the stage, and Martin's bed behind the table. The imagined window is above Martin's bench. The door is on the right side, behind the bench. Use oldfashioned clothes. The women wear ankle-length dark dresses. The old woman has a shawl over her head. The pilgrim wears a long cloak, tied at the waist with a girdle. Stepanitch wears an old military coat.
(MARTIN IS SITTING AT HIS BENCH, WORKING ON A SHOE. A PILE OF OTHER SHOES IS ON THE FLOOR TO HIS LEFT)

NARRATOR: Martin the cobbler sits by the window;
Watch how his work is nimble and neat!
Over his head the people are passing.
Martin can tell them simply by their feet.

CHORUS
He knew them by their boots.
He never saw their faces.
He knew them by their boots,
Their heels, and toes, and laces.

NARRATOR: These are some shoes he fitted with toecaps.
These he had sewn wherever they split.
These needed heels, and these needed patches.
These needed padding so that they would fit.

CHORUS
He knew them by their boots.
He never saw their faces.
He knew them by their boots,
Their heels, and toes, and laces.

NARRATOR:	Leather and felt boots, polished and dull boots;
	People in new boots, people in old;
	Slippers and sandals, shoes and galoshes,
	Boots he had stitched, and boots that he had soled.

CHORUS

He knew them by their boots.
He never saw their faces.
He knew tham by their boots,
Their heels, and toes, and laces.

NARRATOR:	That is the way with Martin the cobbler,
	Here as he sits and works at his seat.
	Most of the day he cannot see people;
	Yet all the time he knows them by their feet.

CHORUS

He knew them by their boots.
He never saw their faces.
He knew them by their boots,
Their heels, and toes, and laces.

In a little town in Russia, more than a hundred years ago, there lived a shoemaker named Martin Avdeitch. He lived in a basement room, which possessed but one window. This window faced on to the street, and through it a glimpse could be caught of the passersby. It is true that only their legs could be seen by Martin as he sat working; but that did not matter, as Martin could recognize most people by their boots or shoes alone. Martin was given plenty of business, because his work was promptly done and lasted well, and his prices were moderate. His wife had died many years earlier, leaving him with a boy three years old. Martin lived in lodgings with the boy, who began to grow up and help him, and to be his great joy. But God had not seen fit to give Martin happiness in his child. The boy fell sick and died. Martin mourned for him bitterly, and murmured against God. His life seemed to him to be empty.

(THERE IS A KNOCK AT THE OUTER DOOR. MARTIN GOES TO ADMIT THE PILGRIM, AS THE NARRATOR CONTINUES. THEY SIT AT THE TABLE, AND CONVERSE IN DUMB SHOW.)

One day an old peasant pilgrim, a travelling preacher, came to Martin's door. They talked together, and Martin told him of his great sorrow. He said that he had no wish left except for death.

| PILGRIM: | You should not speak like that, Martin. You must learn to live for the God who gave you life, not for yourself. |

MARTIN: But how am I to live for him?

PILGRIM: Tell me first, can you read?

MARTIN: Yes, I can.

PILGRIM   Then take this, Martin Avdeitch. Inside this book you will find the
               answer to all your problems.

MARTIN: Thank you, but— (HE LOOKS DOUBTFULLY AT THE BIBLE, AND
               BEGINS TO SEARCH FOR MONEY IN HIS POCKETS.)

PILGRIM: No, no. Do not offer me any payment. If you receive what this book
               has to give, you will owe more than you could ever pay.

(THE PILGRIM IS SHOWN OUT BY MARTIN. THE LIGHT GROWS DIMMER AS MARTIN
RETURNS. THE MUSIC OF THE OPENING SONG IS PLAYED SOFTLY AS HE PUTS HIS
WORK AWAY, THEN GOES TO THE TABLE AND LIGHTS THE CANDLE. THE NARRATOR
SPEAKS MEANWHILE.)

Now at first Martin only meant to read from the Bible on festival days; but from
the beginning it gave him great comfort. Indeed he became so engrossed that he
would read until his candle burned low. All day he would work hard and well, and
at night he would read.
(MARTIN HAS PICKED UP THE BIBLE. HE NOW SITS AND HOLDS IT CLOSE TO THE
LIGHT.)

MARTIN: 'And unto him that smiteth thee on the one cheek offer also the
               other; and him that taketh away thy cloke forbid not to take thy
               coat also. Give to every man that asketh of thee, and of him that
               taketh away thy goods ask them not again. (MARTIN SHAKES HIS
               HEAD IN WONDER.) And as ye would that men should do unto you,
               do ye also to them likewise. (HE TURNS TO ANOTHER PAGE.)
               And why call ye me Lord, Lord, and do not the things which I say?
               Whosoever cometh to me, and heareth my sayings, and doeth
               them, I will show you to whom he is like: he is like a man which built
               a house, and digged deep, and laid the foundation on a rock.

But he that heareth, and doeth not, is like a man that without a foundation built a house upon the earth.' (HE REMOVES HIS SPECTACLES AND RUBS HIS EYES.) Is my house founded upon the rock? I hope so; but it is so easy for me, sitting here by myself, to fall into sin. May the Lord help me to stand firm! Ah well, it is time to go to bed. (HE STARTS TO RISE AND BLOW OUT THE CANDLE, BUT STOPS AND SITS AGAIN.) Yet I must read one chapter more. 'And Jesus turned to the woman, and said unto Simon the Pharisee, "Seest thou this woman? I entered into thine house, and thou gavest me no water for my feet; but she has washed my feet with tears, and wiped them with the hairs of her head. Thou gavest me no kiss; but this woman since the time I came in hath not ceased to kiss my feet. My head with oil thou didst not anoint; but this woman hath anointed my feet with ointment." 'Thou gavest me no water for my feet...My head with oil thou didst not anoint...' I am just like that Pharisee. I drink tea, and think only of my own needs. If the Lord himself should come and visit me, would I receive him any better?

If Jesus came to my house
Would I be on the watch?
Would I know his tread,
And his hand upon the latch?
Would I be unworthy
Of so great a guest?
Would I try to give him
Warmth and care and rest?

Simon was a Pharisee,
Rich and full of pride;
Yet he did not welcome
Jesus to his side.
Am I any better
Than a Pharisee?
Would he find a welcome
If he came to me?

(THE MUSIC CONTINUES SOFTLY. MARTIN'S HEAD NODS. AFTER A PAUSE A VOICE IS HEARD FROM THE DIRECTION OF THE WINDOW.)

VOICE: Martin!

MARTIN: Who is there? (HE LOOKS UP, STARTLED)

VOICE: Martin, it is I, Jesus. Look into the street tomorrow! I am coming to visit you.

(MARTIN STANDS UP, RUBS HIS EYES, SHAKES HIS HEAD, THEN BLOWS OUT THE CANDLE AND GOES TOWARDS HIS BED. BLACKOUT. THE MUSIC OF THE LAST SONG IS PLAYED SOFTLY. WHEN THE LIGHTS SLOWLY COME BACK, HE IS SITTING AT HIS BENCH WORKING. DURING THE NEXT NARRATION HE FREQUENTLY LOOKS UP AT THE WINDOW.)

Next day Martin could not get out of his head the words which he had heard, or else fancied, as he sat asleep. Whenever a pair of boots passed, he peered upwards to see the face of the wearer, even when he knew the boots. The doorkeeper passed, and a watercarrier, and some other familiar figures. Then an old soldier, a veteran of Tsar Nicholas' army, shuffled by in old, patched boots, carrying a shovel. He stopped near the window and began to clear the snow.

(THE SOUND OF A SCRAPING SHOVEL IS HEARD. MARTIN PEERS UP EAGERLY)

MARTIN: Oh, I must be getting into my dotage! It's only old Stepanitch clearing the snow; and just because he comes by I jump to the conclusion that Christ has come to visit me. (HE LOOKS UP AGAIN.) He's too old to be doing that work, and he's half frozen. I wonder if he'd like some tea. Oh, that reminds me. The samovar must be ready. (HE GOES TO THE STOVE AND BREWS THE TEA. THEN HE WALKS TO THE DOORWAY.) Stepanitch! Stepanitch! Come down here and warm yourself! You must be freezing.

STEPANITCH: Oh, Christ reward you, Martin! My bones are almost cracking. (HE STANDS AT THE DOORWAY, STAMPING HIS FEET.)

MARTIN: Come right in! Don't worry about your boots! I'll wipe them—I'm used to it. (MARTIN KNEELS AND WIPES STEPANITCH'S BOOTS.) A stove and a samovar are good friends in weather like this. Come and sit down, and we'll empty this teapot together.

(MARTIN GOES TO THE STOVE AS STEPANITCH SITS C. MARTIN GIVES HIM A CUP OF TEA, AND GOES BACK TO THE STOVE TO POUR HIS OWN. BY THE TIME HE RETURNS, STEPANITCH HAS DRUNK HIS CUP IN ONE GULP AND SET THE CUP UPSIDE DOWN ON THE TABLE. HE WIPES HIS MOUTH WITH HIS SLEEVE.)

MARTIN: Oh, you're ready for another cup.

STEPANITCH: Thank you, Martin Avdeitch.

(MARTIN FETCHES ANOTHER CUP OF TEA, THEN GOES R. TO LOOK UP AT THE WINDOW. STEPANITCH LOOKS AT HIM, PUZZLED.)

STEPANITCH: Are you expecting somebody?

MARTIN: Expecting somebody? Well, to tell you the truth, I am, and I am not.

(MARTIN SITS AT THE TABLE AND IN MIME BEGINS TO SPEAK AND GESTURE. STEPANITCH LISTENS ATTENTIVELY.)

Martin told Stepanitch about the words which he had heard the night before, and how the Lord had said that he would visit him that day. Then he filled Stepanitch's cup with tea once more.

MARTIN: Drink it up! It will do you good. (HE SITS.) You know, I often call to mind, Stepanitch, that when Jesus walked this earth there was never a man or woman, however humble, whom he despised; and how it was chiefly among the common folk that he lived. It was from among them, people like you and me, sinners and working folk, that he chose his disciples. 'Whosoever,' he said, 'shall exalt himself, the same shall be abased; and whosoever shall abase himself, the same shall be exalted. You call me Lord,' he said, 'yet will I wash your feet. Whosoever,' he said, 'would be chief among you, let him be the servant of all. Because,' he said, 'blessed are the lowly, the peacemakers, the merciful and the charitable.'(STEPANITCH HAS FORGOTTEN HIS TEA. HE SITS STILL, WITH TEARS IN HIS EYES.) Oh, Stepanitch, I'm talking too much. You must drink your tea.

STEPANITCH: (RISING) I thank you, Martin Avdeitch. You have taken me in, and fed me body and soul.

MARTIN: You must come back. It gives me joy to have a guest to share my tea. (STEPANITCH GOES OUT. MARTIN FINISHES HIS TEA, AND PUTS AWAY THE CUPS. HE GOES BACK TO WORK, HUMMING THE OPENING TUNE AND WATCHING THE WINDOW.)

MARTIN: Who's this? A woman with a baby! Look how thin her clothes are! I must ask her in out of the wind. (HE GOES TO THE DOORWAY.) My good woman! Won't you bring your baby in? It's warm in here. Come in and wrap the child up! (SHE ENTERS. SHE IS YOUNG, HER CLOTHES THIN, HER FACE EXPRESSING ANXIETY AND SUFFERING.) Sit there and feed him! You'll be near the stove.

WOMAN: I cannot feed him. I have had nothing to eat myself all day.

MARTIN: Nothing to eat? Well, well, I'll find you something. (HE GOES TO THE STOVE.) Here! Some hot soup. Now let me hold the baby. It's all right. I have had a little one of my own. (HE TAKES THE BABY, AND SITS. SHE DRINKS THE SOUP FROM THE BOWL. MARTIN WIGGLES A FINGER IN FRONT OF THE BABY'S FACE AND CLICKS HIS TONGUE.) There! Soon it will be your turn to eat.

WOMAN: You are a friend in great need, sir. When I came to your window I was losing hope.

MARTIN: Have you nothing warmer to wear?

WOMAN: I had a warm shawl, but I had to sell it to buy food. You see, sir, I am a soldier's wife, and my husband was sent to a distant station eight months ago. I have heard nothing of him since.

MARTIN: So he has never seen his baby yet?

WOMAN: No. At first I got a place as a cook, but when the baby came they said they could not do with him. That was three months ago. I have had no work since, and now I have spent all of my savings. I tried to get taken as a wet nurse, but nobody would have me. They said I was too thin. Today I have been to see a tradesman's wife. She had promised to take me on; but when I arrived today she told me to come back next week.

MARTIN: Have you a place to live?

WOMAN: Yes. Thank God my landlady is good to me, and gives me shelter even when I cannot pay for it. Otherwise I would not know how to bear it all.

MARTIN: Here! Hold your baby! (HE HANDS THE BABY TO HER, AND GOES TO THE BED. HE PULLS OUT AN OLD TRUNK FROM BENEATH IT, RUMMAGES FOR A MOMENT, AND PRODUCES A WORN JACKET. HE PUTS IT AROUND HER SHOULDERS.) There! It's a poor old thing, but it will at least serve to cover you.

(SHE LOOKS AT THE JACKET, AND THEN AT MARTIN. SHE BURSTS INTO TEARS.)

WOMAN: I thank you in Jesus' name, sir. Surely it was he who sent me to this house.

MARTIN:	(LAUGHING) He did indeed put me by my window; but it was not for you that I was looking. (AGAIN HE TELLS THE STORY OF THE VOICE IN MIME.)

So Martin told her about his dream—if it was a dream—and why he was watching so closely when she stopped by his door. Then she thanked him, and went on her way. Martin returned to his work.

(THE WOMAN HAS RISEN, THANKED MARTIN, AND LEFT. THE OPENING SONG IS PLAYED SOFTLY WHILE MARTIN RETURNS TO HIS BENCH AND BEGINS TO WORK. THEN LOUD VOICES ARE HEARD FROM THE STREET.)

OLD WOMAN:	I've got you, you little wretch!
BOY:	Let me go! Let me go!

(MARTIN PUTS DOWN HIS WORK AND HURRIES OUT. IT WILL PROBABLY BE EASIEST TO ACT THIS SCENE IN FRONT OF THE WORKROOM. BLACK OUT THE MAIN STAGE. THE OLD WOMAN ENTERS FROM R, HOLDING THE BOY BY THE COLLAR OF HIS SHIRT. MARTIN COMES TO MEET THEM C)

OLD WOMAN:	Don't you try to deny it. You stole my apple!
MARTIN:	Now, now, my good woman. Let go of him, please! Pardon hm, for the good Lord's sake!
OLD WOMAN:	Pardon him! Not until he has felt the policeman's stick!
BOY:	I never took it, I tell you. Let me go!
MARTIN:	Now, let him go, please! He won't do it again. (SHE RELEASES THE BOY, WHO TRIES TO RUN AWAY. MARTIN CATCHES HIM.) No, you don't, my lad! You must say you are sorry. I saw you take that apple.
BOY:	(CRYING)I'm sorry, lady. I did take it. I'm sorry. I was so hungry.
MARTIN:	There now. I will give you one. (TO THE WOMAN) Don't worry! I'll pay you for it.
OLD WOMAN:	Yes, but you spoil him by doing that! He ought to have a sound beating, so that he won't want to sit down for a week.
MARTIN:	That may be our way of giving rewards, but do you think it is God's way? If he ought to be whipped for taking one apple, how about you and me and our sins?

(SHE LOOKS AT HIM FOR A MOMENT, THEN SHAKES HER HEAD)

OLD WOMAN: I know, sir, I know. I had seven children of my own at home once. Now I only have my daughter and my grandchildren. But you should see them run to meet me when I come home from work. Aksintka will go to noone else. 'Granny,' she calls, 'Dear Granny, you look tired!' (SHE PAUSES.) Oh, God go with him! Everyone knows what boys are like.

(SHE STOOPS TO LIFT HER BASKET, BUT THE BOY TAKES IT FROM HER)

BOY: No, let me carry it. It will be on my way home.

(AS THEY GO OFF TOGETHER L. MARTIN WATCHES THEM, SMILING)

MARTIN: She forgot all about her money. (HE TURNS TO GO INTO THE HOUSE. BRING ON THE LIGHTS. MARTIN IS NOW BACK BY HIS BENCH) Now where are my spectacles? There they are! I must put my work away and light the lamp. (THE TUNE OF 'If Jesus came to my house' IS PLAYED SOFTLY. MARTIN PICKS UP A BOOT, LOOKS AT IT, AND NODS CONTENTEDLY. HE PUTS HIS WORK AWAY AND COMES TO THE TABLE. HE LIGHTS THE CANDLE) Now for my Bible. (HE FETCHES IT FROM THE BED, AND SITS) That's funny! It seemed to open of its own accord. (HE STARES AT THE OPEN BIBLE)

(THE FOUR VOICES IN THE FOLLOWING SCENE COME FROM THE CORNERS OF THE STAGE, WHERE THE DAY'S VISITORS STAND IN SHADOW.)

STEPANITCH: Martin!

MARTIN: (STARTLED) Yes? Who—

STEPANITCH: Martin! Don't you know me?

MARTIN: Who are you?

STEPANITCH: It is I, Stepanitch.

YOUNG WOMAN: Martin!

MARTIN: Yes?

YOUNG WOMAN: It is I, Father.

OLD WOMAN: And I, Martin.

BOY: And I, sir.

(MARTIN MOVES HIS EYES SLOWLY FROM CORNER TO CORNER. THEN HE PUTS ON HIS SPECTACLES, AND HOLDS THE BIBLE CLOSE TO THE CANDLE. WE SEE HIS FACE BRIGHTLY LIT, VERY CALM AND RADIANT, AS HE BEGINS TO READ SLOWLY)

MARTIN: Yes...yes. I understand. 'For I was hungry, and ye gave me meat. I was thirsty, and ye gave me drink. I was a stranger, and ye took me in. Inasmuch as ye have done it unto one of the least of these my brethren, ye have done it unto me.'

(DURING THE FOLLOWING LINES, WHICH ARE SUNG EITHER BY THE INDIVIDUAL CHARACTERS OR BY THE CHORUS, MARTIN READS ON FOR A LITTLE WHILE, THEN TAKES OFF HIS SPECTACLES AND BURIES HIS HEAD IN HIS HANDS. HE IS A MAN AT PEACE)

STEPANITCH: I was hungry, and you gave me meat.

YOUNG WOMAN: I was hungry, and you bade me eat.

OLD WOMAN: I was thirsty, and ready to sink.

BOY: I was thirsty, and you bade me drink.

(LIGHTS COME UP GRADUALLY. THE FOUR VISITORS COME FORWARD. THE YOUNG WOMAN WITH HER BABY SITS C. STEPANITCH STANDS BEHIND HER, AS THOUGH HE WERE JOSEPH CLOSE TO MARY. THE BOY SITS AT HER FEET. THE OLD WOMAN SITS TO ONE SIDE. THEY ALL JOIN WITH THE CHORUS IN SINGING THE FINAL SONG. MARTIN STANDS TO ONE SIDE, JOYFUL)

> Who is my neighbor?
> He whose cry I hear.
> Who is my neighbor?
> He whose need is near.
> Who is my neighbor?
> He whose plight I see.
> Who is my neighbor?
> He who calls on me.

(THE PILGRIM HAS KNOCKED AT THE DOOR, AND MARTIN LEADS HIM IN. HE JOINS THE GROUP C, STANDING, AS THE SONG CONTINUES.)

> He is my neighbor
> Who will hear my cry.
> He is my neighbor
> Who will not pass me by.
> Who is my neighbor

In my hour of grief?
He is my neighbor
Who will bring relief.

Go and do likewise!
Never close your door!
Go and do likewise!
Seek the sick and poor!
Find out your neighbor!
Serve your God above!
Go, seek your neighbor!
Fill the world with love!

(DURING THE FINAL LINE MARTIN BLOWS OUT THE CANDLE AND THE LIGHTS FADE.)

Seven:

HOW MUCH LAND DOES A MAN REQUIRE?
+ (hard, but try it!))

CHARACTERS: PAKHOM, a Russian peasant
VERA, his wife
ANNA, her sister
THE DEVIL

This story has the same theme as the parable of the Rich Farmer: beware of greed, which can spoil the lives of even decent, happy people.
In the countryside of Russia a peasant named Pakhom lived with his wife. Their home was small. Pakhom was a tenant farmer, working for a landowner; but they were contented. One day Vera, Pakhom's wife, was sitting at a table with her sister from the city, Anna, who was paying them a visit.

ANNA: I don't know how you can be content to live like this, Vera.

VERA: LIve like what? There's nothing wrong with our lives.

ANNA: Here you are, buried in the country, with nothing to do but slave away at farm work—

VERA: What's wrong with farm work? We eat good food, not the stuff you buy from city shops. We breathe good air—

ANNA: But it is so boring! Life in the city is full of variety—never a dull moment. Here every day is the same: milking, ploughing, hoeing, weeding, spinning. It would drive me mad! And your husband talks about nothing but crops and cows.

VERA: My husband is a good man. You'd better watch your husband, with all those fancy women walking the streets in the city—

PAKHOM: (ENTERING) Now, Vera, don't get excited! You two bickering again?

VERA: Anna keeps telling me that our home is dirty and cramped—

PAKHOM: Yes, I know. Anna likes the city, and we like our lives here. I wouldn't live there for all the gold in the world. I'm happy here.

ANNA: You're not much more than a landowner's slave.

PAKHOM: Well, if you put it like that there is one thng I would like before I die.

VERA: What is that, husband?

PAKHOM: I would like to own some land—only a little, but my own land. If I had that, not even the Devil himself could make me complain.

Now the Devil was hiding behind the stove in Pakhom's home, and he heard what Pakhom said. He began to laugh, and stepped out from his hiding place; but they could not see or hear him.

DEVIL: (ON ONE SIDE OF THE STAGE) Not even the devil himself— We'll see about that, Pakhom. I must make some changes in your life.

Sure enough, Pakhom heard of a small patch of land which he could just manage to buy, by using his small savings and borrowing the rest of the money. But owning this land did not make him any happier. In fact it brought new worries. Cattle from his neighbors' herds strayed on to his land, and poachers broke his fences and stole his property. As a tenant farmer he had never worried about this, but now he resented the tenants and became their enemy. Moreover he found that his small patch of land was not enough. Once again he and Vera were sitting at their table, with Pakhom looking at a sheet of paper.

VERA: What are you worrying about now?

PAKHOM: I'm not worrying—just thinking how different things would be if we owned more land.

VERA: More land! We were far happier when we did not own any.

PAKHOM: Nonsense! The only trouble with this land is that it is not rich enough. Today I heard of some wonderful land a few miles away—

VERA: You don't mean you're going to buy it and move?

PAKHOM: Why not? We have to step up in the world, Vera. This house is far too small. and—

VERA: You sound like my sister. You never used to worry about the house or the land.

PAKHOM: Well, now I know what I want. I shall buy this land.

VERA: Heaven protect us! I hope you know what you are doing!

Pakhom and Vera moved to a bigger house, with more land. Pakhom grew quite rich, but Vera was not happy in her new home. One evening they were sitting in their living room, when there was a loud knock on the door.

VERA: Who could that be?

PAKHOM: Well, go and see! (VERA GOES TO THE DOOR AND OPENS IT. AT THE DOOR IS THE DEVIL, RICHLY DRESSED AS A MERCHANT)

DEVIL: Good evening, Ma'am. May I ask you a favor? I have come a long way, and need water for myself and my horse.

PAKHOM: (LOOKING UP) Come in, sir! Don't keep the gentleman out in the cold, Vera! Fetch some tea! Of course, sir, we will let you have anything you need. Won't you sit down?

DEVIL: That's very kind of you. (LOOKING AROUND) You have a fine home here, and a good farm.

PAKHOM: Good enough, I suppose. I often wish it were larger, and closer to the river. Where are you from, sir?

DEVIL: Oh, I live across the big river, to the east, in the land of the Bashkirs.

PAKHOM:	Is it rich land?
DEVIL:	(LAUGHING) They say it is the richest in all the world. We only have one trouble. Thank you, Ma'am. (VERA HAS BROUGHT CUPS OF TEA)
PAKHOM:	See to the gentleman's horse, Vera. (SHE GOES OUT) Only one trouble?
DEVIL:	We have all this wonderful land, and not enough people to cultivate it.
PAKHOM:	But—is there land available, then?
DEVIL:	Available? We would do anything to find good farmers.
PAKHOM:	How much does the land cost?
DEVIL:	Nothing. We allot land by the day.
PAKHOM:	I don't understand.
DEVIL:	It's quite simple. You may have as much land as you can encircle in a day.
PAKHOM:	But—that would be a huge amount of land.
DEVIL:	More than enough! You must come and be one of us.
PAKHOM:	(TO VERA, AS SHE RETURNS) Vera, this gentleman has given me incredible news. Be ready to pack up. We're leaving for the Bashkir country.
VERA:	What madness is this?
DEVIL:	No madness, lady. I have told your husband how he may find all the land he needs, with no cost. Now I must be leaving; but I hope to see you soon.

In spite of Vera's protests, Pakhom made her pack all that they could carry, and they left for the east. They crossed the great river, and came at last to the land of the Bashkirs. A smiling man met them, and introduced himself as the chief; but in reality he was the Devil in another disguise. He brought them to his tent, and gave them food and drink. Then he explained to Pakhom how he could rise at dawn next day, and walk around all the land he could possibly want. Pakhom slept badly, because he was tired and excited; but at dawn he was all ready to go.

DEVIL:　　　　　Remember, there is only one rule. I will be here on this mound, and before the sun sets you must come and touch this cap.

VERA:　　　　　Be careful, Pakhom! Don't try to go too far.

PAKHOM:　　　　Stop worrying! This is the greatest day of our lives.

DEVIL:　　　　　There comes the sun. Off you go, Pakhom!

(THIS SCENE CAN EITHER BE DESCRIBED, OR ACTED, AS PAKHOM MAKES A LONG CIRCLE AROUND THE AUDIENCE, TALKING TO HIMSELF)

PAKHOM:　　　　There! I must rest and drink some water. (HE DRIVES IN A PEG, AND DRINKS FROM A BOTTLE) Steady, Pakhom! Not too fast. Oh, this is wonderful land! Now, time to turn back. (HE DRIVES IN ANOTHER PEG) Head for the mound, Pakhom. Oh, look! That land across the gully. It's too good to be true. (HE STRUGGLES THROUGH THORNS IN A GULLY, AND ENCIRCLES LAND ON THE HILL. THEN HE TURNS BACK, AND IS CAUGHT BY THE THORNS AGAIN) Now hurry! Oh, God, I must be in time! (PANTING AND STAGGERING, HE REACHES THE FOOT OF THE MOUND) All lost! The sun is gone!

DEVIL:　　　　　(FROM THE MOUND) We can still see the sun up here, Pakhom. One more effort! (PAKHOM CRAWLS UP THE MOUND, REACHES FOR THE CAP, BUT FALLS FLAT JUST SHORT OF IT. HE LIES STILL)

VERA:　　　　　Oh, Pakhom! Why did you have to be so greedy? If only we had stayed in our cottage! (SHE KNEELS BY HIM)

DEVIL:　　　　　No use, woman. He wanted land, more and more land. We will give him all he needs: six feet of earth for his grave.

Eight:

WHO IS MY NEIGHBOR?

(for reading radio style)

A friend of mine, a minister, told me that one evening his High School students were discussing violence in a house facing on a London street. The majority argued that we are growing more civilized, and that violence is gradually becoming less of a problem. Suddenly there was a noise outside: shouting and quick footsteps, then screams. They ran out and found the situation which this play imagines: a boy half killed by thugs. This was about forty years ago. Are things better or worse in the 21st century than they were in the 19th or 15th or any other century of our history? And what can we do? This play is for reading or radio-style presentation.

CHARACTERS: UNCLE DAN, 50's
     PETE, a college student
     Mr. and Mrs. SCHWARTZ, and NANCY, 17
     JUDY and DAVE, a young couple
     RUSTY and BO-BO, gang members, 18
     BUD, gang member, 16
     BARTENDER
     GIUSEPPE, 18
     Two AMBULANCE DRIVERS

It is a hot, sultry evening on a city street. Uncle Dan and Pete are walking past a large apartment building. We can hear a baby crying. A boy goes by on a skateboard. From a window above Nancy calls out, 'Hi, Uncle Dan!' and he greets her in reply.

PETE: That kid will wear a rut in the sidewalk.

DAN: if he hasn't already, he never will. Where can a kid skate in this neighborhood? The street is the only playground.

PETE: Does everyone around here call you Uncle Dan?

DAN: Most of the kids, and some others. If you stay around long enough, and walk with an artificial leg, you get to be known. Come in! Have some coffee.

PETE: Thanks.

DAN: You can tell me more about college, and that psychology course.

PETE: O.K. If you promise to listen.

In the Schwartz's apartment Nancy is restless.

FATHER: There's that baby yelling again.

NANCY: Get with it, Dad! Babies have to cry. Maybe he's as bored as I am. I wish there was something to do.

FATHER: You never stop complaining. Haven't you any homework?

NANCY: I've done it. Anyway it's too hot to study.

MOTHER: Turn on the TV.

NANCY: I don't want to watch TV. I want to go out and do something.

MOTHER: Well, you can't. Not at this time of night.

FATHER: I'm going to bed. Read a magazine. Anything to get away from your bellyaching.

Close by, Dave and Judy, recently married, are also under stress from the heat.

JUDY: Dave, put down that paper and talk to me! (HE SLAPS THE NEWSPAPER DOWN ANGRILY) We have to talk about money. Are we going to be able to make the payments?

DAVE: Judy, I told you. I don't know. It depends on my commissions.

JUDY: And if we can't?

DAVE: Don't think about it now. It's going to be O.K.

JUDY: So you say. Am I going to be out in the street because my husband can't earn a decent salary?

DAVE: I earn as much as most guys, but where it all goes I don't know. We have to be more careful.

JUDY: Careful! Look at me—my clothes—this room! How dare you—

DAVE: I didn't mean it that way. Hey, let me fan you. (HE PICKS UP THE PAPER AND USES IT AS A FAN)

JUDY: That feels good.

DAVE: Don't worry, honey! We'll come through this—honest!

JUDY: I didn't mean to complain, Dave. With the baby coming I get worried—and it's so hot in here.

DAVE: Yeah, sultry, like a storm coming up. That might clear the air.

In Uncle Dan's small first floor apartment Pete has prepared the coffee.

PETE: Ready, Uncle Dan

DAN: Black for me, Pete. (PETE BRINGS THE CUPS) Thanks. Now back to our debate. What you're saying is—or your professor—the kids on the street who steal or commit crimes aren't responsible. We haven't made enough social progress to solve their problems.

PETE: That's right; but we're making the progress. We need to understand what makes people violent or antisocial—why they're frustrated. Then we can educate them out of it—not put them behind bars.

DAN: Does crime go down in proportion to the number of college degrees we hand out?

PETE: It's not that simple. But give it time. We're getting there.

In a bar around the corner Rusty, Bobo, and Bud have been drinking. They order another drink from the bartender.

BARTENDER: Look, fellas, you don't want any more. I shouldn't be serving you. You're under age.

RUSTY: Who said anything about age?

BARTENDER: This kid's not more than sixteen.

BOBO: If you don't want trouble you fetch us those drinks.

BARTENDER: You'll find trouble enough when the cops catch up with you.

RUSTY: We can deal with the cops.

BARTENDER: If that's the kind of damfool stuff they raise you on nowadays, I give up!

(HE SLAPS DOWN THEIR DRINKS)

Back in Uncle Dan's room the debate goes on.

DAN: You keep talking about progress. Seems to me we haven't made much in thousands of years. Are we better than Athens, or Rome?

PETE: Look around you: better hospitals, better schools—

DAN: And printing presses and radios and movies and TV and computers and the Internet. Take the kids along this street. They get ten times the book learning a kid two thousand years ago would have gotten, but in a crisis—

PETE: You don't believe education is making any difference?

DAN: When do you have to get back?

PETE: It's only 9.30. I've another hour.

DAN: Good! Then I'll move to the real heart of the matter. You ask, will education change human nature. I'll tell you something, Pete. There's only one thing that keeps us—some of us—from being wild animals, and that is love—being loved and needed and having someone care about us; and in reverse—caring about them. It's a two way street. Without it, we're no better than dogs running wild.

PETE: I know. I wish the text books had more to say about that. You'd make a great teacher, Uncle Dan.

DAN: Flattery will earn you more coffee.

PETE: I'll fix it—and one for you.

In the Schwartz apartment Nancy is at the window, humming a song.

MOTHER: Quiet, Nancy! Your father's trying to sleep.

NANCY: What a night! How can it be so hot? I'll try pushing the window clear up. (SHE DOES SO) No more air to be had, I guess. (FOOTSTEPS AND WHISTLING BELOW) Mom, there's Giuseppe leaving the delicatessen.

MOTHER: (APPPROACHING WINDOW) Where? Oh, yes. He's a goodlooking boy. Nice too; always whistling.

NANCY: Kind of square, but I guess he's O.K.

MOTHER: Who are those three boys?

NANCY: Where?

MOTHER:	Coming the other way.
NANCY:	Never saw them before. Hey, they're real creeps!
MOTHER:	Oh, God! Look what they're doing!
NANCY:	They're moving in on Giuseppe.

In the street, the gang members were looking for trouble.

BUD:	(IN A THICK VOICE) Who you pushing?
GIUSEPPE:	I don't push nobody—
RUSTY:	He said you were pushing.
GIUSEPPE:	I don't mean to push. I'm sorry.
BOBO:	He's a jerk. That's what he is.
BUD:	Rusty, he pushed me.
RUSTY:	Let's get him. (SOUNDS OF A STRUGGLE)
GIUSEPPE:	Let me go! Oh, God! (SCREAMING)

The noise was heard by many people: first by Nancy at her window,

NANCY:	Oh, no! Look!
FATHER:	What's going on? What's the matter, Nancy?
NANCY:	They're beating up Giuseppe!
MOTHER:	Do something, George!
FATHER:	Nothing I can do. It's not our business. Dirty little swine!

And by Dave and Judy.

JUDY:	Dave, these boys are kicking and beating a kid . We've got to stop them!
DAVE:	How? We can't do anything.

JUDY: You mean you won't! Well, I can. I'm calling the police.

DAVE: If you do that you'll have to give your name. Then we'll be involved. Let the kids work it out!

JUDY: Work it out! In the morgue? They're killing him.

DAVE: Someone will do something. I don't want you interfering.

   Giuseppe wriggled free, and staggered along the street, chased by the three gang members.

GIUSEPPE: Madre mia! Someone help me!

PETE: (INSIDE DAN'S APARTMENT) What's going on out there?

DAN: (AT WINDOW) My God, it's Giuseppe! Let's go! Grab that whistle on my desk, and blow it for all you're worth. I'll tackle them.

PETE: You may get hurt.

DAN: I've got to stop them before they kill him. (OUTSIDE) Get away, you punks!

RUSTY: You keep out of this, pegleg.

DAN: Why, you young— (HE WADES INTO THEM, AND HOLDS BUD, THEY SURROUND HIM. PETE'S WHISTLE SOUNDS FROM A DISTANCE)

BOBO: Cops!

RUSTY: Down the alley! (THEY RUN)

BUD: Don't leave me, Rusty! Aaah! You're breaking my arm!

DAN: I'll break more than your arm if you try to get away.

PETE: You O.K., Uncle Dan?

DAN: Sure. I can still deal with a drunken schoolboy. We'll get the other two when the cops come. Easy, Giuseppe boy! It's all over. We'll take care of you.

BUD: He pushed me! We was walking along peaceful and—

DAN:	Shut up! You can tell your lies to the police. We need an ambulance. (LOOKING UP AT THE WINDOWS AND CALLING LOUD) Have any of you called the police? I'm talking to you up there. Did you call the police? Or an ambulance? In God's name what's wrong with you? There's a boy down here, dying, maybe.
DAVE:	O.K., Uncle Dan. I'll call.
DAN:	Tell them an ambulance. Pete, hold on to this kid.
PETE:	With pleasure.
BUD:	Let me go! I tell you, he—
PETE:	Be quiet! You make me sick.
DAN:	Now, Giuseppe, easy! Your friends are here.
GIUSEPPE:	Thanks, Uncle Dan.
DAN:	Youre a brave man, Giuseppe. Worth a dozen of those punks. Help's on the way.
PETE:	God! he looks terrible. Isn't there something we can do?
DAVE:	Keep him still, and hope they haven't hurt his spine or his kidneys. God knows they tried!
PETE:	It's all so stupid. I can't believe—
DAN:	Progress, huh? This doesn't fit your psychology course. Progress wasn't quick enough to save Giuseppe. (AMBULANCE SIREN) Over here! (RUNNING STEPS)
Ist MAN:	O.K. On the stretcher.
2nd MAN:	Who did it?
DAN:	Other kids. His name's Giuseppe Grandi. Lives down the street.
Ist MAN:	Thanks. We'll leave the police to get the details.
2nd MAN:	Let's go. (AMBULANCE DRIVES AWAY)

DAN:

God help him, poor kid! (LOUD) You people up there! What are you staring at? The show's over, unless you want to wait for the cops to take this little rat away. But I warn you, you'd better not be looking when the police arrive. You might be wanted as witnesses. You might be involved, and that would never do, would it? (SIREN) Yes, I'm tallking to you! A boy gets half killed under your eyes, and you didn't even move a finger—a finger on a telephone. You might get hurt, or someone might ask you questions. What kind of neighbors are you? And what are you going to do next time? Only remember—next time it could be you!

Any Graven Image

The next four plays have a common theme. The Second Commandment reads: 'Thou shalt not make to thyself any graven image.' That literally meant making an idol, a statue or cult object before which people bowed down in prayer. You might suppose that this is a long outdated commandment. Who is likely to carve a piece of wood or stone into a god in our society? But the danger of worshipping a graven image is much more subtle and pervasive than it would appear.

A graven image may be defined as anything which you value or worship too much, so that it takes you away from God and from the right balance of your life. If you look at it in this way it is easy to see how many people bow down to an idol.

It may be money. Paul did NOT say: 'Money is the root of all evil.' He said: 'the LOVE of money is the root of all evil.' Go to any casino and you will see people whose lives are being devastated by a craving for money. But money is only one of the obsessions which may ruin our lives. Power, sex, greed for things other than money: obsessions come in all shapes and sizes. Things which start out as wonderful aims can turn into mean cravings. You can make an idol of your stamp collection, your video games, your piano, in fact anything which monopolizes your time and energy at the expense of a well controlled, unselfish life.

In the first of these plays it is Denise Gibson's house which is her graven image. I wrote this play after being taken to visit a lady in just such a house: I could never forget it. In the second it is Dene Peck's tennis racket. In the third it is Elise Morgan's desk. In the fourth it is something which it seems hard to call an idol: Anastas Bata's love for his dead wife. He found out that he needed to free himself from this just as much as Denise needed to free herself from her obsession with her house.

Nine:

THE PERFECT HOUSE+ (hard to act)

CHARACTERS: BOB GIBSON, 50's
DENISE GIBSON, his wife, 50's
AMADEO, their houseman
LESTER SUMMERFIELD, their architect
A MAN who happened to be close by
Doctor BARROW
Injured CHILDREN

It is midafternoon in Denise Gibson's new house. AMADEO, preoccupied, is looking around the lavishly furnished living room. He is close to the door leading to the patio when DENISE enters from the other side.

DENISE: Amadeo!

AMADEO: Yes, Mrs. Gibson.

DENISE: Have you checked that everything is in place?

AMADEO: All looks good, Mrs. Gibson. They do a nice job.

DENISE: They forgot the carpeting for the platform. I had to yell at them.

AMADEO: It's all right now. Don't you worry!

DENISE: Good! I'll come and take a look. I'd like to test the sound system. That's the first thing to go wrong. You'd better help me. Oh, that reminds me— (SHE STANDS NEAR THE PATIO DOORS, WRITING A NOTE ON A PAD. BOB ENTERS FROM THE PATIO)

BOB: What's on your mind, honey? Where's Amadeo off to in such a hurry?

DENISE: He's going to help me do a final checkup.

BOB: Relax! You pay professionals to do all that.

DENISE: You're too trusting, Bob. When you're paying all that money to bring in a singer like Lee Holden you'd better make sure everything's perfect. I'll be back in a minute. (FRONT DOOR BELL) Who could that be? Will you see? I need to chase after Amadeo.

(SHE GOES OUT TO PATIO. BOB OPENS DOOR. ENTER LESTER)

BOB: Hi, Lester! Come on in!

LESTER: Afternoon, Bob. I couldn't stay away—too curious to see the house all ready for the party. I know you're too busy for a visitor, but—

DENISE: (FROM PATIO) Who is it, Bob?

LESTER: It's me, Denise. Lester. I had to come by and see how my handiwork looks for its first test.

DENISE:	(STILL OUTSIDE) You're an hour and a half early for the party.
LESTER:	I know. I have to go home and pick up Sally. Wow, Bob! Denise has really gone overboard. (HE LOOKS OUT AT THE PATIO)
BOB:	It's her big day, Lester.
LESTER:	And yours?
BOB:	This sort of thing means more to her—the house, the party, and so on. If it fulfils what she wants, that's fine with me.
LESTER:	Well, you know what I've said all along. I've been designing fairsized homes out here for twenty years, and I thought this was too big for the two of you. I still don't agree with everything Denise insisted on having, but I have to hand it to her. She knows her stuff and she sticks to her ideas.
BOB:	That's right. She does. I can see what you mean. Takes some living up to, a place like this. But I'm an outdoor nut, anyway. I think I'll get used to it.
DENISE:	(ENTERING) Hi, Lester! Nice of you to stop by before the crowd arrives.
LESTER:	(EMBRACING HER) Denise, you're a marvel! It's what you wanted, and it's perfect. How many are coming this evening?
DENISE:	Two hundred and sixty, without the gate crashers. And this is one time when I really want the gate crashers to see my house.
LESTER:	Two hundred and— Wow! You think big, don't you?
DENISE:	I could stop the clock forever today. All the years we've been trailing around the world after Bob's job I've dreamed of this: my own house, and guests filling it. And I mean house, and I mean filling. You've given us all of that. Thanks, Lester! (SHE KISSES HIM)
LESTER:	Don't thank me! You're my most profitable clients. It's odd, you know. I haven't often cared so much about a job, and I certainly never before battled with a client to reduce the scale of her plans. I'll be frank with you, though. I hope you enjoy the house as much on the normal days—you know, the golfing and dishes days.

DENISE: Don't worry! We will, won't we, Bob?

BOB: Sure, honey, sure.

LESTER: That reminds me, Bob. We haven't had that game yet. How do you like the course?

BOB: It's fine. I'm a little rusty after being out of the country for so long; but once this party's out of the way I should be playing most days. Give me a week or two, and I'll take you on.

LESTER: Well, I must hurry home, or Sally will wonder how we're going to get here on time. Good luck, Denise! You're on the launching pad, ready to soar into space. Speaking of luck, you had your rain at the right moment. Seems to be all over now.

BOB: Yeah. The forecast is good for the evening.

DENISE: It had to be. California sun is one of the things I paid for. Comes with the house.

LESTER: Everything looks fresh after that shower. Roads are still a bit slippery, especially around that new construction on Mirabelle.

BOB: Most people will come the other way, from town.

LESTER: So long, then. I'll be back later.

BOB: (AT DOOR) Bye.

DENISE: I must hurry, Bob, and put myself together.

BOB: (EMBRACING HER) You look nicely put together to me. I'll see what Amadeo's up to. It all looks great, Denise.

DENISE: Thanks, Bob. It had to be great. We're going to show them the Gibsons have come to town. (SHE GOES OFF ONE WAY, AS AMADEO ENTERS FROM THE PATIO THE OTHER SIDE. HE IS HUMMING)

BOB: You sound happy, Amadeo.

AMADEO: Sure makes a lot of fuss, this party, but I think everything's straight. Flowers O.K. Platform O.K. Caterers O.K.

BOB: You've done a great job. I think it's all coming together. (HE LOOKS OUT ACROSS THE PATIO) The valet parking people will have their work cut out after the rain.

AMADEO: The Band should come soon, and the bartenders. I wonder—
(FROM A DISTANCE COMES THE NOISE OF THE SCHOOL BUS SKIDDING, CRUNCHING AGAINST A WALL, AND OVERTURNING)

BOB: What in—

AMADEO: The bus! The school bus! All those kids!

DENISE: (RUNNING IN) What was that noise?

BOB: I'm afraid it was the school bus. I'm going—

DENISE: You can't leave now, Bob. The Band will be coming. (BOB TAKES NO NOTICE, AND RUNS OUT OF THE FRONT DOOR) Amadeo, check whether they have arrived, will you?

AMADEO: Sure, Mrs. Gibson, but hadn't we better wait—

DENISE: We can't wait. We have too many problems of our own to worry about other people's. (SHE GOES BACK TO HER ROOM. AMADEO STANDS IRRESOLUTE. BOB RUNS IN)

BOB: It was the school bus. Small car skidded at the corner, and they hit it and lost control. 'Fraid there are some kids badly hurt.

AMADEO: Oh, my God!

BOB: I told them this is the nearest house and phone. Some of them will be here in a minute. We'll need mattresses on the patio deck, and boiling water. I'm trying to think—

AMADEO: Yes, sir. (HE RUNS OUT)

BOB: (CALLING AFTER HIM) And sheets. (HE GOES TO PHONE) Get me the police. There's been an accident— Police? There's been a bad accident halfway up Flower Hill, on Garnet—3800's. Yes, Garnet. School bus. My name's Gibson, Bob Gibson, 3846 Garnet. I'm bringing as many as I can to my house. O.K. Hurry, please!

DENISE: (ENTERING) Whatever was that all about?

BOB: I'm afraid it's really bad, honey. School bus overturned. I told them to bring the injured kids here.

DENISE: You told them—

BOB: Listen, Denise, hurry! You know what to get ready.

DENISE: Are you telling me they're coming to my house?

BOB: Of course they are—and to any other house where they can be helped. Now—

DENISE: They can't come here. Our guests will be arriving. Use your head, Bob—

BOB: Don't be crazy! These are kids—dying, some of them. For God's sake—

DENISE: They'll spoil everything. Not now, Bob! (AMADEO IS SEEN ON THE PATIO)

BOB: That's right, Amadeo. Put them there!

DENISE: Have you both gone mad?

BOB: I'll be there in a minute to help you.

AMADEO: Yes, sir.

DENISE: (HYSTERICAL) I'll hate you forever if anyone tramples through my house today. I'll hate you, do you hear?

BOB: For God's sake stop wasting time! We may need the spare mattresses off the beds—

DENISE: (RUNNING TO FRONT DOOR) Bob, I'm locking the door.

BOB: (RUNNING TOWARDS HER) You must be out of your mind!

DENISE: Take your hands off me! (THEY STRUGGLE, AND SHE FALLS. BOB OPENS THE DOOR AS A CAR ARRIVES)

BOB: Now get to work, Denise, or get out of our way!

DENISE:	(STILL ON THE FLOOR) I'm finished with you, I tell you—finished! (SHE STANDS WITH HANDS CLENCHED, WATCHING, AS BOB GOES OUT AND RETURNS CARRYING A CHILD)
BOB:	That's O.K., son. We'll look after you. Amadeo! (HE CARRIES THE CHILD OUT TO THE PATIO, THEN RETURNS WITH A MATTRESS, AS A MAN ENTERS THE FRONT DOOR WITH A CHILD IN HIS ARMS)
MAN:	This girl's bleeding badly. We did our best—
BOB:	(SETTING DOWN THE MATTRESS CENTER) Here, on the mattress. Amadeo! Bandages and hot water. She's unconscious. I wish I knew more about this.
MAN:	I'll get back. There are more. (HE GOES OUT)
DENISE:	Bob, are the ambulances coming?
BOB:	Shouldn't be long now. Poor kid! (ANOTHER CAR IS HEARD) Here come some more. We'll put them in the patio.
DENISE:	I—I'll bandage this girl. You look after the others.
BOB:	(TO THE MAN WHO CARRIES IN ANOTHER CHILD) Out here, will you? (THEY GO OUT, BUT WE HEAR HIM) That's right. A doctor should be here any minute. (THEY REENTER) How many were injured, do you know?
MAN:	About fifteen; and two dead, the driver and a child.
BOB:	Fifteen! My God! Amadeo, we'll need more of everything—sheets, hot water—
MAN:	A station wagon with five or six kids went around to your back entrance. I'll see if I can help. (HE GOES OUT TO THE PATIO. AMBULANCE SIREN HEARD)
BOB:	Thank God—the first ambulance, and a doctor, I hope. (SIREN STOPS. RUNNING FEET. ENTER DOCTOR BARROW)
BARROW:	I'm Doctor Barrow. Are the casualties all in here?
BOB:	In here or on their way. We're doing what we can—

BARROW: (KNEELING BY THE GIRL) Good.

BOB: This girl looks bad.

DENISE: I did my best to stop the bleeding.

BARROW: Yes. (SOUND OF ANOTHER AMBULANCE)

BOB: I'll direct them to the other entrance, and I'll see if any of the kids out there looks like an emergency. (EXIT BY FRONT DOOR)

BARROW: I'll be with you in a minute. Are you Mrs. Gibson?

DENISE: Yes.

BARROW: You did a good job. She should be all right.

DENISE: I'll see what's happening out here. (SHE GOES TO THE PATIO. BARROW WORKS ON THE GIRL. THEN DENISE RUNS IN) Doctor Barrow!

BARROW: Yes?

DENISE: Come quickly, please. It's this boy—

BARROW: Coming, Mrs. Gibson.

(HE FINISHES THE DRESSING, COVERS THE GIRL WITH A SHEET, AND HURRIES OUT. LIGHTS FADE TO A BLACKOUT. SILENCE. THEN A SIREN, FADING INTO THE DISTANCE. LIGHTS UP SLOWLY. THE GIRL HAS GONE. A BLOODSTAINED SHEET LIES ON THE MATTRESS. BOB AND BARROW ENTER SLOWLY FROM THE PATIO)

BOB: (LOOKING AT HIS WATCH) Five o'clock! Not much more than an hour. It seems like ten years!

BARROW: I'll bet it does. Well, Bob, I'll be getting along.

BOB: Thanks for everything, doctor.

BARROW: It's for me to thank you—and Mrs. Gibson. You did a wonderful job, opening your home and doing all you could for them so quickly. You may have saved two or three lives. But I'm sorry for what it has done to your house.

BOB:	If it helped to save any of those children, what the hell does the house matter?
BARROW:	Not everyone would say that. Good night, Bob, and God bless you! (THEY SHAKE HANDS)
BOB:	Good night, Doc.
BARROW:	Give your wife my very best. She's quite a lady, Bob.
BOB:	Yes, she is. I'll tell her.
BARROW:	One day I'd like to call on you, and we'll really get acquainted.
BOB:	Acquainted? You mean, with a martini in one hand, and all the trimmings? Sounds strange to say it, but I think I prefer it this way. That is—
BARROW:	I know what you mean. 'Bye! (HE GOES OUT. BOB CROSSES TO PHONE)
BOB:	Operator, get me the Police, please. Hello. Police? This is Bob Gibson, Garnet Road. We—oh, you know all about it. Yes. Listen, in less than an hour two hundred or more people are due here. Yes, big party. Out of the question now. Yes, it's a mess, and—uh-huh. (PAUSE) You can do that? Have a patrolman at the corner of Garnet and Mirabelle? That's great. It's been on radio? And TV? A lot of the guests will know. Thanks for your help. Yes, you're right. Plenty to be done here. Goodbye.

(HE PUTS THE PHONE DOWN SLOWLY, LOOKS TOWARDS DENISE'S ROOM, CROSSES TO CENTER, PICKS UP THE SHEET, THEN DROPS IT, AND GOES TO AN ARMCHAIR. HE SITS, AND COVERS HIS HEAD WITH HIS HANDS. DENISE ENTERS QUIETLY, AND STANDS LOOKING AT HIM. HE LOOKS UP)

BOB:	Hello, Denise.

(SHE SUDDENLY KNEELS AND PUTS HER HEAD ON HIS KNEES)

DENISE:	Bob, I—
BOB:	Don't try to talk now, Denise. You're exhausted.
DENISE:	There's something I must say.

BOB: All right, then. Say it, if it helps.

DENISE: (LIFTING HER HEAD AND DRAWING BACK FROM HIM) When you ran out of that door to offer my house to those strangers I hated you, Bob. I told you so, and it was true. I hated you. And I hated those children, dead or alive. I said to myself, why does it have to happen to me? Why destroy what I've sweated blood to build up? And I hated every one of you when you came through the door.

BOB: Even the little girl?

DENISE: Yes, her too. Oh, I wanted her to live, and I did as good a job as I could stopping her bleeding; but I hated her because she was in my house and her blood was on my new rug.

BOB: Denise, don't!

DENISE: Then out on the patio, when that little boy, Terry, died, I couldn't stop it, but I tried—God knows, I tried! And I didn't hate him. We always wanted children, and we couldn't have them. I suppose I've shut off that side of me for too long. But I didn't hate him. I knew he mattered. He mattered much, much more than the party—more than the rug, the Band, and—that meant that he really mattered. Oh, Bob!

BOB: Now let me tell you something. When you were screaming at me there at the door I thought it was the end for us. I knew that I couldn't stay in a house which means more to my wife than human lives. It's a silly house, anyway.

DENISE: (SLOWLY) Yes, it's a silly house. (PAUSE)

BOB: The girl's name is Becky. The driver was her father. He died.

DENISE: Oh, no! (SHE BURIES HER FACE ON HIS KNEES)

BOB: I have their address. Her mother has four other kids. I'm going around in the morning, to see what I can do.

DENISE: Can I go with you?

BOB: Sure, if— (PAUSE) What about tonight? Do you want to go out— get away?

DENISE:	No. I'd rather stay here, if you don't mind.
BOB:	That's what I'd like too. It's where we belong tonight.
DENISE:	In a minute I'd like to call Amadeo, and we'll all three have some eggs and coffee in the kitchen. Then I'd like to clean up our home.
BOB:	Tonight? You're not too tired?
DENISE:	No, I'm not too tired—not for that.
BOB:	Funny, you calling it home. Do you know, until that moment, in my mind, it has always been 'the new house'—and was I scared of it!
DENISE:	I know. Inside, I realized that, and resented it. (SHE RISES AND STANDS CENTER) Bob, this house was a craving, for the things life hasn't given us—yet. Bob, I think I'm cured, but I'm going to need your help. (SHE CALLS LOUD) Amadeo! (SHE LIFTS BOB FROM THE CHAIR) Come on, Bob! How would you like your eggs?

Ten:

THE CHAMPION+ (hard to act)

CHARACTERS:	DENE PECK, 35 JILL, his wife, 33 BARRY EDMUNDS, 25 Doctor GEORGE YORK BILL JAEGER, Dene's financial adviser A driver on the freeway A radio announcer

The action of this play goes from a locker room at the National Tennis Center to the home of Dene and Jill Peck, with short scenes on the freeway and at the homes of Dene's doctor and financial adviser. It is not an easy play to act, but suitable for a dramatic reading. It begins in the locker room. BARRY EDMUNDS is rubbing his hair with cream and combing it, with a radio close to him.

ANNOUNCER:	(QUICK, EXCITED) Zarnik to the forehand, Dene Peck deep to the backhand. He's running in. Zarnik a weak return, and Dene puts that away easily. (APPLAUSE) He's looking like a champion today, and this quarterfinal match is safely in his hands.
BARRY:	Attaboy, Dene!

ANNOUNCER: Peck serves. That's a fault, over the sideline. Now a spinning second service. Zarnik returns halfcourt. Peck a halfvolley, Zarnik's chasing it, he lobs, but it's short. Peck is there. He—(Ooohs FROM CROWD)—well, well! For Dene Peck that was a bad miss. Wait a minute! He's bent double: could be a bad cramp.

BARRY: Oh, no!

ANNOUNCER: No. He's O.K. He goes back to serve, and he has that grim, tough look we know so well, the look of a man who refuses to lose. He serves—an ace! (CHEERS) That brings him to match point. Match point for Dene Peck in this quarterfinal of the U.S. Open. which he has won twice before. Here he is, ready to serve. He serves. That's it! That's the match! (CHEERS)

BARRY: Good for Dene! That's the stuff! (TURNS OFF RADIO. HE IS COMBING HIS HAIR, PHONE RINGS) Hello. Oh, hi, Jill! Wasn't it great? Yeah, I will. He'll be here in a minute. What? Oh, I don't know. Cramp, maybe. Made no difference, anyway. To take Zarnik in three sets is really something. Sure, I'll give him the message. So long, Jill.

(HE PUTS PHONE DOWN, WHISTLES)

DENE: (entering) Hi, Barry!

BARRY: Dene, you old rascal! How do you do it? It was great!

DENE: Thanks. Zarnik was tough in the third set, but he didn't quite make it.

BARRY: You just missed Jill. She said to congratulate you and what was all that about a cramp?

DENE: Oh, I don't know. I've been having a bit of it lately. Pain in the chest. Hurts like hell for a minute, then goes away.

BARRY: Well, it's hot, and you're thirty-five. A lot of people wonder how you do it.

DENE: A man is the age he allows himself to be. Jill didn't waste any time calling.

BARRY: You're a lucky man to have a wife like her.

DENE: You're telling me. Oooh! (HE BENDS OVER FOR A FEW SECONDS, HOLDING HIS CHEST)

BARRY: You ought to see a doctor, Dene.

DENE: I will, after the final.

BARRY: (Laughing) You have to beat Al Brock first. I don't envy him, if you play like today. But look after yourself!

DENE: It's nothing.

BARRY: Take a shower. You look wiped out.

DENE: I will. It'll be good to be home. Drop around if you can.

(SCENE CHANGES TO A FREEWAY: SOUND ONLY. CARS DRIVEN FAST; THEN SUDDEN BRAKING, DOOR SLAMMED, QUICK STEPS)

VANESSI: What the—you swerved straight into my lane. Are you drunk or something?

PECK: I'm sorry. I had a sudden cramp.

VANESSI: Cramp! You—hey, I know you. Aren't you Dene Peck? I was watching your match earlier.

DENE: That's right. I'm sorry.

VANESSI: My name's Vanessi, Vince Vanessi. Mr. Peck, aren't you feeling good?

DENE: I'll be O.K. Just this sudden cramp.

VANESSI: You'll have to watch out. Sure I can't do anything for you? Call a doctor?

DENE: No, no. I'm just sorry it happened. I'll be careful.

VANESSI: Well, luckily there's no damage. Take care—and good luck!

(WE HEAR DENE MAKING CALLS)

DENE: Doctor York, please. (PAUSE) George? Dene Peck. Could I drop around tonight? Just routine, but I'd like to ask you something. Thanks. It was rough today, whatever the score said. Around eight then? Thanks. See you. (A SECOND CALL) Hi, Sally! Dene Peck. Is Bill in? I'd appreciate it. (PAUSE) Bill? Oh, thanks. I'm doing fine. Never played better. Look, Bill, can you spare a few minutes tonight? Say 8.30? Fine, then. I'll drop by. Sorry to bother you at night, but you know my crazy schedule. O.K. See you.

(SCENE: THE PECKS' LIVING ROOM. JILL CARRIES A TRAY OF ICED TEA FROM THE KITCHEN. SOUND OF A CAR. SHE OPENS DOOR)

JILL: Hi, darling!

DENE: Hello, honey! (A LONG EMBRACE)

JILL: You made it again!

DENE: Did you think I wouldn't?

JILL: Never. It must be awful in that heat. You had me worried.

DENE: Why? It was in the bag all the way—

JILL: No. I mean when you were all doubled up in the last game, and Barry—

DENE: (ANGRY) Why can't they mind their own business? Can't I miss a tennis ball without everyone analyzing it and—

JILL: Relax, darling! I've made iced tea. Sit down! Even you can't go through two weeks of national tennis without some strain—

DENE: Not you too! Strain—how I hate that word! You get to be thirty-five, and they're all waiting for you to drop dead. (HE SITS DOWN, EXHAUSTED)

JILL: Don't snap my head off, darling! We have a free evening, and no match tomorrow. Stay home and put your feet up!

DENE: That's right. We have a day to ourelves. Where can I take you, Jill? The beach? A movie? Dress up and have dinner at Maxie's?

JILL: Dene Peck, I don't want to go anywhere. (SITS AT HIS FEET) I love you, darling, and I just want us to be together.

DENE: That makes two of us. I'm sorry I got worked up.

JILL: I understand. Whatever you say, it is a strain playing in front of all those cameras and crowds. We have a beautiful home. Let's enjoy it. After supper we'll sit here and listen to some music.

DENE: I promised I'd go and call on Bill for a few minutes.

JILL: Tonight? What a time to worry about Income Tax! You never give yourself a rest. You always act as if you were running from the baseline to the net. No, I mean it. You really do.

DENE: I'm sorry, darling. Wait until tomorrow. I'll promise not to stir. A day here, with you, is my idea of paradise.

JILL: Mine too. Tomorrow you can read the headlines instead of making them.

DENE: That's right. (SUDDENLY HE PICKS HER UP AND HOLDS HER) Oh, Jill! You're the only thing that matters, Looking after you. I—

JILL: You what, Dene?

DENE: Oh, nothing. I'm so glad to be home. Let's drink that iced tea!

(AT DOCTOR YORK'S, DENE IS LYING ON A COUCH STRIPPED TO THE WAIST)

YORK: Over on your back. (PAUSE) You say it was only for a few seconds each time?

DENE: That's all. Dizziness, and this tightness in the chest. I felt my heart thumping pretty hard.

YORK: O.K. Sit up and put your shirt on.

DENE: What's up, Doc?

YORK: Something I've warned you would come one day, but you never listened.

DENE: Does anybody listen?

YORK: Some folks listen so hard they hear three times as much as I tell them. This time you have to listen. You've come to the end of the road, Dene—end of the court, I suppose I should say.

DENE: You mean I'm not fit to play tennis?

YORK: Uh-huh. What happened to you today was not surprising. The thing I admire about you is that you have always done more than the body is capable of doing. You have a row of championships under your belt because you wouldn't lose.

DENE: O.K., O.K., so I try to win. What of it?

YORK: You race that engine of yours, more than anyone I've ever treated, and it's beginning to protest. Trouble is, a human being only has one engine.

DENE: Come on, George! Tell me what I have to do.

YORK: What do tennis players do at your age?

DENE: Go on playing tennis, some of them—and winning.

YORK: Not many. Oh, back in the past there may have been a few: Borotra, Rosewall, Gonzales—you know more about it than I do. But you win on guts and talent. You drive yourself beyond the limit. I'm telling you you can't do that any more. It'll kill you.

DENE: Kill me?

YORK: Exactly that. These spasms are nervous tension, but your heart has had all the stress it can take. Same with a diver or an astronaut. Championship tennis is a young man's game—or woman's. Give up, Dene! Keep a sports store, or use your reputation to turn to something else.

DENE: What if I don't have anything else?

YORK: You'll find it. You're not a dumb athlete with no brain. And Jill will help you—

DENE: Jill? You mean sit around and let my wife work for me? No, George!

YORK: I didn't say that. But she wants to share whatever you do. She can't be on the court, but you know she cares about every ball you hit. There are other things in the world beside forehands and backhands, Dene.

DENE: Are there? If you start on the circuit at seventeen, what else is there at thirty-five—except forehands and backhands?

YORK: Plenty more. Thank God you have the right wife to help you see it! Anyway, my job is to tell you that you've reached the end of big tennis. I mean that.

(AFTER A MUSIC BRIDGE WE SEE DENE AND BILL JAEGER SITTING)

DENE: (accepting a drink) Thanks, Bill. Sorry to bother you so late.

BILL: That's O.K. Fire away!

DENE: How much would I be worth, Bill—I mean, if anything happened to me?

BILL: Well, well! I've been trying to get you to concentrate on that question for years. You know the answer: very little.

DENE: You mean, if I—smashed up on the highway, Jill would be in financial trouble?

BILL: Well, it's relative, isn't it? You and Jill live at a high standard. Plenty comes in, but you spend it, Dene.

DENE: All of it?

BILL: You don't save much. She puts by a little, but you're no help. I've tried to tell you.

DENE: Sure, and I wouldn't listen. Too busy winning matches.

BILL: What's the trouble?

DENE: Oh, today a car nearly hit me. Made me do some thinking.

BILL: So you came straight to me, late in the evening after a tough match? I'll check out what you're worth and send you a memo about ways to cut down and set more aside. And we'll look into upping your insurance.

DENE: Insurance? You mean, on my life?

BILL: Sure. A great ox like you won't have much trouble with the company.

DENE: (SLOWLY) No. So you'll let me know what I'm worth. Yeah. Yeah, Bill, I'd like to know that. It's about time.

(BACK TO THE LIVING ROOM. DENE AND JILL ON THE COUCH, HIS ARM AROUND HER. A CLASSICAL RECORDING FINISHES)

DENE: Don't move, darling. I'll find the Dvorak.

JILL: No, stay. It's been like a dream today—just us at home.

DENE: We don't do it enough, do we?

JILL: Don't put on another. Why don't you go to bed? Al Brock's a lot younger than you.

DENE: I can beat him. He needn't think he can tire me.

JILL: Don't give him the chance.

DENE: He'll be back in the locker room before he knows what hit him. Want some milk and cookies before bed?

JILL: I'll fix it.

DENE: You sit there. I want to wait on you.

JILL: Oh, Dene. All right. I'll sit still. (SHE SITS, THOUGHTFUL, WHILE HE GOES TO THE KITCHEN) Found everything?

DENE: Yeah. Just coming up. (PAUSE. HE COMES THROUGH THE KITCHEN DOOR, CARRYING A TRAY. SUDDENLY HE LETS OUT A LOUD 'Ooh!', AND DROPS THE TRAY. HE STAGGERS AND FALLS TO HIS KNEES)

JILL: Dene! (RUNS TO HIM) What is it, darling?

DENE: (VOICE CAREFULLY CONTROLLED) It's O.K., honey. I guess I tripped on the rug. I'm O.K.

JILL: You're sure?

DENE: (ANGRY) I said so, didn't I? I'll clean this up.

JILL: No, Dene. You sit down. I'll do it. I—

DENE: (SHOUTING) I'll clean it up, do you hear? I'm not helpless.

JILL: (AFTER A PAUSE) I'm sorry. Of course, you do it. I'll fix some more milk.

DENE: Jill, forgive me. I'm all churned up. Two more matches and it will be over.

JILL: (LAUGHING) That's right, darling—two. That's why you never lose—you don't even think about it.

DENE: (KISSING HER) Jill, you're wonderful. Oh, Jilly, I hope I can always make you as happy as we've been today!

JILL: Just stay around, darling. That's all it takes. And don't think I need to be wrapped in cotton wool. You've treated me today as if I would break in pieces if someone sneezed.

DENE: I wanted to show you how much I care for you.

JILL: I know that, darling. Give me a chance to show you too. Now let go of me, and we'll have that milk.

(THE LOCKER ROOM AS BEFORE. RADIO ON, BUT ROOM EMPTY. APPLAUSE AS LIGHTS COME UP)

ANNOUNCER: They're towelling themselves, and taking a drink. The heat must be fierce out there. Dene Peck, defending his title, 35 and still winning—with that bulldog look on his face; and young Al Brock, looking thoughtful, as he well may, because up to now he has no answer to Peck's speed and concentration. Now, Brock to serve, with Peck up 5-2 in this first set. He serves—fast to the backhand, but Peck makes a great return—a clean winner. (APPLAUSE) What a backhand down the line! 0-15. Brock ready to serve again. Down the center line—it's good— Wait! What's happened to Peck?

— 294 —

(CROWD MURMURS) He's down on the court, holding his chest—looks in bad pain. The umpire is calling for help. Dene's getting up, motioning them away. He's picking up his racket, but—oh, he's down again, on his knees. If this is cramp it's a bad attack. Young Brock is helping. They're lifting him on a stretcher—

(DURING THE LAST LINES DOCTOR YORK HAS HURRIED IN. HE TURNS OFF THE RADIO, CLEARS A COUCH, AND PUTS DOWN HIS BAG. AFTER A PAUSE, ENTER DENE, LEANING ON BARRY EDMUNDS)

YORK:	On the couch, Dene.
BARRY:	There, Dene. Easy!
YORK:	Keep everyone else out, will you?
BARRY:	Sure. I'll stand guard outside the door. (HE GOES OUT)
YORK:	Well, you old warrior, let's have a look at you. Lie back.
DENE:	(TRYING TO SIT UP) I have to—
YORK:	Listen. I'm giving the orders. You answer yes or no. Like last time? Dizziness and chest pain?
DENE:	Yes.
YORK:	Mm. I hoped you'd get through this week. It was useless telling you to drop out. So I came along today to keep an eye on you. (ENTER JILL AND BARRY. SHE KNEELS BY DENE)
JILL:	Oh, my poor Dene!
BARRY:	I reckoned I was right to let Jill in, Doc.
YORK:	You're the best medicine he has, Jill. Thanks, Barry. (BARRY GOES OUT)
DENE:	Jill, I—
YORK:	Now you be quiet! An ambulance willl be here soon, and the three of us will ride to the hospital. I don't think any serious harm has been done today.
JILL:	But—what is it, George?

YORK: No real mystery. It's a man of thirty-five pretending to be ten years younger. He's had enough. I told him a couple of days ago.

JILL: He's not—seriously sick? Tell me, George. I need to know.

YORK: No, I don't think so—except in his head. I'm one of your greatest fans, Dene, but this can't go on. If you live a quiet life you'll be as healthy as any of us. I don't mean quiet like an invalid, but avoiding the kind of circus act you've been putting on. You'll have a good life, and a long one.

BARRY: (OPENING DOOR) Ambulance is here, Doc.

YORK: Good. We'll hope to have you home by tomorrow.

(FINAL SCENE, IN THE LIVING ROOM. CAR DOOR CLOSED OUTSIDE. DENE AND JILL ENTER SLOWLY)

JILL: There, darling. You're home.

DENE: (FLAT VOICE) Yes.

JILL: Rosa and I moved the couch over. You can get sun or shade. Just pull the cord.

DENE: (SITS HEAVILY) Yes.

JILL: There are more pillows if—

DENE: (HEAD IN HANDS, SOBBING) Oh God, God, God!

JILL: Dene, my darling, talk to me! Don't shut me out! We can face anything if we share it.

DENE: We have to face it some time.

JILL: Face what, angel?

DENE: I had one thing to give you: my physical fitness. As long as I could win tournaments I could give you this house, travel, clothes, everything. Now it's gone. I'm useless. I don't have anything else. No money, because I was too dumb to save it. It's all gone—everything.

JILL: Stop talking nonsense, and listen! You don't know how wrong you are. I—I don't quite know how to say this, without it sounding mean or crazy. And I'm not either of those things, am I? Except that I'm crazy about you.

DENE: Go on!

JILL: I'm not doing this very well. I've often wanted to talk about it, but—well, you weren't an easy person to talk to about some things. You see, darling, all your fitness, and—yes, your strength—they've been a barrier between us.

DENE: A barrier? How—

JILL: Because you wouldn't allow yourself to need anyone or anything—and in a way that included me. Oh, I know how much you love me, but—

DENE: But you haven't been happy. My God, Jill! I can't take—

JILL: No, no, no! I don't mean that at all. I love you, and I know why you had to be so strong and independent. It's a part of you. But it made you do things for me which you had no need to do.

DENE: I wanted to give you everything. I wanted—

JILL: Dene, I'll tell you my wish, and prayer, for both of us. I want you to need me. You're going to be as strong as ever, my darling, but strong in a new way. And I'll be strong too, because you will need me. I'm not talking about nursing you. In a few days you will be as healthy as ever. I mean all the years ahead—the wonderful years.

DENE: But what are we going to do?

JILL: I don't know; but I feel very happy—not anxious about that. This time last year we knew exactly what was ahead of us: Davis Cup, Australian Open, Rome, Paris, Wimbledon, California, Miami, U.S. Open. I was a real expert on flights and airports and hotels. I'd wake up in a plane, see mountains or clouds below me, and have to think hard where we were—what the next hotel would be, and the next meal because of time zones. It's been exciting, and you were wonderful wherever we went. But I'm not going to live on memories—not for Dene Peck or anyone else.

DENE:	(AFTER A PAUSE) Do you know something, Jill?
JILL:	What?
DENE:	You have more guts than all the champions I have ever played against. And I never knew it—I never knew. I've been blind. (LOOKS AT WATCH) Hey, the final's due to start in three minutes. Let's turn it on. Mind you, Al Brock has no right to be out there; but I'd like to see how he deals with Bill Farrell.
JILL:	I'll switch it on. And don't let's have an argument about who has courage. Which channel?

Eleven:

THE EMPIRE+ (hard to act)

CHARACTERS:
ELISE MORGAN, about 40
MR. DRESNER, her assistant
SALLY, her secretary
Mr. ZUCCO, President of the Company
ALEX KANDINSKY, a storekeeper, 50's
TANYA, his wife
Mrs. FERNHOLTZ, a customer
JANITOR

Elise Morgan is the regional head of a national company. Their business is the renting out of all kinds of furnishings and appliances. She lives alone in an apartment, her only companion being her cat. She is at home late one evening.

ELISE:	Hunter! Come along, boy! Here's your nightcap. Nice warm milk. (SHE PUTS THE MILK DOWN, SITS, AND LIFTS THE CAT) Bedtime, Hunter. (PUTS CAT DOWN) We've had a nice evening, haven't we? Finish your milk. We'll turn on the radio. It's time for him to say goodnight. (SHE TURNS ON RADIO, MUSIC FINISHES, THEN A VOICE)
ANNOUNCER:	And now this is Con Stobart wishing you all goodnight and happy dreams. Listen again tomorrow on WGBM. Until then, once again good night!
ELISE:	Good night. (SHE SWITCHES RADIO OFF. A PAUSE) Good night. (SHE SOBS SOFTLY)

In Mr. and Mrs. Kandinsky's corner store Tanya is at the checkout counter.

TANYA: $3.75, 4, 5, 10. That's it, Mrs. Fernholtz.

FERNHOLTZ: Thank you, Tanya. I'll be seeing you. Goodbye!

TANYA: Goodbye! Come back soon! (FERNHOLTZ GOES OFF) Alex!

ALEX: (FROM OFF STAGE) Coming, Tanya!

TANYA: Time for you to go.

ALEX: (ENTERING) Yes, it's time.

TANYA: You have to persuade them to let us keep the furniture.

ALEX: I'll try. You know they don't run a charity. They're hard people.

TANYA: Miss Morgan will help us. She's been here so often to buy things for her cat. She'll help us: I know she will.

ALEX: We can only hope for the best.

TANYA: I know. But, oh God, don't let them strip our store! What would we do?

ALEX: I'll be going. Keep hoping. Don't worry too much. (HE KISSES HER)

In Elise Morgan's office at Global Furnishings Dresner is standing by her desk. She has not yet come in.

DRESNER: Sally!

SALLY: (ENTERING) Yes, Mr. Dresner.

DRESNER: Miss Morgan will be here in a minute. I need the monthly figures.

SALLY: Here they are.

DRESNER: Thanks. She should be pleased. Her idea really worked out.

SALLY: Pleased? Will you know if she is?

DRESNER: I know. She won't show it. And yet—

SALLY:	That sounds inhuman—and that's not Miss Morgan. It frightens me—all that ability and charm, but you never see the real person. I've only worked for her for three months—
DRESNER:	And I for four years. I've watched her build up a little empire here, with that desk as the throne. The place runs like clockwork—and through it all I like her; but as for personal life—
SALLY:	I know. I wish she would let us in and share—
DRESNER:	There's the buzzer. She's in the building.
SALLY:	I'll be next door if you need me. She's expecting Zucco.
DRESNER:	Yes. He called to say he'll be here soon. I hope he has some good news. (SALLY GOES OUT. DRESNER LOOKS AT REPORT. ENTER ELISE)
DRESNER:	Good morning, Miss Morgan.
ELISE:	Good morning, Mr. Dresner. Any news of Mr. Zucco yet?
DRESNER:	He called to say he would be here in a few minutes.
ELISE:	I want to look over the mail order report before he arrives.
DRESNER:	This is it. I knew you'd need it. You're going to be pleasantly surprised.
ELISE:	I doubt it. I believed in the plan all along. This bears out what I predicted.
DRESNER:	It sure does. You pushed it through. Zucco and the Board were pretty skeptical.
ELISE:	It's my business to know our market. I ought to know what I'm doing after twenty years here. That will be all, Mr. Dresner. I need to read this report.
SALLY:	(ENTERING) Excuse me, Miss Morgan. Mr. Dresner, you're wanted out here if you have a minute.
DRESNER:	Coming. (HE GOES OUT. ELISE SITS AT HER DESK READING. AFTER A PAUSE, BUZZER)

ELISE:	Yes?
DRESNER'S VOICE:	Miss Morgan, there's a man here named Kandinsky. He's very anxious to talk to you personally.
ELISE:	Kandinsky? What does he want?
DRERSNER:	I'll come in and tell you, shall I?
ELISE:	Oh, I suppose so.
DRESNER:	(ENTERING) Kandinsky and his wife operate that small store on 8th and Drummond.
MORGAN:	Oh, yes, I remember. Well, if he must come in, let's get it over.
DRESNER:	Miss Morgan—
ELISE:	Yes?
DRESNER:	This man Kandinsky—he says he knows you. You walk by on your way home, and sometimes buy cat food—
ELISE:	That has nothing to do with our business.
DRESNER:	No, but that's why he specially wanted to see you. It's the usual story. They rent stuff from us, and they're behind on their payments. They're nice people—always helping someone in the neighborhood—
ELISE:	I'm sure they are; but could we run this business if we listened tio every sob story?
DRESNER:	No. Only it's tough on some of these people.
ELISE:	They ought to think of that before they enter into commitments.
DRESNER:	Yes. You're right, of course. I'll send him away.
ELISE:	I will deal with it myself. Send him in.
DRESNER:	What's the use, if —

ELISE:	Mr. Dresner, will you please stop wasting time and bring Mr. Kandinsky in?
DRESNER:	Just as you say, Miss Morgan. (OPENS DOOR) This way, Mr. Kandinsky. Miss Morgan will see you. (HE GOES OUT. KANDINSKY ENTERS)
ELISE:	Sit down, Mr. Kandinsky.
ALEX:	Thank you, Miss Morgan. I appreciate—
ELISE:	I'm afraid I have to tell you that you have come on a vain errand. I'm sure you understand that we can't run a business like this unless we stick firmly to the terms of a contract.
ALEX:	Yes, yes. I understand. I promised my wife—
ELISE:	We have fifty thousand clients like you in this city alone.
ALEX:	Fifty thousand. Yes. But you see, Miss Morgan, it's the store. We have clients too. You come yourself once in a while. If we have to close down—
ELISE:	That, literally, is your business. We have ours, and it isn't a charity. If I hadn't learned that twenty years ago I wouldn't be here now.
ALEX:	You work here twenty years?
ELISE:	Yes, but that has nothing to do with—
ALEX:	No, no. But most days I watch you go by, on the sidewalk on Drummond; so when I get the notice, saying we lose our things if we can't pay, I think, 'She knows our store—buys a magazine sometimes, or cat food. Maybe I can ask her for time—'
ELISE:	I'm truly sorry, Mr. Kandinsky. The answer has to be no. Good morning. (SHE WALKS TO THE DOOR AND OPENS IT, AS SALLY IS ABOUT TO COME IN)
SALLY:	Oh, Miss Morgan. I came to tell you Mr. Zucco is on his way up.
ELISE:	Thank you, Sally. See Mr. Kandinsky out, please.
ALEX:	Goodbye, Miss Morgan. Thanks for seeing me.

(ELISE WALKS TO DESK AND PICKS UP REPORT. AFTER A PAUSE ZUCCO ENTERS)

ZUCCO: Hi, Miss Morgan! Guess what! I've got big news for you.

ELISE: Shall I come through to your office?

ZUCCO: No, no, Sit down. We can talk here.

ELISE: I expect you mean the mail order program. I'm just reading—

ZUCCO: No, no. Oh, I know all about that. You proved us wrong—showed that you were the smart one. It's one more feather in your cap. But I've got much bigger news than that.

ELISE: Bigger?

ZUCCO: Be ready for a shock. I've sold this plant.

ELISE: (AFTER A PAUSE) You've—what?

ZUCCO: Sold the plant. Lock, stock, and barrel. We've realized for some time that it was a losing proposition in the long term. Only your savvy kept it going. Now we have a wonderful deal, which opens the way for bigger things—for you too.

ELISE: You mean—this office—my job—

ZUCCO: What's so special about this place? You'll get a hefty bonus, and I can offer you a much bigger job in our new headquarters: Vice President in charge of services. You can name your own price.

ELISE: My price—yes. (SHE SITS BACK AND CLOSES HER EYES)

ZUCCO: Hey, are you O.K? I didn't think—I'll fetch you some water.

ELISE: It's quite all right, Mr. Zucco. I congratulate you on the deal. It is a shock, but please don't worry about me. I will be all right.

ZUCCO: I must run and make some calls. I'll see you later. I wanted you to be the first to know.

ELISE: Thank you. (HE GOES OUT. ELISE SITS BACK. THEN SHE WRITES A SHORT NOTE, PUTS IT IN AN ENVELOPE, AND LEAVES IT ON HER DESK. SHE RISES AND PRESSES BUZZER.)

SALLY: (ENTERING) Yes, Miss Morgan?

ELISE:	Sally, I'm going home now. Will you ask Mr. Dresner to come in for a minute?
SALLY:	Yes, Miss Morgan.
ELISE:	And Sally—
SALLY:	(TURNING BY DOOR) Yes?
ELISE:	You've learned your job well. I'm grateful to you—
SALLY:	(SURPRISED) Thank you, Miss Morgan. I'll fetch Mr. Dresner. (SHE GOES OUT. ELISE STANDS BY DESK, RUNNING HER FINGERS ACROSS IT.)
ELISE:	(TO DRESNER, ENTERING) Bob, I'm going home. Everything is in order here. (AGAIN SHE TOUCHES THE DESK)
DRESNER:	Yes. It's been a big shock to all of us. Especially you. Can I drive you home?
ELISE:	I've walked home every day for twenty years. I think I can manage. This note is for Mr. Zucco. I would like him to have it tomorrow morning, not today.
DRESNER:	I'll see to it.
ELISE:	Then I think that's everything. Goodbye, Bob.
DRESNER:	Goodbye, Miss Morgan. Don't—
ELISE:	Don't what?
DRESNER:	Oh, nothing. I like this place too, and I've appreciated working under you. But it's a logical step for Zucco, and—after all, it isn't places that matter, but people.
ELISE:	People. Yes, of course. Good night! (SHE GOES OUT. DRESNER PICKS UP NOTE, AND STANDS LOOKING AT ELISE'S DESK)

A few minutes later Tanya Kandinsky is at the check out counter.

TANYA:	Alex! Come here! Miss Morgan just went by.

ALEX: Now? Must be something wrong. She never leaves the office early.

TANYA: Alex, now is your chance. You've got to go and ask her—at home. She may feel different at home.

ALEX: It won't do any good, Tanya.

TANYA: Maybe, outside that office—

ALEX: I guess it's worth a try. I'll finish putting these cans on the shelves. Then I'll go.

Elise went home, climbing the stairs and opening her apartment door. Her cat ran to meet her.

ELISE: Hello, Hunter! (SHE PICKS HIM UP) My only friend. Your bowl's empty. (SHE FETCHES MILK FROM THE KITCHEN AREA, AND A GLASS OF WINE. SHE SETS THE CAT'S BOWL BY HER CHAIR, AND SITS) There! Something for you, and for me. I need it, Hunter. They've taken away my life. They expect me to begin all over again. (PAUSE. SHE SOBS) But I can't, Hunter, I can't. We were all right here. I could bear it, with you—and the office. Oh, God, it isn't fair! He didn't even ask me—and I can't go on. (PAUSE) We're going away, Hunter. It won't hurt you, and I want you to come with me. (SHE WALKS TO THE KITCHEN AREA) Look, we can just lie here, with this cushion under my head, and we'll go to sleep. When the radio man says good night we'll be here, but we won't hear him. Goodbye, Hunter dear! I want to go to sleep now. I'm so tired.

(A SOB, THEN SILENCE. PAUSE. SOUNDS OF CAT MEWING, THEN SCRATCHING DOOR. PAUSE, THEN DOORBELL FOLLOWED BY KNOCK)

ALEX: (OFF STAGE) Quiet, pussycat! You'll scratch the paint. What's the trouble? You want to get out? (REPEAT BELL AND KNOCK) Miss Morgan! (PAUSE) Miss Morgan!

JANITOR: (OFF STAGE) Hey, you! What's going on? Who are you?

ALEX: Do you live here?

JANITOR: I'm the janitor. What—

ALEX: I think there's trouble in Miss Morgan's apartment. (CAT SCRATCHING)

JANITOR: Miss Morgan? She just came in. Wait a minute? Do you smell—

ALEX:	Quick! Open the door. (SOUND OF KEY. THEY RUN IN)
JANITOR:	My God! She's killed herself.
ALEX:	Call an ambulance! (JANITOR RUNS OUT. ALEX HALF CARRIES, HALF DRAGS ELISE OUTSIDE) Merciful God! Don't let it be too late. Miss Morgan, don't die!

It seemed strange in Miss Morgan's office. Sally was restless, and did not know what to do. Then the telephone rang.

SALLY:	Global Furnishings, Miss Morgan's office. Mr. Zucco is not here at present. Yes, I can connect you with Mr. Dresner. (ENTER DRESNER) Oh, Mr. Dresner, it's Grace Hospital. They asked for Mr. Zucco, but—
DRESNER:	The hospital! What—(AT PHONE) Hello. Yes, I am Miss Morgan's assistant. What? (PAUSE) Oh, my God, no! She's—yes, of course. Just a minute. (TO SALLY) Miss Morgan went home and tried to commit suicide. Turned on the gas.
SALLY:	Oh, no! She—
DRESNER:	They think she'll make it. Someone found her. They want her next-of-kin. Can you look that up? We must have it.
SALLY:	Yes. (SHE GOES OUT)
DRESNER:	(AT PHONE) We'll have it in a moment. She never talked about her family, but— Here it comes. Well, Sally?
SALLY:	(VOICE BARELY UNDER CONTROL) It says: 'Next-of-kin: none. In case of emergency contact the President, Fidelity State bank.' Oh, dear God! She had nobody. Don't you see? Nobody! I wish I had known—

Elise was lying in a hospital bed, motionless, when Alex Kandinsky entered her room quietly.

ALEX:	Miss Morgan, are you awake?
ELISE:	(NOT MOVING. VOICE FLAT) Yes, I'm awake.
ALEX:	It's me. Kandinsky.
ELISE:	(SLOWLY) Kandinsky. Yes, I remember.

ALEX: I don't want to disturb you, but I thought you'd like to know about your cat.

ELISE: (SOBBING) Poor Hunter!

ALEX: No, no. He's O.K. He's with Tanya—that's my wife—and me.

ELISE: You have Hunter?

ALEX: Sure we have him, and he's fine. You're not to worry about him.

ELISE: Thank you. It is kind of you to care for him, and to come here to tell me.

ALEX: His name's Hunter?

ELISE: Yes.

ALEX: You know he saved your life?

ELISE: Hunter saved—I don't understand.

ALEX: Well, you see, I'm outside your door, and I hear scratching and whining, and I know something's wrong in there. So me and the janitor, we open the door.

ELISE: So you saved me.

ALEX: No, no. I just happened to be there. Hunter saved you.

ELISE: (AFTER PAUSE) Mr. Kandinsky, what were you doing outside my door?

ALEX: We won't talk about that now. Time for me to go.

ELISE: I must know.

ALEX: I tell you, it doesn't matter. I'll come back tomorrow—

ELISE: I think I know. You followed me home—to ask about the payment. You heard Hunter, and—(SHE TRIES TO SIT UP)

ALEX: Miss Morgan, what are you doing? You can't sit up.

ELISE:	Oh yes, I— (SINKS BACK) I guess you're right. Mr. Kandinsky, hand me that phone, please.
ALEX:	You shouldn't be—
ELISE:	Please! What time is it? 9.30. Mr. Dresner should be there. Operator, get me OR 6-3000, please. Yes. (PAUSE) Mr. Dresner. please. (PAUSE) Mr. Dresner? This is Miss Morgan. Yes. Thank you. We can't talk about that now. I want you to do something for me. Find Kandinsky's file—Alex Kandinsky, you remember? I'm sending a check to cover his payment—
ALEX:	You—no, no!
ELISE:	That would be nice, one day. And bring Sally, but not just yet. I'll give you the check when I see you. Make sure nobody takes anything from Kandinsky's store. Thank you. (SHE HANDS THE PHONE TO ALEX)
ALEX:	Miss Morgan, I didn't come here to—
ELISE:	You don't want payment for saving my life. I know that. I'm not doing it for you, but for myself.
ALEX:	I don't understand.
ELISE:	I'll try to explain it to you. A long time ago I had a bad experience. There was a man, and he—well, it wasn't pleasant, and I let it hurt me far too much. I shut love out of my life—made sure that it wasn't going to hurt me any more. I made work my life. It could have been worse. It was good work, and I was proud of it. There was Hunter too. But yesterday I had a shock, and there was nothing to fall back on, nothing to live for.
ALEX:	I'm sorry you had trouble, but—
ELISE:	Let me finish. This morning I found out that I was not dead. I was in despair. But I think you changed that, Mr. Kandinsky. I'm not sure of anything yet, but I think you did something. You make me feel as if I had run away—which is true. You make me want to look for the warm things again, the things that matter. If the world is like that, I may want to start again. I can only start by giving—not paying, giving. Do you see?

ALEX: (AFTER A PAUSE) You know something, Miss Morgan? I figure that, if you pay that money, a whole lot of what's in my store belongs to you—

ELISE: But I tell you, I—

ALEX: O.K., so you gave it to me and to Tanya. That's good, Miss Morgan. We need it, and we'll take it. But that means I have a right to share something too. Tanya and I, we talked this over. We want to help you—take care of you until you're on your feet again. You need someone to look in on you here, run errands? You tell us what you need. She and I, we want to do that.

ELISE: (AFTER A PAUSE) Let me think about it. My mind isn't clear enough to know what I need. But, Alex—thank you, and Tanya. I know you mean it, right in your heart. Nothing else matters, does it?

ALEX: You ought to rest now.

ELISE: I will.

ALEX: When you're ready to leave the hospital I'll shop for things you'll be needing, groceries, unless— Because Hunter is happy with us, you could come to our home for a few days while you find your feet. It's small, our place, but Tanya would look after you. (PAUSE) Does that make sense?

ELISE: Yes, it makes sense. (SHE LIES BACK, EYES CLOSED) It makes a great deal of sense, Alex. Come again soon!

Twelve:

CAMELS FOR THE ARK (hard to act)

CHARACTERS: ANASTAS BATA, Late 60's
JIMMY TODD, 10, his neighbor
HENRY BELL, 60's
LAURA BELL, his wife
STEVE CARTWRIGHT, 60's
Doctor LEE, 60's

Henry Bell is a victim of a very common ailment: retirement boredom. It had seemed a wonderful prospect, to be free of the office and the commute—but free for what? His wife worries about him, but does not know how to change the situation. Two miles away lives Anastas Bata, a retired cabinetmaker and craftsman. Nobody could have guessed that they needed each other, or that they would ever meet.

Anastas Bata is lying on a couch in his small den. The furniture is simple and oldfashioned. There is a sound of a ball bouncing repeatedly, and whistling. Then silence.

JIMMY: (FROM OFF STAGE) Mr. Bata. I'm sorry. It was my ball again. Would you mind throwing it back?

BATA: Come through and get it, Jimmy. Door's open.

JIMMY: Coming. (PAUSE, KNOCK, AND JIMMY ENTERS)

BATA: Come on in.

JIMMY: Thanks, Mr. Bata.

BATA: Go through the kitchen. (JIMMY GOES OUT, AND RETURNS)

JIMMY: I've got it. Thanks. Hey, are you sick, Mr. Bata?

BATA: Just my leg. It's sore. Won't last long. Run along now.

JIMMY: O.K.

BATA: Oh, wait! Take this bread out for the birds, will you? Leave it by the birdbath?

JIMMY: Sure. (HE GOES OUT AND RETURNS) Thanks for letting me come through the house.

BATA: That's all right. Those balls sure do bounce high.

JIMMY: I practice tennis against the wall. Sometimes I'm a bit wild. Can I tell my Mom you're sick? You need someone to—

BATA: (SHARPLY) No! (GENTLY) I'll be O.K., Jimmy.

JIMMY: I'll see you. Thanks.

BATA: You come any time. And don't worry about me. (JIMMY HAS LEFT) I'll be all right.

Meanwhile Laura Bell was working on her front lawn when Steve Cartwright came through the gate.

STEVE: Mrs. Bell?

LAURA: Yes. Mr. Cartwright, isn't it?

STEVE: You have a good memory. We met at the newcomers' reception in the Rec Center.

LAURA: And we never followed up on it. You know what it's like moving house.

STEVE: Do you like the house?

LAURA: Oh, the house is fine.

STEVE: You don't sound very enthusiastic.

LAURA: A house is a house. And this town is fine. We have to learn how to adjust to Henry being retired. He'll be back in a minute.

STEVE: Just retired, is he?

LAURA: Yes, from a shipping office.

STEVE: I've come from the Community Service group to ask you both a favor.

LAURA: There's Henry now. He took the dog for a walk. That's the big event of the day.

STEVE: Good morning, Mr. Bell.

LAURA: Henry, this is Steve Cartwright, from—

HENRY: I remember meeting you, Steve. Nice to see you again. I'll put Duke in the yard, and be back in a minute.

LAURA: Come inside. (THEY ENTER A PLEASANT LIVING ROOM. HENRY COMES IN BY ANOTHER DOOR) Sit down, Steve.

STEVE:	Let me get straight to the point. You gathered at that meeting what we try to do. We're a group of men and women, no particular affiliation, though many come from the churches. We call ourselves the Brooms—that's why I wear this. (HE SHOWS THEM A SMALL METAL BROOM IN HIS LAPEL)
HENRY:	That's original.
STEVE:	One of our members had the idea. You remember the story about the woman who lost one of her ten coins, and stirred up the whole neighborhood quarreling with her husband and searching for it? Our point is, she would never have found it without her broom, which could reach into hidden corners. So we call ourselves brooms, and look for the hidden people.
HENRY:	Why hidden?
STEVE:	Many reasons. When we began to look we found people lonely, or left out, sick, or misfits. We don't preach to them, but if they accept it we visit them and see if they need anything.
LAURA:	Sounds great. How many of you are there?
STEVE:	Active, about twenty. On the fringes, perhaps fifty more. We need more active members.
HENRY:	What exactly does a member do?
STEVE:	We give you a name and address, and a note of what we know. Then you call on the phone or knock on the door, and take it from there. You may or may not be welcome, and you may or may not accomplish anything; but we know that it is worth trying.
HENRY:	You want us to see if we can help?
STEVE:	I have a specific request for you, if you're not too much tied up.
HENRY:	Tied up? To be honest I'm lost—haven't found out how to deal with retirement.
STEVE:	Good! I mean, good in the sense that perhaps you need what I'm asking you to do; and if Laura will try to help too one of our women members will get in touch with her.

HENRY: What is my assignment?

STEVE: (TAKING OUT A SHEET OF PAPER) Anastas Bata: B-A-T-A. I have his address here, and a phone. All we know is that he is a widower, retired, came from Czechoslovakia, and has been laid up with a bad leg. His doctor tips us off to visit some of his patients.

HENRY: You want me to visit him?

STEVE: If you will. It may not lead anywhere, but you'll be sweeping in a dark corner.

HENRY: Let me have the information. I'll see what I can do.

STEVE: Thank you. Here it is. I must be on my way. I'll ask Ann Quintana to get in touch with you, Laura. I hope you'll get to know more of our members. You have my number there, and a sheet telling you more about the Brooms.

LAURA: I'm glad you thought of us. We'll be seeing you.

Anastas Bata is lying on his couch, lonely and in pain. Jimmy Todd knocks at his door.

BATA: Come in! Why, Jimmy!

JIMMY: My Mom sent you some soup, Mr. Bata.

BATA: Thanks, Jimmy, and tell your Mother thanks. Put it over there, will you? (AS JIMMY CARRIES THE PITCHER TO THE KITCHEN AREA DOCTOR LEE WALKS IN)

LEE: Door was open, so I came on in. How are you doing, Stas?

BATA: Oh, Doctor! You know Jimmy Todd? His mother just sent me some soup.

LEE: I know Jimmy. We had his tonsils out last year. Hi, you young rascal!

JIMMY: Hi! Hope your leg's better soon, Mr. Bata.

BATA: Thanks, Jimmy. Don't forget to thank your Mother. (JIMMY GOES OUT)

LEE:	That's good that you have neighbors who care about you. Let me look at that leg. (HE EXAMINES IT) H'm. Hurts pretty bad, uh?
BATA:	Ja.
LEE:	Well, it's beginning to mend, but you were a stubborn old cuss not to call me earlier. I know it's a problem, living alone. But we caught this in time, and the drugs are working. You're taking them the way I said?
BATA:	Yes, Doctor.
LEE:	We have to do something about your meals, and keeping this place in shape. Otherwise we may have to get you to a hospital.
BATA:	No, no.
LEE:	We'll try to avoid it. You have no relatives?
BATA:	Just my daughter, in Pittsburgh. She can't come—has her own children.
LEE:	Well, we'll have to think. Meanwhile you take that medication. It may clear up soon. (BELL RINGS) Hey, you're busy today.
BATA:	I don't know who it can be. Come in!
HENRY:	(ENTERING) Mr. Bata?
BATA:	Ja, I am Bata.
LEE:	I'm Doctor Lee. Come on in.
HENRY:	My name's Henry Bell. You don't know me, but Steve Cartwright, from Community Services, gave me your address.
BATA:	My address?
HENRY:	Yes. He heard you were sick, and asked me to look in. See if there's anything you need.
LEE:	It's good of you to come. Anastas could do with some company, while this leg is keeping him out of action.

HENRY: What's the trouble?

LEE: Nothing that won't clear up soon. I must be going. I'll call again in a day or two, Stas. Nice to meet you, Mr. Bell.

HENRY: And you, Doctor. So long. (LEE GOES OUT)

BATA: Please, you sit. I would get up, but—

HENRY: Don't you move. (SITS) Comfortable place you have here.

BATA: Yes. Everything close: bed, chair, TV.

HENRY: And your kitchen and yard through there?

BATA: You please have some coffee.

HENRY: If you will too. Let me fix it.

BATA: On the counter. Cups above. (THEY GO ON TALKING AS HENRY FETCHES TWO CUPS)

HENRY: Anything in yours?

BATA: No. Just coffee.

HENRY: Does that leg give you a lot of pain?

BATA: For two weeks, ja. But Doctor Lee fixed it good now.

HENRY: Have you lived here long?

BATA: Before I give up work, I live here with Maria, my wife. But she died nine years ago.

HENRY: Where before that?

BATA: I was born in Bratislava. When I was sixteen my father said to me: Life is hard here. America is the future. We're going there. So we came, fifty-two years ago.

HENRY: And you found your opportunity?

BATA:	I worked with him. He teach me woodwork and carving. All my life I work hard, and it was good. Then my Maria died, and Anna—that's my daughter, is in Pittsburgh.
HENRY:	How long ago did you give up working?
BATA:	Nine years. I stop when Maria died.
HENRY:	I've been retired only three months, and I haven't got used ot it yet. Nine years! Look, Mr. Bata—am I saying it right?
BATA:	Call me Anastas. if you like.
HENRY:	Good. My name's Henry. I'd appreciate it if you'd let me stop by and talk once in a while. There's not too much for a retired man to do in this place.
BATA:	I would like that, Henry.
HENRY:	Well, I'll be going— (AS HE GETS UP HE DROPS A PACKAGE) Oops! That was clumsy. I hope nothing broke.
BATA:	What's in there?
HENRY:	(UNWRAPPING THE PACKAGE) Camels. Sounds odd, I know, but that's what they are. Camels for the Ark. Noah's Ark. I bought an Ark for one of my grandchildren—oh, it must be seven years ago. Each birthday I give her a pair of animals. She'll be twelve next week. This is the year for camels.
BATA:	(TAKING THE CAMELS) Tt, tt . What camels! It is bad work, not right for Noah's Ark. I'm sorry, I—
HENRY:	No, don't apologize. It's hard to find anything carefully made, These were the best I could see. Is this the kind of thing you used to make?
BATA:	I carved the arms of the chair you sit in.
HENRY:	You—did this? I'm no judge, but it looks wonderful work.
BATA:	I make that for Maria forty years ago: two doves.

HENRY: What a craftsman you were! Well, Anastas, I mustn't overstay my welcome. It has been a pleasure meeting you.

BATA: It is good that you come. Always you will be welcome.

HENRY: Don't get up. I can—

BATA: No, no. I get up. It's bad to sit too long. See? I'm on my feet.

HENRY: Fine! But remember what the doctor said about rest. I'll come again soon.

BATA: Ja, soon.

In the Bells' home Laura answers the telephone.

LAURA: Hello. Oh, Mr. Cartwright, this is Laura. Friday? Yes, we'd like that. Henry isn't here. He went to see Mr. Bata. Henry says he's a real character, and very friendly. I heard from Ann Quintana, and we're meeting next week. We'll see you on Friday, then. 6.30. Thanks for calling.

Meanwhile Henry was back at Anastas Bata's home, sitting close to him.

HENRY: It hit me last night, when I was packing up those wretched little camels for Celia. My wife thought I was dreaming, but I have to ask you. Will you carve something simple and beautiful to take their place?

BATA: I carve? Since I gave up work I have not touched my tools, not one time. No, no, Henry! My hands are dead,

HENRY: That's not true—and I'll take a bet on one thing: you didn't throw your tools away or sell them.

BATA: No. I did not do that.

HENRY: Then where are they?

BATA: Wait, Henry. I have told you—

HENRY: Anastas, where are your tools?

BATA: In the workshop the other side of the yard. They must be rusty.

HENRY: So what? Listen, Anastas, Your hands are no more dead than mine. We could fit up a small bench with a lathe. I made a sketch over my coffee this morning.

BATA: (SHAKING HIS HEAD) But, I—

HENRY: No, you listen to me. Last night it came to me that you are meant to carve these camels. Why else did I happen to bring that junky package when I called on you? I won't take 'no' for an answer. If you don't mind, I'm going to take a look in that workshop.

BATA: I do not mind, but I cannot—

HENRY: That's good. I'll go and see what I can find. (HE GOES OUT)

BATA: (SLOWLY, SITTING ALONE) The Ark of Noah. If my hands are not dead!

In the Bells' kitchen Laura is busy, when Henry comes in whistling.

LAURA: You sound cheerful.

HENRY: I am. Just off to see Stas, and show him Celia's letter.

LAURA: It meant a lot to you, didn't it, getting him to do that work?

HENRY: It surely did. Somehow it did something to me as well as to him. (THEY EMBRACE) I'll be back before lunch.

LAURA: I doubt it. (LAUGHING) You two seem to forget about time. Here, don't forget the pie.

Anastas Bata is working at a small bench which he has set up in his den. Henry knocks at the door and enters.

HENRY: Hi, Stas! How's it going?

BATA: You look and see.

HENRY: I certainly will. What in the—what have you got there?

BATA: He is the panther. Always I like the panther. He is strong, yes, but graceful.

— 318 —

HENRY: Stas, that is like the arms of this chair. Wonderful work!

BATA: It is like the chair, yes. I make that chair when I was alive. I make it for Maria. I loved her, and when she died, I could not work. My hands were dead. Now, because you came to my door, I am alive again.

HENRY: I have something to read to you. Listen to this. (HE SITS) It's from Celia.

BATA: Ach, Celia. The little lady with the Ark. Yes, read it, please.

HENRY: She says: 'The camels are so beautiful that they make the other animals feel ashamed.'

BATA: She is a sweet child.

HENRY: Wait! There's more. 'Please tell Stas that I know he loved my camels very much, and already I love them too. That makes us close.'

BATA: (AFTER A PAUSE) Thank you, Henry. That letter is good.

HENRY: You know, Stas, I have a kind of confession to make to you.

BATA: How—a confession?

HENRY: Yes. You see, the first day I came here, I thought I came out of charity—I suppose you'd call it that. The Community people sent me, and I thought you needed a friend.

BATA: Ja, a friend. Everybody needs friends.

HENRY: If I thought at all, I suppose I felt I was doing you a kindness. It was a shock when I found out that I needed you, not the other way around. That's the plain truth, though.

BATA: No. Both. Two, like the camels, yes? (JIMMY'S BALL FALLS IN THE YARD)

HENRY: Hey, what was that?

BATA: Another friend. I think sometimes God sends that ball over the fence, so that my friend comes to fetch it back. (A KNOCK) Come on in, Jimmy!

JIMMY:	(ENTERING) Sorry, Mr. Bata. Do you mind If I go through?
BATA:	Come on in, Jimmy! Yes, fetch your ball—but don't forget to take the bread for the birds. It's on the counter.

Thirteen:

PILGRIM'S PROGRESS
(hard to act, but good scenes)

This play is based on John Bunyan's book. The Director must decide which scenes are to be acted, and which to be narrated. A Narrator and half a dozen Voices can effectively present the play as a reading; but some of the scenes are easy to act, like Christian's dialogues with Evangelist and Worldly Wiseman. Others present greater problems: Is the slough scene to be visible or confined to words? Are the lions to be imagined or represented by actors? Is there to be a realistic Apollyon? With at least thirty-five roles and a Chorus the Director will probably wish to use his actors in multiple roles.

The extent to which the play is being acted will affect the need for costumes. Of the basic characters I would suggest that Christian should wear a shirt and pants of subdued colors, and sandals. ('Rags' meaning simple, unadorned clothes.) He carries a backpack. Evangelist needs a robe or cassock. White would be most suitable. WORLDLY WISEMAN should be flashy: perhaps a top hat and gloves.

FAITHFUL and HOPEFUL are similar to CHRISTIAN—different colors but not too bright. If a Vanity Fair jury is being presented live, make each a caricature of his or her qualities. (Bunyan made them all male, but it would certainly be appropriate to provide a mixed jury.)

LANGUAGE: Following Bunyan, I have been inconsistent over the use of 'thou' and 'you'. The Director may prefer to eliminate 'thou'—which could very easily be done. Hymnals contain musical settings of HE WHO WOULD VALIANT BE.

CHARACTERS: NARRATOR
CHRISTIAN
EVANGELIST
PLIABLE
HELP
WORLDLY WISEMAN
SIMPLE, SLOTH, and PRESUMPTION
TIMOROUS and MISTRUST
WATCHFUL
APOLLYON
FAITHFUL
FIRST, SECOND, and THIRD CITIZENS OF VANITY FAIR
JUDGE

BLIND-MAN, NO-GOOD, MALICE, LOVE-LUST, LIVE-LOOSE, HEADY,
HIGH-MIND, ENMITY, LIAR, CRUELTY, HATE-LIGHT, IMPLACABLE,
members of the Jury
HOPEFUL
MAN by the River
WOMAN by the River
FIRST SHINING MAN
SECOND SHINING MAN
KING
CHORUS

CHORUS

He who would valiant be
'Gainst all disaster,
Let him in constancy
Follow the Master.
There's no discouragement
Shall make him once relent
His first avowed intent

To be a pilgrim.

(DURING THE FOLLOWING NARRATION CHRISTIAN ENTERS AT THE WORDS, 'I SAW A MAN.')

As I walked through the wilderness of this world, I lighted on a certain place where was a Den, and I laid me down in that place to sleep; and as I slept I dreamed a dream. I saw a man clothed with rags, standing in a certain place, with his face from his house, a book in his hand, and a great burden upon his back. I looked, and saw him open the book, and read therein; and, as he read, he wept, and trembled; and, not being able longer to contain, he brake out with a lamentable cry saying:

CHRISTIAN: What shall I do to be saved?

(EVANGELIST ENTERS R.)

EVANGELIST: If this be thy condition, why standest thou still?

CHRISTIAN   Whither must I fly?

EVANGELIST: Do you see yonder wicket-gate?

CHRISTIAN: No.

EVANGELIST: Do you see yonder shining light?

CHRISTIAN: I think I do.

EVANGELIST: Keep that light in your eye, and go up directly thereto.

(EVANGELIST GOES OFF R. CHRISTIAN OFF L.)

Now I saw that Christian set out on his pilgrimage with a neighbor of his as companion, named PLIABLE. They drew near to a very miry slough, that was in the midst of the plain; and they, being heedless, did both fall suddenly into the bog.

(IF THE SCENE IS BEING ACTED, CHRISTIAN AND PLIABLE ENTER, FALL, AND CRAWL ACROSS STAGE. PLIABLE THEN STRUGGLES OUT, AND GOES OFF. CHRISTIAN SPEAKS TO HELP WHILE STRUGGLING ON HIS KNEES. HELP ENTERS AND PULLS HIM OUT. IF THIS IS NOT ATTEMPTED, THE VOICES ARE HEARD OFF STAGE.)

PLIABLE: Ah, neighbor Christian, where are we now?

CHRISTIAN: Truly I do not know.

PLIABLE: Is this the happiness you have told me all this while of? May I get out again with my life, you shall possess the brave country alone for me.

And with that, Pliable gave a desperate struggle or two, and got out of the mire on that side of the slough which was next to his own house: so away he went, and Christian saw him no more. Still Christian struggled on towards the other side; but he could not get out, because of the burden which was upon his back. Then a man came to him, whose name was HELP.

(IF THE SCENE IS BEING ACTED, HELP NOW ENTERS)

HELP: What are you doing there?

CHRISTIAN: I was bid to go this way by a man named Evangelist; but I fell into the slough.

HELP: Why did you not look for the steps? Give me thy hand!

So he drew him out, and set him upon sound ground, and bid him go on his way. Now, as Christian was walking solitarily by himself, he espied one far off, come crossing over the field to meet him; and their hap was to meet just as they were crossing the way of each other. The gentleman's name that met him was Mr. WORLDLY WISEMAN; he dwelt in the town of Carnal Policy.

(WORLDLY WISEMAN ENTERS THROUGH THE AUDIENCE. AS HE GOES ON TO THE STAGE HE MEETS CHRISTIAN, WHO HAS ENTERED)

WORLDLY WISEMAN: How now, good fellow! Whither away after this burdened manner?

CHRISTIAN: I am going to yonder wicket-gate before me; for there, as I am informed, I shall be put into a way to be rid of my heavy burden.

WORLDLY WISEMAN: Why not get rid of thy burden with all speed?

CHRISTIAN: That is what I seek for; therefore I am going this way.

WORLDLY WISEMAN: Who bid thee go this way to be rid of thy burden?

CHRISTIAN: A man that appeared to me to be a very great and honorable person; his name, as I remember, is Evangelist.

WORLDLY WISEMAN: I beshrew him for his counsel! There is not a more dangerous and troublesome way in the world. How camest thou by that burden at first?

CHRISTIAN: By reading this book in my hand.

WORLDLY WISEMAN: I thought so. Fool, thou art meddling with things too high for thee, and running upon desperate ventures to obtain thou knowest not what. Let me advise thee what to do.

CHRISTIAN: Pray, sir, do.

WORLDLY WISEMAN: In yonder village, which is called Morality, there dwells a gentleman whose name is Legality; a very judicious man, that has skill to help men off with such burdens as thine.

Now was Christian somewhat at a stand; but he concluded that his wisest course was to take this gentleman's advice.
(CHRISTIAN HAS BEEN LOOKING UNCERTAIN. NOW HE MAKES UP HIS MIND.)

CHRISTIAN: Sir, which way is it to this honest man's house?

WORLDLY WISEMAN: Go up that hill, and the first house you come at, is his.

(WORLDLY WISEMAN GOES OFF. CHRISTIAN MIMES CLIMBING A STEEP HILL, MOPPING HIS BROW WITH A HANDKERCHIEF. HE LOOKS AROUND NERVOUSLY. AFTER A PAUSE EVANGELIST ENTERS)

So Christian turned out of his way; but as he climbed his burden seemed heavier, and he did quake with fear. Then Evangelist drew near to him, and looked upon him with a severe countenance.

EVANGELIST: What dost thou here, Christian? Did not I direct thee the way to the little wicket-gate?

CHRISTIAN: Yes, sir, but I met with a gentleman—

EVANGELIST: The man that met thee is one Worldly Wiseman, and rightly is he so called. Thou must abhor his turning thee out of the way, and laboring to make the Cross odious to thee.

CHRISTIAN: Sir, what think you? Is there hope? May I now go back and journey up to the wicket-gate?

EVANGELIST: Thy sin is very great; yet will the man at the gate receive thee. Only take heed that thou turn not aside again, lest thou perish from the way.

(EVANGELIST AND CHRISTIAN GO OFF SEPARATELY)

Now I saw in my dream that the highway up which Christian was to go was fenced on either side with a wall, and that wall was called SALVATION. Up this way therefore did burdened Christian run, but not without great difficulty, because of the load on his back. He ran thus till he came to a place somewhat ascending, and upon that place stood a Cross, and a little below, in the bottom, a sepulchre. So I saw in my dream that just as Christian came up with the Cross his burden loosed from off his shoulders, and fell from off his back, and began to tumble, and so continued to do, till it came to the mouth of the sepulchre, where it fell in, and I saw it no more. (CHRISTIAN HURRIES IN) Then was Christian glad and lightsome, and said, with a merry heart:

CHRISTIAN: He has given me rest by his sorrow, and life by his death.

(CHRISTIAN FLINGS UP HIS ARMS AND JUMPS IN THE AIR, THEN KNEELS)

I saw then that he went on, even until he came at a bottom, where he saw, a little out of the way, three men fast asleep, with fetters upon their heels. The name of the one was SIMPLE, another SLOTH, and the third PRESUMPTION.

(THE THREE HAVE CRAWLED ON STAGE AND LIE FACING THE AUDIENCE.)

CHRISTIAN: You are like them that sleep on the top of a mast, for the Dead Sea is under you, a gulf that has no bottom. Awake, and come away! I will help you off with your irons.

SIMPLE: I see no danger.

SLOTH: Yet a little more sleep.

PRESUMPTION: Every vat must stand on its own bottom; what is the answer else that I should give thee?

(THESE THREE CRAWL OFF STAGE)

Now there came two men running to meet Christian. The name of the one was TIMOROUS, and of the other MISTRUST.

CHRISTIAN: Sirs, what is the matter? You run the wrong way

TIMOROUS: We were going to the city of Zion; but the further we go the more danger we meet with.

MISTRUST: Just before us lie a couple of lions in the way, whether sleeping or waking we know not.

(THEY RUN OFF)

CHRISTIAN: You make me afraid; but whither shall I fly to be safe? If I go back to mine own country, that is prepared for fire and brimstone. I must venture. To go back is nothing but death; to go forward is fear of death, and life everlasting beyond it. I must go forward.

(CHRISTIAN GOES OFF)

Thus he went on his way. He lift up his eyes, and behold there was a very stately palace before him, the name of which was Beautiful. So he made haste and went forward, that if possible he might get lodging there. Now before he had gone far he entered into a very narrow passage, where he espied two lions in the way. (CHRISTIAN ENTERS, WALKING SLOWLY.) Then he was afraid; but the Porter at the lodge, whose name is WATCHFUL, cried unto him:

WATCHFUL
(OFF STAGE) Is thy strength so small? Fear not the lions, for they are chained, and are placed there for trial of faith. Keep in the midst of the path, and no hurt shall come unto thee.

Then I saw that Christian went on, trembling for fear of the lions, but taking good heed to the directions of the Porter. He heard them roar, but they did him no harm.

(IF A REALISTIC ROAR CAN BE HEARD ON TAPE, MAKE USE OF IT)

CHORUS
Whoso beset him round
With dismal stories
Do but themselves confound;
His strength the more is.
No foes shall stay his might,

Though he with giants fight;
He will make good his right
To be a pilgrim.

And now, in the Valley of Humiliation, poor Christian was hard put to it ; for he had gone but a little way before he espied a foul fiend coming over the field to meet him.

(CHRISTIAN ENTERS. IT IS PROBABLY BEST TO MAKE APOLLYON A VOICE OFF STAGE, RATHER THAN TO ATTEMPT AN ELABORATE COSTUME.)

His name is APOLLYON. He was clothed with scales like a fish (and they are his pride); he had wings like a dragon, feet like a bear, and out of his belly came fire and smoke, and his mouth was as the mouth of a lion.

APOLLYON: Whence come you, and whither are you bound?

CHRISTIAN: I am come from the City of Destruction, and am going to the City of Zion.

APOLLYON: By this I perceive thou art one of my subjects.

CHRISTIAN: But I have let myself to another, even to the King of Princes.

APOLLYON: I am an enemy to this Prince. I hate his person, his laws, and his people.

CHRISTIAN: Apollyon, beware what you do; for I am in the King's highway, the way of holiness.

(CHRISTIAN WALKS FORWARD)

APOLLYON: I am void of fear in this matter. Prepare thyself to die!

With that Apollyon threw a flaming dart at Christian's breast, and drove him backward; but Christian had a shield in his hand, with which he caught it. Apollyon threw darts as thick as hail, by the which he wounded Christian in his head, his hand, and his foot. Their sore combat lasted for above half a day, even till Christian was almost quite spent. Then Apollyon, wrestling with him, gave him a dreadful fall, and the sword flew out of his hand.

APOLLYON: Ah, I have thee now! Here will I spill thy soul.

But Christian nimbly stretched out his hand for his sword, and caught it.

CHRISTIAN: Rejoice not against me, O mine enemy! (APOLLYON GIVES A LOUD CRY.) Nay, in all these things we are more than conquerors through him that loved us.

And with that Apollyon spread forth his dragon's wings, and sped him away. Then there came to Christian a hand, with some of the leaves of the tree of life, the which he took, and applied to the wounds that he had received in the battle, and was healed immediately. He also sat down in that place to eat bread, and to drink of the bottle which was given him a little before; so, being refreshed, he addressed himself to his journey, with his sword drawn in his hand.

CHRISTIAN: (ENTERS CARRYING A SWORD) I know not but some other enemy may be at hand.

Now as Christian gazed from a little ascent in the way, he saw before him one FAITHFUL. (FAITHFUL COMES THROUGH THE AUDIENCE TO THE STAGE.) Christian ran, and got up with him. Then they went very lovingly on together, and had sweet discourse of all things that had happened to them in their pilgrimage.

(CHRISTIAN AND FAITHFUL EMBRACE, AND WALK OFF. DURING THE NEXT NARRA-TION A GROUP OF CITIZENS OF VANITY ENTER , CARRYING SIGNS READING: 'Vanity Fair;' 'City of Vanity;' 'Come to the Fair!' 'Buy! Buy!')

Presently they saw before them a town called VANITY, in which there is a fair kept. Beelzebub, Apollyon, and Legion contrived to set up this fair long ago, right by the way to the Celestial City. Now Christian and Faithful must needs go through this fair; and behold, even as they entered, all the people in the fair were moved, and the town itself in a hubbub about them.
(CHRISTIAN AND FAITHFUL ENTER)

FIRST CITIZEN: Who are these? Their raiment is truly strange.

SECOND CITIZEN: Are they bedlams?

THIRD CITIZEN: And their language!

CHRISTIAN: Sirs, we speak the language of Canaan—

FIRST CITIZEN: An outlandish speech! Who can understand it?

SECOND CITIZEN: Come, what will you buy?

THIRD CITIZEN: Let us see your money1

ALL CITIZENS: Buy! Buy!
(CHRISTIAN AND FAITHFUL ARE SURROUNDED)

CHRISTIAN: Turn away mine eyes from beholding Vanity!

FIRST CITIZEN:	Away with them!
SECOND CITIZEN:	Put them in a cage!
THIRD CITIZEN:	Bring them to the judge!

(CHRISTIAN AND FAITHFUL ARE DRAGGED OFFSTAGE)

So the men of the fair put them in a cage, and made their feet fast in the stocks. They beat them pitifully, and hanged irons upon them. Then they brought them before a Judge, and a Jury of the people of Vanity. The Jury spent but little time, and unanimously concluded to bring Faithful in guilty.

(THE JURY SCENE MAY BE HEARD FROM OFF STAGE. IF IT IS ACTED ON STAGE, EACH JURY MEMBER BRINGS HIS OR HER OWN CHAIR, AND THEY SIT. CHRISTIAN AND FAITHFUL STAND UNDER GUARD. THE JUDGE IS SEATED CENTER, PREFERABLY ON A SMALL PLATFORM. IF THERE ARE WOMEN ON THE JURY THE JUDGE ALTERS THEIR TITLES ACCORDINGLY)

JUDGE:	Let me hear your verdicts. First the foreman, Mr. Blind-Man.
BLIND-MAN:	I see clearly that this man is a heretic.
JUDGE:	Agreed. Mr. No-Good?
NO-GOOD:	Away with such a fellow from the earth!
JUDGE:	Excellent! Mr. Malice?
MALICE:	I hate the very looks of him.
JUDGE:	And I also. Mr. Love-Lust?
LOVE-LUST:	I could never endure him.
JUDGE:	Nor I. Mr. Live-Loose?
LIVE-LOOSE:	Nor I; for he would always be condemning my way.
JUDGE:	Mr. Heady, what say you?
HEADY:	Hang him! Hang him!
JUDGE:	All in good time. Mr. High-Mind?

HIGH-MIND: He is a sorry scrub.

JUDGE: And you, Mr. Enmity?

ENMITY: My heart riseth against him

JUDGE: Mine also. Mr. Liar?

LIAR: He is a rogue.

JUDGE: How say you, Mr. Cruelty?

CRUELTY: Hanging is too good for him.

JUDGE: Fine words ! Mr. Hate-Light?

HATE-LIGHT: Let us despatch him out of the way.

JUDGE: Mr. Implacable, you are the last of our Jury.

IMPLACABLE: Might I have all the world given me, I could not be reconciled to
               him; therefore let us forthwith bring him in guilty of death!

ALL: Guilty of death!

(CHRISTIAN AND FAITHFUL ARE SURROUNDED AND CARRIED OFF BY THE SHOUT-
ING JURY. THE STAGE IS EMPTY)

They therefore brought Faithful out, to do with him according to their law; and
first, they scourged him, then they buffeted him, then they lanced his flesh with
knives; after that they stoned him with stones, then pricked him with their swords;
and, last of all, they burned him to ashes at the stake. Thus came Faithful to his
end. Now I saw that there stood behind the multitude a chariot and a couple of
horses, waiting for Faithful, who was taken up into it, and straightway was carried
up through the clouds, with sound of trumpet, the nearest way to the Celestial
Gate. But as for Christian, He that overrules all things so wrought it about that he
for that time escaped them, and went his way.

(CHRISTIAN AND HOPEFUL ENTER, TOGETHER WITH TWO OTHER PILGRIMS, A
MAN AND A WOMAN.) So he journeyed on, and with him went one HOPEFUL.
Now at length they came in sight of the gate of the City of Zion. I further saw that
betwixt them and the gate was a river; but there was no bridge to go over. The
river was very deep. The Pilgrims were much stunned, but they that went with
them said:

MAN: You must go through, or you cannot come at the gate.

CHRISTIAN: I know not how I can get across. Are the waters all of a depth?

WOMAN: No. You shall find it deeper or shallower as you believe in the King of Zion.

(MIME THE CROSSING OF THE RIVER)

HOPEFUL: Come, Christian! Let us address ourselves to the crossing of the water!

CHRISTIAN: I sink in deep waters! The billows go over my head!

HOPEFUL: Be of good cheer, my brother! I feel the bottom, and it is good.

CHRISTIAN: Ah! I shall not see the land that flows with milk and honey.

HOPEFUL: Keep your head above water, Brother Christian! I see the gate, and men standing by to receive us.

CHRISTIAN: Nay, it is you they wait for, Hopeful, only you.

HOPEFUL: Be of good cheer, I say! Jesus Christ maketh thee whole!

CHRISTIAN: Oh, I see him again! And he tells me, 'When thou passest through the waters I shall be with thee, and through the rivers, they shall not overflow thee.'

Then they both took courage, and Christian found ground to stand upon. So it followed that the rest of the river was more shallow. Now upon the bank of the river they saw two shining angels, who waited for them.

(IT IS RECOMMENDED THAT THESE VOICES SHOULD COME FROM OFF STAGE, WHERE A BRIGHT LIGHT SHINES)

FIRST ANGEL: We are ministering spirits, sent forth to help those that shall be heirs to salvation.

SECOND ANGEL: Here is Mount Zion, the heavenly Jerusalem, the innumerable company of angels, and the spirits of just men made perfect.

FIRST ANGEL: Call at the Gate, good Christian!

SECOND ANGEL: Tell the King who has come!

(THE DEEP VOICE OF THE KING IS HEARD FROM FAR OFF)

KING: Open the gate! Enter ye into the joy of your Lord!

(CHRISTIAN AND HOPEFUL GO OFF TOWARDS THE LIGHT)

So I saw that Christian and Hopeful went in at the gate; and lo, as they entered, they were transfigured, and they had raiment put on them like gold. But glorious was it to see how the open region was filled with horses and chariots, with trumpeters and pipers, with singers and players on stringed instruments, to welcome the pilgrims as they went up, and followed one another in at the beautiful gate of the City.

CHORUS

Since, Lord, thou dost defend
Us with thy spirit,
We know we at the end
Shall life inherit.
Then fancies flee away!
I'll fear not what men say.
I'll labor night and day
To be a pilgrim.

Fourteen:

GOD'S TUMBLER
(for reading, or production as a musical)

This play was written as a musical, and the score is available. The action takes place in the marketplace of a French town, then close to the walls of the Abbey, and finally at various points inside the Abbey. All this is presented on an empty stage, with only one chair or bench used in some scenes.

Costume is at the discretion of the Director. Simple modern dress in bright colors is recommended for the Chorus; black, brown, or white habits for the monks, leotards and some brightly colored clothes for the Tumbler and his servants. The Narrator speaks from a podium at the side of the stage opposite the piano and Chorus.

Lighting will depend upon the building in which the play is produced. If, for example, it is part of a church service, daylight or full lighting will probably be unchanged. If a stage is used, and lights are available, spots may be used effectively in the second half of the play.

The version of the play given here assumes that the TUMBLER is a dancer as well as an actor. In that case it is a play full of action, with rapid changes of scene.

See the notes at the end of the play for other possible ways of presenting it.

CHARACTERS: THE TUMBLER, a man in his 30's
PIERRE)
LOUIS)   his boy servants
TWO LORDS
TWO LADIES
BROTHER ALBAN
THE ABBOT OF CLAIRVAUX
BROTHER ELDRED
VOICE OF GOD
NARRATOR
CHORUS OF VILLAGERS

We are telling a story of France in the Middle Ages. It begins in the square of a country town. On three sides, sitting on benches or standing behind them, there is a crowd of people of all ages and stations in life. (HE POINTS TO THE AUDIENCE AND CHORUS) In the center the Tumbler dances, (PIANO INTRODUCTION BEGINS) leaping and somersaulting like the brilliant acrobat he is. He is a man loved and sought after wherever he goes.

(THE TUMBLER ENTERS AND DANCES. OTHER DANCERS MAY JOIN WITH HIM IN THIS OPENING DANCE)

Once a wonderful Tumbler
Used to journey through France.
All the people came when they heard his name,
And their feet began to dance.

CHORUS
Dancing, dancing, till the end of the day.
All the people of France began to dance
When the Tumbler came their way.

He was slender and graceful;
He was nimble of limb;
And all day long there was joy and song
When the dance was led by him.

CHORUS
Dancing, dancing, in the markets of France.
All the people came when they heard his name,
And their feet began to dance.

(SLOWER)
But the Tumbler was weary.
There was pain in his heart.
While the crowds went mad he was tired and sad,
And he longed to rest apart.

CHORUS
Dancing, dancing, till the end of the day.
Though his feet danced quick he was tired and sick,
And you might have heard him pray:

TUMBLER: Oh give me peace!
Oh God, give me peace!
My soul is weary,
Oh give me rest and peace!

(THE DANCE IS NOW FINISHED. THE TUMBLER BOWS REPEATEDLY, WHILE THE
CHORUS CLAPS AND CHEERS. HE IS VERY TIRED AND MOVES AS IN A DREAM.
PIERRE AND LOUIS CARRY AROUND PLATES AMONG THE AUDIENCE, AS THOUGH
COLLECTING MONEY. THE TUMBLER COLLAPSES ON TO A BENCH OR CHAIR ON THE
SIDE OF THE STAGE OPPOSITE TO THE CHORUS. THE TWO LORDS AND LADIES AP-
PROACH HIM)

FIRST LORD: Tumbler, come to my house!
Come with me and dine!

FIRST LADY: You shall eat from golden plates
All that's rich and fine.

SECOND LORD: Tumbler, come to my house!
You shall have the best!

SECOND LADY: You are worn and weary.
Come with me and rest!

(THEY SAY ONE LINE EACH OF THE FOLLOWING VERSE.)
You shall have linen and satin and silk,
Butter and honey and cheeses and milk.
You shall have silver and gold as well.
Servants will come when you touch a bell.

TUMBLER: I thank you, my Ladies, and you, my Lords. I thank you from my
heart. But my dancing has made me weary, and I would rest alone.
My servants will see to my wants. I bid you goodnight, and I thank
you for your kindness.

(THE LORDS AND LADIES DEPART, SAYING, 'GOODNIGHT, TUMBLER! GOODNIGHT!' PIERRE AND LOUIS HAVE BEEN WATCHING FROM A DISTANCE. THEY NOW APPROACH HIM)

PIERRE: Master, are you sick?

LOUIS: Master, you look pale.

TUMBLER: Never mind, Pierre! Never mind, Louis! I shall recover when I have sat and rested. Yet in truth it is not my limbs only that are tired, but my heart and my spirit.

PIERRE: Shall we go to the inn and see that your supper is ready?

LOUIS: Shall we prepare wine for you, Master?

TUMBLER: Yes, yes. See that everything is ready. Another inn, another supper, another bed. Perhaps I should have gone with one of the fine Lords or Ladies, and lain between silken sheets, with servants to give me hot baths and pour my wine.

PIERRE: We shall look after you, Master.

TUMBLER: I know it, I know it. How many inns have we slept in, you and I? How many times have I danced since last winter? Well, never mind! I am rich; I am famous throughout France. But in truth I love none of it, except that I love to dance, and to set the feet of Lords and peasants dancing. And even of that I grow weary, and yearn for peace.

LOUIS: Come to the inn, Master!

(THE BELLS HAVE BEGUN TO RING SOFTLY)

TUMBLER: Yes, I will come. Stop! What bells are those? I saw an Abbey as we rode by, but we travel so far and so fast that half the time I do not know where we are.

PIERRE: This is Clairvaux, and those are the Abbey bells.

TUMBLER: Clairvaux! I have heard of it. The good Bernard was Abbot there. Clairvaux! The bells have a sweet tone.

LOUIS: Will you come now, Master?

TUMBLER: Go to the inn, both of you. I want to listen to the bells. Perhaps I shall walk to the Abbey while the sun is setting.

LOUIS: Yes, Master. I will take the money bag.

PIERRE: It is heavy tonight!

TUMBLER: Yes, take it, my sons. I wish that my heart would grow lighter when the bag grows heavier! But enough of that: go to the inn!

PIERRE and LOUIS: Yes, Master.

(THE TUMBLER SITS AGAIN, AND LISTENS. THE FOLLOWING SONG MAY EITHER BE SUNG BY THE CHORUS OR BY A SOPRANO SOLOIST)

> The bells are ringing to call you home.
> The bells are ringing, and bid you come.
> They say that pain can cease,
> That you may find release,
> That there is rest and peace
> If you will hear.
> The bells are ringing to speak to you.
> The night is falling, and rest is due.
> From all the fever and labor and fear
> The bells are calling, if you will hear.

(THE TUMBLER WALKS SLOWLY UPSTAGE TOWARDS THE SOUND OF THE BELLS. AFTER HESITATING, HE MIMES KNOCKING AT A DOOR. SOON BROTHER ALBAN COMES OUT. HE IS A CHEERFUL MAN OF MIDDLE AGE)

ALBAN: Good evening, sir, and welcome!

TUMBLER: Greetings, Father!

ALBAN: No, no. Not Father. I am only a lay brother, sir, whose task it is to watch the door and help strangers.

TUMBLER   You give welcome to all who come?

ALBAN: All but rogues; and sometimes they are welcome too. But come in, sir! You look tired. Abbot Benedict would scold me if he knew that you were standing out here in the darkness.

            Yes, everyone may enter,
            To wash and rest and feed.
            So come inside, for the door is wide

For a man in need.
And I am here to welcome
The stranger at the gate.
I would think it shame if you called my name
And I made you wait.

You are no casual beggar.
You are no wandering tramp.
With clothes so fine, and shoes that shine,
You bear a rich man's stamp.

We ask no prying questions.
We take you as you come.
You may work or pray, you may sleep all day,
You may speak or be dumb.

(ALBAN MOTIONS THE TUMBLER TO SIT)

Now sit there, and I will tell the Abbot that we have a guest. For indeed you must not stir from here tonight.

TUMBLER: I have a lodging at the inn, and my serving boys—

ALBAN: Your serving boys may fend for themselves until morning. Hot milk or mulled wine is what you need, and a square meal, with a long night's sleep to follow.

(MEN'S VOICES FROM THE CHORUS BEGIN THE CHANTING OF 'Remember, O Lord.')

TUMBLER: What is that chanting?

ALBAN: It is some of the brethren on their way through the cloister to the Chapel. Now make yourself at home, and listen till I come.

MALE VOICES: Remember, O Lord, what thou hast wrought in us, and not what we deserve; and, as thou hast called us to thy service, make us worthy of our calling. Amen.

(THE TUMBLER SITS WITH HIS HEAD BURIED IN HIS HANDS. THEN HE LOOKS UP)

TUMBLER: Make me worthy of my calling? Oh God, I have no calling, but to dance and tumble. How useless I am, with all my fame and finery!
Oh for peace of heart! For peace of heart!

The Tumbler was made welcome at the Abbey, first as a guest and then as a novice. He sent for his servants, gave them a generous portion of his money, and delivered the rest to Abbot Benedict. He said a loving farewell to Pierre and Louis, who went away sorrowful, for they had loved their master well. (THIS FAREWELL

SCENE SHOULD BE ACTED OUT IN MIME AS THE WORDS ARE SPOKEN) France soon forgot the Tumbler, and he for his part began to try to learn to be a good monk—a task which he did not find easy.

(THE TUMBLER HAS MOVED TO ONE SIDE, AND WE SEE HIM IN MIME WORKNG AT A CARPENTER'S BENCH. HE MAKES A FALSE BLOW WITH HIS HAMMER, AND THE WOOD FALLS TO THE GROUND. AT THAT MOMENT THE ABBOT HAS COME CLOSE TO HIM)

ABBOT: It seems that your hands are not as deft as your feet, Brother Tumbler. Let me see this work that you have done.

TUMBLER: I have tried hard, Father Abbot, but it is bad work, and I know it.

ABBOT: There at least you are right. In the garden, you dug up Father Juniper's asparagus when you were trying to sow cabbages. In the kitchen, you upset a skillet over Brother Matthew, and broke four earthenware dishes. You can neither read nor write, so that the manuscript room is hardly the place for you. In truth, Brother, I am at a loss to know just how best you can serve Almighty God.

TUMBLER: (SOFTLY, TO HIMSELF) I can dance.

ABBOT: What was that?

TUMBLER: I am sorry, Father. I was thinking faroff thoughts. I will try harder at my work, and perhaps God will give me grace to become a passable gardener or carpenter even yet.

(A BELL TOLLS FOR THE NEXT THIRTY SECONDS)

ABBOT: There is the bell for Vespers. Go and prepare yourself; and do not worry too much about your bruised thumbs or botched work. As long as nobody has to depend on eating your cabbages, or use this box (which may the good Lord forbid!) God will watch your heart rather than your hands.

(THE BELL CEASES TOLLING. WE SEE THE TUMBLER GO TO ONE SIDE OF THE STAGE, AS THOUGH HIDING, AND THEN CROSS TO THE OTHER AND KNEEL)

But the Tumbler did not go to Vespers. Instead he waited in the Cloister until the rest had gone into the Chapel, then stole down to the Crypt, where there was a small Chapel of Our Lady. He prayed long at the altar steps, and as he prayed he seemed to hear music. His whole body began to tingle, and his feet itched to dance.

TUMBLER: (STILL KNEELING) Oh God! What use am I? It is as the Abbot said. I can do nothing right, and I am sick. Yet here I feel at home, and close to you. Can I do nothing to serve you?

VOICE OF GOD: You can dance. (THE TUMBLER LOOKS UP, ASTONISHED) One gift I gave you, Tumbler, which no other man in France shares; and that gift you sacrificed to serve me here. I have often watched you dance on village greens and in city squares. Dance for me now, and do me service!

(THE TUNE OF THE FOLLOWING SONG BEGINS SOFTLY, AND SLOWLY. IT GROWS LOUDER AS THE VOICES ARE HEARD)

TUMBLER: Whose was that voice? And what is this music? Pierre? Louis?

(WE DO NOT SEE THE BOYS, BUT THEIR VOICES COME FROM FAR AWAY, BEHIND THE ALTAR)

PIERRE: Dance, Master! It was God who called you.

LOUIS: Dance for him, and for the Virgin Mary, Master!

(AS THOUGH IN A TRANCE THE TUMBLER SLOWLY TAKES OFF HIS HABIT AND BEGINS TO DANCE, AT FIRST HESITANTLY, THEN WITH MORE AND MORE FLUENCY. HE SINGS AS HE DANCES. WHEN THE DANCE IS DONE HE FALLS AND BEGINS TO COUGH AND SOB)

TUMBLER: I can give you dancing,
I can dance and sing.
I can tumble and leap and turn:
That is what I bring.
Only by my dancing
I can play my part.
All my love is here in my feet;
I'm dancing with my heart.

There's no gift of hand or head that I am fit to bring.
There's no work that I can do to serve my God and King.

I can give you dancing.
I can dance and sing.
I can tumble and leap and turn
That is what I bring.

At the end of the dance the Tumbler sank exhausted at the foot of the altar, coughing; but for the first trime since he arrived at the Abbey he felt fulfilled. Every day he slipped away into the Crypt and danced. At length one of the brothers, Eldred, noticed his absence from Vespers.

(THE TUMBLER IS STILL KNEELING AT THE ALTAR. ELDRED ENTERS STEALTHILY ON THE OTHER SIDE OF THE STAGE, AND HIDES IN THE SHADOWS)

Eldred was not a bad or vindictive man; but monks are very much like other men, and perhaps he envied the Tumbler his fame in the outside world, or despised his clumsiness in the work of the Abbey. At all events, consumed by curiosity, he noted one evening where the Tumbler lurked in the Cloister. Then he too slipped away through the shadows and followed him. He saw the Tumbler dance, but he did not hear the music, because his ears were not attuned to it.

(THE TUMBLER IS NOW IN SHADOW. WE SEE ELDRED ON THE OTHER SIDE OF THE STAGE.)

ELDRED: It's disgusting, it's disgusting,
      All his posturing and lusting!
      Bowing to the Altar like the Devil at his prayers!
      He's revolting, quite revolting,
      With his juddering and jolting!
      Somersaulting openly upon the Altar stairs!
      It's disgusting, quite dis—

(THE ABBOT HAS ENTERED QUIETLY, AND ELDRED BECOMES AWARE OF HIS PRESENCE)

ABBOT: What is the matter, Brother Eldred? You look angry and upset.

ELDRED: It is nothing, Father Abbot. I—

ABBOT: Nothing? I am sorry that you can look so deeply and sadly moved by nothing. When there is anger in a man's heart, especially if he be a monk, better to let it out and draw its sting.

ELDRED: Indeed, Father, you are right. But when it means causing harm to a fellow Brother—

ABBOT: I see. (HE PAUSES) Even so, you had better let me be the judge of that. Such harm also may best be cured by the open light of truth. What has made you so full of indignation, Brother?

ELDRED: Truly, Father, it is a sight which I have just seen, and which I little thought ever to see in a house of God.

(THEY WALK OFF TOGETHER, ELDRED GESTICULATING AS HE TELLS HIS STORY. THE TUMBLER IS STILL LYING AT THE ALTAR STEPS)

And so Brother Eldred told the Abbot; and the Abbot, who was a good and wise man, said little, but made Eldred promise, on his oath of obedience, to say nothing of what he had seen. Then the Abbot went to the quiet of his cell, and prayed.

(THE ABBOT ENTERS AND KNEELS, AT A DISTANCE FROM THE TUMBLER, FACING THE AUDIENCE)

ABBOT: O God, show me what is right for your servant and our brother, the Tumbler! You have taught us that as monks we should do unto you true and laudable service; and noone could wish to carry out your bidding more than he does. Yet all that he can do well is to dance; and I have never read nor heard that to turn somersaults is to pray—though to be sure, Lord, King David danced before your altar. O Lord, you know that the Tumbler is not long for this world, being grievously sick, and that he is a good man, generous of heart. Teach me what I should do!

(HE REMAINS KNEELING DURING THE FOLLOWING NARRATION)

In the morning the Abbot awoke, knowing what he should do. All that day he went about his duties. The hours of the monastic life passed in their usual rhythm of work and worship, in the eating of meals and in the brief period of relaxation. When the time for Vespers came, the Abbot went to the Chapel in the Crypt, hid himself, and watched.

(THE TUMBLER IS STILL LYING MOTIONLESS. THE ABBOT GOES TO THE OPPOSITE SIDE OF THE STAGE. THE MUSIC BEGINS, AND AGAIN THE TUMBLER DANCES. THE DANCE IS SHORTER AND WILDER THAN BEFORE, AS THOUGH HE IS DRIVING HIM-SELF TO FINISH IT. HE FALLS SUDDENLY, IN A PAROXYSM OF COUGHING, WHILE THE MUSIC IS STILL AT ITS HEIGHT. THE ABBOT RUNS FORWARD TO KNEEL BY HIM, AND THE MUSIC STOPS)

TUMBLER: Oh, Father Abbot, I—

ABBOT   Do not be afraid, my son!

TUMBLER: But I am afraid. You saw me?

ABBOT: Yes, I saw you dance.

TUMBLER: I have sinned, Father, and I know that now I shall not be able to stay here. I have abused your goodness; for night after night I have come here and danced. But I swear that I did it because I was hungry and thirsty to do God service, and to give him thanks.

ABBOT: Which is what you have done, my son.

TUMBLER: You mean that you—

ABBOT: I mean that when I watched you my heart was more full of thankfulness than it has been for many a year, perhaps more than it has ever been; and full of humility also.

TUMBLER: But—I don't understand. You don't want to send me away? You can punish me in some other way?

ABBOT: I am not going to send you away. I do not think that either you or I will live much longer in this world. I am old, and you are sick. I hope that we shall make our pilgrimage together; and proud should I be to come to my Lord with such a friend beside me! But I enjoin upon you one thing, on your vow of obedience. Each day you must dance here alone; for it is your service to him who gave you such grace and strength. Do not overtax yourself, but dance to give thanks. That is your carpentry, your gardening, your reading and writing, yes, and your cooking and your prayer. Our walls will rejoice with the pulse of your dancing, for it too is sacred.

(DURING THE NEXT NARRATION THE ABBOT AND TUMBLER REMAIN STILL.)

So he danced every day. And it came about that one night, as he danced, the Tumbler seemed to see his servants again, Pierre and Louis, welcoming him; and his mother and father, whom he dearly loved; and a great crowd that watched and took pleasure in his dancing: but it was a crowd of angels, not of peasants; and the music was the music of a heavenly choir.

(THE TUMBLER HAS SLOWLY RISEN AND COME DOWNSTAGE. HE GAZES OUT OVER THE AUDIENCE, WITH A LOOK OF JOY ON HIS FACE. HE DANCES BRIEFLY AND GENTLY BEFORE SLIPPING TO HIS KNEES AND THEN TO THE GROUND. THE ABBOT HAS LEFT THE STAGE)

Had you been there, you would have seen the Tumbler stumble, fall, and rise no more; for in that hour his body was shed away. But his spirit danced out of earthly life, and danced right through the gates of heaven, which lay wide open before him. On the other side the trumpets sounded for him, in the rhythm and joy of his dancing; and the Angels rejoiced, as men and women on earth had rejoiced, at his grace and beauty.

(IF OTHER DANCERS TOOK PART IN THE OPENING SCENE, THEY MAY COME THROUGH THE AUDIENCE DURING THIS NARRATION, RAISE THE TUMBLER UP, AND DANCE OUT DOWN THE CENTER AISLE. OTHERWISE IT IS BEST IF HE LIES STILL, AND THE FINAL DANCE IS LEFT TO THE IMAGINATION.)

CHORUS
Dancing, dancing, up to heaven so high!
All the alngels sang, all the trumpets rang,
When the Tumbler's feet danced by.

ADDITIONAL NOTES ON PRODUCTION.

Some companies or congregations may wish to act this play, but conclude that without an outstanding dancer-actor it is not possible. With imagination and ingenuity the play can be presented in different ways.

The simplest format is that of a narration. The Narrator tells the whole story, with the Chorus standing next to him around a piano. Other voices read the lines allotted to the different roles:Tumbler, Abbot, servants, etc.

Between this and a full production there may be compromises. The dancing may be imagined, but the scenes acted. There are ten acting roles, not including the Narrator and the Voice of God. If there are not actors available to fill all these roles, some scenes may be acted and some told by the Narrator. He (or she) could for example describe the scenes involving Brother Alban and Brother Eldred; and the lines allotted to the Lords and Ladies could be spoken and sung by Chorus members rather than on stage.

Fifteen:

SATAN'S GUIDE TO THE TEN COMMANDMENTS

This is an experiment in Bible study. The narration and scenes are intended for reading or simple presentation, followed by discussion. The Guide has been written with adult groups in mind, but it could well be used with high school or junior high school groups. One way of using the Guide is to assign roles and read it straight through, then go back and discuss it stage by stage. Another way would be to read it in sections. A natural stopping place occurs at the end of the Second Commandment. A minimum of six people are needed to play the roles. More may be used if roles are not doubled.

SATAN

Good morning. My name is Satan—now don't look so upset! I don't have horns, or cloven feet. I'm your friend, and I want to explain why I am here with you today. I have come to talk to you about Moses and those Ten Commandments. (HE BECOMES ANGRY AND UPSET)

Oh, it's no use. I can't control myself when I think of that man. He has given me more trouble than any other of those miserable humans whom HE (POINTING UPWARDS) created. Until Moses came along I was doing very well. They all had their different religions—gods of the sky and the sea, of lust and war and wind and fire—but it was all superstition and fear. They would sacrifice anything and anybody, from their grandmothers to their prize bulls, to save their skins. The idea that the gods wanted them to do good—whatever good may be—never occurred to them.

Then everything changed. Why did that stupid Egyptian princess have to get all sentimental, and pull dear little Moses out of the bulrushes? Pharaoh was quite right to kill all those dangerous little Jew boys. They were getting out of control. But little Moses was pampered, and raised like an Egyptian prince—only to stab Egypt in the back.

HE staged a great photo op—a burning bush, a voice like Charlton Heston, and Moses trembling there on the mountain with his shoes off. And HE said to Moses, 'There is only one God'—ONE GOD! What about me? Haven't I done more for men and women than HE has? And what about Zeus and all the rest, and the friendly little spirits whom I can keep under control? But Moses believed him, and went back to Egypt to raise hell—no, that wasn't well put. They went off into the desert, where they ought to have starved; but HE gave them manna to eat and water out of bare rocks. Then HE summoned Moses up another mountain and showed him those TEN COMMANDMENTS. I have never got over it—never! None of the religions which humans had invented before that time had suggested that God LOVED them, or—just as bad—that HE wanted them to love HIM, or—worse still—that believing in HIM meant that you should keep a series of laws which are ruinous to my whole work. Curse Moses! Curse the day when he lugged those stone tablets down the mountain! Things have never been the same for me since.

You see, if you take them seriously—which, thank Lucifer and all the spirits of Belial, you don't—I am finished!

One God:

no idols:

no swearing:

regular worship:

real family life:

no war:

sexual purity:

respecting other people's property:

no lies about their characters: not even any envy?

I ask you! How could I operate under those conditions? So ever since Moses ran at the mouth and told those miserable Jews to keep the Ten Commandments I have been fighting to see that nobody listens. As you will see from some of the pictures I will show you, I don't have too much to worry about. The Commandments are on plenty of walls and in every Bible. You even fight about whether they should be allowed in your oh, so secular schools! But that doesn't matter as long as nobody actually OBEYS them!

THE FIRST COMMANDMENT

Take number One. Let me show you one of my favorite places of worship: the Church of All Saints and Mammon in Bucksville, New York (actually there are similar churches in every State). What a sensible congregation! They have two altars: a beautiful one for HIM, and over here a silver table, with a Golden Calf above, and a green altar cloth woven out of dollar signs. HE says you cannot serve God and Mammon, but believe me they try!

THE SCENE WILL HAVE TO BE DESCRIBED, UNLESS YOU RECRUIT A CHOIR. THEY HAVE OLD, FRAYED ROBES, AND SLOUCH IN DRAGGING SANDALS ON THEIR FEET. THEY CARRY TWO BANNERS, BEARING THE SIGN: HALF AND HALF. A SLOPPY MINISTER WALKS IN FRONT OF THEM.

MINISTER: Our choir will now lead you in singing the hymn in your leaflet: WE ARE THE CHILDREN OF LIGHT.

CHOIR
We are the children of light,
And we worship the Lord with half of our might.
We half believe in God above,
And we practice half of Christian love.
We worship God, just half and half,
But we also keep an eye on the Golden Calf.

That's the kind of anthem I like. But I'm worried about their new Rector. He is teaching them one of his horrible prayers: ALL THINGS COME OF THEE, O LORD, AND OF THINE OWN HAVE WE GIVEN THEE. Sacrilege! It's not true! I give you far more than HE does—all you want, anything you ask! So here's to the Golden Calf! Long may he fight the good fight against Moses and his abominable laws!

THE SECOND COMMANDMENT

I often have a good laugh over the second commandment. I have sat in churches and heard preacher after preacher say that all ten are out of date, and should be thrown out, especially number two. Only primitive peoples long ago, they say, made idols of wood or stone and bowed down before them.

Well, I have news for you, Mr. Liberal Preacher. Maybe wood and stone are out of date, but idols are alive and well. I could take you to the homes of many of your Vestrymen—and nowadays Vestrywomen—where idols are worshipped as reverently as the Moabites worshipped Chemosh or the Tyrians Ashtoreth. One of my favorite couples are Moron and Myopia Pitts, members--sort of—of Saint Croesus-close-to-the-Market.

Hush! They are praying to their graven image!

(MAN AND WOMAN KNEEL BEFORE A LUXURIOUS COMBINED COMPUTER, PRINTER, TV)

MORON: (BOWING TO THE GROUND) Great Lord of Television, King of All Channels, forasmuch as without Thee I would quickly perish, feed me, I pray, with thy soothing sounds and narcotic images!

MYOPIA: Modem, goddess of the Internet, fling open the gates of knowledge, however useless!

MORON: Pour out upon us, O Gateway to whatsoever is trivial and titillating, the abundance of thy blessed e-mail!

MYOPIA: O Holy Tube, source of all power and might, cleanse me, I pray, with thy sweet soap! Thrill me with thine honeyed romance! Terrify me with thy spinechilling violence! Update me on the market every three minutes! Uplift my soul through thy servants the TV Evangelists! Banish all disturbing thoughts of reality from my mind!

MORON: And, of thy goodness, Most Merciful Screen, guide me through thy blessed commercials so that I may buy only those things which are pleasing in thy sight!

MYOPIA: Then at the last, Lord, zonk me out with sheer exhaustion and ecstasy, so that I may be ready to greet thee again at the dawn of another day!

BOTH: Praise the Tube! Amen.

I could show you any number of other graven images along your street, if we had the time. DIVES GRUBB lives close to you, with his computer and his ulcer, making more money in order to—make more money. Wasn't it sad when that day trader lost it and shot a bunch of his fellow grubbers? Sad for you, that is: I thought it was a day to remember.

Then there's your neighbor DOTTIE PEEVEY, whose idol is her ghastly little daughter, Evie Peevey. She dresses her like a doll, and has turned the poor kid into a spoiled mess—just the kind of child I love.

Let me tell you a secret. Those first two commandments are the only ones that make me tremble with fear. If the nasty little humans kept those two, they wouldn't need any others. Worship one God, and you will love your neighbor, however unattractive he may be. Refuse to set up your idols, and you won't need to worry about laws of honesty or purity or greed. That is why I go all out to teach those human scum to find graven images: gold, silver, flesh, celluloid, digital, no matter, so long as you bow down to them and worship them. Graven images are my bread and butter—and I can never have enough of them.

THE THIRD COMMANDMENT

No need to waste much time on commandment number three. You all take the name of the Lord your God in vain, even when you are hardly conscious of it. I can hear your thoughts, you see, not just what you say out loud. I heard you last Sunday in that fashionable church of yours, saying HIS creed, which you have repeated so many times that it long since ceased to mean anything: 'I believe in God the Father Almighty—just look at Flora! How can she wear such a ghastly hat?' And later, kneeling and peering through your fingers: 'Give us this day our daily bread—I don't know how the Stimsons can appear in church after what has been said—and forgive us our trespasses.' If that isn't taking HIS name in vain I don't know what is—mumbling prayers while you are thinking things which you would hate him to hear. And those cheap little swearwords. Of course you don't mean anything when you say 'O God!' because there is a hole in your stocking, or 'Christ Almighty!' when someone cuts in front of you. At least you'll know from now on that you give somebody some pleasure when you take HIS name in vain: me, your friend, Satan.

THE FOURTH COMMANDMENT

Now I want to show you how John and Mary Hope have observed commandment number four: REMEMBER THAT THOU KEEP HOLY THE SABBATH DAY. They were married at Saint Paul's just over twenty years ago. Such a lovely wedding! No expense spared. Here they are, first of all later that year, in bed together.

MARY: John, wake up! It's 8.30 We promised Father Maniple that we would come regularly, and it's a month since—

JOHN: Oh, not today, Mary, for God's sake. No, I don't mean that. I mean, we were up late, and this is the only day we get to sleep in.

MARY: O.K., but we did promise.

JOHN: Besides, you're pregnant. Soon we shall be having the baby baptized, and then we'll start a regular routine.

Now take a look at them seven years later.

JOHN: Hurry up, Mary! We ought to leave.

MARY: You don't have to get the kids ready. Can't you come and help me?

JOHN: If you aren't ready we'd better skip it. It's too much hassle getting them down there in time.

MARY: If you'd just put Tom's shoes on, instead of complaining—

Now we will look in on them soon after their twentieth anniversary.

MARY: How about going to the 9 o'clock, John?

JOHN (YAWNING): Oh, I dunno. There was some point in it while the kids were around, but now—

MARY: We have more time now. I'd like to get back in there, join the Women's Guild—

JOHN: I know what you mean. Maybe I'll sign up for softball. But I need to clean the pool this morning. Anyway, since old Canon Thurifer left it hasn't been the same.

MARY: I know; and I can hardly find my place in the new books.

JOHN: It's only a couple of months to Christmas. Let's go then.

MARY: Fine! Then perhaps after the first of the year we can start going regularly.

After the first of the year! Some of my favorite words. But isn't it a comfort to know that John and Mary wil be buried in the memorial garden? May they rest in—well, I'm not sure where. HE has such a sloppy habit of forgiving even people like them.

THE FIFTH COMMANDMENT

I've been a little worried and upset about the Fifth Commandment recently. HONOR THY FATHER AND THY MOTHER? That was a joke in the good old Sixties. I had it made. Honoring your parents was out—I mean OUT! Anyone over thirty, parents, teachers, clergy, the military, the pigs, was included among the enemy. I've lost some ground since then, but not too much.

Just before Christmas last year I looked in on two families. The score was 1-1. You can't win 'em all. This family is just the kind I enjoy.

READ OR ACT

GRANNY IS COMING FOR CHRISTMAS

After scene one SATAN says: 'But things are not always so good for me.'
After scene two he says: 'Horrible! All that sentimental nonsense! Ugh! I must do something to spoil their Christmas.'

THE SIXTH COMMANDMENT

But we must move on to number six. Luckily men and women have been killing each other ever since Cain began it; but those same head-in-the-clouds preachers make light of this commandment. We respectable Christians don't kill people, they say, except when our heroes go to war, when killing is the proper thing to do. Only in Agatha Christie do you find corpses in the sacristy or the vicarage.

What they don't realize is that you can commit murder with your tongue at the drop of a hat—a mixed metaphor, but I'm sure you understand me. Take a look at my favorite member of Saint Jude's-under-the-Grapevine, EVE DROP. She and her friend BLABBA MOUTH are enjoying a cup of coffee. It takes them less than two minutes to commit murder.

BLABBA: How is your new Assistant doing?

EVE: Very well, considering—

BLABBA: What do you mean, considering?

EVE: Well, you know—the stories we've heard.

BLABBA: No, I don't know. Do tell me!

EVE: I'm not sure that I ought to pass it on. All I've heard are rumors, indirectly.

BLABBA: You know you can trust me. The only thing I heard about him is that he came from somewhere in Texas.

EVE: That's right. There had been some kind of trouble in his parish.

BLABBA: What trouble?

EVE: Nobody quite knows. All we can say for certain is that he was out of a job, and our Rector took him in. You know our Rector: anyone can pull the wool over his eyes.

BLABBA: But there must be some kind of evidence behind the rumors. What are people saying?

EVE: That's just it. Nobody knows. He was Youth Minister at this place in Texas.

BLABBA: Ooh! That's a touchy area. We know all about that at Saint Philip's

EVE: Well—you said it—I didn't. One of our members read about a case in Texas, but that may just be a coincidence.

BLABBA: Well, yes. Texas is a big place. Of course it might be something to do with money.

EVE: Like what happened at the Cathedral, you mean? Yes, it could be that. And then there's his wife—

BLABBA: Ooh! I didn't realize he was married.

EVE: Oh, yes, he's married; and some of us wonder—I mean, there's nothing against her. They met when he was in Seminary.

BLABBA: That's bad for a start. We all know what those Seminaries are like nowadays—everyone living together, and farout courses—

EVE: You see, she has this job at a Doctor's office, and the baby, so she can't be around the church very much. And he—

BLABBA: What? Go on!

EVE: Well, he does spend a lot of time with the choir, and the Altar Guild—

Beautiful! You see what I mean? Murder by association, insinuation! Nothing that Eve said was an actual lie. Those two don't need to lie. All they need to do is to let their dirty little minds savor mischief and malice. I love them!

THE SEVENTH COMMANDMENT

As for adultery, which poor old Moses hoped to squelch by commandment number seven, it was always a losing battle. Well, you know that. In the days before women's liberation respectable men kept their mistresses around the corner, or looked for prostitutes. In some ways it was tougher on the women in those days, but I was often able to help them to compensate with discreet little affairs. Now of course anything goes—though I'm not sure that AIDS has helped me. It actually makes some people more careful—not for religious reasons, I need hardly say, but out of sheer terror.

To suit our modern culture I have my chapels, as I sometimes call them, to annoy HIM: singles bars. Soft lights, a bartender who will hear your confession much more sympathetically than any prissy priest, musack in the background, plenty of alcohol—Satan's sacrament, on the rocks—and how they pair off doesn't really concern me too much. That is where Walt and Helen met.

(HELEN IS SITTING AT A BAR COUNTER. WALT ENTERS)

WALT:	Hi! Mind if I join you?
HELEN:	Be my guest.
WALT:	Scotch on rocks, Felix. Another for you?
HELEN:	Thanks. Martini. Felix knows how I like it.
WALT:	Are you married?
HELEN:	You could say I am. The way my husband treats me the marriage is a joke.
WALT:	Where is he tonight?
HELEN:	Working late. Work, work, work, if that's really what he does. I'm bored to tears with sitting at home. How about you?
WALT:	I've moved out. Midge never really understood me from the start. It was a big mistake. You could say I grew out of the marriage, and she stayed put. Cheers!
HELEN:	Cheers!

Simple! That's all it takes to break up two marriages: a little boredom, a spoiled husband, some suggestive TV commercials, a couple of drinks, and next thing you know it's 'My place, or yours?' It's not even called adultery nowadays. You don't want an ugly name for something so natural and blameless.

THE EIGHTH COMMANDMENT

As for stealing, that's another laugh—one of Satan's all time favorite belly laughs: THOU SHALT NOT STEAL. Let's look at a couple of men for a change. They usher every Sunday at All Saints.

PETE:	Sit down, Jim.
JIM:	Thanks.
PETE:	That's terrible news about Sally Porter.
JIM:	What happened?
PETE:	Didn't you hear? She was caught shoplifting.

JIM: Sally? I can't believe it!

PETE: I know. It's hard to imagine anybody doing something like that—I mean anybody from the church. I can truthfully say I've never stolen so much as a piece of candy in my whole life.

JIM: Me too. I see you've got a new TV.

PETE: Yeah, just bought it last week. We turned in the old one to the church sale. Took a big tax deduction on it.

JIM: You mean you got away with that?

PETE: Why not? And we hardly ever rent a movie. My son copies them for us.

JIM: I can see you're pretty smart.

PETE: Believe me, you have to be smart nowadays, if you want to avoid paying everything you've got in taxes. Pay by cash, and keep no records—that's my motto.

JIM: Hey, I see you've got that great new book on Yosemite. I saw it at the store, but I couldn't afford it. Oh, it's not yours, is it? It has Nellie Grove's name in it.

PETE: Yeah, I borrowed it from Nellie. I never seem to get around to returning it.

JIM: Well, I must be on my way. Darn it, it's raining, and I lost my umbrella at church a week or two ago.

PETE: I'll see you to the car. (HE PICKS UP AN UMBRELLA)

PETE: Wait a minute! That IS my umbrella. How did you—

PETE: No kidding! I must have picked it up by mistake after coffee hour.

JIM: You have the hell of a nerve, stealing my umbrella.

PETE: What do you mean, stealing? I told you, I never stole anything in my whole life.

Oh, no. He never stole anything in his life. He just acquires things, and cheats the IRS—all the kinds of backhand stealing that you enjoy too.

THE NINTH COMMANDMENT

So we come to number nine: FALSE WITNESS. You don't have to go to court to bear false witness. All you need to do is to blacken your neighbor's reputation, or lie to get yourself out of trouble. If somebody else gets hurt, too bad! You must look after Number One.

That's how Don felt, when he sideswiped another car, on his way home from a lively party. He and his wife Maureen are sitting in the car at the side of the road.

DON: Quick! Change seats! You were driving.

MAUREEN: What do you mean, I—

DON: Don't argue! You don't drink. They'll throw the book at me if they find I had a few drinks.

MAUREEN: I don't have my driver's licence, and—

DON: O God, how stupid can you be? But we can say you forgot. Move over!

MAUREEN: I was driving. I forgot. Tell your own lies, Don. I'm not perjuring myself. It was your fault, and you know it.

DON: My fault? That idiot could easily have swerved out of my way. I couldn't see him when I passed the bus. Now will you—

MAUREEN: No, I won't! I'm sticking to the truth. That old man didn't have a chance to avoid you.

DON: Old? You saw him? Great! We can blame it on him. Shouldn't be driving at night at his age.

MAUREEN: When are you going to stop kidding yourself, Don? I've had enough. You drink too much, you get mad about the game on the radio, and then you expect me to take the blame and shelter you from reality. Here comes the police car.

DON: (IN TEARS) O God! I'll lose my licence. I swear I'll never touch a drink again before driving. if you'll just—no, it's no use. You're right. Yes, Officer. I'm afraid I was responsible. I hope nobody in the other car was hurt.

Too bad Don took responsibility. He was just below the legal level for drunk driving, so he got off lightly. He is off the bottle for now, but I have hopes that it won't last. One day I'll think of a way to get even with that selfrighteous Maureen.

THE TENTH COMMANDMENT

So all we have left is greed and envy: THOU SHALT NOT COVET. I'm going to enjoy this one. I hardly know which way to turn to show you how everyone does it. That Russian fellow Tolstoy put it as well as anyone. Remember his story of Pakhom the peasant and his poor wife? Take a look at them!

(Here your actors should present number 6 in this series, HOW MUCH LAND DOES A MAN REQUIRE?)

SATAN: (AFTER THE SCENE HAS BEEN PRESENTED) So you see? If I can turn a decent man like Pakhom into a greedy scrounger, I can win every time.

VOICE OF GOD: (FROM FAR AWAY) No, Satan. Not every time. You don't like losing, do you? But you often do lose. Ten short laws, carved on stone three thousand years ago: however much they are abused and broken, they still have power in millions of hearts. You are darkness, Satan, and darkness is strong; but light is stronger. Light shines in the darkness, and the darkness cannot put it out.

Sixteen:

A VIETNAM PARABLE

This is a radio style presentation. It can either be presented by one Narrator, or by a Narrator with Voices. If the latter plan is adopted, the text must be modified. Words such as 'Davidson said' and 'he cried' will be omitted. Read the text carefully to make these small changes. For example, on the second page omit the words, 'He put a meaningful emphasis on the last word,' because the actor will have done this when he says, 'Good evening, Corporal.' But leave in the following words: 'Davidson made no reply.'

CHARACTERS: GENERAL GODSON (CORPORAL DAVIDSON)
THE SERGEANT
PETE, JIM, JOHN, PHIL, AND TOM, soldiers

Who was Jesus Christ? What was he, and what is he, in relation to God and humanity? How you answer that question decides the direction of your life.

He himself often approached important questions through parables. Parables are illustrations, designed to help and provoke thought. They do not aim to tabulate answers. So this parable is to be used as one means of approach to the central truth of our Christian faith.

It is a timeless story, and it could be set in many contexts: the soldiers could be Roman legionaries or part of Napoleon's army, or caught up in either of the World Wars. But I am calling it A VIETNAM PARABLE because that war still evokes powerful images, even for those who have been born long after it was over.

In a difficult period during that agonizing war, one of the Chiefs of Staff in Washington was a General named GODSON. He was a fine soldier and a good man. The war troubled him greatly. Above all he took to heart the distance which separated him, in his Washington office, from the men who were doing the fighting. Never in his long career as a soldier had he experienced such a gap in understanding.

General Godson made a decision. He put it to the other Chiefs of Staff, and eventually they agreed with his proposal. This was that he should drop out of Washington quietly, ostensibly absent on an inspection tour, and assume a new personality. He would go to Vietnam, not as a visiting VIP, to fly in, inspect, and return, but as a fighting man among fighting men.

He did just that. One of the frontline units was joined by a new Corporal, named CHRIS DAVIDSON. At this point in the parable we might turn to a verse in Saint Paul's letter to the Philippians, in which he describes what Jesus did when he took on a new identity. 'He emptied himself,' says Paul. Many versions of the Bible say, 'He humbled himself.' That is what General Godson did. He emptied himself of rank and privilege, of safety and comfort and power.

When Corporal Davidson joined the unit, he began to affect many people's lives. It was not that he threw his weight about. He was quiet, and spent a good deal of his time alone; but he was certainly not a loner, for he enjoyed the company of all those who were around him. The strange thing was that he seemed almost more at home with the troublemakers, the scroungers, and the potsmokers than with those who obeyed all the regulations. He even befriended the girls who followed the army from place to place. They were not used to having friendship offered to them. Some of them didn't like it, but others had their lives changed completely by Davidson's friendship.

He was not a rebel against army rules. What he did was to show his men, through his own example, that the spirit of a rule mattered more than the letter. 'After all,' he would say, 'the army is made for man, not man for the army.' His unit reached a high standard of discipline, because the men learned to understand what discipline really meant.

His companions often quoted things which Davidson said; but they were more impressed by what he was than by his words. He was not holier-than-thou in his dealings with a bunch of ordinary sinners, but they greatly admired his quiet courage, his humanity and compassion and gentle humor.

Soon after he arrived, Davidson was praying by himself one day. He wanted to be alone, so as to think out ways in which he could best perform the job which he had undertaken. But a Sergeant followed him. This was a man who often seemed to be hanging around the camp, though nobody knew his name or which unit he belonged to. He spoke now to Davidson in a halfjoking, ingratiating tone of voice.

'Good evening, Corporal.' He put a meaningful emphasis on the last word.

Davidson made no reply.

'You know, Davidson, if you are who I think you are, you really have it made. You and I, working together, could—'

'You and I are not working together,' Davidson said.

'But we could be. Look, if you were to go to Saigon, tell them who you are and what you have come to do, and broadcast to the whole army—you could offer then new incentives and benefits—'

'Men don't live by incentives and benefits', Davidson said quietly. 'What they need is love and understanding and honest leadership.'

'Of course, of course,' said the Sergeant, quickly switching his line of attack. 'I absolutely agree with you. But they also need a victory to restore their morale. Persuade the powers-that-be to drop a nuclear bomb on a city, and we can advance straight through to Hanoi. You can go home and run for President. With me to organize your campaign—'

'Get out!' said Davidson.

'Dont be a fool! I have a lot of influence—'

'I'm sure you have,' Davidson said. 'So have I. Thank you for finally showing me how not to use it. Now leave me alone!'

The Sergeant went away, muttering angrily to himself:

'You wait, Davidson, or Godson, or whatever you call yourself. I'll be even with you yet.'

Davidson was a puzzle to his superiors. The Officers saw in him a superb soldier. They gave him more than his share of dangerous and responsible assignments. But both the Chaplains and the Doctors had misgivings about him. Those Chaplains who knew him personally admired him, and spoke warmly of his character and influence. Those who heard about him at second hand were more critical. What was a Corporal doing, they wondered, building up his following among the men? Was he starting some kind of new sect, which could upset and threaten the establishment?

One Senior Chaplain decided to find out for himself, discreetly. He paid a call on Davidson late one evening. He came away disturbed, and uncertain what to think about this strange man. He had gone prepared to tell Davidson some home truths. Somehow it ended up the other way around.

Then there were Doctors who had their doubts about Davidson. Stories circulated about his socalled 'cures'. Men who had been undergoing treatment in drug clinics, without getting any better, were heard to say that they had been healed by Davidson. They couldn't explain how he had healed them. Doctors who examined them could only say that their condition had certainly improved, for no apparent reason. A report was sent to headquarters, and a careful watch was kept on Davidson, to see that he was not practicing medicine without a licence, using some kind of quack remedies.

Davidson's friends heard about this, and were discussing it with him one day. It was then that he told them the story of the Good Vietnamese. During an engagement with the enemy, he said, a G.I. was wounded, and left lying on exposed ground. He called out to his companions to help him. Now there was a Chaplain sheltering with the men close by, and also a Doctor. They were brave men, but they agreed that anyone who ventured out there would be killed long before he could reach the wounded man. For the moment, they could do nothing.

Davidson did not say that they were wrong; but he went on to describe how there was a young Vietnamese man also watching. His village had been overrun so many times that he had no idea which side he was on, but he knew that he was on the side of pity and love. It tore at his heart to see another man die for lack of help.

To everyone's astonishment he began to crawl out from his shelter. He shouted out something which the Americans could not understand. Then a strange thing happened. An enemy machinegunner trained his weapon on the rescuer, and was about to kill him; but he suddenly realized what the situation was, and he did not fire. So the Good Vietnamese was able to tie a rough dressing on the man's wound, give him a drink of water, and support him back to safety.

'It makes you think, doesn't it?' Davidson said. 'Just what is healing? Prescriptions? Text books? Or care coming from the heart?'

That was the way he talked about things. He did not criticize people who were trying to do their jobs, but he would go beyond the obvious explanations of a man's actions, to explore his motives.

One night a number of Davidson's friends were sitting with him. Jim and John were there, and Pete and Andy, Tom and Matt and a few more. Some of them formed a closely knit group by now, friends to whom he had given nicknames like 'Rocky' and 'The Thunderers' and 'Eager Beaver.' They had grown to love and depend on these evening talks. Now one of them asked: 'Do you have a family, Chris?'

He didn't answer for a moment. He was thinking of his wife and children back in Washington, and wondering whether he would ever see them again. He pointed, first to the group of friends around him, then towards the village, and finally the other way, where they knew the enemy to be.

'There is my family,' he said. 'We're human beings, aren't we? We belong to the family of man.'

Once another of his friends—Phil was his name—suddenly asked him: 'Who are you really?'

'I'm Chris Davidson, your Corporal. Why? Who do you think I am?'

'I don't know,' Phil said. 'You're different, somehow.'

'We talk about it all the time,' said Pete. 'One guy says you look like Abraham Lincoln come back to life. Someone else said he saw a picture of some highup, a General or something—and he swore it was you.'

Nobody could quite remember what Davidson said in reply to this. He seemed to change the subject. He talked about the need for all of us to know who we are, and the importance of real communication and concern between people fighting side by side, and their Officers, and so on right through to the people at the top, including the President.

That was the odd thing about Davidson. You asked him one question, and he pointed the way towards an answer—but that meant asking more and bigger questions. He certainly made you think.

The end of the parable is bound to be an anticlimax. It cannot come close to the original truth. But let us try to imagine an ending.

Davidson's unit was in an exposed position near a frontline village. His friends always remembered afterwards that at supper that night he talked about many things: the meaning of service and sacrifice, of friendship and dedication and courage. What they hardly noticed was that one man—he looked like the Sergeant, but nobody could be quite sure—slipped away from the group into the shadows. I believe that this was a man who had come to hate Davidson, and was burned up with jealousy. Satan entered into him—or was he Satan himself? The probability is that he conveyed a message to the enemy, giving the disposition of the unit, with the result that they attacked unexpectedly that night. But this could not be proved, because next day the Sergeant was found hanging from a tree.

The attack came. Davidson's men were outnumbered and had to withdraw. A hut in the village caught fire. Davidson knew that there were people inside. He ran to try to put out the fire. He stamped on the blazing straw, until his feet were badly burned, and he tried with charred hands to open the door. His friends pulled him back, but they were driven off by heavy fire. They had to leave him for dead. They were stricken with grief for this man whom they all loved; but they knew that it was the kind of death he would have chosen, trying to rescue some of his family.

Davidson was not dead. Some Vietnamese sheltered him and carried him to a field hospital. He was taken to Saigon, and recovered; but he had scars on his hands and his feet. He knew that this was the end of his mission. He could not fight any more, and he needed to go back and make use of all that he had learned. He went to another friend, a fellow General, and told him what had happened. The astonished General lent him a uniform, and arranged transport for him to Washington.

On the way to the airport Davidson, now once again Godson, passed through the city. His unit had been pulled back from the front line. It happened that he came face to face with two of his closest friends, Pete and John. They were staggered when they saw him. One of them cried: 'My God! Who are you?' The other ran into a cafe where their friend Tom was sitting.

'Tom!' he shouted. 'Come out here! It's Chris!'

'Don't be crazy!' Tom said. 'Chris is dead.'

But he came. He saw the scarred hands, and believed.

Davidson told them that he was General Godson, and that he was on his way back to Washington. He swore to them that never again, if he could help it, would soldiers in the front line have reason to feel cut off from the men who gave the orders from far away.

John asked him: 'You mean you and General Godson are one and the same person?'

'That's right,' said Chris. 'If you have seen Corporal Davidson, you have seen General Godson.'

At the end of the parable we may ask a question not easy to answer: Who was Corporal Davidson? He drew a Corporal's pay, had a Corporal's I.D., fought a Corporal's battles. Was he at that time General Godson?

If you tried to put it in a formula, you would have difficulty in explaining the whole truth. And in the much greater case of Jesus, Son of God, Son of Mary, Son of David, the Church has not found the question easy to answer. I don't think anyone has ever improved upon Saint Paul's simple description: 'He emptied himself.'

Let this mind be in you, he wrote, which was also in Christ Jesus; who, being in the form of God, thought it not robbery to be equal with God, but made himself of no reputation—emptied himself—and took upon him the form of a servant...Wherefore God has highly exalted him.

Who was Jesus Christ? What was he, and what is he, in relation to God and humanity? Upon your answer to that question depends the whole course of your life.

Verse Plays

These plays were written as musicals. I have left some music references in the text, in case you wish to order the score of a play. They are also suitable for reading and discussion. Costumes for a performance should be modern and simple. Props should not be hard to make. A skilful pianist can handle all of the music, but the presence of other instruments enriches the presentation. A large chorus is desirable.

OLD TESTAMENT

NOAH*
JOSEPH AND HIS BROTHERS
JOB*

NEW TESTAMENT

THE PRODIGAL SON*
THE WEDDING FEAST*
THE GOOD SAMARITAN*
GOOD FRIDAY*
A PENNY A DAY
THE UNJUST STEWARD

*Scores arranged by Pamela Stubbs
For the plays not marked "*" I have a melody line score

Noah

Bible reference Genesis 6-9

CHARACTERS: Noah
Noah's wife
Shem, Ham, and Japheth, their sons
Wives of the three sons
Voice of God
Mahalaleel
Chorus

NOAH was first presented at the Bishop's School, La Jolla, CA in 1965

(A TABLEAU OF SOME CHORUS MEMBERS FORMS ON STAGE: A WOMAN WITH A SHOPPING BASKET, A BUSINESSMAN WITH A BRIEFCASE, A BOY WITH A SKATE-BOARD, AN ATTRACTIVE GIRL, ETC. DURING THE OPENING LINES THEY FREEZE)

CHORUS LEADER
It was the morning of the world.
The sun was fair upon the earth;
And by the mighty hand of God
The sons of men had come to birth.

(TABLEAU MEMBERS PERFORM APPROPRIATE ACTIONS DURING NEXT FOUR LINES)

CHORUS
Look at them now, the seed of Adam,
Crown of the Creator's plan!
Noble and mean and proud and fearful—
What a piece of work is man!

(TABLEAU FIGURES FREEZE AGAIN)

CHORUS LEADER
There was a village on a hill,
Where man and woman used to toil;
And by the labor of their hands
They made a living from the soil.

(TABLEAU FIGURES INTERACT)

CHORUS

Look at them now, the friends of Noah,
Living as best they can!
Sinners and saints and cheats and heroes—
What a piece of work is man!

(TABLEAU MEMBERS GO OFF. A PATIO COUCH IS PLACED L.C., WITH A POT-
TED PLANT BESIDE IT. WHILE THE TUNE OF THE NEXT SONG IS PLAYED ON
THE PIANO, NOAH ENTERS AND LIES ON THE COUCH. HE BEGINS TO READ A
MAGAZINE)

CHORUS LEADER

In the cool of the evening,
When his labor was done,
Noah sat in his garden
To see the setting sun;
And he heard a voice calling
In the cool of the day

VOICE OF GOD (OFFSTAGE: VERY LOUD)

Noah, you have found favor!
Noah, rise and obey!

(NOAH SITS UP AND LISTENS. HE MAKES NOTES ON A PAD)

CHORUS

Make an ark of gopher wood, at the bidding of the Lord.
Make an ark of gopher wood just fifty cubits broad.
Make an ark of gopher wood and see that it is strong,
O, make an ark of gopher wood three hundred cubits long.
Make an ark of gopher wood, at the bidding of the Lord.
Make an ark of gopher wood, and put all the beasts on board.
Make an ark of gopher wood and build three stories high,
O, build it fast and fit it with a mast, if you're anxious not to die.

(NOAH HURRIES OFF ONE SIDE, AS HIS WIFE AND FAMILY ENTER FROM THE
OTHER)

WIFE: Noah! Noah!

SHEM: What's the matter, Mother?

HAM: Is anything wrong?

WIFE: I'm not really sure. Your father has been acting strangely today.

JAPHETH: Yes, I noticed he was restless . What do you think it is?

WIFE:	You know he sometimes gets these fits when he thinks he is talking to God.
SHEM'S WIFE:	Yes. I think he should see a doctor.
HAM'S WIFE:	Has he been at it again?
WIFE:	I don't know; but something funny was going on out here a few minutes ago, and he hurried away before I could stop him.
JAPHETH'S WIFE:	Hurried away?
SHEM:	It's really most disturbing.
SHEM SINGS:	It is really most disturbing when Father listens to God.
SHEM'S WIFE:	It's a thing that needs more curbing, when Father listens to God.
HAM'S WIFE:	It's a sin against convention when he does what he has done.
SHEM:	It can only lead to tension with Shem, his eldest son.
HAM:	You can see that I'm regretful when Father listens to God.
SHEM'S WIFE:	It can only make us fretful when Father listens to God.
JAPHETH'S WIFE:	When he talks of being guided, then I wonder where I am.
HAM:	What the good Lord has provided is good enough for Ham.
JASEPH:	There's a note of frenzied drama when Father listens to God.
JASEPH'S WIFE:	How I wish things could be calmer when Father listens to God!
HAM'S WIFE:	We believe in laws and morals, but when Father goes so wild
JASEPH:	It can only end in quarrels with Japheth, his youngest child.
SHEM:	Can't you do anything about it, Mother?
WIFE:	What can I do? He's a good man, and if he thinks God has spoken to him nothing will change his mind.

HAM: So we just have to wait and see?

WIFE: Yes, wait and see, and pray God to be good to us. Don't worry, children! What Noah does will be right; but I hope it won't upset us all too much.

(SHE SINGS):   I want to live peacefully
Here where I've lived so long.
I want to live quietly
Here where we all belong.
I don't want any excitement.
I don't want new places to go.
I'd like things to stay
Just this way—
And to live in the land I know,
Home is here, where the corn grows high.
Home is here, where the stream runs by,
Where every face is the face of a friend;
Where my life began, and my life should end.
Home is here, where my children grow.
Home is here, with the things I know;
With the village folk, and the corner store—
While I have all this I want nothing more.
                Home is here! Home is here!

(THE SONG IS REPEATED BY WIFE AND FAMILY.)

(NOAH COMES ON DOWNSTAGE, WHILE HIS WIFE AND FAMILY FREEZE. HE CALLS OUT TO MAHALALEEL, WHO IS AT THE BACK OF THE AUDIENCE)

NOAH: Mahalaleel!

MAHALALEEL: Hello, Mr. Noah! What can I do for you at this time of the evening?

NOAH: I came to ask whether you have any gopher wood that I can buy?

MAHALALEEL: Gopher wood? Certainly I have a little. What do you want it for?

NOAH: I'm going to build an Ark.

MAHALALEEL: An Ark? I don't know that I'm quite clear what an Ark is. How big is it?

NOAH: Three hundred cubits long, fifty broad, and three stories high.

MAHALALEEL: Eh? Have you been drinking again by any chance? Who in the world would want an Ark that size?

NOAH: It's the word of the Lord. Don't ask me to explain it. Let me have all the gopher wood that you can spare. I shall start to build in the morning. Now I must go and call on Admah and Mizraim. Good night, Mahalaleel!

MAHALALEEL: Good night, Mr. Noah! Gopher wood, to build an Ark! What next?

(NOAH APPROACHES THE FAMILY CENTER.)

NOAH: Hello, dear! Hello, boys and girls!

WIFE: Well, Noah. Where have you been?

SHEM: Yes, Father. What is this all about?

NOAH: I'll tell you. You have a right to know. You see these plans? (HE UNROLLS A BLUEPRINT.) Well, they come from God, and they're urgent. Let me explain.

(HE SINGS):

I'm going to make an Ark of gopher wood, at the bidding of the Lord.
I'm going to make an Ark of gopher wood, which I really can't afford.
I'm going to make an Ark of gopher wood and caulk it all with pitch. Yes,
I'm going to make an Ark of gopher wood, though you couldn't call me rich.

(SECOND VERSE IS SUNG BY NOAH, WIFE, AND FAMILY. SONS BRING ON THE ARK AND ASSEMBLE IT CENTER.)

I'm going to put a window in the Ark, and build three stories high.
And out of the window of the Ark I can send the birds to fly.
I'm going to make an Ark of gopher wood three hundred cubits long.
Yes, I'm going to make an Ark of gopher wood and see that it is strong.

(THIRD VERSE SUNG BY CHORUS, SOME OF WHOM CROWD AROUND THE ARK. SOME CHORUS MEMBERS SPEAK PARTS OF THESE LINES, INTERSPERSED WITH DERISIVE LAUGHTER.)

And all the people said, 'What a crazy man to build that monstrous boat!

You're a hundred miles from the nearest sea and the thing will never float.
Come and look at the folly that Noah's built! It really is a lark
To see him wasting all that gopher wood on a crazy kind of Ark!'

NOAH: Good! We're all ready for the animals.

WIFE: All right, boys and girls. Let in the animals!

(DURING THE NEXT SONG THE ANIMALS ENTER THROUGH THE AUDIENCE,
AND ARE LINED UP LEFT BY THE FAMILY. DANCING AND ANIMAL SOUNDS
CAN BE ADDED AT THE DIRECTOR'S DISCRETION. THE SONG IS SUNG BY ALL
EXCEPT WHERE INDIVIDUAL LINES ARE MARKED.)

>   There will still be cats and dogs,
>   Praise the name of the Lord!
>   Sheep and chickens, ducks and hogs,
>   Praise the name of the Lord!
>   There will still be kangaroos,
>   Praise the name of the Lord!
>   Foxes, wolves, and caribous,
>   Praise the name of the Lord!

SHEM: The buffalo and the crocodile and the elephant and giraffe,

HAM: The fierceness of the lion and the sweetness of the calf,

JAPHETH: The rattlesnake with its rattle, the hyena with its laugh,
>   Praise the name of the Lord! Praise the name of the Lord!

>   There will still be skunks and moles,
>   Praise the name of the Lord!
>   Tigers' cubs and horses' foals,
>   Praise the name of the Lord!
>   There will still be polar bears,
>   Praise the name of theLord!
>   Mice and monkeys, rats and hares,
>   Praise the name of the Lord!

WIFE I: The platypus and rhinoceros and the bison and the bee,

WIFE 2:   The pelican and the penguin and the cormorant from the sea.

WIFE 3:   The parakeet and canary and the nightingale in the tree,
>   Praise the name of the Lord! Praise the name of the Lord!

NOAH: All ready? Put the ramp in place!

SHEM:	All set, Father!
HAM:	Who's first?
JAPHETH:	Step up, you two!

(THE ANIMALS PASS BEHIND THE ARK AND OFFSTAGE DURING THE NEXT SONG.)

ALL:	Open the door, and let in the animals!
	We must get them in before the sky turns dark.
	Put down the ramp, and drive up the animals!
	We'll find room for two of every kind in the Ark.
	Drive up the horse! Drive up the mare!
	God says we have to take just one pair.
	Drive up the bull! Drive up the cow!
	Drive up the pig with his wife the sow!
	Open the door, and let in the animals!
	The lion and the lioness will lie with the lamb.
	Put down the ramp, and drive up the animals!
	The he-goat, the she-goat are following the ram
	Drive up the dog! Drive up the bitch!
	He-cat and she-cat, it's hard to tell which.
	Drive up the stag! Drive up the deer!
	Room for two of everything alive up here!
	Open the door, and let in the animals!
	We must get them in before the sky turns dark
	Put down the ramp, and drive up the animals!
	We'll find room for two of every kind in the Ark!
NOAH:	That's it, then. All together on board!
CHORUS MEMBER	On board? But it's dry land.

(LAUGHTER FROM CHORUS)

WIFE:	Oh, Noah! Are you sure that you're right?
SHEM:	Yes, Father. Are you sure that you're right?
WIFE:	Are you sure that you're right, husband Noah?
	For I feel very much in the dark.
	Are you sure that you're right, Father, husband Noah?
	For I don't want to live in an ARK.
FAMILY:	Are you sure that you're right, Father Noah?

All the world seems to think that you're wrong.
Are you sure that you're right, Father Noah?
Shall we be shut in here very long?

CHORUS:
(SOME LAUGHING AND SPEAKING THE LINES)
Are you sure that you're right, Father Noah?
Are you crazy as you would appear?
Are you sure that you're right, Father Noah?
You'll excuse us if we seem to jeer.

Are you sure that you're right, Father Noah?
If you're right then its time to be off.
Are you sure that you're right, Father Noah?
We must choose to go in or to scoff.

(NOAH, WIFE, AND FAMILY NOW STAND IN THE ARK, NOAH AT THE WHEEL.)

NOAH: All aboard! Goodbye, friends!

CHORUS MEMBER: Goodbye! Let us know if you feel seasick! (LAUGHTER)

CHORUS:
And all the people said, 'What a crazy man to build that monstrous boat!
You're a hundred miles from the nearest sea, and the thing will never float.
Come and look at the folly that Noah's built! It really is a lark
To see him wasting all that gopher wood on a crazy kind of Ark!'

(THUNDER AND LIGHTNING. CHORUS SHRINK BACK IN PANIC, SOME CRYING OUT. FAMILY REEL AND SWAY.)

ALL (EXCEPT
NOAH AND WIFE):   There came a kind of distant murmur.
There came a gentle, growing hum.
There came a muffled sound which shook the ground,
Like the throb of a beating drum.

O, Father Noah, steer for all you're worth!
If a precious few don't survive with you
Man will need a second birth.
There came the noise of rolling waters.
There came the hiss of swirling mud.
There came a plunging roar, and the people saw
That this was the threatened flood.
O, Father Noah, steer for all you're worth!

— 367 —

If a precious few don't survive with you
Man will need a second birth.

(DURING THE NEXT VERSE SOME CHORUS MEMBERS SCREAM AND SHOUT
WORDS SUCH AS 'HELP! HELP! I'M DROWNING!')

There were shouts of fear and terror,
For they had no place to hide.
They were crushed and drowned on the highest ground
By the racing, hungry tide.

O, Father Noah, steer for all you're worth!
If a precious few don't survive with you
Man will need a second birth.

When the wave hit (NOAH AND FAMILY REEL) Noah's vessel
It began its crazy course.
It seemed to plunge and sink on disaster's brink
In the cruel whirlpool's force.
O, Father Noah, steer for all you're worth!
If a precious few don't survive with you
Man will need a second birth.

(AFTER A FINAL ROLL OF THUNDER IT IS QUIET. NOAH SINGS.)

I'm looking for the land which the Lord has promised,
Warmed by the kindly sun.
I'm looking for the land which the Lord has promised,
After the flood is done.
I'm looking for a home for my sons and daughters,
Where the corn and the vine will grow.
I'm looking for a home for my sons and daughters,
Where the quiet streams will flow.
It's a long time to wait, and my heart is worn,
Watching the waters swell;
But I don't lose faith, 'cause the Lord has sworn
To bring us where all is well.
I'm looking for the land which the Lord has promised,
Soon as the flood goes by.
I'm looking for the land which the Lord has promised,
Soon as the earth is dry.

(SONG IS REPEATED BY NOAH AND WIFE, WITH THE FAMILY HUMMING.)

WIVES: Not so much wind.
Not so much rain.
Perhaps life is going to be normal again.
If things were restored

By the grace of the Lord,
I don't think I ever would dare to complain.

ALL: We used to complain if the sun was hot.
We used to complain if the sun was not.
We used to complain of the wind and the rain.
We certainly weren't contented with our human lot.
We used to complain if the clouds were low,
We used to complain of the ice and snow.
We used to complain, again and again,
That things were inconvenient and that God should know.

SONS AND WIVES: The house wasn't big enough for all our needs.
The garden was so difficult, with all those weeds.
The kitchen was inadequate and cold and damp.
It was smoky in the living room with that oil lamp.
The neighbors were a nuisance, making all that noise.
The girls were almost worse than those intolerable boys.

ALL: The village wasn't really near enough for us.
Too many other people crowded on the bus.
We used to complain and forget to pray.
We used to complain every night and day;
But we'll never complain if ever again

SONS: We have a home to live in,

WIVES: Our own home to live in,

ALL: A dry home to live in
In the same old way.

NOAH: It's true. There's not so much wind.
And the rain has stopped.

HAM: But what's the use of that, if the whole world is covered with
water?

JAPHETH: And salt water at that. We shall all die of thirst soon.

NOAH: Don't give up hope. God gave us the Ark, and if we trust him
we shall find a way out.

WIFE: I hope so, husband; but all this water is certainly depressing.

NOAH, WIFE,
AND FAMILY: Is there ever going to be
Anything but sea?
Are we ever going to see
Anything but sea?
It would mean a lot to me
Just to look at a tree.
Lord, set me free
From the power of the sea,

(SONG IS REPEATED.)

CHORUS LEADER: And God made a wind to pass over the earth, and the waters asswaged; the fountains also of the deep and the windows of heaven were stopped. And Noah sent forth a dove, to see if the waters were abated from off the face of the ground; but the dove found no rest for the sole of her foot, and she returned. And he stayed yet another seven days, and again he sent forth the dove out of the ark; and the dove came in to him in the evening; and lo, in her mouth was an olive leaf pluckt off; and Noah knew that the waters were abated off the earth. And God spake unto Noah, saying, Go forth of the ark, thou, and thy wife, and thy sons, and thy sons' wives with them. Bring forth with thee every living thing that is with thee.

(DURING THE NEXT SONG THE ANIMALS ARE USHERED OUT OF THE ARK BY THE FAMILY, AND RETURN TO THEIR ORIGINAL PLACES THROUGH THE AUDIENCE.)

ALL: Bring forth with you everything!
Praise the name of the Lord!
Man and beasts cry out and sing!
Praise the name of the Lord!
Take the roof right off the Ark!
Praise the name of the Lord!
Dance and leap and run and walk!
Praise the name of the Lord!

SHEM: The buffalo and the crocodile and the elephant and giraffe.

HAM: The fierceness of the lion and the sweeetness of the calf.

JAPHETH: The rattlesnake with its rattle, the hyena with its laugh

ALL: Praise the name of the Lord!
Praise the name of the Lord!

> God brought Noah safe and sound,
> Praise the name of the Lord!
> Back again to solid ground.
> Praise the name of the Lord!
> Japheth too, and Ham, and Shem,
> Praise the name of the Lord!
> And their wives along with them,
> Praise the name of the Lord!

WIFE 1:   The platypus and rhinoceros and the bison and the bee.

WIFE 2:   The pelican and the penguin and the cormorant from the sea.

WIFE 3:   The parakeet and canary and the nightingale in the tree,
               Praise the name of the Lord!
               Praise the name of the Lord!

(BEFORE THE END OF THE SONG THE SONS REMOVE THE ARK R. DURING THE FOLLOWING NARRATION NOAH, WIFE, AND FAMILY FREEZE DOWNSTAGE. AS THE RAINBOW IS REVEALED AT THE BACK OF THE STAGE, THEY KNEEL.)

CHORUS LEADER: And God blessed Noah and his sons, and said to them, Be fruitful, and multiply, and replenish the earth! And I, behold, I establish my covenant with you, and with your seed after you. I do set my bow in the cloud, and it shall be for a token of a covenant between me and the earth.

(NOAH, WIFE, AND FAMILY ARE KNEELING DURING THE NEXT SONG.)

WIFE: When men were broken and scattered,
               Their heads all bruised and bowed,
               God showed his sign in a sunlit sky,
               And set his bow in the cloud.
               And still his covenant made of old
               Is strong, and must endure;
               And in rain or sun we must follow him
               Whose love is always sure.

CHORUS
When rainclouds darken the heavens,
And storms frown out of the sky.
The Lord will turn his face again
And set his bow on high.

NOAH: For fires and floods and winds will come
To try man's strength and faith;
And man himself, through war or hate,
Will tread the road of death.

CHORUS
But those who wait for the sunlight,
And trust in God as their friend,
Will watch his rainbow shine in peace
When the floods are come to an end;
For the light and the life and the love of God
Are more than the storm can bend.

(NOAH, WIFE, AND FAMILY RISE. THE FAMILY CIRCLE AROUND THE SIGNPOST.)

SHEM: Eu - rope?

(THEY PRONOUNCE THE NAMES WITH DIFFICULTY)

HAM :   A - si –a?

JAPHETH: A - fri - ca?

WIFE 1:   A - me - ri - ca?

WIFE 2:   Aus - tra - li- a?

WIFE 3:   Europe for me!

HAM: And Africa for me!

SHEM: How about it, Father? Shall I try America?

NOAH: No. It's too soon for that, my son. Stick to Asia!

(DURINGTHE NEXT SONG NOAH BLESSES EACH KNEELING PAIR IN TURN, HIS WIFE STANDING BESIDE HIM.)

CHORUS
So the sons of Shem went one way,
And the sons of Ham went another;
And the sons of Japheth travelled far
From the sons of either brother.
Yes, the sons of Shem went one way,
And the sons of Ham went another;
And the sons of Japheth travelled far
From the sons of either brother.

Shem, Ham, and Japheth
Spread far the human stock;
But it all went back to Noah's faith
Which was firm and strong as rock.

(SHEM AND HIS WIFE START OUT RIGHT THROUGH THE AUDIENCE, SING-
ING THEIR VERSE A CAPPELLA. DITTO HAM TO LEFT DURING HIS VERSE, AND
JAPHETH DURING HIS.)

SHEM AND WIFE: We're starting out on a journey.
It may be hard and long.
We're starting out on a journey
And we sing a pilgrim song.

HAM AND WIFE: We're starting out on a journey,
And if we're clothed and shod
We shan't need much on the journey
As we tread the way of God.

JAPHETH
AND WIFE: We're starting out on a journey.
It's a simple road to take.
We shan't need much on the journey
If we make it for his sake.

(NOAH AND WIFE WAVE TO THEM.)

ALL: We shan't need much on the journey,
And what we have we'll spend;
For all we shall need is a faithful heart
When the journey comes to an end,
Yes, all we shall need is a faithful heart
When the journey comes to an end.

JOSEPH AND HIS BROTHERS

BIBLE REFERENCE: GENESIS 35, 37, 39-50.

CHARACTERS: Jacob
Rachel, his wife
Their twelve sons
Midianite merchants (optional)
Potiphar and his wife (optional)
Pharaoh's Butler

Pharaoh's Baker
Guards
Pharaoh's wise men

The story dictates that this is a play with a male cast, but there is no reason why many of the brothers should not be played by females. The pace and success of the play depend largely on the quick exchanges among the ten brothers, both in the songs in which they sing individual lines, and in their spoken dialogue. To find ten actors who will combine as a team in these scenes will be the main challenge for the director. I have included Rachel in the story. Her death is described in Genesis 35: l6; but in 37: 10 Jacob asks Joseph 'Shall I and thy mother bow down ourselves to thee?' The balance of the story is enhanced by her part in it.

CHARACTERS: Jacob
Rachel, his wife
Joseph, their son
Benjamin, their youngest son
Joseph's ten brothers
Pharaoh of Egypt
Potiphar, Captain of the Guard
Pharaoh's chief butler
Pharaoh's chief baker
Jailer
Soldier

CHORUS, whose members play different roles

JOSEPH AND HIS BROTHERS was first presented at The Bishop's School, La Jolla, California, in 1966.

(THE PLAY OPENS INSIDE THE HOME OF JACOB AND RACHEL. THEY ARE SITTING AT A TABLE. RACHEL IS SEWING JOSEPH'S COLORED SHIRT. JOSEPH, A BOY OF 17, AND BENJAMIN, 10, ARE ALSO AT THE TABLE. THE OTHER BROTHERS MOVE IN AND OUT, TALKING, DURING THE OPENING VERSE.)

NARRATOR   In the land of Canaan,
Ages long ago,
Jacob, son of Isaac,
Watched his children grow.
Some were born of Zilpah, or fed at Leah's breast;
But the sons of Rachel
Jacob loved the best.

CHORUS
Now she took rich wool and the hair of a goat,
And she made for Joseph a many-colored coat.
It was dyed all shades with many-colored dyes,
And it made him hateful in his brothers' eyes.

(RACHEL IS NOW TRYING THE SHIRT ON JOSEPH. THE TEN BROTHERS IN A GROUP TOGETHER ARE POINTING, LAUGHING, AND SHOWING THEIR SCORN AND DISLIKE FOR THEIR BROTHER)

> For his brethren used to see their father dote
> On Joseph in his many-colored coat;
> And his father's doting and his mother's sighs
> Made Joseph hateful in his brothers' eyes.
>
> It was sad to see those elder brothers gloat
> At the boy who had the many-colored coat.
> For his father and mother could never realize
> That it made him hateful in his brothers' eyes.

JOSEPH: Are you coming to supper now, Reuben?

REUBEN: No, thank you, brother. I shall wait. I might be in the way.

JOSEPH: Are you angry with me?

SIMEON Angry? Why should we be angry?

(THE TEN BROTHERS STAND IN A CLOSE GROUP AWAY FROM THE TABLE.)

REUBEN: A coat of many colors   On his back!

SIMEON: A coat of many colors,   While I wear black!

LEVI: A coat of many colors   To flaunt all day!

JUDAH: A coat of many colors,   While I wear gray!

ZEBULUN: A coat of many colors!   I call it mean!

ISSACHAR: A coat of many colors,   While I wear green!

DAN: A coat of many colors,   Bright and new!

GO
AD: A coat of many colors!   Mine is faded blue!

ASHER: A coat of many colors!   What a sight!

NAPHTALI: A coat of many colors!   Mine is old and white!

(JOSEPH STANDS C. AS HE SPEAKS THE BROTHERS GATHER AROUND HIM.)

JOSEPH:	I dreamed a dream last night. Perhaps, if I tell it to all of you, one of you can explain to me what it means.
SIMEON:	Perhaps!
JUDAH:	Tell us your dream, brother dear!
LEVI:	Yes, I am sure we would all like to hear about it.

JOSEPH:
Last night I dreamed a dream,
For the Lord sent a sign.
All your sheaves in the field
Bowed down before mine.

BROTHERS:
Joseph is a dreamer! Dreams that he is king!
We are all his slaves, and must obey in everything!

JOSEPH:
Last night I dreamed a dream;
It was clear to see.
The sun and moon and stars
Bowed down before me.

BROTHERS:
Joseph is a dreamer! Dreams that he is best!
We must be his servants, who will bow at his behest!

(ALL LEAVE THE STAGE WHILE THE BEGINS TO SPEAK. THE BROTHERS RETURN ALMOST IMMEDIATELY, AND SIT OR STAND IN A GROUP L. SOME OF THEM MAY CARRY SHEPHERD'S CROOKS. SOME ARE WARMING THEIR HANDS AS THOUGH AT A FIRE. JOSEPH DOES NOT ENTER R. UNTIL THE LINE 'Why should we serve this dreamer?')

So his brothers envied Joseph. But his father remembered the dreams, and wondered what they meant. Joseph's brothers went to feed their father's flocks. Jacob sent Joseph to join them; and Joseph met a traveller, who told him 'They are gone to Dothan.' So Joseph followed them; and when they saw him afar off, they conspired against him to kill him.

(ONE OF THE BROTHERS POINTS R. OFF STAGE, AND THEY ALL LOOK IN THAT DIRECTION AS THEY SING.)

BROTHERS:
Behold, this dreamer cometh,
Wearing his colored gown!
Behold, this dreamer cometh!
Quick! Let us strike him down!

He is the cause of envy;
He is the cause of strife.
Why should we serve this dreamer?
Come! Let us take his life!

SIMEON: Come here, dreamer!

JUDAH: Welcome, brother!

LEVI: Come nearer, so that we can bow down to you!

SIMEON: Tie him up, and throw him into the pit!

REUBEN: Don't hurt the boy!

JUDAH: Oh, no! We shan't hurt him.

LEVI: Take the coat, and smear it with goat's blood!

SIMEON: Yes, and we can tell Father that an evil beast devoured him.

(THEY STRIP JOSEPH OF HIS COLORED SHIRT, TIE HIM UP, AND PUSH HIM OFF-STAGE L.)

LEVI: There you go, mother's darling!

SIMEON: Go to sleep down there. Sweet dreams!

BROTHERS
(LAUGHING)   Sweet dreams!

CHORUS

So they tied his hands, and mocked him with their wit;
And they threw him down a deep and rocky pit;
For they would not dare to strike a brother dead,
But they left him there, and sat them down to bread.

(THE BROTHERS SIT AROUND THE FIRE, LAUGHING AND EATING.)

Yes, they stripped him of his many-colored coat,
And they dipped it in the blood of a goat.
Then they took that coat, now stained a crimson red,
To convince their father that his son was dead.

But God did not mean Joseph to die. While the brothers were still sitting near the pit, there came by Midianites, merchantmen. The brothers saw a chance of profit for themselves. They lifted Joseph out of the pit, and offered him for sale to the merchantmen. They paid twenty pieces of silver for the boy, and took him with them on their way to Egypt. The brothers were delighted with their good fortune.

BROTHERS
(TWO: lines each)   Twenty pieces of silver,
To be rid of this pest!
    Twenty pieces of silver,
    And my conscience at rest.

Twenty pieces of silver!
Modest payment indeed!
    Twenty pieces of silver!
    Don't accuse me of greed!

Twenty pieces of silver!
They could have him for ten!
    Twenty pieces of silver
    Not to see him again!

(THE MERCHANTS HAVE GONE OFF R. THE BROTHERS GO OFF L. TWO CHAIRS ARE PLACED C. JACOB AND RACHEL ENTER AND SIT. THE BOY BENJAMIN STANDS BY HIS MOTHER. SOON THE BROTHERS ENTER FROM L, AND KNEEL BEFORE JACOB. REUBEN OFFERS HIM THE BLOODSTAINED COAT. JACOB AND RACHEL BREAK DOWN AND WEEP. BENJAMIN KNEELS AND TRIES TO COMFORT THEM, WHILE THE BROTHERS, ASHAMED, GO OFF L.)

CHORUS
Jacob mourned for his son,
Mourned for his son, and refused to be comforted.
Jacob mourned for his son,
Mourned for his son, and refused to be comforted.

JACOB AND RACHEL: For I will go down into the grave mourning.
    I will go down into the grave, to my son, mourning.

CHORUS
Jacob mourned for his son,
Mourned for his son, and refused to be comforted.

(THEY GO OFF L. DURING THE NEXT CHORUS THE MERCHANTMEN COME ON SLOWLY FROM R. JOSEPH, WITH HIS HANDS TIED, IS IN THE MIDDLE OF THEM. POTIPHAR ENTERS FROM L. HE BARGAINS WITH THEM, AND TAKES JOSEPH OFF L.)

CHORUS
Midianites, merchantmen,
Took Joseph down to Egypt.

Midianites, merchantmen,
Sold Joseph there in Egypt.
In the house of Potiphar
The boy was bought and sold.
Merchantmen of Midian
They traded him for gold.
Midianites, merchantmen,
Sold Joseph there in Egypt.
Midianites, merchantmen.

(THE MERCHANTMEN GO OFF R. JOSEPH, HIS HANDS NO LONGER TIED, IS
PUSHED ON STAGE FROM L. HE FALLS TO HIS KNEES.)

JOSEPH: I'm eating my heart away
For love of my fatherland.
I'm eating my heart away.
Oh wind, that blows on land and sea,
Be bearer of my word!
Oh wind, that blows on land and sea,
When will my cry be heard?
Oh, when will my cry be heard?

I'm eating my heart away
For love of my fatherland.
I'm eating my heart away.
Oh Lord, who rules in earth and sky,
When will you turn and heed?
Oh Lord, who rules in earth and sky,
Pity me now in my need,
Oh, pity me now in my need,

I'm eating my heart away
For love of my fatherland.
I'm eating my heart away.
Oh birds, that fly by land and sea,
Be mindful of my plight!
Oh birds, that fly by land and sea,
Bend to my father your flight,
Oh, bend to my father your flight.

I'm eating my heart away
For love of my fatherland.
I'm eating my heart away.

(THE NEXT SCENE, IN POTIPHAR'S HOUSE, COULD BE MIMED, WITH JOSEPH
REJECTING THE ADVANCES OF POTIPHAR'S WIFE. UNLESS THIS IS DONE SKIL-

FULLY IT IS BETTER OMITTED. IN THAT CASE JOSEPH REMAINS ON STAGE. AT THE END OF THE NARRATION GUARDS BRING ON THE BUTLER AND BAKER, HANDLING THEM ROUGHLY, AND LEAVE THEM WITH JOSEPH.)

When Potiphar, an Officer of Pharaoh, bought Joseph from the Midianites, Joseph found favor in his sight. Potiphar made him overseer of all that he possessed. But after he grew to manhood Potiphar's wife cast her eyes upon Joseph, and sought to make him her lover. Joseph would not betray his master, but she accused him of doing her violence. So Potiphar threw Joseph back into prison. After this Pharaoh was angry with his Chief Butler and his Chief Baker. They were cast into the same prison as Joseph. The Butler and the Baker each dreamed a dream. The Butler dreamed of a vine with three branches, which bore fruit. He took juice from the grapes, and set it before Pharaoh. The Baker dreamed that he had three baskets upon his head. The topmost basket contained bakemeats for Pharaoh; but the birds came and ate them from the basket.

(ALL THREE PRISONERS HAVE MIMED SLEEP. THE BUTLER AND BAKER AWAKEN, AND TELL JOSEPH THEIR DREAMS IN MIME. DURING THE NEXT CHORUS JOSEPH INTERPRETS THE DREAMS TO THEM.)

CHORUS

Pharaoh's butler dreamed a dream
In his prison cell.
Joseph told him what it meant,
The son of Israel.
Told him he would soon be back
Serving Pharaoh's wine
Told him, in his darkest day,
The sun would surely shine.

Pharaoh's baker, when he dreamed,
Also wondered why.
Joseph's heart was sad for him,
For he must surely die.
Pharaoh on his birthday feast
Had that baker slain;
But the butler was restored
To his place again.

(AS THE SONG ENDS GUARDS ENTER FROM R.)

GUARD
(TO THE OTHERS):   Set this man free! Take the other to his death!

(GUARDS GO OFF WITH THE BUTLER AND BAKER R. JOSEPH GOES OFF L.)

While Joseph was still in the prison Pharaoh also dreamed. In one dream he saw seven lean cattle which came after seven fat cattle and devoured them. Then he saw seven thin ears of corn which devoured seven fat ears. He told his dreams to his wise men, but none of them could interpret what he had seen.

(A CHAIR IS BROUGHT ON AND PLACED C. SEVERAL OF PHARAOH'S WISE MEN ENTER FROM EACH SIDE. THEY FORM AN AGITATED GROUP. THE FOLLOWING LINES ARE SPOKEN SWIFTLY, EACH INDIVIDUAL TAKING A SHORT PHRASE.)

WISE MEN: Pharaoh's dreaming, dreaming, dreaming!
                  What shall we do?
                  Call the interpreters! Call the necromancers!
                  Call the Priests of Osiris and isis!
                  Pharaoh's dreaming, dreaming, dreaming!
                  What does it mean?
                  Seven fat kine, seven lean kine;
                  Seven rich ears, seven thin ears.
                  Pharaoh's dreaming! Pharaoh's dreaming! Pharaoh's dreaming!
                  What shall we do?

(PHARAOH HURRIES ON FROM R. AND STANDS C.)

PHARAOH: Can noone tell me what my dreams mean?

BUTLER: (KEELING BEFORE THE PHARAOH)Your Majesty, I have thought of a man who might tell you the truth; one whom, to my shame, I have forgotten and used ungratefully.

PHARAOH: Who is he? Where is he to be found?

BUTLER: (STANDING) I remember, in the prison,
                  There was a man in chains with me.
                  When I dreamed, he told me the meaning,
                  Turned it, and made it plain to see.
                  His name? Ah yes! His name was Joseph.
                  I will go and fetch him here.
                  He may tell this dream for Pharaoh.
                  He may make their meaning clear.

(PHARAOH SITS ON THE CHAIR. THE BUTLER GOES OFF. DURING THE NEXT NARRATION JOSEPH IS LED ON, STILL IN HIS JAIL CLOTHES. HE KNEELS IN FRONT OF PHARAOH. MIME THEIR EXCHANGE OF WORDS, AND JOSEPH'S EXPLANATION OF THE DREAMS. PHARAOH JUMPS UP, EMBRACES JOSEPH, AND PUTS HIS RING ON JOSEPH'S FINGER. THE BUTLER BRINGS A GOLD CHAIN,

WHICH PHARAOH PUTS AROUND JOSEPH'S NECK. THEN PHARAOH GOES OUT, AND JOSEPH SITS ON THE CHAIR, SURROUNDED BY THE WISE MEN.)

Then Joseph was brought from his cell, and he knelt before Pharaoh in his prison garb. Pharaoh told him his dreams, and Joseph made plain to him the meaning of them. So great was Pharaoh's joy that he gave orders for Joseph to be set over all the land of Egypt. All through the seven years of plenty Joseph built storehouses in which he set aside great stocks of every crop. When the famine came all the people of Egypt begged Joseph to sell them food.

(A CROWD OF EGYPTIANS ENTERS. SOME KNEEL BEFORE JOSEPH, SOME STAND, AS THEY BEG FOR FOOD.)

EGYPTIANS
CHORUS MEMBERS: All the men of Egypt came to him, Joseph! Joseph!
You could hear them cry his name to him, Joseph! Joseph!
Give us barley! Give us wheat!
Give us grain, or give us meat!
We are starving! We must eat! Joseph! Joseph!

All the people came and sighed to him, Joseph! Joseph!
Rich men, poor men, came and cried to him, Joseph! Joseph!
Give us barley! Give us wheat!
Give us corn, or give us meat!
We are starving! We must eat! Joseph! Joseph!

We will pledge our lands and lives to you, Joseph! Joseph!
All our children and our wives to you, Joseph! Joseph!
Give us barley! Give us wheat!
Give us corn, or give us meat!
We are starving! We must eat! Joseph! Joseph!

(DURING THE NEXT NARRATION A CROWD OF PEOPLE OF ALL COLORS AND RACES COME BEFORE JOSEPH, PLEADING FOR FOOD.)

Men and women came from other lands also, to buy from Joseph, because word had spread that there was corn in Egypt. Jacob also said to his sons, 'Go to Egypt and buy corn, that we may live, and not die!'

CHORUS: Then from far and wide came the folk of every land.
There was corn in Egypt!
They came by the mountains, and they came by the sand.
There was corn in Egypt!
They came by the rivers and they came by the seas.
They came with their money and they came with their pleas.
They came there to Joseph and they fell on their knees.
There was corn in Egypt.

From the north and the south, from the west and the east.
There was corn in Egypt!
All the rich and the poor, all the greatest and the least.
There was corn in Egypt!
They came by the rivers and they came by the seas.
They came with their money and they came with their pleas.
They came there to Joseph and they fell on their knees.
There was corn in Egypt!

Then the sons of Jacob set their beasts on the way.
There was corn in Egypt!
They journeyed from Canaan both by night and by day.
There was corn in Egypt.

(THE TEN BROTHERS ENTER FROM L. THEY ARE WEARY AND RAGGED. THEY KNEEL BEFORE JOSEPH.)

They came by the rivers and they came by the seas.
They came with their money and they came with their pleas.
They came there to Joseph and they fell on their knees.
There was corn in Egypt!

(THE AUDIENCE KNOWS THAT JOSEPH RECOGNIZES HIS BROTHERS. HE RISES FROM HIS SEAT AS THEY KNEEL, AND STARES AT THEM. THEN HE SITS DOWN AGAIN. AT THE CLOSE OF THE SONG HE GESTURES TO THE PEOPLE AROUND HIM TO LEAVE. THE STAGE IS EMPTY EXCEPT FOR JOSEPH AND HIS BROTHERS.)

JOSEPH: What men are you, and what is your country?

REUBEN: My Lord, we are from Canaan, sons of Jacob. We were twelve brothers, but one is dead, and the youngest is at home with his parents.

JOSEPH: How do I know that you are not spies, come to see the nakedness of the land?

SIMEON: No, my Lord. We are not spies. We have come only to buy food.

JOSEPH: Then if your story is true prove it! Send and fetch this youngest brother to me! One of you shall stay as hostage here in prison. Guards!

(GUARDS ENTER AND BIND SIMEON. HE IS LED OFF RIGHT, WHILE THE OTHERS BOW TO JOSEPH AND THEN GO OFF LEFT.)

Joseph sent his brothers home with sacks of corn, and put back in the sacks the money which they had paid. They told Jacob and Rachel how they had

been received in Egypt. He would not let them take Benjamin from his side.
(CHAIRS ARE SET C. FOR RACHEL AND JACOB. BENJAMIN STANDS BESIDE
THEM. THE BROTHERS ARE IN FRONT OF THEM ON EITHER SIDE.)

JACOB: No, I tell you, no! I will not let Benjamin go!

REUBEN: Not let him go? He must go!

JACOB: I have lost one of the two sons on whom my heart was set,
                   because he went with you. Must the other also be lost?

LEVI: You have other sons, Father!

ISSACHAR: Yes. Do you care nothing for us?

DAN: Must Simeon rot in an Egyptian jail?

GAD: And the rest of us starve to death?

(IN CONTRAST TO THEIR ANGER, REUBEN SPEAKS MORE GENTLY.)

REUBEN: Let him go, Father! It is for the best.

JACOB:
(BOWING HIS HEAD) He is your son also, Rachel. Must we let him go?

RACHEL: Yes, husband. I think that our son Joseph would have wished
                   us to let Benjamin go, to save all of our family and those who
                   depend on us; but it breaks my heart also.

(SHE SINGS.)
                        I'm eating my heart away
                        For one who has left my side.
                        I'm eating my heart away.

JACOB AND RACHEL: Oh Lord, who rules in earth and sky,
                        Shine on us with your light!
                        Oh Lord, who rules in earth and sky,
                        Show me the path that is right!
                        Show me the path that is right!

JACOB: I'm eating my heart away
                   For one who has long been lost.
                   I'm eating my heart away.

JACOB AND RACHEL: Oh Lord, who rules in earth and sky,
When will you turn and heed?
Oh Lord, who rules in earth and sky,
Pity me now in my need!
Pity me now in my need!

RACHEL: You must go, Benjamin, for the sake of us all.

JACOB: Yes, my son. You must go. May God's blessing be upon you, and upon you also, Reuben, and you, my sons. You are all dear to us, and the fate of God's people is in your hands.

(ONE CHAIR IS LEFT ON STAGE C. DURING THE FOLLOWING NARRATION JOSEPH ENTERS AND SITS.)

When the famine grew sore again Jacob at last let Benjamin go; but his heart was broken, and so was the heart of Rachel. The ten brothers returned to Egypt.

(GUARDS BRING IN THE BROTHERS FROM R. THEY BOW BEFORE JOSEPH.)

JOSEPH   You are welcome back, my friends. Peace be with you!

REUBEN: We have brought our youngest brother Benjamin, sir, as you commanded us.

JOSEPH: So you are Benjamin. Greetings! Guards, bring the prisoner Simeon to join us! You have journeyed far, and there is a feast in readiness for you.

(SIMEON IS LED ON R., AND EMBRACES HIS BROTHERS. THEY ALL GO OFF L., WITH JOSEPH. THE GUARDS GO R. THE STAGE IS EMPTY FOR THE NARRATION.)

After they had feasted together Joseph sent his brothers on their way home with a supply of corn. And again he had their money placed in their sacks. But he told his Steward to put in Benjamin's sack the golden cup from which he always drank, and which he used in his prophecies. Then Joseph sent his servants to arrest the brothers, and to threaten that the one in whose sack the cup was found should become Joseph's slave. They found the cup in Benjamin's sack. Then the brothers were once again led into Joseph's presence.

(JOSEPH IS SEATED C. THE BROTHERS ARE LED ON FROM L., WITH BENJAMIN IN FRONT, HELD BY A GUARD.)

GUARD: This is the one, my Lord. The cup was in his sack.

JOSEPH: Then he must be my slave for the rest of his life.

JUDAH	(KNEELING)My Lord, this is our youngest brother. Ever since our other brother was lost to us this youngest boy, Benjamin, has been the apple of his father's eye. That was why he did not come with us on our first journey.
REUBEN:	Our father Jacob could scarcely bear to let Benjamin come this second time, my Lord. If we leave Benjamin here, never to see his father and mother again, I do not know how to face them with the news.
LEVI:	I beg of you, sir, to be merciful, and to let me take his place. I will be your slave, if that must be; but in God's name let him go!
SIMEON:	You have shown mercy to me, mighty Prince. If you have ever known the precious bond between father and son, I beg you to grant this prayer of ours! Take any of us, but not my youngest brother!

(JOSEPH HAS BEEN SITTING WITH BOWED HEAD, HIS HANDS BEFORE HIS EYES. NOW HE LOOKS UP, OVERCOME BY EMOTION.)

JOSEPH:	Free him, and leave us alone! (BENJAMIN'S GUARD FREES HIM, AND GOES OFF R. JOSEPH STANDS.) Reuben, Judah, Benjamin—all of you, my brothers! I am Joseph! Yes, you may well stare at me, but it is true. I am Joseph, whom you meant to kill, and then sold as a slave. But God sent me before you to Egypt, to prepare the way—to save your lives, and the lives of my father and my mother.

(THE BROTHERS FALL TO THEIR KNEES AND HIDE THEIR FACES.)

REUBEN:	Joseph!
JUDAH:	Oh God, forgive me!
LEVI:	I cannot face you. it makes me afraid.

(IN THE FOLLOWING SONG THE BROTHERS SPEAK INDIVIDUAL LINES. THEY RE-MAIN KNEELING, WHILE JOSEPH GOES FROM ONE TO ANOTHER, TAKING THEIR HANDS. HE RAISES BENJAMIN AND EMBRACES HIM C.)

BROTHERS
(INDIVIDUAL LINES): I'm afraid of Joseph! What is he going to do?
I'm afraid of Joseph, and it scares me through and through.
I have earned his hatred, I have earned his scorn,
And my mind is fearful, and my heart is torn.

ALL: I'm afraid of Joseph! What is he going to do?
                        I'm afraid of Joseph, and it scares me through and through.

(INDIVIDUAL LINES)   If he seeks for justice, he can strike me dead;
                        For my guilt is heavy on a brother's head.

ALL: I'm afraid of Joseph! What is he going to do?
                        I'm afraid of Joseph, and it scares me through and through.

(INDIVIDUAL LINES)   If he seeks for vengeance, that is in his hand.
                        Then my life is forfeit for the deed I planned.

ALL: I'm afraid of Joseph! What is he going to do?
                        I'm afraid of Joseph, and it scares me through and through.

JOSEPH: (STANDING C.) Do not be afraid! Stand up, all of you, please!
                        God has brought good out of evil, a blessing out of violence and
                        hatred. Soon you shall go to Canaan, and fetch my father and
                        my mother. They shall live here on good land which i will give to
                        them and to you. After all my years of loneliness and exile I will
                        see them again. So this is a day of joy, not of vengeance.

REUBEN: We will bring them, Joseph. But can you truly forgive us?

BROTHERS
(STILL KNEELING):   Yes, Joseph. Forgive us if you can!

JOSEPH: Forgive you? It is for God to forgive, and for God to punish.
                        It was his hand which guided us to this hour. Let us use his
                        mercy to serve him better.

                        You meant to do me evil.
                        You tried to take my life.
                        But God can bring a blessing
                        From man's most bitter strife.

                        You cursed me for a dreamer,
                        And envy filled your breast.
                        But God can take our passions
                        And turn them for the best.

                        For he has brought me riches,
                        And he has brought me fame.
                        He chose me out to serve him,
                        And to exalt his name.

I have come safe through danger;
I have come safe through pain.
At last my God has brought me
To my loved ones again.

(DURING THE FINAL NARRATION JACOB AND RACHEL ENTER, AND EMBRACE JOSEPH. FOR THE FINAL CHORUS ALL OF THE CHORUS MEMBERS MAY COME ON STAGE AND STAND BEHIND THE FAMILY OF JACOB.)

Joseph and his brothers rejoiced together. Then the brothers returned to Canaan, and told their mother and father the glad news that Joseph was indeed alive, and had prospered in Egypt. They were overcome with joy. Jacob settled in Egypt, on the rich land which Joseph gave to him and to his family. He and his sons prospered, and he died happy . The twelve sons of Joseph became the fathers of the twelve tribes of Israel.

ALL:
Oh praise God in his holiness!
Praise him in the firmament of his power!
Praise him in the high notes!
Praise him in the low notes!
Praise him on the trumpet and the psaltery and harp!
Praise him with the timbrels!
Praise him with dances!
Praise him with the strings and the wind and the organ!
Praise him! Praise him!
With the clash of the loud, highsounding cymbals!
Let everything that hath breath
Praise the Lord!

JOB

CHARACTERS:
Job
His wife
Their three daughters
Eliphaz, Bildad, and Zophar, Job's friends
Satan
Messenger
Voice of God
Maidservants
Chorus

JOB was first presented on BBC/TV in 1963, and was awarded first prize in the Monte Carlo UNDA film festival a year later.

(THE SETTING IS THE LIVING ROOM OF JOB'S COMFORTABLE HOME. THE

STAGE IS BRIGHTLY LIT, AND EVERYONE IS DRESSED FOR A PARTY. AS THE
BEGINS TO SING, JOB, HIS WIFE, FAMILY, AND FRIENDS ENTER AND GROUP
THEMSELVES AROUND THE HOST AND HIS WIFE. MAIDSERVANTS CIRCULATE
WITH TRAYS OF FOOD AND DRINK.)

CHORUS LEADER: If you saw Job at home
At supper with his wife,
You'd say that they were a lucky pair
And had a happy life.

CHORUS
With cattle in the stable
And sheep upon the hills,
Job had the best of everything,
And money to pay the bills.

CHORUS LEADER: Job had a family party.
All his friends were there.
If you saw them all together
You would say their luck was rare.

CHORUS
The table was well laden
With fruit and meat and fish.
The servants hurried to and fro
With every kind of dish.

CHORUS LEADER: But all of his good fortune
Could never turn his head.
His servants thought the world of him,
And this is what they said.

CHORUS
We like Job; he's a very good master.
We like Job; he's a very good master.
We like Job; he's a very good master.

MEN: Nobody's afraid of.

WOMEN: Everybody's fond of.

ALL: Everybody likes old Job!

JOB: Shall we dance, my friends?

(THE OPENING SONG IS PLAYED SWEETLY, IN WALTZ TIME. JOB DANCES WITH
HIS WIFE, THE THREE DAUGHTERS WITH ELIPHAZ, BILDAD, AND ZOPHAR.

(SATAN ENTERS RIGHT AND WATCHES CONTEMPTUOUSLY, THEN GOES AND WHISPERS TO THE PIANIST. THE TUNE CHANGES TO HOT, BLARING JAZZ. SATAN TAKES JOB'S WIFE AND BEGINS TO DANCE A WILD TWIST. THE THREE FRIENDS LEAVE THE DAUGHTERS, AND DANCE WITH THE MAIDS. JOB HURRIES TO THE PIANO, AND THE MUSIC RETURNS TO WALTZ TIME. THE ORIGINAL DANCERS RETURN. SATAN SITS LAUGHING TO ONE SIDE.)

JOB: My children, I pray you remember
That Jehovah has blessed us indeed;
And those whom he blesses with plenty
Must give freely to others in need.
Thank God for all his blessings!
To him be glory and praise!
Thank God for all his blessings!
Gladly our voices we raise.
For all the things that he gives, for the light upon our way,
For all the love and the care that he shows us every day,
For the food upon the table, and the roof above our head,
God be prais-ed and worshipp-ed, O God be prais-ed and worshipp-ed!

SERVANT: Dinner is served, Mrs. Job.

WIFE: Shall we go in, my friends?

(ALL GO OFF EXCEPT SATAN, WHILE THE PIANO PLAYS THE OPENING TUNE AGAIN. HE WALKS TO THE TABLE UPSTAGE, AND TASTES THE PUNCH WITH DISGUST. HE POURS SOMETHING FROM A SMALL BOTTLE INTO IT, AND LAUGHS AS HE STIRS THE MIXTURE. MEANWHILE HE IS SINGING.)

CHORUS LEADER: Satan used to spend his time
Waiting, waiting;
Finding things that he could spoil,
Hating, hating.
There was nothing he could make,
So he loved to crush and break,
Killing for destruction's sake,
Waiting, hating.

(A TELEPHONE RINGS: EITHER A WHITE TELEPHONE ON A SMALL TABLE TO ONE SIDE, OR A CELL PHONE WHICH SATAN TAKES FROM HIS POCKET.)

SATAN: Hello!

VOICE OF GOD: Satan, from whence have you returned?

SATAN: From wandering to and fro in the earth,
Thinking of death and thinking of birth;
Watching men waste their sweat and breath
In their twilight life between birth and death.   I
I saw them mouthing their empty prayers,
And grabbing as much as each one dares.
If ever things take a turn for the worse,
Man's beautiful blessings turn to a curse.

VOICE OF GOD: Did you consider my servant Job?

SATAN: Job? Job?
Job is a model of human piety.
Job is a pillar of high society.
Job behaves with complete propriety.
But make him suffer—leave him in the lurch—
And you'll see if he sticks to his pew in church.
Job leads a privileged existence;
His virtue depends on your assistance.
Job has no magical resistance.
Let me take his cushion away,
And you'll see what Job will have to say!

VOICE OF GOD: Are you sure that that is true, Satan?

SATAN: I will prove it, if you give me leave.

VOICE OF GOD: You may test his faith, but you must not put his life in danger.

SATAN: Test his faith! He has no faith.
Faith is a house of cards.
One push, and over it goes.
Faith is a myth;
Faith is a farce,
As adversity very soon shows.
Let me plague Job,
Let me tempt Job!
Don't protect Job,
Don't exempt Job!
And I'll show him to you in a different light,
Whining and cursing because of his plight.

(SATAN GOES OFF. THERE IS A CLASH OF CYMBALS OR DRUM AS THE MES-
SENGER RUNS IN L.)

MESSENGER: Master! Master!

(JOB HURRIES IN FROM THE OTHER SIDE AND MEETS THE MESSENGER C. HE BENDS OVER HIM.)

JOB: What is the matter? What is your news?

MESSENGER: The news is terrible.

(HE MIMES THE TELLING OF THE NEWS.)

CHORUS LEADER: The news is bad for Job.
      The messenger looks grim.
      He says that thieves have seized the flocks
      and murdered all save him.

JOB (DOWNSTAGE
CENTER):   What the Lord gave the lord hath taken away.
      What the Lord wills his people must obey.
      May the souls of his servants rest in peace,
      And to do his will may I never cease!
      What the Lord gave the Lord hath taken away.
      Blessed be the name of the Lord!

(THE PIANO PLAYS THE INTRODUCTION TO THE FRIENDS' SONG AS THEY DANCE THEIR WAY ON AND STAND CLOSE TO JOB.)

FRIENDS: When your heart is feeling like a lump of stone,
      It is sad to have to bear the pain alone.
      In this situation, luckily for him
      Job has got some friends like
      Eliphaz, Bildad, and Zophar the Naamathite.

(EACH SAYS HIS OWN NAME IN EACH VERSE)
      In this situation, luckily for him
      Job has got some friends like us.

      It would be a terrible catastrophe
      If you could not call upon a friend like me.
      In this situation, what a lucky thing
      Job has got some friends like
      Bildad, Zophar, and Eliphaz the Temanite!
      In this situation, what a lucky thing
      Job has got friends like us.

When your sins have left you in a dreadful state,
And you can't do anything but pray and wait,
In this situation, luckily for Job
He can call on friends like
Zophar, Eliphaz, and Bildad the Shuhite.
In this situation, luckily for him
Job can call on friends like us.

JOB: What the Lord gave the Lord hath taken away.
What the Lord wills his people must obey.
May the souls of his servants rest in peace,
And to do his will may I never cease!
What the Lord gave the Lord hath taken away.
Blessed be the name of the Lord!

WIFE: Blessed be the name of the Lord? I curse his name and so
should you. It is a lie, a lie, a lie!

JOB: Wife, be calm! Come with me and pray!
Perhaps God calls him to a brighter day.
We must have faith, even when things look black.
God gives us love, and we must love him back.

WIFE: God gives us love! His love is all a lie!
Now all I want is to curse God and die!

(THE LIGHTS FADE. JOB, WIFE, AND SON GO OUT, WHILE THE SATAN TUNE IS
PLAYED SOFTLY. SATAN ENTERS AND STANDS CENTER UNDER A SPOT, TENSE
AND FRUSTRATED.)

VOICE OF GOD: Satan, from whence have you returned?

SATAN: From wandering to and fro in the earth,
Thinking of death and thinking of birth;
Watching men waste their sweat and breath
In their twilight life between birth and death.

VOICE OF GOD: Has my servant Job forsaken me?

SATAN: Skin for skin, yea, all that a man hath will he give for his life.
But put forth thine hand now and touch his bone and his flesh,
and he will curse thee to his face. Job has borne nobly the pain
and death of others—oh, yes, nobly! Let us see how he will
bear his own pain.

(BLACKOUT. ROLL OF DRUMS. FROM OFFSTAGE JOB CRIES OUT IN PAIN. A FEW

SECONDS LATER A SPOT COMES ON C. AS JOB STAGGERS ON, FOLLOWED BY HIS WIFE. HE COLLAPSES, AND SHE STANDS BY HIM. HE IS COVERED WITH SORES.)

WIFE: Now will you not curse God and die?

JOB: Though I curse the day on which I was born, I will not curse God. Only so can I guard my integrity.

WIFE: Your integrity! How can you speak of that, when we would all be better dead?

Why do we have to be born,
If this is the world we are born in?
Why are we sentenced to live,
If this is the way of our living?
Why give us hearts that can love,
If love must be tortured and riven?
Why give us life, which is better not given?

Why do we bother to pray,
If this is the fruit of our praying?
Why give our service to God,
If this is the God we are serving?
Why should we worship his name,
Amid all our pain and our grieving?
Curse God and die, and have done with believing.

JOB: I cannot curse him. I cannot live without integrity.

I will keep my integrity as long as I have breath;
For without my integrity my life is only death.
All the pain and the wounds cannot make a slave of me,
If I can guard my integrity.

I will keep my integrity as long as I survive;
For without my integrity my soul is not alive.
Though his flesh be destroyed, and his soul in agony,
Yet man can live with integrity.

Now my faith is my shield in perplexity,
While I strive to remain what the Lord would have me be.
Though his limbs are in chains, yet a man is truly free
If he can guard his integrity.

(HE CROUCHES CENTER, WHILE HIS WIFE SHRINKS BACK TO ONE SIDE. THE FRIENDS COME IN, WHISTLING THE TUNE OF THEIR FIRST SONG. THEY STAND CLOSE TO HIM AND SPEAK THEIR LINES, SINGING THE REFRAIN.)

ELIPHAZ: When things are turning worse and worse.

ALL: What a man needs is friends,

BILDAD: When he has grievous wounds to nurse.

ALL: What a man needs is friends.

ZOPHAR: When Providence's blows have struck.

ELIPHAZ: (Though he may call it 'cruel luck.')

BILDAD: And foes are keen to stir the muck.

ALL: What a man needs is friends; What a man needs is friends.

ZOPHAR: When suffering makes his spirit weak.

ALL: What a man needs is friends.

ELIPHAZ   When hostile tongues are quick to speak.

ALL: What a man needs is friends.

BILDAD: When he is left without defense,

ZOPHAR: And difficulties are immense,

ALL: He longs for folk with common sense.
                What a man needs is friends,
                What a man needs is friends.

                When your heart is feeling like a lump of stone,
                It is sad to have to bear the pain alone.
                In this situation, luckily for him,

                Job can call on friends like
                Eliphaz, Bildad, and Zophar the Naamathite.
                In this situation, luckily for him,
                Job can call on friends like us.

When your sins have left you in a dreadful state,
And you can't do anything but pray and wait,
In this situation, luckily for Job,
He can call on friends like
Zophar, Bildad, and Eliphaz the Temanite.
In this situation, luckily for Job,
He can call on friends like us.

ELIPHAZ: We have come to talk to you, Job, out of our great regard for your character and position.

BILDAD: This is a moment when no true friend could withhold advice.

ZOPHAR: You must remember that all this cannot have happened to you without good reason.

ELIPHAZ: Listen to what we say, and be sure that it is said for your own good.

JOB: Leave me alone! I have sinned—I know that I have sinned; but what does God want me to do? Can he not pardon me, instead of marking me down for destruction and making my life a burden too hard to bear? O God! You have poured me out as milk and curdled me like cheese. You hunt me down like a lion. Why was I born at all? Could I not have died in my mother's womb, and been carried straight to my grave? Leave me alone for the little time that I have to live!

ZOPHAR: Somebody must answer these lies of yours. I wish that God could speak, and show you his wisdom.

BILDAD: He is punishing you far less than you deserve, and it is blasphemous for you to try to examine his conduct.

ELIPHAZ: Stretch out your hand toward him, and put your wickedness away!

JOB: My friends, I am sure that you are very wise—none wiser. But I have some understanding also. It is you who are the liars, and who speak wickedly in God's name I will trust in him, though he slay me; but I will maintain my own ways before him. O God! Make me to know my transgression and my sin; but do not break a leaf driven to and fro, and haunt all my footsteps!

ZOPHAR: You crafty, ignorant windbag! What do you know that we do not know, you, who drink iniquity like water?

BILDAD: So we are vile in your sight? You would like the world changed to suit you, no doubt—the rocks moved!

ELIPHAZ: A hypocrite never triumphs for long. He may swallow down riches, but he vomits them up again.

JOB: I tell you, you cannot kill hope in me, though you kill pity in yourselves. For I know that my Redeemer liveth, and that he shall stand at the latter day upon the earth. And though after my skin worms destroy this body, yet in my flesh shall I see God!

ZOPHAR: Liar!

BILDAD: Sinner!

ELIPHAZ: Hypocrite!

JOB (Kneling): I'll believe in God as long as I can,
If I have to believe alone.
I'll believe that this is part of his plan;
But my heart isn't made of stone.
I'll believe he shares all our hurts and cares,
Even when it is hard to feel.
I'll believe that he watches over me,
But my heart isn't made of steel.

(A ROLL OF DRUMS. THE FRIENDS SHRINK BACK INTO THE DARKENED STAGE. JOB AND HIS WIFE KNEEL C. AND LOOK UP.)

VOICE OF GOD: Who is this that darkeneth counsel by words without knowledge? Gird up thy loins like a man! For I will demand of thee, and answer thou me!

Can you draw Leviathan with a hook?
Can you write the power of God in a book?
Did you make the Pleiades?
Did you frame the seven seas?
Can you draw Leviathan with a hook?

Can you yoke the unicorn to the plough?
Can you make the Behemoth's head to bow?
Can you cause the buds to spring?

Can you paint the peacock's wing?
Can you yoke the unicorn to the plough?

Have you seen the place where the dead must go?
Do you know what womb concealed ice and snow?
Can you make the eagle fly;
Stay the bottles of the sky?
Have you seen the place where the dead must go?

Where were you when the earth was born?
When the stars sang to greet the dawn?
Did you give the heavens their laws?
Did you shut the sea with doors?
Where were you when the earth was born?

(THIS SONG MARKS THE CLIMAX OF THE PLAY, IT ENDS WITH ANOTHER CLAP OF THUNDER OR ROLL OF DRUMS, DURING WHICH THERE IS A BLACKOUT. JOB, HIS WIFE, AND THE FRIENDS GO OFF. THE TUNE OF ' WHAT THE LORD GAVE' IS PLAYED SLOWLY, PREFERABLY ON A TRUMPET. JOB QUICKLY CHANGES AND REMOVES SIGNS OF HIS AFFLICTION. FULL LIGHTS COME ON, AND JOB, HIS WIFE, AND THE FRIENDS ENTER. THEY EXCHANGE GREETINGS.)

CHORUS LEADER
So the Lord blessed Job,
And he came back home.
The Lord blessed Job and caused him to rejoice.
Yes, the Lord blessed Job,
And he came back home;
And Job blessed God with a mighty voice.

(THE FRIENDS KNEEL IN FRONT OF JOB C.)

ELIPHAZ: Pardon us, Job!

BILDAD: We have sinned before God.

ZOPHAR: We spoke foolishly, Pardon us!

JOB: I will pray God to pardon you. We have all sinned, but God is
              good to those who repent.

(DURING THE NEXT VERSE THE TWO MAIDSERVANTS COME ON, ONE CARRYING A BABY GIRL. TWO OTHER SMALL GIRLS, JOB'S DAUGHTERS, ALSO COME FORWARD AND JOIN JOB AND HIS WIFE. THE WIFE TAKES THE BABY INTO HER ARMS.)

CHORUS LEADER
So the Lord blessed Job,

And he gave him daughters,
Jemima, Karen-Happuch and Kezia.
And he lived at home
With his wife and his daughters.
And his wife loved Job, and Job loved her.

CHORUS(AND ALL
ON STAGE):

And they all thanked God
For his gifts and his blessings.
They all gave God both glory and praise.
Yes, they all thanked God
For his gifts and his blessings;
And Job had joy for the rest of his days.

JOB:

Thank God for all his blessings!
To him be glory and praise!

ALL:

Thank God for all his blessings!
Gladly our voices we raise.

For all the things that he gives, for the light upon our way;
For all the love and the care that he shows us every day;
For the food upon the table, and the roof above our head,
God be prais-ed and worshipp-ed!
O, God be prais-ed and worshipp-ed!

NOTE: A musical version of JONAH has been published separately by Players press. For information about the play write to them at P.O.Box 1132, Studio City, CA 91614.

From the New Testament

The Prodigal Son

Bible reference Luke 15 11-32

CHARACTERS:
The Father
The Mother
The Elder Brother
The Prodigal Son
Three temptresses
Girl in the tavern
Satan
The Steward
Chorus

THE PRODIGAL SON was first presented on BBC/TV in 1963, and published by Samuel French, also in 1963, in a shorter form than the present play.

(THE SCENE IS THE FAMILY LIVING ROOM. THE STAGE IS EMPTY EXCEPT FOR A TABLE, SET FOR FOUR PEOPLE. FATHER ENTERS R, READING A NEWSPAPER, AND PULLS A CHAIR FROM THE TABLE TO SIT C. MOTHER ENTERS, CARRYING A TRAY)

FATHER: Need any help, Mary?

MOTHER: No, thanks, Joe. It's all in. How was your day?

FATHER: Fine! We're heading for a good harvest.

MOTHER: Were the boys with you?

FATHER: Pete was there, helping Manuel. John never showed up.

MOTHER: It always seems to be that way.

FATHER: I know. The men on the ranch all like John, but—

MOTHER: And the girls! He only needs to turn on that charm—

FATHER: But Pete is the one who does all the work.

MOTHER: I'll call them for supper.

FATHER No, I'll do that. (HE GOES TO ONE SIDE.) Pete! John!

ELDER BROTHER
(HURRYING IN): I'm ready for it. That was some day.

FATHER: Have you seen John?

ELDER BROTHER: I've heard him—or rather his stereo, full blast. He gets back from the beach when he thinks dinner is ready.

MOTHER: Then why isn't he here?

ELDER BROTHER: Because he's taking a shower—what else? And I need to hurry. I've got to get back to the barn before dark and check with Manuel—

PRODIGAL
(HURRYING IN)   What's for dinner?

MOTHER: Oh, John! We've been waiting for you.

ELDER BROTHER: Some of us have work to do.

FATHER: All right. Let's sit down and say a blessing.

(THEY SIT MOTHER WITH HER BACK TO THE AUDIENCE, ELDER BROTHER ON HER RIGHT, PRODIGAL ON HER LEFT. THEY ALL HOLD HANDS EXCEPT FOR PRODIGAL.)

PRODIGAL: Do we have to hold hands like kids?

FATHER: If you want to eat dinner with us, John, you give thanks with the rest of us.

(THE FATHER SINGS THE FIRST LINE, THEN THE OTHERS JOIN IN.)
>
> Thank God for all his blessings!
> To him be glory and praise!
> Thank God for all his blessings!
> Gladly our voices we raise.

(THEY EAT IN SILENCE. LIGHTS NARROW TO A SPOT OVER THE TABLE.)

CHORUS LEADER: A certain man had two sons.
> A certain man had two sons.
> One stayed at home, and was solid and slow.
> The other said, 'O let me go!'
> The other said, 'O let me go!'

(AS THE NEXT CHORUS BEGINS ONE OF THE MAIDSERVANTS ENTERS, AND STEPS UP ON TO THE TABLE, UNSEEN BY ALL BUT THE PRODIGAL. SOME KIND OF STEP WILL BE NEEDED FOR HER. SHE HOLDS OUT HER HANDS, AND RAISES THE PRODIGAL TO HIS FEET. HE SWINGS HER DOWN R.C., AND BEGINS TO DANCE WITH HER.)

CHORUS
> He wasn't a boy, and he wasn't a man.
> He was halfway between when the story began.
> He was young, he was restless, he didn't know why,
> But he knew there were things he was longing to try.
> He was hungry for life, and he wasn't content
> To remain in the place where his youth had been spent.
> He was headstrong and bold, and he hadn't a care.
> He was burning to go, but he didn't know where.

(THE OTHER TWO MAIDSERVANTS HAVE JOINED THE FIRST. THEY ARE THE TEMPTRESSES OF THE PRODIGAL, AND EACH DANCES WITH HIM, OFFERING HIM WHAT HE WILL FIND IF HE GOES OUT INTO THE WORLD ONE MAY HAVE A SURF BOARD, ONE A MOTOR CYCLE HELMET, ONE EVEN A NEEDLE—OR THEY CAN CONVEY THEIR MESSAGE BY DANCING. THE REST OF THE FAMILY CONTINUE TO EAT, NOT SEEING THE PRODIGAL'S DREAM. THE PIANO PLAYS THE SONG A SECOND TIME. BEFORE IT ENDS THE DANCERS VANISH, AND THE PRODIGAL RETURNS TO HIS SEAT)

CHORUS LEADER: A certain man had two sons.
                      A certain man had two sons.
                      One stayed at home, and was solid and slow.
                      The other said, 'O let me go!'
                      The other said, 'O let me go!'

(THE PRODIGAL JUMPS UP FROM HIS CHAIR, AND MOVES RESTLESSLY AROUND THE TABLE AS HE SINGS)

PRODIGAL: Give me the portion of mine inheritance!
                      Give me the money that's mine to spend!
                      Give me the portion of mine inheritance!
                      I want to live till it comes to an end.
                      Give me everything I'm entitled to!
                      It's unfair of you to refuse.
                      Give me the money in cash immediately!
                      I'm old enough to spend all that I choose.

(THE FATHER PRODUCES A BAG OF MONEY FROM HIS POCKET)
                      I want to go, I want to live,
                      I want to take what life can give.
                      I want to have all of the things
                      That a purse full of money always brings.
                      (HE SNATCHES THE BAG)
                      Give me the portion of mine inheritance!
                      I want to live before I must die.
                      Give me the money that I'm entitled to!
                      I'm in a hurry to say goodbye!

CHORUS (SPOKEN)
He's in a hurry to say goodbye!

PRODIGAL :   I'm in a hurry to say—goodbye!

(LIGHTS OUT. THE FAMILY GO OFF, AND THE TABLE IS CLEARED AWAY. SOME LIGHT ON THE FRONT OF THE STAGE REVEALS THE PRODIGAL, WHO ENTERS

WITH A PACK ON HIS BACK, WHISTLING AND WALKING CONFIDENTLY. THE
CHORUS BEGINS THE NEXT SONG. THE PRODIGAL EMPTIES HIS PACK BEFORE
COMING ON AGAIN TO WALK BACK ACROSS THE STAGE. HE IS LOOKING AT A
MAP, AND WALKING MORE SLOWLY. HE SITS TO ONE SIDE AS THE SONG ENDS)

CHORUS

He went into a far country.
Watch him make his way.
He went into a far country,
Seeking a place to stay.
Will he find in a far country
Friends to take him in?
Will there be in a far country
Ways that lead to sin?

(A BED HAS BEEN PLACED L.C. DOWNSTAGE. ON IT THERE IS A JUMBLED MIX-
TURE OF BEDDING, CLOTHES, BOOKS, ETC. THE MOTHER COMES IN, STANDS BY
THE BED, AND SINGS)

MOTHER: An empty room, and a rumpled bed,
     The clothes he wore, and the books he read,
     All of them meaningless, all of them dead!
     Whatever happened to love?
     Oh, whatever happened to love?

     What happened to our love,
     The thing that mattered most?
     What stole away our happiness,
     Until our dream was lost?
     What happened to our trust,
     Our laughter and our joy?
     What happened to the tenderness
     That tied us to our boy?

     At the back of the closet the treasures are piled
     From the days when he chattered and laughed and smiled.
     Whatever happened to my little child?
     Whatever happened to love?
     Oh, whatever happened to love?

     What happened to the days
     When he came running in
     With tousled hair, and dirty face,
     All eager to begin
     To pour out all the tales

Of things that he had done—
Of joys and triumphs, plans and dreams—
What happened to my son?
What happened to our love?
What happened to our love?

(DURING THE LAST FOUR LINES THE FATHER HAS COME ON. HE JOINS IN THE
LAST LINE, AND THEY EMBRACE. THE SPOT GOES OUT, THEY GO OFF, AND THE
BED IS REMOVED. A MOMENT LATER FULL LIGHTS COME ON, AND A GROUP
FROM AMONG THE DANCERS AND CHORUS ENTERS. THEY FORM A TABLEAU
OF A SIDEWALK, STANDING RIGID WHILE THE PRODIGAL WALKS BETWEEN
THEM, SINGING)

CHORUS
Faces! Faces! Faces! Faces!

PRODIGAL I stand on a lonely sidewalk,
      Here where I am not known.
      I swim in a sea of faces,
      But always I am alone.
      Don't turn away from me!
      A friendly glance, a moment's touch,
      A trivial word—I don't ask much,
      To reach to my lonely heart,
      While I stand in a world apart.

CHORUS
Faces! Faces! Faces! Faces!

PRODIGAL: I pass on my eager journey
      Into a distant land,
      And watch for a smile of welcome
      Or the clasp of a helping hand.
      Don't turn away from me!
      Look in my eyes, and give a smile!
      It only takes a little while
      To break through the edge of pain—
      And I feel like a man again!

(ONE OF THE DANCERS HAS REACHED OUT TO HIM, AND THEY GO OFF ARM
IN ARM. THE REST GO OFF AS THE LIGHTS ARE LOWERED. WHEN THE STAGE IS
CLEAR THE LIGHTS RETURN. THE FATHER COMES ON TO ONE SIDE, THE ELDER
BROTHER HURRIES ON THE OTHER SIDE. THEY MEET C)

FATHER: Is everything all right, Pete?

ELDER BROTHER: Of course, *Sir!* Why should anything be wrong? I do my brother's work as well as my own, and nobody cares—

FATHER: You know that's not true.

ELDER BROTHER: Oh, leave me alone! All you think about is Mother's lost darling.
It makes me sick!

(HE RUNS OFF)

FATHER: O God in heaven! Make us a family again!

(HE GOES OFF. A SPOT SHOWS THE PRODIGAL, SITTING TO ONE SIDE READING HIS MAP)

PRODIGAL: There seem to be several people
Locked up inside of me,
Fighting a constant battle
For my identity.
Sometimes they keep me prisoner.
Sometimes they set me free.
Is one of them my true being?
Is one of them really me?

Who am I? Just a dreamer of dreams.
Who am I? Just a failure, it seems.
No—a hero, the idol of the crowd,
Timid, or arrogant, humble, or proud.
Who am I?

There seem to be several voices
Crying inside my heart,
Sometimes they sound in discords,
Each with a different part.
They're crying for recognition,
And sometimes I stop my ears;
For sometimes they bring me gladness,
And sometimes they bring me tears.

Who am I? I'm all ready to go!
Who am I? Why, the star of the show!
Included, respected—neglected, ignored;
Assured, or bewildered—ecstatic, or bored.
Who am I?

There seem to be several people
Sewn up inside my skin.

Struggling to take possession.
Is one of them going to win?
For I want to know my meaning,
And I want to find my way.
Yes, I want to know why my heart beats so fast
While tomorrow follows today.

Who am I? Just a dreamer of dreams.
Who am I? Just a failure, it seems.
No—a hero, the idol of the crowd;
Timid, or arrogant, humble, or proud;
Accepted, rejected, aggressive, withdrawn,
Never consistent—uplifted, or torn—
A soul, or a robot; a mask, or a face;
Animal, or spirit—I must know my place.
Who am I?

(WHILE THE CHORUS SINGS THE NEXT VERSE TWO TABLES ARE PLACED C.
AND RC. TWO CHAIRS ARE AT EACH TABLE. THE BOY AND GIRL, BOTH YOUNG
AND ATTRACTIVE, COME AND SIT RC. MEANWHILE THE PRODIGAL HAS GOT
UP AND GONE OUT. OFFSTAGE HE TEARS HIS SHIRT AND SMEARS HIS FACE
WITH BLOOD. FULL LIGHTS ARE NOW ON. SATAN AND A WAITRESS—ONE OF
THE TEMPTRESSES— ENTER. SHE STANDS NEAR THE TABLE C. THE PRODI-
GAL LIMPS ON, AND IS GREETED EFFUSIVELY BY SATAN IN MIME. SATAN
SEATS HIM , AND TELLS THE WAITRESS TO BRING HIM A DRINK. SATAN MAY
BE SMARTLY DRESSED AS A MAITRE' D. THE WAITRESS GOES BETWEEN THE
TWO TABLES, FILLING THE PRODIGAL'S GLASS WHEN HE HAS DRUNK IT. HE
IS OBVIOUSLY NEAR COLLAPSE. SATAN SITS AT HIS TABLE AND PRODUCES
A SET OF DICE. THEY PLAY, AND THE PRODIGAL WINS. HE LAYS HIS WALLET
ON THE TABLE. THEN HE LOSES TWICE. SATAN ORDERS HIM ANOTHER DRINK,
AND SIGNALS TO THE WAITRESS TO DROP SOMETHING IN IT. THE PRODIGAL
SWAYS FORWARD, HIS HEAD DROPPING, BUT SATAN AROUSES HIM AND
POINTS TO THE GIRL AT THE OTHER TABLE. THE PRODIGAL MAKES A HALF-
HEARTED ATTEMPT TO APPROACH HER, BUT THE BOY PUSHES HIM BACK
INTO HIS SEAT. THE WAITRESS TAKES HIS WALLET, BUT SATAN SNATCHES IT
FROM HER. THE PIANO PLAYS THE INTRODUCTION TO THE GIRL'S SONG,
AND SHE SINGS FROM HER PLACE AT THE TABLE)

GIRL: You can buy everything,
               Money cannot fail;
               But you can't buy happiness,
               And love is not for sale.
               You can buy flattery,
               Comfort, and advice;
               But you can't buy happiness,

And love has got no price.

Food and friendship, clothes and drink,
Luxury and sex;
Music, murder, scent or mink—
You can pay by checks.

You can buy everything;
Money has its way;
But you can't buy happiness—
There is no price for happiness—
And love won't let you pay.

(SATAN DOES NOT LIKE THIS SONG. HE HURRIES TO THE PIANO, AND ORDERS
THE PIANIST TO PLAY A JAZZED UP VERSION OF THE TUNE, THE OTHER TWO
TEMPTRESSES COME ON, AND TOGETHER WITH THE WAITRESS THEY DANCE
WITH THE PRODIGAL. HE CAN HARDLY STAND, BUT THEY PUSH HIM FROM ONE
TO ANOTHER. AS THE MUSIC ENDS HE FALLS. ACCOMPANIED BY A DRUM ROLL,
SATAN AND THE DANCERS DRAG THE PRODIGAL OFFSTAGE. THE FAR COUNTRY
TUNE IS PLAYED ON THE PIANO, AND THE TABLES AND CHAIRS ARE MOVED OFF.
A LITTLE PUFFED WHEAT OR OTHER CEREAL IS SPRINKLED C. WHEN THE MUSIC
ENDS, THE PRODIGAL CRAWLS ON, SEES THE FOOD, AND BEGINS TO EAT IT
GREEDILY. SATAN COMES ON LAUGHING, AND STANDS OVER HIM. HE IS CARRY-
ING A CANE, WITH WHICH HE PRODS HIM DURING THE NEXT SONG)

SATAN: Now I've caught him!
            Here's another victim and I've caught him!
                  He will not escape me,
            For his money is vanished, and he finds he is banished
                  And alone with me In the pigsty—
            Literally and morally the pigsty!
                  I will keep him prisoner.
            He will find life is hollow while he still has to wallow
                  With the pigs and me!

                  I must screen him
            From the kind of love that could redeem him.
                  Never in the future do I mean him
                  To escape my clutches and be free.

                  I'm his master,
            Leading him to ruin and disaster!
                  He's an easy victim;
            With his wine and his ladies he will soon come to Hades
                  And be friends with me!

(THE PRODIGAL, STILL GROVELLING ON THE GROUND, BEGINS TO SING. SATAN'S LINES ARE SPOKEN.)

PRODIGAL
and SATAN: I'm in Hell!
You certainly are well on the way.
I'm in Hell!
It's up to me to see that you stay.
I'm hungry, I'm dirty, I haven't any friends.
That's usually the way this kind of thing ends.
I'm lonely, I'm desperate, my clothes are in tatters.
And you've no way out. That's the thing that really matters.
I'm in Hell!
Ah well, my boy, you've no one else to blame.
Living Hell!
Alive or dead, it's very much the same.
I feed on scraps that are left in the gutter.
Sad, sad words for a lad like you to utter.
I sleep on straw that is foul and musty.
You do look a little bedraggled and dusty.
O God, I'm sorry!
That's quite enough of that—no praying!
Please, please forgive me!
Whatever is the young fool saying?
Perhaps my father will give me pardon.
He won't, I tell you! His heart will harden!
O merciful God, am I damned for ever?
You can't go back, I tell you Never! Never! NEVER!

(A CLASH OF CYMBALS. THE PRODIGAL SINKS DOWN, SOBBING. THEN THE GIRL'S VOICE IS HEARD FROM THE BACK OF THE HALL.)

GIRL (SOLO):   You can buy everything;
Money has its way.
But you can't buy happiness;
There is no price for happiness;
And love won't let you pay.

(THE PRODIGAL LISTENS EAGERLY, AND BEGINS TO PULL HIMSELF UP TO HIS KNEES. WHILE HE SINGS THE NEXT SONG HE GRADUALLY STANDS UP, AND DURING THE LAST VERSE STAGGERS DOWN THE STEPS TO THE CENTER AISLE AND ON TO THE BACK OF THE HALL. SATAN WATCHES IN ANGER AND FRUS-TRATION, AND GOES OFF.)

PRODIGAL: I will rise and go to my father,
And tell him of all my sin.

I will knock at the door, and entreat him
To open and let me in.

I have been the cause of his sorrow,
And brought disgrace on his name.
I have sinned so much against heaven
That I must return in shame.

I will say that I am not worthy
For his love to cherish and save.
I will beg for food and for shelter,
And live as a humble slave.

For the meanest place in his castle
Is sweeter than life to me;
The home that I have forsaken,

The home where I long to be.

(A CHAIR IS PLACED L.C. THE FATHER SITS ON IT AND OPENS A BOOK. THE
MOTHER ENTERS, AND STANDS BY HIM.)

MOTHER: You didn't hear any news of John in town?
                No, my dear. No news; but there will be one day.

FATHER: No news, but we keep on praying.

MOTHER
AND FATHER: No news, but we're hoping still.
                No news, but we keep on saying,
                He will return when it is God's will.'
                He may be living.

                He may be dying.
                He may remember.
                He may forget.
                We keep on searching,
                We keep on trying,
                For God is love and we trust him yet.

                No news!
                But we keep on praying.
                No news!
                But we're hoping still.
                No news, but we keep on saying
                He will return when it is God's will.

The time will come when he will be yearning
To find the home where he lived and grew.
Our hearts are set for our son's returning,
And every morning our love is new.

No news, but we keep on praying.
No news, but we're hoping still.
No news, but we keep on saying,
He will return when it is God's will.

(THE ELDER BROTHER ENTERS ONE SIDE, SATAN ON THE OTHER. SATAN BLOCKS HIS WAY AND ACCOSTS HIM.)

SATAN: Excuse me a moment, Sir.

ELDER BROTHER: Who are you? What do you want?

SATAN: I have come to give you news about your brother.

ELDER BROTHER: *What? My brother?*
                 There's a message he was very keen to send.
                 So I'm glad to have the chance
                 To prepare you in advance.
                 Understand that I am speaking as a friend.
                 I have come to let you know that he's returning.
                 What? Returning?
                 You will want to make him welcome, I am sure;
                 For whatever he has done
                 He is still your father's son,
                 And has had a lot of suffering to endure.

                 What he needs is understanding and forgiveness.
                 What? Forgiveness?
                 To be treated as if nothing were amiss.
                 Now that all his cash is spent
                 He is ready to repent.
                 Greet him gladly with a brother's loving kiss.

                 It will not, I think, affect your own position.
                 My position?
                 There is plenty left for you and him to share.
                 He has forfeited his claim,
                 But you could not bear the shame
                 Of denying him your tenderness and care.

— 410 —

So be ready any moment to receive him.
Me? Receive him?
Degradation has not robbed him of his charms.
You will shortly have the joy
Of welcoming the boy,
When he throws himself into his father's arms.

(SATAN GOES OFF ONE SIDE, LAUGHING; THE ELDER BROTHER THE OTHER
SIDE. THE GIRL FROM TE TAVERN ENTERS AND STANDS C.)

GIRL: I wonder what happened to that boy I saw here. Oh, I know he
was high on drugs, and he made a pass at me; but there was
something about him, something lovable and also vulnerable
and sad. I'd like to meet him again; and wherever he is I hope
he will find friends. It can be lonely out there sometimes.

There are times when the world seems far too big,
And your strength seems far too small;
And to fight for the things you value most
Is to beat at a hard stone wall.
You can't stop war, or crime, or smog,
Or the strife of race with race;
But close at hand, if you turn your eyes,
There is pain on a lonely face.

Reach out and touch a lonely person!
Reach out and hold an empty hand!
For every time your love goes out to a lonely person
It falls like rain on a thirsty land.

There are times when you feel that to act alone
Is a useless thing to do;
For the pain of the world is far too deep
To be changed by me or you.
But every deed which we honor most
Goes back to a brave one's choice;
And close at hand, if you stop to hear,
Is the sound of a lonely voice.

CHORUS

Reach out and touch a lonely person!
Reach out and hold an empty hand!
For every time your love goes out to a lonely person
It falls like rain on a thirsty land.

Yes, every time your love goes out to a lonely person
It falls like rain on a thirsty land.

(SHE GOES OFF. THE PRODIGAL IS AT THE BACK OF THE HALL, AND SINGS UNACCOMPANIED.)

PRODIGAL   I will rise and go to my father,
And tell him of all my sin.
I will knock at the door and entreat him
To open and let me in.

(HE BEGINS TO DRAG HIMSELF SLOWLY UP THE CENTER AISLE. THE FATHER ENTERS, AND STANDS GAZING OUT OVER THE AUDIENCE—PERHAPS WITH BINOCULARS. HE SEES HIS SON IN THE DISTANCE, AND CRIES OUT 'JOHN!' THEN HE TURNS AND RUNS OFF, CALLING 'MARY! COME QUICKLY! HE'S HERE!' THE MOTHER RETURNS WITH HIM, AS THE INTRODUCTION TO THE NEXT SONG IS PLAYED. HALFWAY UP THE AISLE SATAN COMES AND KNEELS, BEGGING THE PRODIGAL TO STOP; BUT WITH HIS EYES ON HOME THE BOY SIMPLY DOES NOT SEE HIM. SATAN SLINKS AWAY IN DISGUST AS THE PRODIGAL STAGGERS FORWARD. THE FATHER RUNS TOWARDS HIM. THE PRODIGAL COLLAPSES A FEW FEET SHORT OF HIM. THE FATHER LIFTS HIM AS HE SINGS)

FATHER: Come home! Come home! Come home to me!
Come home! Come home! Come home to me!
My son was lost, and he is found again;
From far away I heard his voice.
He left his home, and is returned again.
I bid him welcome, and rejoice.

FATHER AND
MOTHER: Come home! Come home! Come home to me!
Come home! Come home! Come home to me!
Fling wide the gates, and bid him come again!
Let trumpets call and bells resound!
My son was lost, and he is home again!
My son was lost, and he is found!
Come home! Come home! Come home to me!
Come home! Come home! Come home to me!

(AFTER EMBRACING HIS MOTHER, THE PRODIGAL MAY GO AND GREET MEMBERS OF THE CHORUS IF THE STAGE MAKES THIS APPROPRIATE. ALSO THE STEWARD COMES ON AND WELCOMES HIM. THEN THE FATHER AND MOTHER LEAD HIM OFF, AND THE STEWARD BEGINS TO SUMMON THE OTHER SERVANTS TO PREPARE A FEAST. THIS IS AN OPPORTUNITY FOR A DANCE ROUTINE.)

STEWARD: Put the best wine out on the table!
                    See that nothing shall lack!
                    Bring the fatted calf from the stable,
                    And welcome the Prodigal back!
                    Call the men who are out at the reaping;
                    Bid them hasten, and come!
                    Wake up those who are resting or sleeping!
                    Welcome the Prodigal home!
                    Call them here for the feast and the singing!
                    Let the messengers run!
                    All the bells in the castle are ringing
                    To welcome the Prodigal Son!

(THE PREPARATION OF THE FEAST CONTINUES WHILE THE CHORUS REPEATS THIS SONG. AS THEY END, THERE IS A CLASH OF CYMBALS OR DRUM ROLL AS THE ELDER BROTHER ENTERS. THE SERVANTS FREEZE)

ELDER BROTHER: Why all this fuss?
                    What has he done to deserve it?
                    Why all this fuss?
                    It makes me sick to observe it!
                    I'm told thast he has spent his time with harlots and with thieves,
                    And eaten up the refuse that a pig or chicken leaves;
                    But when he comes back crawling, what a welcome he receives!
                    Why all this fuss?

                    Why all this fuss?
                    Isn't it all rather hearty?
                    Who thinks of us?
                    Why haven't I had a party?
                    It does me no good slaving here, as far as I can see.
                    I'm just a humble stay-at-home, no need to think of me!
                    Far better be a prodigal, and get your pardon free!
                    Why all this fuss?

                    Why all this fuss?
                    What an absurd way to treat him!
                    Why all this fuss?
                    This is a strange way to greet him!
                    He's cut his father's heritage effectively in half.
                    His conduct is disgraceful—and it really makes me laugh!

As soon as he comes whining home, you kill the fatted calf!
Damn all this fuss, I say! Damn all this fuss!

(AS HE FINISHES, THE FATHER AND MOTHER ENTER WITH THE PRODIGAL, NOW
DRESSED IN CLEAN CLOTHES. THEY STAND C, THE ELDER BROTHER BEING TO
ONE SIDE AND THE SERVANTS AT THE BACK OF THE STAGE)

FATHER: Sit down with us to dinner, Pete.

ELDER BROTHER: Dinner? This isn't dinner. This is the great celebration for my
dear brother's return.

MOTHER: Pete—

ELDER BROTHER: It's no use expecting me to join in the festivities. This is for the
favorite—the darling—the Prodigal!

My brother wasted half of your fortune.
I've heard about the stupid things he did.
You kill the fatted calf in his honor;
But you never even gave me a kid—
I can't believe it—
You never even gave me a kid!

(CHORUS MEMBERS COME ON TO THE STAGE AND DIVIDE INTO TWO SEC-
TIONS, ONE R AND ONE L, WITH THE FAMILY MEMBERS BETWEEN THEM)

My brother went and lived in a pigsty.
He's been to every row where he could skid.

CHORUS AND
ELDER BROTHER You're putting all the best on the table;
But you never even gave me (him) a kid—
E,B. *It isn't funny!*
You never even gave me (him) a kid!

ELDER BROTHER: He never even sent you a postcard.
I stayed at home to do as I was bid.

CHORUS AND
ELDER BROTHER: Now look at all the silver and the crystal!
But you never even gave me (him) a kid—
E.B. *It makes me wonder.*
You never even gave me (him) a kid!

ELDER BROTHER: He always was a cheat and a scrounger,
                    A pest, of whom I wanted to be rid.

CHORUS AND
ELDER BROTHER: But now he has returned he's a hero!
                    (SHOUTS OF 'HE'S A HERO!')
                    And you never even gave me(him) a kid—
                    E.B. *The whole thing's crazy!*
                    You never even gave me (him) a kid!

FATHER: Come to the table, and I will tell you a story.

(ALL MOVE BEHIND THE TABLE AND FORM A HALF CIRCLE)

                    There was a good shepherd,
                    Who had a hundred sheep.
                    It was his work, and his delight,
                    His precious flock to keep;
                    And in the heat of summer,
                    And in the winter cold,
                    He fed them on the mountains,
                    And led them to their fold.

                    This shepherd would number
                    His flock from day to day;
                    And he would leave them in the fold
                    If one had gone astray.
                    He left them there together,
                    The ninety and the nine;
                    And said, 'I must seek for
                    This one lost sheep of mine.'

                    Now I am your shepherd,
                    And master of you all;
                    And you, my son, have stayed with me
                    And lived within my hall.
                    Yet those who dwell in shelter
                    Must not grow proud and cold,
                    But welcome home the lost ones
                    Who come back to the fold.

FATHER AND
CHORUS: Yes, those who dwell in shelter
                    Must not grow proud and cold,
                    But welcome home the lost ones
                    Who come back to the fold.

So welcome him with feasting,
And do not count the cost;
For this my (his) son is found again,
My (his) son whom I (he) had lost.

Thank God for all his blessings!
To him be glory and praise!
Thank God for all his blessings!
Gladly our voices we raise.
For all the things that he gives, for the light upon our way;
For all the love and the care that he shows us every day;
For the food upon the table, and the roof above our head,
God be prais-ed and worshipp-ed!
O, God be prais-ed and worshipp-ed!

THE WEDDING FEAST

THE PARABLE CAN BE FOUND IN THE BIBLE IN TWO VERSIONS MATTHEW 22, 1-14, AND LUKE 14, 7-10. THE PARABLE OF THE HUMBLE GUEST IS FOUND IN LUKE 14, 11. THE WEDDING FEAST WAS FIRST PRESENTED ON BBC/TV IN 1964

CHARACTERS: The King
Simon, Barzillai, Elias Invited guests
Three Messengers
The Greedy Guest
The Humble Guest
The King's Steward
The King's Page
Several Servants
The Prince
The Prince's Bride
The Photographer
A Captain
Two Pharisees
CHORUS, who also act as Wedding Guests

DRESS should be modern, simple, and cheerful. Instead of 'wedding garments' use corsages and boutonnieres. A crown is enough to distinguish the King.

SCENERY and PROPS should be very simple: a table and chair for the King, later moved to one side and used by the Greedy Guest; crutches, etc., for the halt and the lame, eyepatches for the blind. The Feast can be imaginary.

STAGING: the play is designed to fit into any building. All that is required is an acting area, with space to one side for a piano and the Chorus. Except for the delivery of the invitations, all the action takes place in the King's Palace.

(DURING THE OPENING CHORUS THE KING IS SEATED AT A TABLE, WRITING
BUSILY. HE HANDS THE STEWARD A CHECK OR BAG OF MONEY IN THE MIDDLE
OF THE SECOND VERSE, AND GIVES A LETTER TO EACH OF THE THREE MESSEN-
GERS AT THE BEGINNING OF THE THIRD VERSE)

CHORUS

A King made a marriage for his son
And sent men to summon everyone.
He wrote the invitations
To friends and to relations,
And all the noblemen in the land,
To come to the wedding he had planned.

He told all his servants to prepare
A feast for the wedding with due care.
He gave them all they needed,
Until they had succeeded
In doing all the things he had planned.
It was the finest wedding in the land.

He sent out his messengers to say
The time of the wedding and the day.
Then gladly he awaited
What he anticipated
Would be a joyful day for the land,
The day of the wedding he had planned.

(THE KING AND HIS SERVANTS GO OFF, OR A CURTAIN IS DRAWN TO CONCEAL
THEM. THE THREE MESSENGERS ENTER, AND STAND AT DIFFERENT POINTS AT THE
FRONT OF THE STAGE, L.C., C., AND R.C. DURING THEIR SONG THEY MIME KNOCK-
ING AT THREE DOORS. A DANCE SEQUENCE MAY BE FITTED TO THIS SONG)

MESSENGERS   Opportunity's coming.
Watch his hurrying feet!
What kind of a reception
Is he going to meet?
Don't be deaf when he's knocking!
Don't look at him askance!
Opportunity's coming.
This is your golden chance.

Hello, Mister Opportunity! Why are you at my door?
Come in, Mister Opportunity! What are you waiting for?
You will see my door unlock,
Soon as I hear you start to knock.
Step up, Mister Opportunity! Show me something more!

Thank you, Mr. Opportunity! Glad you came my way.
Welcome, Mister Opportunity! It's my lucky day.
What are you holding in your hand?
Let me try to understand!
Surely, Mister Opportunity, you have come to stay.

(AT THE END OF THE SONG SIMON, BARZILLAI, AND ELIAS COME ON AND
STAND AT THE THREE IMAGINARY DOORS. THE MESSENGERS KNOCK AGAIN,
AND DELIVER THE LETTERS. EACH OF THE INVITED GUESTS MIMES WRITING A
FEW WORDS ON THE INVITATION AS HE SPEAKS HIS VERSE.)

SIMON: Simon the Pharisee thanks the King
For the invitation to his son's wedding;
But business reasons, he is sorry to say,
Will keep him from being free that day.

LORD BRAZILLAI: Lord Barzillai is deeply grieved
To refuse the invitation which he has received.
He has taken a wife himself, and so
Regrets that he will be unable to go.

DOCTOR ELIAS: Doctor Elias is most upset
That he has to express his deep regret.
His farming interests keep him tied,
And his time is completely occupied.

ALL THREE: (CLOSE TOGETHER, CENTER)
We find it sad to refuse the King,
Whom we like to obey in everything.
Our regrets, of course, are quite profuse,
But we all with one accord would like to make excuse.

(THEY GIVE THE LETTERS BACK TO THE MESSENGERS AND WALK OFF, EX-
PRESSING THEIR CONTEMPT. THE KING IS AGAIN SEEN AT HIS TABLE, WITH THE
STEWARD STANDING BESIDE HIM, NOTEBOOK IN HAND)

KING: Steward, we must reckon
What we shall need,
With a hundred thirsty throats
And a hundred mouths to feed. Wine?

STEWARD: Eighty flagons. (HE NOTES THIS DOWN.)

FOOTMAN: A letter for you, Sire.

KING:	Put it on the table.
	Logs for the fire?
STEWARD:	Logs from the forest.
KING (OPENS LETTER)	What does he say?
STEWARD:	Lamb and beef and mutton.
KING:	Josiah will be away.
STEWARD:	Boar's head and venison.
FOOTMAN:	Sire, I bring another.
STEWARD:	A whole ox for roasting.
KING:	What? And his brother?

(HE GROWS MORE ANGRY WITH THE ARRIVAL OF EACH LETTER.)

STEWARD:	Then the fruits and honey—
KING:	This villain shall be hung!
STEWARD:	Oil and grain and cheeses—
KING:	Steward, hold your tongue!

(A CHAIN OF SERVANTS PASS LETTERS ACROSS THE STAGE TO THE KING.)

FIRST FOOTMAN:	Letter after letter
SECOND FOOTMAN:	And the King in a rage.
FIRST FOOTMAN:	Look, here's another!
SECOND FOOTMAN:	Give it to the Page!
PAGE	Sire, let me give you—
KING (SNATCHING THE LETTER)	Here! Let me see!

STEWARD: The messengers are back, Sire.

KING: Bring them here to me!

(THE MESSENGERS ENTER. AS EACH SINGS HIS VERSE HE HANDS THE KING
THE INVITATION WHICH HE IS CARRYING.)

FIRST MESSENGER: Simon the Pharisee thanks the King
                  For the invitation to his son's wedding;
                  But business reasons, he is sorry to say,
                  Will keep him from being free that day.

SECOND
MESSENGER: Lord Barzillai is deeply grieved
                  To refuse the invitation which he has received.
                  He has taken a wife himself, and so
                  Regrets that he will be unable to go.

THIRD MESSENGER: Doctor Elias is most upset
                  That he has to express his deep regret.
                  His farming interests keep him tied,
                  And his time is completely occupied.

ALL TOGETHER: They find it sad to refuse the King,
                  Whom they like to obey in everything.
                  Their regrets, of course, are quite profuse,
                  But they all with one accord would like to make excuse.

(THE KING'S ANGER INCREASES. DURING THE LAST VERSE HE HAS BECKONED
TO A CAPTAIN AND GIVEN HIM ORDERS. HE JUMPS UP FROM HIS CHAIR AS HE
BEGINS TO SING)

THE KING   Go into the highways!
                         Go into the byways,
              That the wedding be furnished with guests!
              Go through the streets and call them here!
              Call them from far and call them from near!
                         Go into the highways!
                         Go into the byways,
              That the wedding be furnished with guests!
              Go to the city, and there proclaim
              That I will welcome the halt and the lame.
                         Go into the highways!
                         Go into the byways,

That the wedding be furnished with guests!
Go out and call the deaf and the blind,
And all the poor men that you can find.
Go into the highways!
Go into the byways,
That the wedding be furnished with guests!

(THE SERVANTS GO OUT AMONG THE AUDIENCE AND BRING THE GUESTS UP
TO THE STAGE. OTHERS MIME THE PREPARATION OF THE FEAST. THE TABLE
AND CHAIR ARE MOVED TO ONE SIDE)

CHORUS
They went into the highways.
They went into the byways,
And the wedding was furnished with guests.
They went through the streets and called them there.
They called them from far and called them from near.
They went into the highways.
They went into the byways,
And the wedding was furnished with guests.
They went to the city, that they might proclaim
That the King would welcome the halt and the lame.
They went into the highways.
They went into the byways,
And the wedding was furnished with guests.
They went out and called the deaf and the blind,
And all the poor men that they could find.
They went into the highways.
They went into the byways,
And the wedding was furnished with guests.

(THE GUESTS ARE NOW LINED UP ACROSS THE FRONT OF THE STAGE. SOME
ARE VERY OLD, SOME BLIND, SOME LAME OR CRIPPLED)

CHORUS
And when the bells began to call
The people gathered in the hall;
And man and woman, girl and boy,
Were glad with laughter and with joy.

(THE STEWARD, ACCOMPANIED BY THE MESSENGERS, COMES FORWARD TO
INSPECT THE NEW GUESTS. HE WALKS UP AND DOWN IN FRONT OF THEM.)

STEWARD: Is this the best that you could find?

HALT GUESTS: Yes, the halt,

LAME GUESTS:	And the lame,
BLIND GUESTS:	And of course the blind.
STEWARD:	Just look at their clothes! Though it's not their fault.
LAME GUESTS:	Yes, the lame,
BLIND GUESTS:	And the blind,
HALT GUESTS:	And of course the halt.
STEWARD:	We asked Lords and Ladies, and look who came!
BLIND GUESTS:	Yes, the blind,
HALT GUESTS:	And the halt,
LAME GUESTS:	And of course the lame.
STEWARD:	We must make the best of it, and be kind
HALT GUESTS:	To the halt,
LAME GUESTS:	And the lame,
BLIND GUESTS:	And of course the blind.
STEWARD:	It's the savor that matters, and not the salt—
LAME GUESTS:	For the lame,
BLIND GUESTS:	And the blind,
HALT GUESTS:	And of course the halt.
STEWARD:	We must carry on, though it's not the same—
BLIND GUESTS:	With the blind,
HALT GUESTS:	And the halt,
LAME GUESTS:	And of course the lame.

CHORUS

> The King had taken pains to make that feast
> A time of joy for greatest and for least.
> By his command, whoever entered there,
> A wedding robe was given him to wear.

FIRST FOOTMAN: Boutonnieres!

SECOND FOOTMAN: Corsages!

PAGE: Wedding garments! The King would like each of you to wear one.

(THE FLOWERS ARE GIVEN TO THE GUESTS. WHEN THIS IS NEARLY DONE, TWO PHARISEES WALK TOWARDS THE STAGE THROUGH THE AUDIENCE. THEY STAND IN FRONT OF THE GUESTS)

FIRST PHARISEE: What a collection!

SECOND PHARISEE: I hope the King is taking steps to separate the real guests from—these!

FIRST PHARISEE: Let us go up higher—to the upper seats!

(THEY PUSH THEIR WAY THROUGH THE ROW OF GUESTS AND GO TO THE BACK OF THE STAGE.)

HALT MAN: Well! He fancies himself, doesn't he?

LAME MAN: Upper seats, indeed! I'm grateful to be here at all.

(THE HALT, LAME, AND BLIND GUESTS SAY THE FOLLOWING LINES TOGETHER.)
> From the grudging heart and the graceless word,
> O deliver me, good Lord!
> From the sneering tone and the lifting brow,
> O deliver me, good Lord!
> From the damning voice, and the eyes gone cold,
> From the grim face set in a cruel mold,
> From the hint half dropped, and the truth half told,
> O deliver me, good Lord!

(DIFFERENT GUESTS SAY THE FOLLOWING LINES.)
> I've never been anywhere like this.
> ALL Isn't it wonderful?
> Me in a palace! It's simply bliss.

ALL   Isn't it wonderful?
Me in a hall with chandeliers,
Wearing the flowers that a Princess wears,
I shall remember it all my years.
ALL   Isn't it wonderful?

(THEY ALL SING)   God make me grateful for friendship and care!
God make me grateful for all that is fair!
God bless the King and the Prince and his Bride!
God give them happiness side by side!

STEWARD: Ladies and gentlemen, make way for the royal party!

(THE KING AND PRINCE AND BRIDE ENTER AND STAND C)

CHORUS
The Prince came with his Bride all dressed in white,
And in that hall it was a gracious sight
To see the people gathered in a ring,
Rejoicing to be guests before their King.

(THE PHOTOGRAPHER ENTERS, AND POSES EVERYONE FOR A GROUP PICTURE.
NOBODY NOTICES THE GREEDY GUEST, WHO GOES TO THE TABLE AT ONE SIDE)

GREEDY GUEST: Cheese? Ham? Shrimps? Beef?
Turkey? Chicken? Asparagus? Egg?
Strawberry? Peaches? Pineapple? Punch?
This should make a substantial lunch.

Get something for nothing!
That's the motto to keep.
Get something for nothing!
Live life on the cheap.
Caviare, sausages, cake, champagne;
Nothing to lose, and plenty to gain.
Better than sitting out there in the rain!

Get something for nothing!
That's the way to be smart!
Get something for nothing!
That is the wise man's part.
Wine and women and dance and song—
Give me a drink, and make it strong!—
Everything tasty that comes along!

Get something for nothing!
That's the way to be smart.

(THE PHOTOGRAPH HAS BEEN COMPLETED. THE CHORUS BEGINS TO SING AGAIN, BUT BREAKS OFF ABRUPTLY WHEN THE KING CATCHES SIGHT OF THE GREEDY GUEST)

CHORUS

The whole assembly burst into a cheer;
A sound which warmed that good King's heart to hear—

(THE CHORUS CONTINUES, NOW SPEAKING)

But he suddenly saw, at the side of the hall,
A man who was taking no notice at all.
He had elbowed his way to the drink and the food,
He was noisy and careless and dirty and rude.
He was munching and swilling, and paying no heed,
For his only desire was to drink and to feed;
And the King was so angry, his eyes started out,
And the guests in the hall heard him suddenly shout.

THE KING: How can you stand there
Without a wedding garment?
Don't you even care
What the party's about?
If it's only greed
Brought you here to my table,
Get you gone with speed,
Or be driven right out!

How did you get by
Without a wedding garment?
Can't you even try
To behave as a guest?
Do you feel no shame
Without a wedding garment?
Go the way you came,
If you know what's best!

(THE KING AND CHORUS MEMBERS HAVE SURROUNDED THE GREEDY GUEST AND DRIVEN HIM OUT. THEN THE KING NOTICES THE HUMBLE GUEST, WHO HAS BEEN KEEPING OUT OF THE WAY SOMEWHERE AMONG THE AUDIENCE. THE KING GOES TO HIM AND LEADS HIM C)

THE KING: Friend, go up higher!
Sit at my right hand!
Friend, go up higher

With the highest in the land!
You, who were humble,
Be my honored guest !
Come to my table!
Eat and drink the best!
You, who were shrinking
From a place of pride,
Eating and drinking
At a poor man's side,
Come by the fire!
Share my wedding cup!
Friend, come up higher!
Come with me and sup!

(THE KING NOW STANDS C WITH THE GUESTS GATHERED AROUND HIM.)

THE KING: Shall we say a blessing, my friends?

ALL TOGETHER
Thank God for all his blessings!
To him be glory and praise.
Thank God for all his blessings!
Gladly our voices we raise.
For all the things that he gives, for the light upon our way,
For all the love and the care that he shows us every day,
For the food upon the table, and the roof above our head,
God be prais-ed and wor-shipp-ed,
Oh, God be prais-ed and wor-shipp-ed!

(THEY ALL BEGIN TO EAT AND DRINK, WHILE THE KING, PRINCE, AND BRIDE
CIRCULATE AMONG THEM)

CHORUS
This is the tale of an earthly King,
Who did a just but a cruel thing;
And of a guest who was rough and rude,
And paid the price of ingratitude.

This is a lesson which Jesus gave
To all the friends he had come to save.
So let the lesson be here renewed,
To keep us all from ingratitude.

Here was a man whose thoughtless greed
Drove the King to a headstrong deed;
For he would not share the wedding food
With a guest who showed ingratitude.

(THE ROYAL PARTY IS NOW CENTER DOWNSTAGE)

        So serve your God with a thankful heart!
        Play your proud or your humble part!
        And wear for him, who is just and good,
        The clean white robe of gratitude!

        O praise God in his holiness!
        Praise him in the firmament of his power!
        Praise him in the high notes!
        Praise him in the low notes!
        Praise him on the trumpet and the psaltery and harp!
        Praise him with the timbrels!
        Praise him with dances!
        Praise him with the strings and the wind and the organ!
        Praise him! Praise him!
        With the clash of the loud, highsounding cymbals!
        Let everything that hath breath
        Praise the Lord!

THE GOOD SAMARITAN

THE PARABLE IS FOUND IN SAINT LUKE'S GOSPEL, CHAPTER 10, VERSES 25-37.

The story explains itself. The respectable passersby find reasons not to stop and help an injured man. The one who stops, and risks danger as well as making a sacrifice of time and money, is a foreigner. More than that, he is a 'Samaritan'. It is important to understand what this meant to the Jewish listeners who first heard the parable.

Samaria was once the capital of the Northern Kingdom of the Jews, Israel. When the Assyrians conquered it in the 8th century B.C.E. they deliberately left it with a mixed population by means of forced migrations—a technique rediscovered in the 20th century. The Jews of Judah, the Southern Kingdom centered on Jerusalem, despised the Samaritans more than other foreigners, thinking of them as renegade Jews. Therefore it was a shocking thing for Jesus to make a Samaritan the hero of his story.

Production of this play is very simple. It can be presented in a church as part of a worship service. There is no need for lighting changes, and there are very few props. On one side of the stage there is a road sign, reading JERUSALEM 15 JERICHO 15. Later, before the song 'Open up the door!', another sign is placed near the center of the stage, reading THE HALFWAY INN.

Dress should be modern and simple, with bright colors. The Priest wears a black robe. The Levite is formally dressed. The Bandits are outlandish and wild. The girl Onlookers are beautifully dressed.

The play can easily be acted by quite young children, but it is also suitable for elders actors.

The Chorus should stand close to the piano to one side of the stage.

During the opening song, 'Is it nothing to you?', slides may be projected, representing human suffering and needs shipwreck: fire, highway accident, refugees, flood, hurricane. In a church setting finish with a representation of the Crucifixion.

CHARACTERS: A MERCHANT
HIS TWO SERVANTS
BANDITS
THREE YOUNG LADY ONLOOKERS
A PRIEST
A LEVITE
THE GOOD SAMARITAN
HIS TWO SERVANTS
INNKEEPER
CHORUS

(THE GOOD SAMARITAN was first presented as part of a BBC Television program, *SEEING IS BELIEVING*, in 1963)

CHORUS: Is it nothing to you, all ye that pass by?
Is it nothing to you if the people die?
Can you close your eyes to the grief and pain?
Can you close your minds to the jailer's chain?
Is it nothing to you?

Is it nothing to you, all ye that pass by?
Is it nothing to you if the lonely sigh?
Can you close your ears when the hungry call?
Can you close your hearts when the wounded fall?
Is it nothing to you?

Is it nothing to you, all ye that pass by?
Is it nothing to you if the stricken cry?
Can you close your eyes to the victim's need?
Can you close your ears when the helpless plead?
Is it nothing to you?

(AS THIS SONG ENDS THE BANDITS APPEAR ON STAGE)

BANDITS: It's a wonderful place for bandits,
The Jerusalem-Jericho road.
We wait for a fat cat merchant,
With a nice, expensive load.
We shout out, 'This is a holdup!
Put down your bags and fly!'
And if he is slow to drop them and go
He can kiss his life goodbye.
The Jerusalem –rusalem –rusalem- rusalem
-rusalem-Jericho road!

It's a wonderful place for bandits,
The Jerusalem-Jericho road.
We live in a mountan hideout,
Where all our loot is stowed.
We wait for a scout to warn us
That a victim is on his way;
Then we wield our daggers and clubs and spears,
And all he can do is pray.
The Jerusalem –rusalem –rusalem –rusalem
-rusalem-Jericho road!

(THE BANDITS HIDE TO ONE SIDE. DURING THE FIRST VERSE OF THE NEXT SONG
THE MERCHANT ENTERS, THROUGH THE AUDIENCE. HE LOOKS AT THE SIGNPOST,
CONSULTS A GOLD WATCH, AND HAS WALKED C BY THE END OF THE VERSE. THEN
WE HEAR SEVERAL SHOTS. HE SPINS AROUND AND FALLS. THE SERVANTS DROP
THEIR BAGS AND RUN OFF, DISREGARDING A GESTURE OF APPEAL FROM THE
MERCHANT. DURING THE SECOND VERSE ONE BANDIT RUNS ON, THEN BECKONS
TO THE SECOND TO FOLLOW HIM. THEY TURN THE MERCHANT OVER ROUGHLY,
AND TAKE HIS WATCH, WALLET, AND THE BAGS DROPPED BY THE SERVANTS.
MEANWHILE THE DIALOGUE BELOW HAS TAKEN PLACE.)

CHORUS

A merchant journeyed down the road,
The road to Jericho.
He took with him a costly load
To bear to Jericho.
He was a man of wealth and pride,
With servants walking at his side;
But thieves and bandits often hide
This side of Jericho, this side of Jericho.

MERCHANT
(AS HE FALLS)   Help me! Simon! Elias! I've been shot.

FIRST SERVANT: Bandits! Let's get out of here!

SECOND SERVANT: Oughtn't we to—

FIRST SERVANT: If we don't hurry, we're dead. Come on! (THEY RUN.)

FIRST BANDIT: Quick! Get his wallet!

SECOND BANDIT: Got it! Is he dead?

FIRST BANDIT: Not yet, but he soon will be. Grab that bag!

SECOND BANDIT: O.K. Behind the rocks before anyone sees us. (THEY RUN.)

(EXCEPT FOR THE MERCHANT, THE STAGE IS EMPTY)

CHORUS
You see him lying in the dust,
This side of Jericho.
His cuts and wounds are bleeding fast,
This side of Jericho.
Unless some kindly passerby
Will not abide to let him lie,
The stricken merchant here must die,
This side of Jericho, this side of Jericho.

(AS THE LAST VERSE FINISHES THERE IS A SHORT DRUMROLL. IN TIME TO THE DRUM THE THREE ONLOOKERS MARCH ON, TURN TOGETHER C., AND STEP OVER THE BODY. THEY ARE BEAUTIFUL GIRLS, BEAUTIFULLY DRESSED, BLASE AND DE-TACHED. THE VERSES ARE SPOKEN, WITH DRUM ACCOMPANIMENT AD LIB).

FIRST ONLOOKER: If a man by the roadside has suffered an assault,
                It's nothing to do with me.

SECOND ONLOOKER: It's risky to help him, and it's probably all his fault.
                It's nothing to do with me.

THIRD ONLOOKER: Why pick on me to stop and lend a helping hand?

FIRST: Why can't an ostrich hide his head in the sand?
                I tell you, it's nothing to do with me.

ALL	It's absolutely nothing to do with me.
SECOND:	If the man next door gets drunk, and beats his wife, It's nothing to do with me.
THIRD	A girl must be practical in twenty-first century life. It's nothing to do with me.
FIRST:	Am I my brother's keeper when he gets into a jam?
SECOND:	Can't you see how overworked and put upon I am? I tell you, it's nothing to do with me.
ALL:	It's absolutely nothing to do with me.
THIRD:	If some faroff Africans are fighting all the time, It's nothing to do with me.
FIRST:	With things as they are, I have to think of every dime. It's nothing to do with me.
ALL:	We want to live our lives in peace and keep them clear of fuss. Of course it would be different if disaster threatened us; But so far it's nothing to do with me. It's absolutely nothing to do with me.

(THEY MARCH OFF AS THEY CAME, AGAIN STEPPING OVER THE BODY. DURING
THE FOLLOWING VERSES THE PRIEST AND LEVITE FOLLOW THE SAME ROUTE
AS THE MERCHANT. THE PRIEST GOES TENTATIVELY TOWARDS THE MERCHANT,
BUT THINKS BETTER OF IT AND HURRIES AWAY. THE LEVITE , WHEN HE SEES
THE MERCHANT, LOOKS AROUND APPREHENSIVELY, THEN RUNS PAST HIM
AND OFFSTAGE. THE MERCHANT MAKES FEEBLE SIGNS TO EACH OF THEM, BUT
COLLAPSES INTO UNCONSCIOUSNESS AS THE LEVITE DEPARTS)

CHORUS
A certain Priest came travelling by
To go to Jericho.
He did not want to let him lie,
This side of Jericho.
He wanted that poor man to save,
And all his wounds to staunch and lave;
But by himself he was not brave,
This side of Jericho, this side of Jericho.

A Levite next came on his way,
The way to Jericho.
He also would have liked to stay,
This side of Jericho.
He was so frightened of his fate,
He did not even hesitate.
He told himself it was too late,
And ran towards Jericho, and ran towards Jericho.

They passed by on the other side.
The road was small, and it was not wide;
But they hurried along with averted gaze,
'Cause they didn't like those bandits' ways.

They passed by on the other side.
The road was small, and it was not wide;
And when they were too much afraid
It was a Samaritan who gave him aid.
It was a Samaritan,
It was a Samaritan,
It was a Samaritan who gave him aid.

(THE SAMARITAN NOW ENTERS, THROUGH THE AUDIENCE. IF HE IS PUSHED IN
A WHEELCHAIR BY HIS TWO SERVANTS IT CAN BE USED IN LIEU OF A 'DONKEY'
TO CARRY THE WOUNDED MAN. HE STOPS TO READ THE SIGNPOST, THEN
SEES THE MERCHANT. HE RUNS TO HIM, LOOKS AT HIS INJURIES, AND MO-
TIONS TO HIS SERVANTS TO PICK HIM UP.

SERVANT 1:   Hadn't we better get out of here quick, sir?

SERVANT 2:   Whoever did this may still be around.

SAMARITAN: We're not going to leave this man to die. Help me lift him.

THEY SET THE MERCHANT IN THE WHEELCHAIR AND GO OFF. A , MAN OR
WOMAN, STEPS FORWARD.

There were other people who passed by on the other side that day. Ed
Robinson was on the way to a golf game. He saw what had happened, but
he did not want to miss his tee-off time. The Johnstons were on their way
to cocktails at the Club. Tom Johnston put on speed to get by quickly. He
knew that Mary might urge him to stop. She would have liked to do so, but
by the time she suggested it it was too late. They agreed that they would
call the Police from the Club, but somehow they forgot. Bud Smelzer slowed
down, then lost his nerve and drove by. Frank Sorley nearly stopped to help,
but, remembering that he was already late for work and would probably be

fired if he were even later, he took a deep breath and hurried on. Maybe you went by. Maybe I did too. We were both in a hurry, I'm sure, and we had good excuses. The world is full of people who are in a hurry, and they all have excuses—some perhaps even good reasons. But wouldn't it be better if we stopped for those who need our help—the injured, the hungry, the lonely, the unloved? Or if we used our imagination and our compassion, to find out who they are and what they need?

(THE FOLLOWING SONG IS SUNG BY THE OR BY ANOTHER SOLOIST, WITH CHORUS LINES AS INDICATED IN THE SCORE.)

SOLOIST: There are times when the world seems far too big,
And your strength seems far too small;
And to fight for the things you value most
Is to beat at a hard stone wall.
You can't stop war, or crime, or smog,
Or the strife of race with race;
But close at hand, if you turn your eyes,
There is pain on a lonely face.

Reach out and touch a lonely person!
Reach out and hold an empty hand!
For every time your love goes out to a lonely person
It falls like rain on a thirsty land.

There are times when you feel that to act alone
Is a useless thing to do;
For the pain of the world is far too deep
To be changed by me or you.
But every deed which we honor most
Goes back to a brave heart's choice;
And close at hand, if you stop to hear,
Is the cry of a lonely voice.

Reach out and touch someone forsaken!
Hold in your arms someone unloved!
For every time your love breaks through to a lonely person
Your soul is cleansed, and your worth is proved.

There will soon be another billion souls
On the face of crowded earth;
But the fact of another billion souls
Won't alter each one's worth.
Saint Francis set the world on fire
When he kissed a leper's cheek—

And so can you, if you turn your eyes,
Reach out, and touch, and speak.

Reach out your hand, and feed the hungry!
Wise men may mock, and call you fool;
But every time your love brings joy to a lonely person
It spreads like waves on a rippling pool.

Reach out and touch a lonely person!
Reach out and hold an empty hand!
For everytime your love goes out to a lonely person
It falls like rain on a thirsty land.
Yes, every time your love goes out to a lonely person
It falls like rain on a thirsty land.

(THE SOLOIST AND LEAVE THE STAGE. THE SIGN MARKING **THE HALFWAY INN** IS PLACED OFF CENTER ON THE SIDE OPPOSITE TO THE CHORUS. THE SAMARITAN ENTERS WITH HIS TWO SERVANTS, WHO ARE PUSHING THE CHAIR CONTAINING THE MERCHANT. THE SAMARITAN MIMES KNOCKING AT A DOOR CLOSE TO THE SIGN. DURING THE FOLLOWING SONG THE INNKEEPER APPEARS C. WITH HIS HELP THE TWO SERVANTS SUPPORT THE MERCHANT INSIDE THE INN. THE SERVANTS TAKE HIM OFFSTAGE. DURING THE LAST VERSE THE SAMARITAN GIVES THE INNKEEPER MONEY. BEFORE THE END OF THE SONG THE PRIEST AND LEVITE ENTER AND STAND TO ONE SIDE, LISTENING)

SAMARITAN: Open up the door! Open up the door!
Here is a man in sorest need.
Bring him succor, and come with speed!
Open up the door!

Carry him gently! Carry him gently!
Take him and give him all that is best!
Give him shelter and care and rest!
Carry him gently!

Treat him with kindness! Treat him with kindness!
Call a physician to ease his pain!
Nurse him back to his health again!
Treat him with kindness!

INNKEEPER(SPOKEN):Excuse me, sir, if I remark
That I am somewhat in the dark.
You are a gentleman, it's clear;
But not, I think, from our Judaea.

Are you perhaps from Galilee?
Or have you come across the sea?
Are you from Sidon or from Tyre?
Excuse me, sir, if I inquire.

Excuse me, sir, if I confess
I don't know whom I now address.
Your wounded friend looks like a Jew;
But—you'll excuse me—who are you?
Who is the victim's next-of-kin,
If he's to stay here at my inn?
And if there is some further fee—
Excuse me, sir—where will you be?

SAMARITAN: I am a Samaritan, and shall return this way.

INNKEEPER, PRIEST,
AND LEVITE: A Samaritan!

PRIEST AND LEVITE (SINGING OR SPEAKING IN TIME TO MUSIC)

We passed by on the other side
The road was small, and it was not wide;
But when we were too much afraid
It was a Samaritan who gave him aid.

CHORUS

It was a Samaritan,
It was a Samaritan,
It was a Samaritan who gave him aid.

INNKEEPER: Is he your friend, sir?

SAMARITAN: He is a stranger to me.

INNKEEPER: A stranger?

SAMARITAN: Yes, but he is my neighbor.

PRIEST: A stranger?

LEVITE: And your neighbor?

INNKEEPER: How can that be, sir?

SAMARITAN: Who is my neighbor?
He whose cry I hear.
Who is my neighbor?
He whose need is near.
Who is my neighbor?
He whose plight I see.
Who is my neighbor?
He who calls on me.

He is my neighbor
Who will hear my cry.
He is my neighbor
Who will not pass me by.
Who is my neighbor
In my hour of grief?
He is my neighbor
Who will bring relief.

SAMARITAN AND
CHORUS: Go, and do likewise!
Never close your door!
Go, and do likewise!
Seek the sick and poor!
Find out your neighbor!
Serve your God above!
Go, seek your neighbor!
Fill the world with love!

A Penny A Day

Bible reference Matthew 20 1-116

A PENNY A DAY was first presented at Saint James-by-the-Sea Episcopal Church, La Jolla, California, in 2002

Production notes: Dress should be contemporary and simple jeans and T-shirts for the Laborers; a large hat for the farmer. The play may be acted without any stage props; but if preferred there may be benches to mark the marketplace, baskets for the Laborers to carry, a large bin into which they empty their loads, and a pay desk in the later scene.

Music a piano may provide sufficient accompaniment, but if other instruments are available they may be used appropriately. Handbells would help the song 'It's the end of another day.'

CHARACTERS: THE FARMER (owner of the vineyard)
LABORERS four groups, with at least four in each group
TOM, JIM, ALEX, Laborers
LEADER OF LABORERS, in first group
OLDER LABORER, in fourth group
TWO YOUNG LABORERS, in fourth group
FOREMAN
CHORUS, which includes the Laborers, but should have other voices in addition

BEFORE THE OPENING SCENE THE SINGS.

There isn't a clock that measures
The work that we do for God.
He doesn't add up the hours or the days,
And he doesn't want us fretting over what he pays.
There isn't a gauge that reckons
The hours that we work for him.

CHORUS

Think of the present, and not of the past!
Don't try to tally the first and the last!
He doesn't watch the clock to see when you start.
The only thing that matters is to do your part.
God judges you by the love in your heart,
The love that you give to him.

(THE SCENE IS THE MARKETPLACE. SEVERAL LABORERS, SITTING OR STAND-ING, ARE TALKING AMONG THEMSELVES AS THE FARMER ENTERS DURING THE OPENING CHORUS)

CHORUS

See a farmer hastening
To the market square,
Hoping he will find the men
To pick his harvest there.
At the vintage season,
Early in the day,
Hear him to the harvesters
Lift up his voice and say.

FARMER: We want men to work in the vineyard.
Harvesters, hear my call!
Men of worth to work in the vineyard.
There is work for you all.
Hurry now at the dawn of the day!
Hurry now, and be on your way
To the vineyard!

Workmen, hasten now to the vineyard!
You will be shown your task.
There is pay to earn in the vineyard,
Plenty for all who ask.
Now the grapes are ripe on the vine.
Hurry there, for the day is fine
In the vineyard!

LEADER
OF LABORERS: Excuse me, sir. What will our pay be?

FARMER: I will pay each of you a penny for the day's work. Do you agree?

LABORERS: Yes, master. We agree to a penny.

(THEY GO OFF, REPEATING THE SECOND VERSE OF THE LAST SONG. JIM AND TOM STAY BEHIND. JIM SLOWLY PICKS HIMSELF UP AND GATHERS HIS GEAR.)

TOM: Come on, Jim. Hurry up!

JIM: What's the hurry? He isn't going to get more than a pennyworth of work out of me.

TOM: It's struck six. Time to begin!

JIM: All right, Tom. All right. That clock's fast. I'll bet he sets it fast on purpose, and slows it down at the end of the day, to get more work out of us.

TOM: What's wrong with you? Got out of bed the wrong side?

JIM: I don't want to be exploited, that's all. I'm coming. Don't rush me!

(THEY GO OUT. THE SECOND GROUP OF LABORERS ENTER ONE SIDE, THE FARMER THE OTHER SIDE)

CHORUS

See him now returning,
As the hours run.
More and more are needed
If the work is to be done.
While the sun is climbing
High into the sky,

Hear him in the marketplace
Lift up his voice and cry.

FARMER: We want men to work in the vineyard!

CHORUS
(Including Laborers): Harvesters, hear his call!

FARMER: Men of worth to work in the vineyard!

CHORUS: There is room for us all.

FARMER: Come to join with those who are there!
I will pay what is right and fair
In the vineyard.

CHORUS
(While second
  group goes off): Workmen, hasten now to the vineyard!
We shall be shown our task.
There is work to do in the vineyard,
Plenty for all who ask.
Now the grapes are ripe on the vine.
Hurry there, for the day is fine
In the vineyard!

(LABORERS FROM THE FIRST GROUP CARRY BASKETS TO AND FRO ACROSS
THE STAGE, SHOWING THAT THE SCENE HAS CHANGED TO THE VINEYARD. JIM
PUTS DOWN HIS BASKET AND LOOKS AT HIS WATCH. TOM IS WITH HIM)

JIM: Lunch bell's late.

TOM: Oh, come off it, Jim! You've spent the whole morning looking
at your watch, when you weren't taking a coffee break or
having a quiet smoke in the rest room. You've hardly done a
stroke of work, except when you thought the Foreman was
coming along.

JIM: I've put in my time, haven't I? I'm not a slave!

TOM: Time is about all you have put in.

(THE LUNCH BELL RINGS.)

JIM: There it goes! Pack up, boys!

(EXIT JIM. ALEX AND A FOURTH MAN, WHO IS THE FARMER IN DISGUISE, HAVE ENTERED. THE FOURTH MAN SITS TO ONE SIDE.)

TOM: There goes the world's champion shirker! Well, I'm going to look for a shady spot. Coming, Alex?

ALEX: In a minute. You go ahead, and I'll join you. (HE GOES ACROSS TO THE FOURTH MAN.) You're new here, aren't you? Will you come and sit with us for lunch?

MAN: Thanks. I think I'll just stay here and rest. I'm going to eat this evening.

ALEX: Here, mate! You look tired out. You need something to eat and drink.

MAN: Don't worry! I'll be all right.

ALEX: Nonsense! You come along and share my lunch. It's plain, but there's plenty for the two of us. Only water to drink, I'm afraid.

MAN: (SOFTLY TO HIMSELF, AS ALEX WALKS AHEAD)A cup of water! Thanks, Alex! I'll come; and I will never forget your kindness.

(THEY GO OFFSTAGE. WHILE THE NEXT VERSE IS SUNG A THIRD GROUP OF LABORERS ENTERS. THE FARMER FOLLOWS THEM.)

CHORUS
Later in the morning
See him come again.
There is need for more men still
To work with might and main.
At the vintage season
None may stay away;
Therefore in the marketplace
Hear him stand and say

FARMER: We want men to work in the vineyard!

CHORUS
Harvesters, hear his call!

FARMER: Men of worth to work in the vineyard!

CHORUS
There is room for us all.

FARMER: Hurry to join with those who are there!
                    I will pay what is right and fair
                    In the vineyard.

CHORUS

Workmen, hasten now to the vineyard!
We shall be shown our task.
There is work to do in the vineyard;
Plenty for all who ask.
Now the grapes are ripe on the vine.
Hurry there, for the day is fine
In the vineyard!

(IT IS NOW LATE IN THE AFTERNOON. A FOURTH GROUP OF LABORERS ENTERS THE MARKETPLACE. AN OLD LABORER SEES TWO YOUNG MEN SITTING, DEJECTED, ON A BENCH.)

OLD LABORER: Out of a job, then?

FIRST YOUNG
LABORER: Out of a job, as usual. It always happens to us.

SECOND YOUNG
LABORER: Me too. The awkward squad, that's what we are.

FIRST Y.L.:   Nobody seems to want me.
                    Where am I going to go?

SECOND Y.L.:   Nobody seems to want me.
                    So what am I meant to do?

FIRST Y.L.:   Everyone seems to think that I'm a nitwit,
                    All that I ask is just a simple niche.

SECOND Y.L.:   Nobody likes to think that he's a misfit.
                    A penny a day would make me feel so rich!

FIRST Y.L.:   Nobody seems to need me.
                    What have I got to give?

SECOND Y.L.:   Nobody seems to need me.
                    So how am I going to live?

FIRST Y.L.:   If I could only find a boss who'd trust me,
                    Then it would have a very quick effect.

SECOND Y.L.:   If I could only find a job—there must be
                Something to give me back my selfrespect.

BOTH Y.L.:   Nobody seems to want me.
                Where am I going to go?
                Nobody seems to want me.
                So what am I going to do?

(THE FARMER ENTERS DURING THE FOLLOWING CHORUS VERSE.)

CHORUS

There is work in plenty
Waiting to be done.
See him now returning
Near the setting of the sun.
Here are others waiting
For a place to go.
If he gives them work to do
They will not be slow.

FARMER: Why do you stand there idle?

LABORERS
(FOURTH GROUP) Because no man has hired us.

FARMER: Why do you stand there idle?

LABORERS: Because no man required us.

FARMER: If you are not the sort who lurk
                Out of the way, and try to shirk,
                Come to the vineyard now and work,
                And you'll get your pay at the end of the day.
                Why do you stand there idle?

LABORERS: Because no man hath hired us.

FARMER: Why do you stand there idle?

LABORERS: Because no man required us.

FARMER: If you are not the sort who shun
                Work that is waiting to be done,
                Off to the vineyard now, and run,
                And whatever is due I'll pay to you.

CHORUS: Workmen, hasten now to the vineyard!
We shall be shown our task.
There is work to do in the vineyard,
Plenty for all who ask.
Now the grapes are ripe on the vine.
Hurry there, for the day is fine
In the vineyard!

(THE MUSIC CONTINUES AS A BRIDGE WHILE A PAYDESK IS SET UP C. THE LA-
BORERS BRING THEIR BASKETS DURING THE NEXT CHORUS, AND EMPTY THEM
INTO A BIN—IN MIME OR WITH ACTUAL BASKETS. THE FOREMAN WATCHES,
MAKING NOTES. THE LABORERS SIT OR STAND TO EACH SIDE OF THE STAGE.
THE FARMER HAS GONE OFFSTAGE)

CHORUS

Evening in the vineyard
Now is drawing close;
So the farmer stands prepared
To pay them what he owes.
First they bring their burdens,
Now the hour is late.
Hear them sing their evening song
By the vineyard gate.

LABORERS: It's the end of another day.
We are ready to make our way.
Work is done, and we all can say
'Time to be gone. Good night!'

We have done our Master's task.
Now it is time to rest.
Fair reward is all we ask.
We have worked our best.

Hear the call of the evening bell!
Night is casting a peaceful spell.
Till the dawn we will say farewell.

(DIFFERENT GROUPS) Time to be gone.   Time to be gone,
Time to be gone.   Time to be gone.
Time to be gone,
      To be gone,
           To be gone,
   Good night!

(THE FOREMAN IS AT THE DESK.)

FOREMAN:	LIne up here, men! Latest arrivals in front!
JIM:	Why? What's it all about?
FOREMAN:	Master's orders. Go on! Get in line!
JIM:	There you are! What did I say? Injustice! Last come, first served!
TOM:	Oh. shut your mouth, Jim!
FOREMAN:	You first, Alex. The Master told me to put you in front.
JIM:	Why him? I worked longer than he did!
FOREMAN:	You what? Worked, did you say? Now see here, Jim! If you want to keep your job here, you stay quiet! You're a lazy, good-for-nothing loafer, and a bad influence.
JIM: (MUTTERING)	Victimization!
TOM:	Here comes the boss!

(THE FARMER ENTERS, AND STANDS AT THE DESK WITH A BAG OF MONEY.)

FARMER:	All ready, Foreman?
FOREMAN:	Ready, sir. The last are first.
FARMER:	Step up, please! Alex, here's your pay.
ALEX:	Why me first, sir?
FARMER:	Aren't you going to see your daughter in the hospital? You'll have to hurry.
ALEX:	How did you know that, sir?
FARMER:	Never mind how I knew. Here's your pay. You worked well.
ALEX:	But, sir, I was only here for three quarters of the day. Do I get a full day's pay?
FARMER:	You get a penny, Alex, like the rest. You were late because

you stopped to fetch old Mrs.Turpin's groceries for her, not because you were lazy.

ALEX: But, sir, how—

FARMER: It's my job to know my men, Alex; just as a good shepherd knows his flock. And then there was the lunch hour, wasn't there?

ALEX: You mean sharing—? That was nothing. I couldn't see a man go hungry.

FARMER: Here's your penny. Come back again, Alex! We need you.

(ALEX GOES OUT. DURING THE NEXT SONG THERE IS MUCH ACTION, AS EACH GROUP COMES TO THE DESK TO BE PAID.)

CHORUS ALL LABORERS

Now at the desk the last came first,
And you'd think that they'd be paid the worst;
But a question passed right down to the back

(ALL WHO HAVE NOT BEEN PAID, IN TWO SECTIONS.)

'What? A penny for men who have been so slack?'
'A penny when they were so slack?'

The next had only worked since three,
But they were rewarded equally.
You could hear them cry at the end of the line

(ALL WHO HAVE NOT YET BEEN PAID, IN TWO SECTIONS.)

'A penny is their share? What will be mine?'
'A penny, eh? What will be mine?

Another group who followed soon
Had a penny for working there since noon;
And the men at the back said cheerfully
(THE REMAINDER, IN TWO SECTIONS.)
'A penny for a half day? Two for me!'
'Still a penny? Then two for me!'

But when those who had borne the heat of the day
Were given a penny for their pay
They threw the coins down in disgust,
And yelled, (FIRST GROUP OF LABORERS TWO SECTIONS)
'We will have more! We must!'
'We want a penny more, and have it we must!'

(THE FIRST GROUP GATHER AROUND THE FARMER TO PROTEST)

> Give us more than a penny!
> You haven't any
> Right to say
> We earned only a penny,
> After so many
> Hours of the day.
>
> These have only worked one hour,
> These have only worked three.
> These have only worked six hours—
> Half as long as we!

(SECOND GROUP JOINS IN.)

> We want more than a penny!
> You haven't any
> Right to say
> We earned only a penny
> After so many
> Hours of the day.

(THIRD GROUP JOINS IN.)

> These came nearly at evening,
> In the cool of the day.
> All the hours that the sun shone
> We have toiled away.
>
> Give us more than a penny!
> You haven't any
> Right to say
> We earned only a penny
> After so many
> Hours of the day.

FARMER: Did you not agree with me for a penny?

LEADER /LABORERS: Yes, sir; but compared with these—

FARMER: Stop! You said you would work for a penny. We said nothing about comparing yourselves with others.

> You were hired for a penny.
> You haven't any
> Right to say
> You earned more than a penny

After so many
Hours of the day.

If these have only worked one hour,
And these have only worked three,
Why should you be complaining?
Leave my job to me!

FARMER AND
CHORUS

(I have)
He has paid you a penny.
You haven't any
Right to say
You earned more than a penny,
After so many
Hours of the day.

FARMER:

All who come to the vineyard
Will be given their due.
What is paid to your comrades
Shouldn't worry you.

CHORUS ALL
 LABORERS

We were hired for a penny.
We haven't any
Right to say
We earned more than a penny
After so many
Hours of the day.

FARMER:

Turn your steps on your homeward way!
Come at dawn for another day!
Work is done, and we all can say
'Time to be gone! Good night!'

CHORUS

We have done our Master's task.
Now it is time for rest.
Fair reward is all we ask.
We have worked our best.

Hear the call of the evening bell!
Night is casting a peaceful spell.
Till the dawn we shall say farewell.

(DIFFERENT GROUPS)

> Time to be gone.   Time to be gone.
> Time to be gone.   Time to be gone
> Time to be gone
>   to be gone
>   to be gone
> Good night!

THE UNJUST STEWARD

BIBLE REFERENCE LUKE 16 1-8

THE UNJUST STEWARD was first presented at All Saints Episcopal Church, Pasadena, California, in 1975.

Production notes No elaborate scenery is required. The simple props are indicated in the text. Modern dress for all characters. Perhaps a clerical robe for Moses and Aaron. Satan smartly dressed in a dark color. Jack and Vera flashily dressed.

Lighting may be used effectively as indicated in the text.

Music: a melody line score. Piano acompaniment is sufficient.

CHARACTERS: VOICE OF GOD
MOSES
AARON
SATAN
MINISTER
JACK STEWARD
VERA, Jack's girlfriend
MR. LORD, the boss
MR. GALETTI, MRS. SCHEER, MR. GOMEZ,
MISS MACPHERSON, debtors to Mr. Lord
TWO COMMENTATORS, a man and a woman
CHORUS, which includes the CHOIR but also additional
voices. A chorus of up to twenty is recommended.

(WITH THE STAGE IN DARKNESS, THE CHORUS BEGINS TO SING. AFTER ONE VERSE A BRIGHT LIGHT COMES ON GRADUALLY, REVEALING MOSES KNEELING C. HE FACES TOWARDS THE LIGHT.)

CHORUS
> God spoke to Moses long ago.
> God spoke to Moses long ago.
> God spoke to Moses long ago
> 'Tell the people of Israel,

The people of Israel,
To serve me with their might.'

God spoke to Moses long ago. (THREE TIMES)
'Tell the people of Israel,
The people of Israel,
To walk in truth and light.'

God spoke to Moses long ago. (THREE TIMES)
'Tell the people of Israel,
The people of Israel,
To fight Jehovah's fight."

God spoke to Moses long ago. (THREE TIMES)
'Tell the people of Israel,
The people of Israel,
To love me with their might.'

(FROM THE SOURCE OF THE LIGHT)

VOICE OF GOD: Tell them to have no other Gods but me, Moses. Tell them that my love is with them, and underneath are the everlasting arms; but they must make no graven image, and must love me with heart and soul and mind.

MOSES: I will tell them, Lord. It will be hard to follow you sometimes, but I will tell them. Lord, if we fail—

VOICE OF GOD: If you fail, return to me with penitent hearts, and I will give you new strength. But do not compromise with evil, or with other gods.

MOSES: I will do my utmost, Lord. (THE LIGHT BEGINS TO FADE AS MOSES CONTINUES.)
Preserve me, O God, for in thee have I put my trust.
O my soul, thou hast said unto the Lord, 'Thou art my God; I have no good like thee.'
But they that run after another God shall have great trouble.
I have set the Lord always before me; for he is on my right hand, therefore I shall not fall.
Thou shalt show me the path of life; in my thy presence is the fulness of joy.

(MOSES GOES OFF WHILE THE STAGE IS DARK. WHEN LIGHTS COME UP AARON IS SITTING AT A DESK R.C., WRITING. SATAN ENTERS L, WITHOUT BEING SEEN BY AARON.)

SATAN:	Good morning, Aaron.
AARON:	(LOOKING UP STARTLED) I beg your pardon. Who– I don't think I know you.
SATAN:	My name is Satan.
AARON:	Satan? Why, you—
SATAN:	Not so fast, Aaron! Before you condemn me so hastily, let me tell you why I have come. You see, I have been watching with admiration all that you are doing for your people
AARON:	I am not the leader of our people. It is my bother Moses—
SATAN:	Exactly. And Moses is a great man, a very great man—in some ways too great a man, Aaron.
AARON:	Too great? How can that be true?
SATAN:	Too great for ordinary people to keep up with him. That is where your wisdom and your gifts come in, if I may say so. Moses goes up to Mount Sinai and talks with God. He enjoys the limelight, and rightly so. He is unique, in a world of his own. But you have your finger on the pulse of the ordinary man and woman, Aaron. That is your strength.
AARON:	Yes, that may be true.
SATAN:	It is true. That is why I have come to give you some advice and help. This is a critical moment for all humanity, Aaron, and you, you alone, are called to be the moderating influence. Moses will come down again from Sinai, after having seen a great vision. But religion, like everything else, must be practical; and nobody could call your brother Moses a practical man. If what he tells the people is far beyond their reach, what is its use?
AARON:	I see that risk; but what do you advise me to do?
SATAN:	To put it simply, see that your people keep their feet on the ground, when he comes down with his head still in the clouds! See that they mix in some common sense with his heady ideals. It is going to depend on you.
AARON:	But—if you are right, how shall I go about it?

SATAN: Compromise is the key—intelligent, sensible compromise. Keep them in touch with reality! Now I suggest that it would be a great idea, for a start, to collect all the gold that the people possess—rings, ornaments, and so on—and melt it down to make a Golden Calf—

(THE LIGHTS FADE OUT, EXCEPT FOR A SPOT ON THE COMMENTATORS, WHO STAND WITH THE CHORUS AT THE PIANO. THEY SING THE NEXT SONG, WITH THE CHORUS SINGING THE WORDS ,'BUILD (or BREAK) THAT GOLDEN CALF! ' WHENEVER THEY OCCUR.)

COMMENTATORS AND CHORUS

Aaron did what Satan told.
Build that Golden Calf!
Gathered all the people's gold.
Build that Golden Calf!
Gathered bracelets, gathered rings,
Gathered all their golden things,
Sang the songs a pagan sings.
Build that Golden Calf!
Moses' anger then was grim.
Break that Golden Calf!
Bitter words they heard from him.
Break that Golden Calf!
'Lord Jehovah gave us birth.
All your gold is nothing worth.
Tread that Calf down in the earth!
Break that Golden Calf!'

(A SPOT SHINES ON THE COMMENTATORS.)

SHE: I'm confused. I thought this was a play about the Unjust Steward. I can't remember the story very well, but I'm sure Moses didn't come into it.

HE: No. you're right. But I think the play is saying that they are part of the same situation.

SHE: Well, I don't understand it yet.

HE: It says in this commentary that the story of the Unjust Steward was a real shocker—the most surprising that Jesus ever told—and he was full of surprises. The clue comes at the end, where he says 'The children of this world are wiser than the children of light.'

SHE: So? What does that mean?

HE: That the bad guys try harder than the good guys, I think. Crooks do better planning than people who are religious. It's not always true. Plenty of people live and work for their faith wholeheartedly; but I think Jesus found himself surrounded by pious people who were ineffective amd hypocritical. He wanted to wake them up with this story. The moral is bad: guys, like Jack Steward, will do anything to succeed. Must good guys are wimps.

SHE: I still don't see how Moses comes into it.

HE: It looked to me as though Satan was scared stiff that Moses really meant what he was saying; so he was trying to soften Aaron up. I mean, if people started taking God's words literally, Satan would be finished.

SHE: They're coming back. Wait a minute! This looks like a modern church.

(STAGE LIGHTS COME ON. MINISTER AND AARON ENTER ONE SIDE. ON THE OTHER SIDE IS A ROW OF CHAIRS. AS SATAN SPEAKS THE CHOIR SHUFFLES IN, ITS MEMBERS SHABBILY DRESSED IN ROBES. THEY STAND IN FRONT OF THEIR CHAIRS, SINGING OUT OF TUNE. IF NUMBERS ARE SUFFICIENT ALTERNATE LINES MAY BE SUNG BY TWO SECTIONS, BUT THE LAST TWO LINES ARE SUNG BY ALL.)

SATAN: You're quite right. It is a church. You may be surprised by the hymn which they are about to sing; but the fact is I have persuaded them that honest compromise is better than hypocrisy. The church is called 'The Temple of God and the Golden Calf.' Perhaps some of you out there would like to join—that is, if you don't already belong to a similar church.

CHOIR (STANDING)
We are the children of light,
We worship the Lord with part of our might.
We come to church, and we pray and sing,
And we half believe in everything.
We half believe in a God above,
And we practice half of Christian love.
We believe in half the Christian creed.
We believe in half of the things we read.
On Sunday it seems a high ideal,
But on Wednesday it doesn't seem quite real.

(DURING THE LAST TWO LINES THEY BOW IN TWO DIRECTIONS.)
> We follow God, just half and half;
> But we also keep an eye on the Golden Calf.

MINISTER: Will you please all be seated? (THEY SIT.) It is a great privilege for me to introduce to you our visiting preacher, Aaron. I know that you have heard something of his work, and of course you all know that he is the brother of the great Moses. I am sure that he has a message of a truly practical kind to give us. I am delighted to call upon him to speak to us. Aaron!

AARON: Thank you, Pastor. May the words of my mouth, and the meditations of our hearts, be always acceptable in thy sight, O Lord, our strength and our redeemer! My friends, it is I who am privileged to be speaking to you, a typical, decent congregation of believers. What I want to say to you today is this. I am a great admirer of my brother Moses—probably his greatest admirer. I know no man whose contact with God is closer or deeper; but what disturbs me about him is this: will he, by setting before us ideals so high that we cannot sustain them, frighten most of us away from religion altogether? Or else, shall we turn into hypocrites, pretending one set of ideals and living by quite different standards? That was why I persuaded my people to make the Golden Calf, while Moses was far away up on Mount Sinai. I feel strongly that we preachers must realize that we are dealing with human beings, not with saints or angels. The Golden Calf represents an honest compromise between God and Mammon. If you are shocked by that idea, ask yourselves whether it is not in fact the kind of common sense religion by which you yourselves are living.

(HE RECITES): It's all very well for Moses,
As he stands on Sinai hill.
It's all very well for Moses.
He has an iron will.
But for people who aren't like Moses
The standards are too high.
So half and half, with a Golden Calf,
I divide my loyalty.

AARON AND CHOIR
It's all very well for Moses,
Conversing with the Lord.
It's all very well for Moses;

It's something he can afford.
But for lesser folk than Moses—
Which means, for you and me—
We must recognize that compromise
Must be religion's key.

(THE CHOIR FILES OUT CLUMSILY, SINGING 'We are the children of light...'
LIGHTS FADE TO BLACKOUT. AARON AND MINISTER ALSO GO OFFSTAGE.
WHEN LIGHTS COME ON AGAIN MOSES IS KNEELING C.)

MOSES: Lord, I have come back up here to pray to you. It's a hard climb, but I need to be as near to you as I can. Lord, you saw what was happening down there. I could hardly believe it when I saw what Aaron had done—my own brother! And to build an idol, a Golden Calf, just when we were trying to find our way to you as our one true God! And you saw what I did. I'm afraid I saw red, Lord. We destroyed the calf so that you would never have known it existed. But since then I've been thinking. Aaron isn't a bad man, I know that. His point of view is that it's better to have most of the people halfway on your side than to have a very few who go all the way in loving and serving you. Which do you want, Lord? Do you want me to rewrite those Ten Commandments? You know what I mean 'Serve God, but only within reason. Honor your father and mother, as long as they are sensible and agree with you. Don't kill, or steal, or commit adultery, unless things become too difficult.' Lord, even up here it's hard to see it all in perspective. But you did speak to me clearly before. So until I know that you have changed your mind I shall stick to what you said then. Most people are going to say that I am hopelessly impractical, and it's going to be a tough time. So please be with me, Lord! Don't let them get away with watering down your word with compromises! I will lift up mine eyes unto the hills, from whence cometh my help. My help cometh even from the Lord, who hath made heaven and earth.

(HIS VOICE FADES. LIGHTS FADE TO BLACKOUT. MOSES GOES OFFSTAGE. THE
CHORUS SING SOFTLY A VERSE OF 'Aaron did what Satan told'. THEN LIGHTS
UP AGAIN ON THE STEWARD'S OFFICE AT LA CRESTA RANCH, ARIZONA. JACK
STEWARD SITS WITH HIS FEET ON THE DESK C. SPEAKING ON ONE OF THE
TWO TELEPHONES IN FRONT OF HIM. VERA, FLASHILY DRESSED, SITS ON ONE
END OF THE DESK, DISPLAYING HER LEGS TO THE AUDIENCE. SHE IS POLISH-
ING HER NAILS.)

JACK: Mrs. Hawkins? Yes, this is Jack Steward. You can't what? You can't pay your rent this month? Well, you know, Mrs. Hawkins, that is your problem, isn't it, not mine. Arrange something? Well, yes, I dare say we could talk it over. But there's no getting away from the fact that Mr. Lord must have his money. Yes, you call around here in the morning. About eleven will be fine. I'll see you then, Mrs. Hawkins. (HE PUTS DOWN THE TELEPHONE.)

VERA: Who was that, honey?

JACK: Old Mrs. Hawkins? Oh, she lives in one of the cottages west of the ranch.

VERA: And she can't pay?

JACK: With a little persuasion she'll pay. Maybe I shall have to lend her some of the money, for a consideration.

VERA: What would the boss say to that?

JACK: What can he say? He spends his time in New York and Florida and Europe, and leaves this place to me to run. I reckon he gets a fair bargain—I do a good job for him. If I make a bit on the side, there's nothing wrong in that. It won't be long now before we can take that honeymoon cruise.

VERA: Sounds good to me. What does the boss do, Jack?

JACK: Better not to inquire too closely. He's one of the big wheeler-dealer financiers, with interests everywhere, some of them shady, I'm sure. He hasn't a clue what's going on here. (TELEPHONE RINGS, HE PICKS IT UP.) Hello! Yes, this is Jack Steward. Put him through. Who? (HE JUMPS TO HIS FEET.) Yes, sir. Yes, of course, I'll come right over. You're coming here—to my office? I wasn't expecting—why yes, sir, of course it's convenient. I'll be seeing you then, Mr. Lord. (HE PUTS THE TELEPHONE DOWN VIOLENTLY.) Holy mackerel! It's the boss—flown in unexpectedly. He's on his way over. Listen, honey, you wait in there. You might meet him if you go out now. Keep out of the way! I'll cope with him. Hurry!

(HE USHERS HER OFF L, STRAIGHTENS PAPERS ON HIS DESK, AND LOOKS AROUND NERVOUSLY. MR. LORD ENTERS R.)

JACK: Why, hello there, Mr. Lord! Good to see you. This is a surprise.

LORD: I'm sure it is. More than that. I'm certain it is quite a shock.

JACK: Oh, I wouldn't say that, sir. You're always a welcome visitor.

LORD: Hardly a visitor, Jack. I do own this place, remember? As for being welcome—I wonder.

JACK: What do you mean, sir?

LORD: I'll tell you what I mean. You think I live a long way away, so you reckon that I don't know what goes on here on the ranch. Well, maybe my ears are sharper than you thought, Jack Steward. I've come to find out the truth.

JACK: I've no idea what this is all about, Mr. Lord.

LORD: You haven't? Well, reports have reached me, never mind from whom, that you're taking too much into your own hands, in more ways than one—robbing me right and left, and wasting my money.

JACK: Robbing you and wasting your money? I'd be interested to know who told you that!

LORD: Never mind who told me! It's up to you to show that they're wrong. I want to be fair. I'll give you a chance to prove that everything's above board. You've got till ten tomorrow morning. Then I'm going through the books. They'd better be in order, or you're fired! Is that understood?

(FADE TO BLACKOUT ON THE LAST WORDS. LORD GOES OFFSTAGE. VERA RETURNS AND STANDS BY JACK AT THE DESK. MEANWHILE SPOT SHINES ON COMMENTATORS.)

SHE: I'd say he deserved it, wouldn't you?

HE: It certainly looks like it. I'm sure Jesus' audience expected it to end that way.

SHE: You mean, next morning he gets caught cheating, loses his job—perhaps goes to jail?

HE: That's the obvious ending, isn't it? Like that other story where the man was made to pay the uttermost farthing. Jack and Vera seem to be in for some weeping and gnashing of teeth. No honeymoon cruise!

SHE: But that's not the way this story ends. Is that what you are saying?

HE: Absolutely. Here they come again! Let's watch

(LIGHTS REVEAL THE OFFICE JACK SITTING, VERA STANDING BY HIM.)

VERA: That sounded pretty bad, Jack.

JACK: You bet it's bad! If I lose this job, Mr. Lord will make it impossible for me to get another. We'll starve!

VERA: What are you going to do?

JACK: We're going to fight, Vera! I've got to think. If he fires me, I have only two choices to dig as a hired laborer, or to beg. Just think of that! I'll do anything—anything—to avoid it.

I can raid a bank, I can forge a check,
I can plan a crime and risk my neck,
I can win at cards with a phoney deck—
But I just won't dig!

CHORUS: No, he just won't dig!
And I just can't beg!
He'd be ashamed of it—he just can't dig!

JACK AND VERA: I must lay myself a golden egg,
Since I just can't dig, and I just won't beg.
I must make a kill that is really big,
For I just won't beg!

CHORUS: No, he just won't beg!
And I just can't dig!
CHORUS He'd be ashamed of it—he just can't dig!

VERA: O.K., Jack. Fight him! What can I do to help?

JACK: We have until ten o'clock tomorrow morning. All right! If that's the way he wants it, he can have it. Where's that list?

VERA: List of what?

JACK: The boss's debtors. Here it is! We'll begin with these four. You take Mrs. Scheer and Miss Macpherson. I'll look after Galetti and Gomez. Use that phone. Tell them to come here—and quick!

(THEY SPEAK ALTERNATELY ON THE TWO PHONES, STANDING ON EITHER SIDE OF THE DESK)

JACK: Mr. Galetti? Come at once!

VERA: Hurry on over Mrs. Scheer

JACK: Mr. Gomez? *Pronto!* Quick!

VERA: Miss Macpherson? We need you here!

(JACK AND VERA REPEAT THE SONG 'I can raid a bank,' SINGING BOTH VERSES TOGETHER. CHORUS LINES AS BEFORE. JACK AND VERA DO A DANCE ROU- TINE. AS THE SONG ENDS THE FOUR DEBTORS ENTER . JACK AND VERA PULL CHAIRS FORWARD FOR ALL OF THEM TOGETHER R.)

VERA: Sit down, Mr. Galetti. All of you please sit down.

GALETTI: What's it all about, Mr. Steward?

SCHEER: Ja, Mr. Steward. Tell us! I don't understand.

JACK: You'll find out in a minute, all of you. Now, Mr. Galetti, let's take you first. I have your account with Mr. Lord here. (GALETTI MOVES TO THE DESK. THE OTHERS REMAIN SEATED.) Do you remember the items on your account?

GALETTI: A hundred measures of oil, Mr. Steward. It's a big burden for a poor man like me,

JACK: Well now, Mr. Galetti, you know that you owe Mr. Lord a hundred measures of oil, and i know it; but Mr. Lord doesn't know it. He has no idea how much oil you owe him. So if I were to take this pen and alter that figure to—what shall we say? Fifty?—it could be a secret between the two of us, couldn't it?

GALETTI: Fifty? Gee, you'd do that for me, Mr. Steward?

— 458 —

JACK: I'm doing it at this very moment, Mr. Galetti. There! You see? I have no great reason to love Mr. Lord. The difference between fifty and a hundred matters a great deal to you, but it isn't going to hurt him. And perhaps one day you may be able to do something for me?

GALETTI: I sure will, Mr. Steward. Only fifty! What a load off my mind!

VERA: (USHERING GALETTI OUT) Goodbye, Mr. Galetti. Mrs. Scheer has a problem too, Jack.

JACK: Well, I'm hopeful that we can handle all these good people's problems helpfully.

SCHEER: It's all that wheat, Mr. Steward. You know how it is. Times have been bad, and the long and the short of it is that I owe a hundred measures.

JACK: A hundred measures of wheat? Hm. That's more difficult. He can do some checking. Suppose we change that figure to— eighty?

SCHEER: That would be a mighty big help, Mr. Steward.

JACK: And you, Mr. Gomez?

GOMEZ: (HURRING TO THE DESK) It's the rent on my place, see? I do my best, but the arrears—

JACK: The arrears amount to a thousand dollars. Is that correct?

GOMEZ: A thousand, or maybe a little over. Gee! It's a lot of money.

JACK: Something tells me that seven hundred would be a more satisfactory figure, Mr. Gomez. there! Not a bad piece of forgery!

GOMEZ: I don't know how to thank you, Mr. Lord—

JACK: I may be able te tell you a way to do just that. Now why don't you help Mrs. Scheer, and we can deal with Miss Macpherson's affairs.

VERA: Come on, Mrs. Scheer.

(VERA SHOWS SCHEER AND GOMEZ OUT.)

JACK: Now, Miss Macpherson. A loan, wasn't it?

MACPHERSON: That's right, Mr. Steward, a loan; and the interest adds up so you wouldn't believe it. I owe Mr. Lord almost five thousand.

JACK: Five thousand? That's funny! Come here, Miss Macpherson! (SHE GOES TO THE DESK.) I could have sworn for a moment that that figure was a three, not a five. You see? Don't you agree that it is a three now?

MACPHERSON Oh, glory be, Mr. Steward! You don't know what this will mean to me!

JACK: Glad to do it for an old friend, Miss Macpherson. We're all old friends and neighbors on the ranch, aren't we? Anything we can do to help each other—

MACPHERSON: You name it, Mr. Steward—I'll do it! You've saved my life!

JACK: Now, I have a great deal of work to do, so I'll have to ask you to leave, Miss Macpherson. Keep in touch!

VERA: Goodbye, Miss Macpherson. Have a nice day! (SHE RETURNS TO THE DESK.) Gee, Jacky, aren't you taking a big risk?

JACK: Risk of what? He's out to ruin me, isn't he? Well, if he fights dirty, so will I! I'm going to look after you and me. if he gets hurt, who cares? Now, honey, let's get down to these account books.

(FROM A DISTANCE OUTSIDE DISCORDANT VOICES ARE HEARD. IT IS THE CHOIR ACROSS THE ROAD, SINGING "We are the children of light.")

VERA: What's that noise?

JACK: That soppy music? That's the church across the road. The dogooders, having their social hour. I'll bet they'd have a shock if they knew what we were up to in here!

VERA: I know one thing. If they ever worked as hard for their God as we're working now, religion would take a sharp turn upwards.

JACK: That'll be the day! They don't know what sweat means. Hand
                   me that ledger, sweetheart!

VERA: Listen!

CHOIR (OFFSTAGE): Fight the good fight with all your might!

JACK: That's no use to me, you children of light!

CHOIR: Cast care aside, lean on thy guide!

JACK: I must help myself. The Lord won't provide!

CHOIR: Lay hold on life, and it shall be—

JACK: Oh, nuts! You sing halfheartedly!

(THE PIANO CONTINUES SOFTLY WHILE JACK AND VERA SPEAK.)

JACK: I must fight my fight with all of my might.
                   Those people in there half believe in right.

VERA: When a crisis comes, and things look tight,
                   You can give up hope for the children of light!

JACK: They can bleat away about faith and prayer,
                   But the children of darkness really care!

VERA: And there's nothing to make the Devil laugh
                   Like the children of light with their half and half.

JACK: (SHUTTING THE LEDGER ON THE DESK)
                   There! That's the best I can do. If I'm fired, we'll see how
                   Mr. Galetti and the others can help.

VERA: You'll blackmail them?

JACK: That's no way to talk, sweetheart. All I will need to do is to
                   show them where their best interests lie. Now cheer up! We'll
                   have that honeymon cruise yet!

(BLACKOUT. JACK AND VERA GO OFFSTAGE.. A SPOT HIGHLIGHTS SATAN L.)

SATAN: On the whole I'm well satisfied with the way things are working out. I have Moses really worried, Aaron preaching compromise, the people in church listening to him and bowing to the Golden Calf; and here at the ranch everything is turning out well. Mr. Lord is being as mean as he can. Jack Steward is fudging the account books. Not one of those pillars of respectability objected to the help he offered them. Ah well! I can usually rely on my followers working a good deal harder than His. (HE POINTS UPWARDS.) Yes, I think the situation is developing according to plan.

(BLACKOUT. SATAN GOES OFFSTAGE. AFTER A PAUSE THE BRIGHT LIGHT FROM MOUNT SINAI SHINES AGAIN, AND MOSES IS SEEN STANDING C.)

MOSES: Lord, did you hear all that?

VOICE OF GOD: Yes, Moses. I heard it.

MOSES: It's terrible to hear that man Jack and his girl treating your Church with contempt, and Satan crowing over us!

VOICE OF GOD: I know, Moses; and you can't help feeling, can you, that he is partly right. That makes it all the worse. Is that what is troubling you?

MOSES: Yes, Lord. Those people in church—from their singing they didn't exactly sound like good witnesses for you, did they?

VOICE OF GOD: No, Moses. They are not bad people, but they are weak. I'm afraid you didn't put an end to compromise when you stamped out that Golden Calf.

MOSES: Must it always be like this, Lord? Will good men always be halfhearted?

VOICE OF GOD: They rise above it sometimes; but I do wish that some of them, instead of dozing in their comfortable pews in church, would take some lessons from Mr. Lord and Jack Steward. I can't help admiring Jack and that girl Vera.

(LIGHTS FADE TO BLACKOUT. MOSES GOES OFFSTAGE. THE CHOIR SINGS SOFTLY THE FIRST VERSE OF 'God spoke to Moses long ago.' WHEN THE LIGHTS COME UP, MR. LORD SITS AT THE DESK. JACK STANDS BESIDE HIM.)

LORD: Hm. It all looks plausible enough.

JACK: Thank you, Mr, Lord.

LORD: But then I would expect that. What I want to find out is the truth behind all these figures.

JACK: The truth is, sir, that this ranch has been making a sizable profit ever since you put me in charge of it.

LORD: Yes, and I'm sure you have made a sizable profit too. Hello! What's this?

JACK: Which, Mr. Lord?

LORD: Mr. Galetti. With all that family to feed, only fifty measures of oil? It sounds far too little.

JACK: It's all there in the books.

LORD: So I see. And Miss Macpherson. She wrote to me in Florida. I thought she mentioned five thousand, not three. Wait a minute! that 3—very clever! Very clever indeed! And others like it, no doubt. Let's take another look at Galetti. Aha! I've got it now! Just how many forged entries are there in this ledger, Mr. Steward?

JACK: Not one that you can prove. You left me here to run this ranch, and I've done my job. You can fire me if you liike, but you can't pin any forgeries on me.

LORD :   (SITTING BACK AND LAUGHING) You know, Jack, I underestimated you. Fix a drink for both of us, and sit down!

JACK: I don't get it, Mr. Lord.

LORD: You don't? Make mine scotch on rocks, and I'll explain.

JACK: Why certainly, sir. Just a moment.

(HE GOES TO A CABINET L. AND RETURNS WITH TWO GLASSES. LORD MEAN-WHILE LOOKS FURTHER AT THE LEDGER.)

LORD: That's better, Jack. Cheers!

JACK: Cheers, sir!

LORD:	See here, Jack. I left you here to run the ranch because I had some big deals to look after—I mean big—and other things. I was too busy to run it myself. Right?
JACK:	That's true, sir.
LORD:	Well, my business is growing, Jack, and it's getting tougher. I need some ruthless, effective lieutenants to help me. So I decided to pay a surprise visit here, and find out what kind of job you are doing.
JACK:	Well, the books are balanced and in order. You can't prove a thing against me.
LORD:	On the contrary, Jack Steward. I've proved that you are just the man I need. You're smart, you're doing a great job–and you're dedicated. Not what those good folks across the road would call dedicated, but we know better than they do. Those forgeries—that was quick thinking, and smooth work. And now you have all those people in your pocket.
JACK:	(STARING AT MR. LORD) You mean—you don't want to fire me?
LORD:	Fire you? Well, only in this sense, that you're far too big a man to waste your talents out here. How about moving to New York? Whatever you're making here—and I mean legally or illegally— I'll double it. But you must be prepared to take responsibility, and the going will be rough and dirty. Now how about it?
JACK:	I can't believe my ears, sir. You bet I'll go to new York!
LORD:	Just you wait, Jack! Together we can do wonders—the sky's the limit!
JACK:	(SPRINGING TO HIS FEET) Just a moment, sir. Vera! Come in here! (SHE ENTERS L.) Mr. Lord, I want you to meet the girl I'm going to marry. Vera, this is the boss.
VERA:	I've heard a lot about you, Mr. Lord.
JACK:	Vera helped me fix the books yesterday, sir.
LORD:	Is that so? Then you'll be a valuable member of our partnership in crime.

JACK: I've been promoted, darling. What do you think about that? I was all ready to be fired, and I've been promoted!

LORD: Fix Vera a drink, Jack! There! Congratulations, both of you!

(THEY RAISE THEIR GLASSES, AND ALL BEGIN TO LAUGH. THE MUSIC OF 'I can raid a bank...' COMMENCES. JACK AND VERA JUMP FORWARD AND BEGIN TO DANCE AND SING. AFTER ONE VERSE LORD JOINS THEM. WHEN THE SONG IS FINISHED THEY RETURN TO THEIR DRINKS, LAUGHING AND TOASTING EACH OTHER. VERA FLIRTS WITH LORD.THEY ALL POINT TO THE LEDGER, AND LAUGH OVER IT. SATAN APPEARS TO ONE SIDE, AND WATCHES THE REST OF THE SCENE WITH OBVIOUS SATISFACTION.)

CHORUS

So Mr. Lord commended Jack Steward
Because he was crooked and smart.
He could plan a crime in doublequick time,
And he made deceit an art.

And if you were only like Jack Steward,
And I were only like Mr. Lord,
We would fight God's fight with all of our might,
With the Spirit as our sword.

Yes, Mr. Lord commended Jack Steward
Because he was crooked and smart.
He could forge and cheat; he was swift and neat
When he played a bad man's part.

And if you were only like Jack Steward,
And I were only like Mr. Lord,
We would serve God's ends more than Satan's friends,
With a strong and glad accord.

Yes, Mr. Lord promoted Jack Steward
Because he was crooked and smart.
When it came to lies, he was shrewd and wise,
Never slack or faint of heart.

So which of us can fight Jack Steward?
And which of us can beat Mr. Lord?
If the Christians dream while the bad men scheme
Then the Cross will be ignored.

(AS THIS SONG ENDS, THE CHOIR APPEARS AT ONE SIDE OF THE STAGE. IT

PROCESSES ACROSS TO THE OTHER SIDE,PASSING IN FRONT OF THE THREE AT THE DESK, WHO WATCH AND LAUGH, AS DOES SATAN.)

CHORUS

We are the children of light,
And we worship the Lord with part of our might.
We come to church, and we pray and sing,
And we half believe in everything.
We half believe in a God above,
And we half believe in Christian love...

(THEY SHUFFLE OFFSTAGE, AND THEIR VOICES DIE AWAY. SATAN HAS POURED HIMSELF A DRINK. HE AND THE THREE AT THE DESK RAISE THEIR GLASSES AS THE LIGHTS FADE TO BLACKOUT)

GOOD FRIDAY

First presented in the Chapel of the U.S.Navy Hospital in Balboa Park, San Diego, in 1965.

There are two ways in which this version of the Good Friday and Easter story can be presented.

It can be acted on stage or in a church setting, more as a pageant than as a play. This is the plan followed in the text.

Alternatively it can be sung by soloists and chorus while a series of slides are shown to the audience. This involves collecting up to one hundred slides, which can be a rewarding task. You should decide what pictures will make the most impact. My selection, built up over many years, includes a blend of famous pictures and sculptures, old and new—Michelangelo, Grunewald, Rouault, and many others—together with photographs, many of them contemporary and changing with each new production.

CHARACTERS: Centurion
Two soldiers
Two followers of Jesus
Two bystanders
Three young ladies onlookers
Two Jewish men
Chorus of bystanders

(WITH THE STAGE IN DARKNESS, THE TUNE OF THE OPENING SONG IS PLAYED SOFTLY. THE LIGHTS COME UP GRADUALLY. ON ONE SIDE OF THE STAGE A GROUP INCLUDING THE FRIENDS OF JESUS, THE BYSTANDERS, AND JEWISH MEN GAZE OUT OVER THE AUDIENCE. DOWNSTAGE ON THE OTHER SIDE THE TWO SOLDIERS ARE PLAYING DICE. THE CENTURION STANDS C. EVERYONE IS

STILL EXCEPT FOR THE SOLDIERS AS THE MUSIC IS PLAYED, AND DURING THE NARRATION)

At dawn on the day when Jesus was crucified there were many people watching and waiting. Very different feelings, different hopes and fears, filled the hearts of men and women in Jerusalem, as that Good Friday began.

(A SPOT MAY FOLLOW THE DIFFERENT GROUPS AS HE MENTIONS THEM)

There were those who hated him, those who loved him, and those who cared little about him either way, but were still affected by what was to happen on Golgotha Hill that day. And there were soldiers, waiting for their orders as the trial of Jesus drew to a close. When Pilate gave in to the pressure of the Jewish leaders, and consented to the crucifixion of Jesus, there was work for the soldiers to do, carpenter's work, to nail to the Cross the Son of God, himself the son of a carpenter.

CENTURION: Take some beams, and make three crosses!
There'll be an execution on Golgotha today!
Take some beams, and make three crosses!
There'll be an execution on Golgotha today.

(WITH CHORUS AND SOLDIERS)
Golgotha! Golgotha! There'll be an execution.
There'll be an execution on Golgotha today.

(ALL OF THE ACTION IN THE NEXT VERSE IS MIMED.)

CENTURION: Nail them firm, and join them tightly!
There'll be an execution on Golgotha today.

Nail them firm, and join them tightly!
There'll be an execution on Golgotha today.
Harden your heart, and do your job!
It's not for a soldier to sigh or sob.
Nail them firm, and join them tightly!
There'll be an execution on Golgotha today.

(WITH CHORUS AND SOLDIERS)
Golgotha! Golgotha! Therelll be an execution.
There'll be an execution on Golgotha today.

CENTURION: Call them out to bear their crosses!
There'll be an execution on Golgotha today.
Call them out to bear their crosses!
There'll be an execution on Golgotha today.

Call them out to bear their crosses!
There'll be an execution on Golgotha today.

(WITH CHORUS AND SOLDIERS)
Golgotha! Golgotha! There'll be an execution.
There'll be an execution on Golgotha today.

(THE LIGHTS FADE OUT. THE SOUND OF HAMMERS IS HEARD OFFSTAGE. THE GROUP DESCRIBED EARLIER PRESS FORWARD TO C, WHERE THE SOLDIERS HOLD THEM BACK)

1st SOLDIER: Keep back, there! Keep back! No crowding around the crosses!

1st JEW: I am an official observer. I—

2nd SOLDIER: Sorry, sir. Governor's orders. You can see all you want from here.

1st FRIEND
OF JESUS: Oh God! It can't be true! It can't be happening!

1st BYSTANDER: Can't we get any closer?

2nd BYSTANDER: I guess not. We'll have to watch from here.

1st BYSTANDER: That's what always happens to me. I'm always on the edge of the crowd.

(IN THE FOLLOWING SONG, LINES MARKED WITH * MAY BE SPOKEN OR SHOUTED.)

1st BYSTANDER: I'm always on the edge of a crowd,
                   Looking over someone's shoulder;
                   Following any noise that's loud,
                   Looking over someone's shoulder.

BOTH BYSTANDERS: "Hosanna in the highest!"
                   That was the cry I heard.
                   "Hosanna in the highest!"
                   So I echoed every word.

2nd BYSTANDER: I'm always on the edge of a crowd,
                   Looking over someone's shoulder;
                   Following any voice that's loud,
                   Looking over someone's shoulder.

BOTH BYSTANDERS: "Hail to the mighty healer!

Blessed be Jesus' name!"
"Hail to the mighty healer!"
They cried, so I cried the same.

1st BYSTANDER: I'm always on the edge of a crowd,
Looking over someone's shoulder;
Following any voice that's loud,
Looking over someone's shoulder.

BOTH BYSTANDERS: "Down, down with the blasphemer!"
The angry voices said.
"Down, down with the blasphemer!"
So I followed where they led.

2nd BYSTANDER: I'm always on the edge of a crowd,
Looking over someone's shoulder;
Following any voice that's loud,
Looking over someone's shoulder,

BOTH BYSTANDERS: "Crucify him! Crucify him!"
That is the leaders' cry.
"Crucify him! Crucify him!"
They shout—and so do I.

1st BYSTANDER: I'm always on the edge of a crowd,
Looking over someone's shoulder;

2nd BYSTANDER: Following any voice that's loud,
Looking over someone's shoulder.

(THE TWO SOLDIERS ARE SITTING DOWNSTAGE ON THE SIDE CLOSEST TO THE
CROSSES. THE CENTURION ENTERS FROM THAT SIDE SLOWLY, AND TOSSES A
ROBE CLOSE TO THEM.)

CENTURION: There's a strange, strange man on the cross in the center,
With his life just ebbing away.
While the nails drove through, still his face was tender,
And I thought I heard him say
"Father, forgive them!" That was what he said.
"Father, I pray to you.
Father, forgive them!" I heard him cry,
"For they know not what they do."

1st BYSTANDER: Who is his father? He asks him to forgive,

1st FRIEND OF JESUS:	Who is his father?
2nd FRIEND OF JESUS:	Tortured now and torn, Can he think of dying as waiting to be born?
1st JEWISH MAN:	He is a blasphemer, dying for his sins.
2nd JEWISH MAN:	He is a deceiver, and falsehood never wins.
1st JEWISH MAN:	We have tried to save him, but he paid no heed.
2nd JEWISH MAN:	Every chance we gave him to be spared and freed.
CENTURION:	Then the thief next door ceased his raging and crying, And I heard his halting word "Oh, remember me," with the voice of the dying, "When you come to your kingdom, Lord!" "I will remember." That was what he said, Love shining from his eyes. "I will remember! Today you shall be With me in Paradise."

(THE THREE YOUNG LADY ONLOOKERS ENTER, AND LOOK OVER THE SHOULDERS OF THE GROUP.)

1st ONLOOKER:	What's happening?
2nd ONLOOKER:	Oh, an execution! How horrible!
3rd ONLOOKER:	Let's get away. It's nothing to do with us.
1st ON LOOKER:	Wait a minute! I want to know who that man in the middle is. Excuse me, sir. Can you tell me who it is up there—the middle one?
1st JEWISH MAN:	A false Messiah.
2ND JEWISH MAN:	His death was unavoidable.
2nd ONLOOKER:	Excuse me. What has the one on the center cross done?
FIRST BYSTANDER:	I don't really know. I overheard someone say it was blasphemy.

2nd BYSTANDER: We're just passing by, like you.

3rd ONLOOKER: Excuse me—

(THE FIRST FRIEND OF JESUS FALLS TO HIS KNEES SOBBING.)

   Oh, I'm sorry. Is he a friend of yours?

1st FRIEND
OF JESUS: He is our Savior.

2nd FRIEND
OF JESUS: We cannot live without him.

1st ONLOOKER: Come on, girls! We can't do anything.

2nd ONLOOKER: No. Let's go, Betty! After all, it's nothing to do with us.

(THEY WALK TO THE FRONT OF THE STAGE. IF THERE IS STAGE LIGHTING A SPOT SHOULD PINPOINT THEM. IN THE FOLLOWING VERSES THEY ARE IDENTIFIED AS ONE, TWO, AND THREE.)

ONE: If a man by the roadside has suffered an assault,
   It's nothing to do with me.

TWO: It's risky to help him, and it's probably all his fault.
   It's nothing to do with me.

THREE: Why pick on me to stop and lend a helping hand?

ONE: Why can't an ostrich hide his head in the sand.
   I tell you, it's nothing to do with me.

ALL: It's absolutely nothing to do with me.

TWO: If the man next door gets drunk and beats his wife,
   It's nothing to do with me.

THREE: A girl must be practical in twenty-first century life.
   It's nothing to do with me.

ONE: Am I my brother's keeper when he gets into a jam?

TWO: Can't you see how overworked and put upon I am?
   I tell you, it's nothing to do with me.

ALL:	It's absolutely nothing to do with me.
THREE:	If three gasping criminals are dying on the cross, It's nothing to do with me.
ONE:	I don't care for bloodshed; but they probably aren't much loss. It's nothing to do with me.
TWO:	Isn't it disgraceful that there's such a wave of crime?
THREE:	I don't know much about it, for I haven't got the time; And surely it's nothing to do with me.
ALL:	It's absolutely nothing to do with me.
ONE:	If some faroff Africans are fighting all the time, It's nothing to do with me.
TWO:	With things as they are i have to think of every dime. It's nothing to do with me,
THREE:	We want to live our lives in peace, and keep them clear of fuss.
ALL:	Of course it would be different if disaster threatened US! But so far it's nothing to do with me. It's absolutely nothing to do with me.

(THEY MARCH OFF IN STEP, AWAY FROM THE CROSSES)

CENTURION:	Then I heard him say to his friend and his mother, As they watched him, silent and grim, That he gave them charge each one of the other, And they took fresh strength from him. "This is your mother!"—That was what he said. "Mother, behold your son! This is your mother!" I heard him cry, When his course was almost run.
	Then his lips would move in a soundless praying, And he whispered many a word; Till he raised his voice in a tortured saying, And I watched him while I heard. "Father, O Father!"—That was what he said. "Have you forsaken me?

Do not forsake me!" I heard him cry,
As he hung in agony.

1st FRIEND
OF JESUS: Is God his Father? And has God ceased to care?

2nd FRIEND
OF JESUS: How can he forsake him, if his Son is dying there?

CENTURION: He had spurned the drug that was there for his easing
When the pain was at its worst;
But he raised his head, now his strength was ceasing,
And I heard him say, "I thirst."
"See, he is thirsting!" They cried below.
"Reach him the draught to drink!"
"See, he is thirsting!" I heard them say,
As his head began to sink.

He's a strange, strange man on the cross in the center,
Who has drawn his dying breath.
In the midst of pain, still his face was tender,
And he seemed to conquer death.
"Now it is finished!"—that was what he said.
"Father, the hour is come.
Into your keeping I give my soul!"
And then his lips were dumb.

(AT THE WORDS "It is finished" THE FRIENDS OF JESUS FALL TO THEIR KNEES
AND HIDE THEIR FACES. THE BYSTANDERS ARE MOVED ALSO AS THEY LOOK
TOWARDS THE CROSSES. THE JEWISH MEN ARE ALSO MOVED. THEY HAVE
COME TO SEE JUSTICE METED OUT TO A BLASPHEMER, BUT THEY ALSO HATE
WHAT IS BEING DONE)

BYSTANDERS: It's sad to see that man die;
Nobody seems to know why.
They say he was a sinner; but he healed the sick.
It's sad to see that man die.

It's sad to see that man killed.
It's sad to see his blood spilled.
They say he was a traitor; but his ways were pure.
It's sad to see that man killed.

It's sad to watch that man now.
It's sad to see his head bow.

They call him a blasphemer; but his words were of love.
It's sad to see that man now.

JEWISH MEN: Stubborn and unbending, he defied the Law.

Now you see the ending he will lie no more!
This is the man who trusted in God that he would deliver him!
This is the man who mocked at our Law and said we should trust in him!
This is the man who led them astray—the 'Christ' from Nazareth!
This is the man whose folly and pride have led him to pain and death!
The soldiers threw dice for Jesus' robe, because they did not want to tear it.
The one with the highest throw took it for his own.
(WE SEE THE SOLDIERS MIME THESE ACTIONS WITH A ROBE WHICH THE CEN-
TURION GIVES TO THEM)

Now the coat was without seam, woven from the top throughout;
And so was the life of him who died, who was God's own son, no doubt.
And the soldiers played at dice that day for the coat that had no seam;
But they tore the flesh of him who died, as they nailed him to the beam.

CHORUS
Oh, my Lord! The coat was woven whole.
Oh, my Lord! You died to save my soul.

A soldier won the seamless coat, and took it for a prize;
And the seamless Lord, from his burning pain, looked down with loving eyes.
For the soldiers played at dice that day for the coat that had no seam;
But they tore the flesh of him who died, as they nailed him to the beam.

CHORUS
Oh, my Lord! The coat was woven whole.
Oh, my Lord! You died to save my soul.

Now the lives of men are frayed and torn, like a robe all frayed and patched;
But the dying Lord was clean and whole, whose brow the thorns had scratched.
And the soldiers played at dice that day for the coat that had no seam;
But they tore the flesh of him who died, as they nailed him to the beam.

CHORUS
Oh, my Lord! The coat was woven whole.
Oh, my Lord! You died to save my soul.

Now the robe that Jesus wore that day was made in a single piece;
And the love of the Lord who wore that robe will live and never cease.
And the soldiers played at dice that day for the coat that had no seam;

But they tore the flesh of him who died, as they nailed him to the beam.

CHORUS

Oh, my Lord! The coat was woven whole.

Oh, my Lord! You died to save my soul.

(THE SOLDIERS GO OFF TOWARDS THE CROSSES. THE FRIENDS OF JESUS REMAIN KNEELING AS THEY SING.)

FRIENDS OF JESUS: I tried to serve him,
Body and soul,
Because I came to him empty,
And he made me whole.
I tried to give him
All that's best of me,
Because I was a prisoner,
And he set me free.

Is there a gift worth giving
To one who has made you live?
A richer and better living
Is all that I have to give.

I tried to serve him,
Body and soul,
Because I came to him empty,
And he made me whole.
I tried to give him
All that's best of me,
Because I was a prisoner,
And he set me free.

(THERE IS A CRASH OF THUNDER OR ROLL OF DRUMS, AND A BRIGHT FLASH. THE CENTURION ENTERS FROM THE DIRECTION OF THE CROSSES)

CENTURION: It is finished! His life is done. Carry him to the grave!

JEWISH MEN: It is finished! The fight is won; but him we could not save.

BYSTANDERS: It is finished! Time to go home. Nothing left to see.

FRIENDS OF JESUS: It is finished! Oh valiant heart, death has set you free!

(THE LIGHTS FADE TO A BLACKOUT. AFTER A SHORT SILENCE A SPOT SHOWS THE THREE ONLOOKERS, TWO SITTING, ONE LYING ON THE FLOOR IN FRONT OF A TV SET—WHICH MAY BE IMAGINED. THEY ARE DOWNSTAGE ON THE SIDE OPPOSITE TO THE CROSSES)

1st ON LOOKER:	I'm bored. What can we do?
2nd ONLOOKER:	Watch TV, I suppose. What's on?
THIRD ONLOOKER:	Let's try to get the news. I'd like to hear about that man we saw on the cross.
1st ONLOOKER:	Oh, who cares about that?
2nd ON LOOKER:	It probably wouldn't mention him anyway. Just another crucifixion. (SHE READS FROM A TV GUIDE) Look, let's get Channel 4. It's the Scarabs.

(SHE TURNS ON THE SET. THEY SIT STILL DURING THE FOLLOWING SONG)

CHORUS
Is it nothing to you, all ye that pass by?
Is it nothing to you, if the people die?
Can you close your eyes to the grief and pain?
Can you close your minds to the jailer's chain?
Is it nothing to you?

Is it nothing to you, all ye that pass by?
Is it nothing to you, if the lonely sigh?
Can you close your ears when the hungry call?
Can you close your hearts when the wounded fall?
Is it nothing to you?

Is it nothing to you, all ye that pass by?
Is it nothing to you, if the stricken cry?
Can you close your eyes to the victim's need?
Can you close your ears while the helpless bleed?
Is it nothing to you?

(THE SPOT FADES, AND THERE IS DARKNESS. SLOWLY LIGHTS COME ON TO REPRESENT DAWN. THE STAGE IS EMPTY. WHERE THE CROSSES WERE OFFSTAGE, THE TOMB OF JESUS IS NOW. LIGHT SHINES FROM IT. DURING THE NEXT SONG MANY PEOPLE COME FROM THE OPPOSITE SIDE AND KNEEL FACING THE TOMB, LED BY THE TWO FRIENDS OF JESUS. THEY ARE RICH AND POOR, SICK AND WHOLE, OF EVERY RACE. THE CHORUS MAY BE A PART OF THIS GROUP ON STAGE)

CHORUS
Comfort ye! Comfort ye!
Comfort ye, my people, saith your God!
Speak ye comfortably to Jerusalem!
Cry unto her that her warfare is accomplished!

Cry unto her that her warfare is accomplished!
Her iniquity is pardoned!
Comfort ye! Comfort ye!
Comfort ye, my people, saith your God!

(THERE IS A FLASH OF LIGHTNING AND A NOISE OF THUNDER)

But the light of the lamp which the cross has lit
Will shine till the world shall end;
For the rocksealed grave could not shut in
The soul of the sinners' friend.
He broke from the graveclothes, burst from the tomb,
And conquered the clouds of night!
For nails and spear and lash and cross
Could never put out that light!

(THE LAST FOUR LINES ARE REPEATED IN A RISING SPIRIT OF TRIUMPH. KNEEL-
ING FIGURES NOW FILL THE STAGE, AND THE LIGHT BRIGHTENS TO DAYLIGHT.
STILL FACING THE TOMB, ALL ON STAGE REPEAT THE EARLIER SONG, WHICH IS
NOW TURNED FROM THE PAST TO THE FUTURE)

CHORUS

I want to serve him,
Body and soul,
Because I came to him empty,
And he made me whole.
I want to give him
All that's best of me,
Because I was a prisoner,
And he set me free.

Is there a gift worth giving
To one who has made you live?
A richer and better living
Is all that I have to give.

I want to serve him,
Body and soul,
Because I came to him empty,
And he made me whole.
I want to give him
All that's best of me,
Because I was a prisoner,
And he made me free.

(ALL TURN TOWARDS THE AUDIENCE FOR THE FINALE.)

All of the peoples,
In every land,

Must hear of this story
And understand.
Tell all the peoples
Of every land,
Love won the victory
By Jesus' hand.
Tell of his caring
So much that he came!
Tell of his sharing
Sorrow and shame!

All of the peoples,
Over the earth,
Must hear of his coming,
Hear of his birth.
Hear of his living
True to his call;
Hear of his dying,
Savior of all.
Tell of his prizing
Poor men as friends!
Tell of his rising,
To the world's ends!

All of the peoples,
In every land,
Must hear of this story
And understand.
Love won the victory
By Jesus' hand.
Tell all the peoples
Of every land!